MW00989487

Tails
of
SHA'AR HAGAI

Tails
of
SHA'AR HAGAI

A Wild Life With Wildlife

Myrna Shiboleth

Sephirot Press

ISBN - 978-0-9802071-1-8

Printed in the USA. First Printing, December 2008
Published by Sephirot Press, Durham, NH
www.sephirotpress.com

To order additional copies, please contact us
orders@sephirotpress.com
Sephirot Press and associated
logos are trademarks of
Sephirot Press.

Designed by: Ian D. Bier

Dedication

To the memory of my parents, Seymour and Shirley Karlin, who out of tolerance, understanding and deep love always let me choose my own path in life.

And to my daughter, Dorcas Aharon, who has survived having me as a mother and has grown up to be a fantastic woman.

Contents

Tails
of
SHA'AR HAGAI

Foreword

When I was a teenager in Chicago, I belonged to a Zionist youth group. We American Jewish teens wanted to show our closeness to Israel, so we met once a week, heard lectures on Israel, sang Israeli songs, had parties on the Jewish holidays, went to a 'kibbutz style' summer camp, and also had a chance to meet other nice Jewish teens. I can't say that at the time I was a particularly committed Zionist. It was more the idea of far away, exotic Israel, the kind of place about which books like *Exodus* were written, with movie stars like Paul Newman starring in the film versions. It was also an acceptable activity in the community in which I grew up. Zionist groups were valid excuses for all sorts of social activities that I wouldn't have had access to otherwise.

The teen years are an idealistic age and the leaders of those groups were idealists through and through. They expected all of us recruits to set a date for *aliyah*, literally Hebrew for going up. We were supposed to immigrate to Israel after high school graduation, preferably with the goal of living on a kibbutz, a large communal farm that embodied the pioneering spirit.

Even in those days I was stubborn. As soon as someone told me what to do, it gave me a valid reason for not doing it. So instead of setting a date for *aliyah*, I quit the group.

Today I live in Israel. As far as I know, I am the only former member of that particular group that does. After thirty years of pioneering in ways that I never would have believed possible in this strangely frustrating but also fascinating place, I am still too stubborn to leave.

What Israel has given me is the possibility to know myself and discover resources within that I never would have known I possessed under other conditions. What I have given to Israel—well, I'll let you be the judge of that...

Chapter One: The Beginning

I was totally unprepared for my first sight of Sha'ar Hagai.

The car turned off the road into what appeared to be a trackless wilderness, about 20 kilometers outside of Jerusalem. My companions announced, "This is the place." I wasn't quite sure what the place was, or even if, among all the plant life, there was a place at all.

We climbed up the hill away from the road. I wish I could say that we hacked our way through the vines, but we hadn't had the forethought to bring a machete. Rather, we pushed our way along the path of least resistance through the overgrowth—if anything ever deserved to be called overgrown, this was it! Suddenly, in front of us was a building. At least it appeared to be a building. Beyond the weeds and tall grass, there seemed to be the top of a wall with a roof connected. When we finally found a door, we squeezed in.

The interior of the house looked like it should have been on the business end of an archaeological dig. All we needed were shovels to get to work. Up to window height, the floors were covered with rubble that appeared to be a combination of fallen plaster, the remains of various Bedouin campfires, and great quantities of sheep droppings. After all, if the Bedouin had been sheltering here, then so had their sheep. But as these buildings had been constructed with walls of thirty-six centimeters of reinforced concrete, despite twenty-odd years of abandonment to the elements and the Bedouin, they were still standing. And when I looked up from the rubble and out the window, the whole panorama of the Judean hills was before me.

Continued exploration showed that there were five buildings, all in similar states of disrepair, although not all were identical in size and arrangement of rooms. It was obvious that whatever we did with this place, there would be a lot of work involved.

This was actually a very historic location. Here the road from the coastal plain to Jerusalem entered the Judean hills. There are few ways through these hills, which although not huge mountains for most countries, by Israeli standards they are indeed good sized and very rocky crags. The primary way through is via a pass which is called *Sha'ar Hagai* or in Arabic *Bab-el-wad*, which means 'gateway to the valley.' This pass has always provided the primary access to Jerusalem. During the War of Independence in 1948, the Arabs took up positions on the mountains above the road to blockade supplies to Jerusalem. Special armored vehicles were used to run the blockade and bring much needed provisions to the beleaguered city, but not all made it through the ambushes. The wrecks of these armored cars remain still today in a place of honor along the road as a memorial to those whose lives were lost in the attempts to go up to Jerusalem.

The buildings we were examining had been built by the British in the time of the mandate, in the 1930s, before Israel existed as a country. The main water line to Jerusalem ran through here, and there was a British built pumping station. At the time it was built, everything was run manually, so on the hillside above the pumping station, these buildings had been constructed for the engineers and workers that ran the pumping station. After the British left in 1948, the buildings had been abandoned. However, they had been built to the same standard as the fortified police stations the British had built: meant to stand up to anything. We even saw signs on a few of the buildings of direct mortar hits from the War of Independence, resulting in minor craters in the wall and a few cracks in the plaster.

It was obvious that there was a great deal of work to be done to make this place livable. But the location was ideal for breeding dogs—isolated, with no near neighbors to complain about barking, but close enough to the main road so that access was easy. This was the spot where we could bring our dream of breeding Canaan dogs to reality.

Thus began Sha'ar Hagai farm.

However did I, a typical middle class 'Jewish American Princess,' from Illinois, heart of the conservative mid-west, get involved in this? Well, life can lead us down paths we never would have dreamed of.

I was a very shy child. I don't remember learning to read, but I seemed to have learned at a very young age, and from then on voraciously devoured everything that came into reach. This often included adult novels that my mother thought she had hidden from me. Books were my best friends, and my favorites among them were books about animals. While my schoolmates played with dolls, I ran up and down the block playing *Lassie* or *Black Stallion*. Although I had only a few other children as favored playmates, I was acquainted and on friendly terms with every dog in the neighborhood, and would walk up and down the alleys petting them over the fences.

My parents, definitely not great animal lovers, never really understood why their daughter always brought home stray dogs and cats. Luckily for them, we lived in the city, so I never managed to adopt any less tame creatures. But I was never allowed to keep any of my rescues.

"When I grow up," I told them, "I will have as many animals as I want!" They didn't really believe me, which was a big mistake.

When I was sent to summer camp, I snuck away to a nearby riding stable where I spent all my pocket money. Holding on for dear life as the horse trotted cross-country, I had a marvelous time. My family remained hopeful that I would outgrow this strange animal obsession, but I was determined that some day my life would be full of animals.

After graduating from university with a respectable degree in art, I took off with a girlfriend on a trip through Europe, with the end station being Israel. Somehow, Israel felt like home. From the moment I got off the plane, I felt comfortable. I loved the beauty of the country, the smell of oranges in the air, the bright sun, and the casualness of life. The people were outgoing and friendly and didn't really care who you were or where you were from; and if you couldn't speak very good Hebrew, well then, sign language was fine. Instead of coming home as originally planned, I spent the next year in Israel, working at whatever came along to support myself. This included teaching horseback riding and working as an extra in the movies. My poor mother didn't know how to tell her friends that her well-brought-up daughter with that respectable university art degree was working with HORSES! My activities were translated into "working on a kibbutz," a choice that was more respectable in our community.

None of these various jobs seemed to promise a big future, though, and finally, after a year, at the heartfelt request of my parents, I came home to give the U.S. another chance.

On my return, I got a dream job. I was hired by Animal Talent Scouts in New York, an agency that trained and handled all types of animals for TV, movies, theatre, advertising and whatever else anyone could imagine using an animal for. Not only could I work with animals, but in the glamorous world of entertainment!

The turnover of employees at ATS was phenomenal. Most of the job applicants were very interested in the glamour side, but not so interested in the cleaning, feeding and training of the animals, which comprised at least 90% of the job. The boss was very demanding and expected everything to be done to a high standard—one of the reasons that she had managed to build up a respected and successful business in a difficult and competitive field. I, however, having been raised and trained by a world-class Jewish mother, was able to live up to the work standards expected of me, and soon began receiving some of the fun assignments.

The first major job that I had for ATS was to handle two dogs, an Old English Sheepdog and a small mixed terrier, in a very successful Broadway musical, *George M!* The dogs had a small but important part; my job was to have them immaculately groomed before show time, get them to the theatre in time, prepare the props needed for their appearance, get them in position at the correct cue, and run around backstage to pick them up as they came offstage after their appearance. I sat backstage with the dogs, too shy to really talk to any of the show biz people, enjoying the atmosphere and the excitement. The dogs also loved going to the theatre, and were always depressed on the days there was no performance. True performers, they knew their cue—when the music preceding their entrance started to play, they jumped up, ready to go on stage to their adoring public.

My next big job was the Radio City Christmas Pageant. The pageant involved a nativity scene, and we provided the animals to go with it—a few donkeys, some sheep, and a camel and a white horse for the Kings. My job was to help in the care and feeding of the animals, which were stabled backstage at Radio City for the duration of the run of the show—about a month or so. This time I didn't get to just sit backstage and let the animals get all the good parts; I had to lead the horse across stage for the pageant. I was dressed in a rather elaborate robe, and an actress playing one of the kings was to ride the horse while dressed in a very heavy velvet jewel encrusted robe and enormous headdress.

The horse had been provided by one of our 'subcontractors'—people who owned trained animals and were listed in our card file—to be called upon when we needed them. This was necessary as it was impossible for us to keep every animal that might possibly be required for any occasion. This horse was an experienced trooper, who knew exactly what it meant to be on stage. He would stand passively in his stall all day, ignoring everything, and would allow himself to be saddled and mounted without a modicum of trouble, but the moment he stepped out on stage in front of the audience and heard the applause, his ears would come up and he would start to prance and curvet, a sort of a prance with feet off the ground, like a highly trained Arabian stallion. To add to the fun, the actress riding him had never been on a horse in her life before this show and was absolutely terrified. My job was to walk the horse across the stage, trying to prevent him from dancing around enough either to damage the props or unseat the actress, who spent the whole time cursing under her breath.

After the show had been running for a week or so, a date was set for publicity photos to be sent to the local newspapers. In order to save the actress from the torture of having to mount the horse an extra time, it was decided that I would be a stand-in. I would ride the horse, dressed in the elaborate costume. The costume was really extremely bulky and very heavy; once dressed in it, I could hardly move and had to be more or less lifted up onto the horse. But at last we were all ready, and the photographers were set. The horse, however, had other ideas. Maybe he missed his customary adulation from the audience, but for whatever reason, he suddenly reared up and threw himself over backwards.

I had enough riding experience to know what to do—but the costume was so heavy that I couldn't move my arms to control the reins, or move my body to throw myself sideways out of his way. Fortunately, I landed on the floor a bit to the side of the horse—and there I remained like a turtle on my back, unable to move from the weight of the costume until someone came to pick me up.

Luckily, none of THOSE photos ever appeared in the press.

The horse was not the only one in that show who liked to play games—there was also his stable mate, the camel. Camels are rather nasty animals capable of kicking in any direction, biting quite savagely, and even spitting if you are otherwise out of reach. This camel was quite well behaved, but he did have his little tricks. His favorite was to stand quietly in his stall with his head turned to watch the people passing by, and then, when someone came into range, to urinate on his tail and flick it at the unsuspecting passersby.

Not all of the jobs I did for ATS were as glamorous; there were also a lot of little jobs that had their own share of excitement. I handled a yak at a local pet fair; he was quite young so only about half the size of a full-grown yak, about the size of a large cow. He was very appealing with soft wavy black hair and large soft black eyes, and all the children were eager to pat him. However, he was not really trained to walk on a halter, and would walk off to inspect anything that looked interesting or edible, dragging me along behind—even a baby yak weighs a few hundred kilos and is quite strong.

There was an innocent-looking white rabbit used for fashion photographs that managed to scratch up the model who didn't know how to hold it properly. She got quite upset and was ready to walk off the shoot, until I showed her that if she held it properly so that it felt secure, it would settle down. Once we even had a goose and a lamb in our office in the center of Manhattan for a few days that were going to be photographed for a children's book publisher. I exercised them by walking them around the streets of New York on leashes. The sophisticated New Yorkers walked right past and ignored us, with only a quick sideways glance indicating that they had noticed something unusual.

We also had several trained llamas that were very popular with clients, but were kept most of the time on the ATS farm in New Jersey. Another one of my jobs was to drive to New Jersey to bring a llama in for an assignment. Having a llama in the back seat of the car on the New Jersey Turnpike had a very interesting effect on the flow of traffic.

My boss wasn't above checking out my qualifications either whenever the opportunity arose. On one visit to the New Jersey farm, she told me, "Go take the pony stallion out for a ride, he needs some exercise." Well, riding wasn't work; it was fun, so off I went. True, the pony didn't seem very enthusiastic, and did seem quite unresponsive to my signals, but we managed to get along together and had a pleasant ride. When I got back, I was informed that the pony hadn't been ridden for several years. "I just wanted to see if you really know how to manage horses," was my boss's comment.

The biggest job I worked on, though, was a series of print and TV advertisements for woolen carpets. For this assignment, we flew out to Salt Lake City, the center of sheep country. The idea was to dye a flock of sheep in the colors of the various woolen carpets, and drive them down the main street of Salt Lake City for photographs. Just to ensure that we would be in control, we brought a trained ewe with us in a dog crate.

Our first view of Salt Lake City was the stockyards, where our flock of sheep awaited us. Although born and raised in Chicago, I had never been to a stockyard. I found the hogs in particular to be fascinating; I had never realized that they were so very big or so fierce. Our sheep were a wild bunch just off the range and not very amenable to being caught and colored, which in the end we did with chalk. This system was decided on as it wouldn't damage the fleece, but no one had really considered how much work it would be or how much time it would take to work colored chalk into the entire fleece of twenty wild sheep. By the time we were finished, there was no thought of anything but collapsing in the motel room—no sight seeing, even though Salt Lake City was very beautiful, and a place I had never been before.

The next morning our rainbow flock was moved to an improvised pen on a side street leading into the main thoroughfare of Salt Lake City, where the filming would be done. Our New York lead sheep was now a beautiful kelly green, and the others were varying shades of gold, red, blue, green and violet. Passersby started to congregate around the pen, staring at the colored sheep. Now, Salt Lake City is the heart of sheep country, but spectators began asking questions we couldn't believe—where we had gotten these colored sheep from, how we got the different shades... My boss had a great time answering, "Well, you see if you breed a blue one like that to a yellow one like this, then you get a green one like that one..."

Traffic was halted and the sheep were paraded down the main street; after several takes, it was decided that the filming had been successful. Now we could fly home.

We got to the airport late, just a few minutes before takeoff time. Quickly checking our luggage through, as well as our little green ewe in the dog crate, who of course was returning to New York with us, we ran to the plane and managed to settle quickly in our seats, just in time to see from the window the baggage handler bringing our luggage up to load on the plane. He started to grab the dog crate to swing it aboard, glanced inside, stopped dead, and looked again. Sticking his fingers in between the grate, he plucked out a twist of wool, looked at it, and held it up to the light. We had done a good job—it was green to the roots.

Our last sight of him was to see him gesturing wildly to his coworkers, "Hey, guys, come take a look at this!"

Chapter Two: Roommates

While living in New York and working for Animal Talent Scouts, I had acquired some roommates, or more accurately, several roommates. By the time I decided to go back to Israel, I had two dogs and eleven cats.

I had found a one-room apartment on the lower West Side in Manhattan, walking distance from the brownstone home of ATS. But it was lonely and I knew very few people in New York. So what better than to get a dog?

I had always loved collies, since I had read *Lassie Come Home* and the Albert Payson Terhune books about collies as a child. So I called up the SPCA to ask if they had any collies for adoption, my budget not really allowing the purchase of a pedigreed dog from a breeder. Yes, they said, there was a tricolor collie dog, about six months old, available for adoption. In the middle of New York's first blizzard of the winter, I went to bring home my new dog, walking home with him most of the length of Manhattan since no taxi driver was about to pick up a dog in that weather.

I called him Degel, which means flag in Hebrew, very suitable to his happy nature and constantly wagging tail. But within a few days, I had also discovered why Degel had ended up in the SPCA shelter looking for a home.

Saying that Degel was destructive would be an understatement. Within a few days he had managed to chew holes in the sofa, strip the plaster off the kitchen wall, and demolish the telephone. But the prize went to the day I came home to find everything completely covered in feathers—Degel had totally demolished a goose down pillow.

My neighbors quickly realized that the screams coming from my apartment when I arrived home from work did not mean that I was being attacked, only that Degel had "done it again."

Since Degel was clearly bored and lonely when I was not at home, I wanted to provide him with a companion. There were always plenty of cats being given away, so, following up an ad in the local newspaper, I brought home two. One was a lovely tortoiseshell and the second a mishmash of gray, white and pinkish orange that her former owners called 'Maltese,' although as far as I know, there is no such thing. The cats soon adjusted to the idea of living with a dog, and the three of them galloped around the apartment playing tag. I doubt that my downstairs neighbors were enthusiastic about the patter of little paws over their heads, but they never said anything. The building I lived in was full of rather strange people, including a former Peace Corps volunteer who had returned with a green Amazon parrot that lived uncaged in his apartment and attacked anyone who came through the door. I seemed to fit right in.

Then one day I found an ad in the New York Times that would forever change my life: someone was selling Canaan Dog puppies. I knew of Canaan Dogs from living in Israel—this was the native breed of Israel, a desert dog that was quite rare even over there. The Canaan was one of the few breeds of primitive dog that still existed. They were a bit larger than the jackals that were native to the Israeli wilderness, and considered a medium-sized dog. They had heads very reminiscent of the other wild canines—wedge shaped, with very mobile prick ears set obliquely, and dark, intelligent, almond-shaped eyes. The body was square in shape and the tail was carried curled over the back, and the movement was quick and athletic. The coat was medium short and very thick as a protection against the harsh conditions of the desert, and came in a wide variety of colors. These dogs had a wild look to them and were obviously survivors.

I had even had a Canaan Dog for a while during the year I was there. He had been given to me by some friends when he was a very small puppy—I had the feeling that they wanted to get rid of him and knew that Myrna, "the crazy animal lover," would never be able to refuse the tiny brown and white bundle. When I asked them what kind of dog he was, the answer was, "Oh, he's a Cana'ani."

Sheikh was a very intelligent and independent fellow who always knew how to get his own way, a trait that I was to learn was not uncommon in the breed. One of his favorite tricks was to run off barking hysterically just when my landlord was feeding his own dog, a rather stupid boxer. The boxer would run after Sheikh to see what was happening, and Sheikh would double back and finish his food before the boxer even discovered that there was nothing to bark at. I had been sorry to leave him behind with a friend when I returned to the U.S.. But what on earth were Canaans doing being advertised in the *Times*?

Calling the number in the ad, I found that it belonged to a kennel in Pennsylvania where they bred Dalmatians, and now had become one of the first breeders in the U.S. of Canaans. The puppies were from one of the first litters to be born in the U.S..

The breed had been 'redomesticated' from the wild or pariah state by Prof. Rudolphina Menzel, an animal behaviorist and cynologist who had immigrated to Israel in the 1930s from Vienna. When asked by the *Hagana*, the predecessor to the Israeli Defense Force, to develop and train dogs for military purposes, she first attempted to use the breeds she was familiar with from Europe; she herself was a well-known boxer breeder. But she found that they all had real trouble working in the harsh climate of Israel. Her observations indicated the existence of a native breed of dog that was well adapted to the conditions; they were found in the wild and also were used as herd and camp guard dogs by both the Bedouin and Druse, native Arab inhabitants of Israel. She began capturing the dogs and found that they were easily domesticated and trained, highly alert and very devoted. Professor Menzel named them Canaan Dogs after the Biblical Land of Canaan, and from then on worked for the establishment of these dogs as a recognized breed.

In the '60s, Professor Menzel sent a few Canaans to the U.S., to the few breeders who were interested in saving this ancient breed. Spatterdash Kennels in Pennsylvania was one of these.

The idea was irresistible—an Israeli dog! My feelings of nostalgia for my year in Israel got the best of me, and I rented a car and drove out to Pennsylvania to see these puppies.

I would not return to New York empty handed. Who could resist puppies? Certainly not me! So a little two-month-old female, white with black spots, officially known as Spatterdash Gimel Wafi, came back to join the crew in my little apartment.

I had purchased a baby's playpen to keep the new puppy in while I was not at home, in the hopes of preserving what was left of my little apartment. It took Wafi about three minutes to decide that the idea of being confined did not suit her, and to jump over the side of the pen. So, another pair of running feet was added to the commotion.

Wafi was a good puppy, usually not prone to trouble. She was, however, very suspicious of anything not familiar to her, the total opposite of Degel, who loved everyone. Wafi was not enthusiastic about New York City; while Degel pranced along looking for someone new to pet him, she skulked along at my side, looking with great suspicion at anyone coming towards us. From a very young age she guarded my apartment, and barked at anyone passing by. Fortunately, I lived on the top floor, so traffic in the hallway was minimal. But it did give me a secure feeling—no one who heard her bark could tell that there was only a half-grown puppy behind that door. Of course, she never approved of my various dates either, and sat behind a chair staring at them and growling under her breath whenever they dared to invade her apartment—not very conducive to a romantic mood.

One guy I liked at the time, Jim, was a musician in the orchestra of the Broadway show the ATS dogs were doing. I had met him while waiting around backstage for our cues. He was a very pleasant fellow, liked the dogs, and was very cute. We made arrangements for him to come over one night after the performance for coffee and TV.

When I entered the apartment with him, Wafi instantly responded with high-pitched, semi-hysterical barking. Who on earth was this, coming into our safe territory, at this time of night?! I calmed her down and tried to get her to come over and say hello, but she refused, retreating to the safety of the corner behind her favorite chair. I thought that she would settle there quietly. My friend sat down on the sofa, I brought the coffee, turned on the TV, and sat down next to him.

17

This was not acceptable to Wafi. She moved forward, took up a position opposite us but just out of reach and watched Jim intently, muttering softly under her breath. When Jim leaned forward to pick up his coffee cup, Wafi's tone escalated to a fierce sounding growl. As he leaned back, the tone again became almost imperceptible. But each time that Jim moved, turned his head in my direction, or tried to say something, Wafi's growl increased to a frightening level—at least to someone who was not experienced with dogs.

Jim was able to take this for only a short time, becoming more and more nervous and uncertain of what the little dog really intended. Despite my reassurances, after a few minutes of this, Jim gave up and left, never to call again.

Of course, like all puppies, there were times when she couldn't resist trouble. One day she and Degel got hold of an old fox fur scarf that I kept for decoration; I ate, breathed, and wore fur for weeks before I managed to clean it all up.

At about this time, my two cats both helped increase the family. My tortoiseshell produced five beautiful kittens, and the 'Maltese' produced three, each as ugly as she was. But of course that was not enough—one of the neighborhood ladies, to be friendly, insisted on giving me another kitten—it had six toes on its feet, so it was good luck, she said. So that made eleven cat and two dogs—and now the patter of fifty-two little feet around the apartment was more like machine gun fire. Things were getting out of hand.

To add to my chaotic life, I was not working only at Animal Talent Scouts. The amount of business ATS had was variable and not enough to keep me on as a full-time employee with a salary that I could live on comfortably. I therefore had to get another job. I started working for the City of New York as a social worker in the Department of Welfare. I soon had the impression that every college graduate that landed in New York without a job spent at least some time working for the Welfare Department. At first it seemed really interesting, but the futility and despair was starting to have a strong influence on me. Somehow I hadn't really pictured myself spending my life living in the middle of New York City in a small apartment shared by a pack of cats and dogs, spending my days trying to convince the indigent that having a job was a good idea.

Although I tremendously enjoyed my ATS job, over the months I found myself feeling restless. Here I was, getting to work with my beloved animals regularly in a glamorous dream job, and something still wasn't right. Finally, I realized that I really missed Israel. After long and hard consideration, I reached a decision to go back to Israel as an immigrant and try to establish my life there.

Chapter Three: Anchors Aweigh

This time, for several reasons, I decided to travel to Israel by ship instead of airplane. First of all, it was much cheaper to take the two dogs by ship than to fly with them. Secondly, I could also take more baggage with me. But primarily it was because I had never traveled by ship, and I knew from the movies that it would be glamorous and exciting.

The first problem was finding a home for all the cats. I certainly did not intend to take eleven cats to Israel with me and I knew from experience that Israel was well populated with cats. But it certainly wasn't easy to find homes for all of them in New York. Finally, though, the last cat was passed on to its new owners.

I bought a good-sized trunk—you have to have a trunk if you are traveling by ship! About half of it was filled with books, the rest with clothes and linens, and on the top, wrapped in canvas, was a saddle, because I was sure that in Israel I would have access to a horse. I had a small suitcase to carry on the ship and I was ready.

The day of embarkation arrived and the dogs and I went down to the pier. The trunk had been sent ahead, but I had to stand in line with my suitcase and the dogs to check in and board. The line seemed to consist entirely of old Greek ladies dressed in long black dresses with scarves over their heads carrying bundles tied up in brown paper. Here and there, interspersed in the crowd, were a few Greek Orthodox priests. True that this was a Greek ship, but I had been expecting something a bit different. In the movies there were always plenty of young, glamorous and fun people on cruise ships. Where were they all? After a long wait I was able to put my suitcase in my cabin—to be shared with two other as yet unknown persons—and to take the dogs up to the kennel on the top deck.

The dogs were not too happy about being closed up in a kennel. They had never been kenneled before, and they looked at me with amazement when I closed the door on them and walked away. Their pitiful whines followed me as I climbed down the steep stairs to the main deck. The facilities seemed to be all right. The kennels were roomy and well protected from the wind and weather, and there was a comfortable dog bed inside. I was allowed to let them loose to run around on the top deck. I also discovered that the dogs would be fed on the same meat that we would eat in the dining hall, so I couldn't object to that.

I returned to the cabin to meet my roommates, who turned out to be two elderly ladies, not Greeks, but Jewish grandmothers traveling to Israel. I figured I could live with them for a week without any problems; hopefully neither of them snored or was an insomniac.

When it was time to depart I went up to the deck to wave goodbye to the shores of New York, like in all the old movies. How exciting, I thought. My first ocean crossing!

As I looked around at the other passengers, I noticed a family standing nearby, and with them a dog. And the dog was a female collie.

"Hi," I said, "What a lovely dog! I have a dog on board too, and he is also a collie. What a coincidence!"

"Really? How odd!" answered a woman about my age. "Where is your dog?"

"Up on the top deck in the kennels," I answered. "How come you're allowed to have your dog down here with you?"

"Since we have a family cabin, they let us keep Honey with us, too," she answered. "My name is Deborah, by the way."

As we talked, we found that we had other interests in common, besides collies. Her family was returning from several years spent in the U.S.. There was Ilan and Liora, the parents, two children, Erez who was 8 and Tamar who was 10, and 'Auntie' Deborah, who had completed her nursing degree in the U.S.. They were now returning home, and would be living in Jerusalem. Maybe this trip wouldn't be so boring after all, I thought.

However, as the ship began to move out beyond the harbor and into the sea, I felt less sure of my potential enjoyment. By the time we were a few hours away from dry land, I was curled up in my bunk feeling totally miserable. I had never pictured myself being seasick; now all I wanted was to quietly die.

At dinnertime, my new friend Deborah came to find me, and discovered me sunk in misery. Sure that the best thing for me was to get up, move around, and get something in my stomach, she dragged me out of bed and towed me in the general direction of the dining hall. I never got any farther than the first public toilet in the corridor, and for a while it looked doubtful that I would give up that sanctuary even to return to my bunk.

By the next day, thanks to calm weather and a massive dose of travel sickness pills, I felt somewhat better, though very guilty about having abandoned my poor dogs. So Deborah and I made our way to the top deck where the kennels were, in the hopes of letting them out to run around a bit.

However, as we got to the top of the metal staircase leading up, we were hit by such a blast of wind that for a moment I was sure that I would be blown overboard. The brisk wind combined with the movement of the ship created such a strong gust that it was almost impossible to stand against it. Holding on to the railing around the deck, we dragged ourselves over to the kennels to find the dogs perfectly all right and well sheltered. But there was certainly no possibility of letting them out.

I found that shipboard life was quite boring, not at all like it is portrayed in the movies. There were no handsome young men dying to make my acquaintance. Since most of the travelers were either old Jewish ladies or old Greeks, the most interesting conversations I had were with the crewmembers, who had little time to chat. I sat in the nightclub in the evenings listening to the bored musicians play for three or four people, wondering where the romance was. Deborah, being more sensible, usually went to bed early.

The dogs seemed to be doing all right, but after a few days we noticed, on our daily, effort-filled visit, they weren't eating well, despite the good meat they were being fed. Deborah and I decided that they, too, might be seasick. What could we do about it? Well, Deborah suggested, we could go to the ship's doctor, pretend that WE were seasick, and ask for pills. That seemed like a reasonable idea.

As office hours came around, we walked into the ship's doctor's office, and Deborah gave him her story about being seasick. He looked at her with a skeptical face—she certainly looked in the pink of health—and then agreed.

"All right," he said, "you can have some pills, but you take the first two here." Deborah had no choice but to swallow the pills before we could leave the office with what we needed for the dogs. I don't think she had to visit the bathroom for two days after that. It did seem to perk the dogs up, though.

After nearly two weeks at sea, we finally approached Haifa and my new life in Israel. But as we came near to harbor, there was one more thing I had to do. Waiting until my two roommates were out, I snuck the two dogs down to the room, and into the shower.

They had become quite grubby from their two weeks on deck under the ship's funnel—I couldn't possibly disembark with dirty dogs! So into the shower we all got, and after some extreme efforts, we all got out, fairly clean. A bit more effort to dry the dogs and the cabin, and we were ready for shore.

Wafi celebrated the return to the homeland of her ancestors by promptly coming into season.

Chapter Four: Settling In

As I didn't have any place to live in Israel, and having just landed on shore with my trunk and two dogs, finding some place to live was my first priority. Finding those accommodations wasn't easy, I soon discovered. I had been accepted to a program at the Hebrew University, a new department in communications, which I thought would be fun and interesting and also give me an opportunity to make use of my artistic talents. But I certainly could not live in the dorms with two dogs. My limited financial situation did not give me a lot of other possibilities either. So for the time being, until I found a place to live, the dogs had to go into a boarding kennel.

I had been told that there was a boarding kennel in Jerusalem, on the grounds of the Jerusalem Biblical Zoo. So that was my first stop.

The Jerusalem Biblical Zoo was a very well-known institution in Jerusalem. In fact, it was the only zoo there, and one of the first in Israel. The original idea had been to collect all the various species of animal mentioned in the Bible and to enable the public to see them. On each cage, as well as the species name and description of the animal, were the quotations from the Bible referring to that particular animal. For instance, you might find the famous quote, "The lion shall lie down with the lamb" (Isa.11:6) on the sign in front of the lion's cage, along with the Latin name, habitat, and other information that is usually found in zoos. And across the way, you might well find the pens with wild sheep. Over the years, the zoo had expanded to include many species of animal that were not Biblical, but the unique philosophy of the zoo remained. The wealth of information provided both about the animals themselves and their ancient connection to this land, in a setting by the hills of Jerusalem with their ancient terraces, stone walkways and walls built of Jerusalem stone, surrounded by the wonderful greenery also with a Biblical connotation—olive trees, figs, grape vines, and such—gave a special atmosphere to this place that was not found in more modern zoos.

I was directed to the zoo director's office, where I met a blonde woman of Valkyrian proportions in a brown leather miniskirt. This was my first introduction to Dvora Ben Shaul, chief biologist and manager of the zoo, a meeting that was to have a profound influence on my life. She was much more interested in meeting Wafi than me.

"Oh my, there is a little Cana'ani," she exclaimed as I entered her office. She leaned over and started to fondle the dogs. "Rudolphina is a good friend of mine and will be excited to hear about this. Your little bitch is probably the first foreign-born Canaan to return to her ancestral homeland! And a lovely collie, too! What are their names?"

"The Ca'naani is Wafi and the collie is Degel," I replied.

"Hebrew names, hmm? Quite appropriate."

After some time spent getting acquainted with the dogs, she finally got around to me.

"So you've come to Israel with two dogs. What are you planning to do here?"

"I am starting a course at the Hebrew University next week, in Communications," I answered.

"And what do you expect to do with the dogs? They won't let them come to class with you, and you can't keep them in the dorms."

"Well, that is my biggest problem at the moment. I need to find a place to live where I can keep them. And it would help if I could find some work to pay the expenses. I really don't know where to start."

As we were talking, a short, slightly plump blond woman of about my age burst into the office. Whatever had been her purpose in coming in was instantly forgotten when she saw Wafi.

26

"A Cana'ani!" she exclaimed enthusiastically, immediately sitting down on the floor next to the dogs and starting to make friends. Wafi was her first interest, but Degel was not neglected.

"This is Israela," Dvora said. "She runs a boarding kennel here in the zoo."

Israela was also an American, who had been living in Israel for several years. She had worked in the U.S. as a dog trainer, and was trying to make her way in Israel working with dogs as well. This, as I would soon discover, was not at all easy.

So the most immediate problem was solved. Degel and Wafi were taken down to the kennel, and I was now faced with the necessity of looking for living accommodations.

During my previous time visiting in Israel I had met Yehuda, a fellow who ran a riding stable in Jerusalem. One of the fondest memories I had, and one that had given me the feeling that I would like to live in Israel, was the memory of a ride we had taken together through the Jerusalem forest. We stopped along the way to eat figs straight from the tree. This kind of stuff was very impressive to a city-bred girl like me. I decided that he would be a good person to get in contact with again. I assumed that since he was an animal person, maybe he would know of a place I could live with my dogs. At the least maybe I could have another ride.

It took me a few days of searching to find him, as he had moved. Finally, after asking around, I found someone who told me where to look. I took a bus to the edge of town, and then started walking down a narrow road into the terraced forest that adjoined the city. Surrounded by tall pines that gave the air a unique freshness, I saw ahead of me a leveled bit of land in the midst of the trees. It was surrounded by a wooden rail fence, and inside was a little house, an open sided shed serving as a stable, a few chickens clucking around, and of course, horses.

As I opened the gate, the door of the house opened, and a tall, black bearded man came out to see who was there. It was my old friend Yehuda. I was doubtful that he would recognize me; after all, we had only had a short acquaintance. But he greeted me as an old friend.

"You haven't been around for quite a while," he said.

"I was back in the States for a year. But now I am going to do a course at the university. Actually, I came around to ask if you might know of somewhere that I can rent a room."

"Won't they give you a room in the dorms?" he asked.

"Well, there is a small problem. I brought my two dogs with me, and they are not allowed in the dorms."

It turned out that he had a room available, which he was willing to let me use in exchange for working part time in the stable. The dogs were no problem either. What luck!

I was eager to move in as quickly as possible, so that I could get my dogs out of the kennel. I found a taxi that was willing to take my trunk, my dogs, and me and we drove down to the stable.

Yehuda showed me my room. It was small but quite sufficient. I started to unpack. It was already late afternoon and was getting quite dim, but looking around, I could see no light switch.

"Yehuda," I called, "where is the light switch?"

"Oh, there isn't any," he replied casually, "I don't have any electricity."

I was stunned. I had never before lived in a place without electricity; even the summer camps that I went to as a kid in the U.S. had electricity.

"Why not?"

"Oh well, it is just typical Israeli bureaucracy. The city won't approve bringing electric lines out here unless I have a particular form, and they are causing me problems with that. These things happen all the time here—you'll see for yourself!"

"But will you be getting it?"

"Sure, eventually. Maybe in a year or two."

It was obvious that I was going to have to learn a new lifestyle. We used small kerosene lamps in the evenings. They gave enough light to read by, which was the only entertainment available other than a small transistor radio. If we needed strong light for some particular purpose, we could light a pressure lamp, also powered by kerosene, but which could be pumped up to give quite a lot of light.

There was also no hot water, unless the day was sunny enough to heat it up. Solar-powered water heaters were very common in Israel and very efficient. Since a good proportion of the year the weather was sunny, most of the time there was plenty of hot water. But for rainy days, a normal household had a backup electrical system to heat the water. On those days, we either heated a pot of water on the gas stove, or showered in cold water.

The dogs, however, loved the place. Wafi, in particular, was very happy to be out of the city in the sort of place a Canaan was intended to be. She wasn't crazy about all the people who showed up to ride and take lessons, but she enjoyed the freedom that she had, and soon showed her talents as a guard dog. Anybody approaching down the little road was greeted by a fury of barking as Wafi ran around keeping well out of reach but giving the alarm that a stranger was coming. On the other hand, she also showed some of the surprising characteristics of the breed that I had not really been familiar with before. She had always gotten along well with the cats while we were living in New York, even cuddling up with them. But I had to admit that I was quite surprised to find her curled up with the stable's baby chicks cuddled against her body as they would have done with a mother hen, and a few of them, who apparently hadn't found a suitable spot, sitting on her head and back.

Since I was living rent free, I decided to find a better use for the housing grant I had from the university. I imported two female collie pups from the U.S., with plans for breeding in the future. Soon, Dawn and Dandi joined the family. My landlord began to wonder if the place was a stable or a kennel.

I had remained in contact with Dvora and Israela from the Jerusalem zoo since my arrival in Israel. We shared many interests, including our love of animals, and in particular, Canaan dogs. One day, after a few months of being in Israel, they told me that they were looking for a place to establish a kennel. The idea was to breed Canaan Dogs, Israel's native breed, and one of the only remaining natural breeds in the world, which would face extinction if it did not become an accepted domestic breed. In order to support the breeding and to make a living, a boarding kennel would also be established. The zoo was not willing for Israela to continue running the kennel there, and she needed to relocate. In addition, Dvora was a breeder of German Shepherds, and Israela of Dobermans. My expanding dog pack apparently convinced them that I was sufficiently crazy to be invited to join their group.

I was thrilled by the idea: what could be better than having a kennel? We soon started to collect additional Canaans as a basis for our breeding. The first two were a young, black and white brother and sister, Nadav and Nurit, from Professor Menzel's kennel, Bnei HaBitachon. After them, a few more were acquired from various sources. The dogs all lived in the kennel in the zoo.

Dvora knew of some abandoned British buildings at Sha'ar Hagai. It was obvious, when we went to inspect them, that to say they needed a lot of work was an understatement. On the other hand, no one seemed to know who they really belonged to or to care much about what happened to them; all of Dvora's efforts to clarify the situation dead ended. None of the authorities minded if we moved in to Sha'ar Hagai—most of them didn't seem to know that such a place existed— and no one wanted to take responsibility for it either.

Meanwhile, I was about ready for a change. I was having a hard time coping with the program of studies at the University. It was 1969, the country had just experienced a major election, and election propaganda was the topic for that year's communications studies. Coming from a democratic country with two political parties, I found it impossible to understand the Israeli political system of twenty or thirty political parties, some of them based on, it seemed to me, nothing. This combined with the difficulties of studying in a foreign language; although my Hebrew was pretty good, it was not really on a university level. I got very frustrated.

Israel was, in general, not an easy place to live in for an American. On the one hand, the general atmosphere was exciting; these were the years just after the Six-Day War, and they were filled with optimism. Anything was possible! No one really cared much about your background or your qualifications. If there was something you wanted to do, then you were welcome to try. People were friendly and welcoming, and ready to make you a part of the group and of the society. There was a feeling of security and safety; we were, after all, invincible! It was possible, for example, to travel anywhere by hitchhiking since no one considered it to be dangerous. I could walk around town late at night without worry, with the only problem being that, especially in Jerusalem, the sidewalks were rolled up by 9 p.m.

But there were some problems. The first was the bureaucracy, which seemed to be an inheritance from the days of the Turks. Getting anything accomplished demanded long-range planning and nerves of steel. The U.S. was not without its bureaucracy but the Middle Eastern attitude of "tomorrow, or maybe the next day...or maybe next year..." was definitely hard to take.

Another difficulty I had was the feeling that everyone seemed to feel entitled to know everything about me the moment they met me. We Americans value our privacy. I found it hard to accustom myself to sitting down on a public bus and having my seatmate, a stranger, ask me where I lived, what my job was, how much I earned, and if I had a boyfriend. This was combined with a tendency for people to stand within about an inch of my face while talking to me; obviously, the 'personal space' in the Middle East was quite a bit less than in America.

However, I found that I was much more adaptable than I would ever have imagined, and was able to cope with this very different lifestyle, although it wasn't easy.

My idyll at the riding stable was also coming to an end. My boss was annoyed that I had other friends and interests, and was no longer happy about all the dogs. One day, after a major disagreement, I found all my possessions in a pile outside in the yard. Obviously, the time had come to move.

Attempts to get some sort of permission to establish a kennel at Sha'ar Hagai proceeded as expected; they were mired down in bureaucracy. And in the meantime, we had collected a number of dogs and space was becoming a problem, as Israela had had to close down her kennel. It was decided that, since I didn't have a place to live any way, I would move out to Sha'ar Hagai with the dogs, and would shortly be joined by the others. Meanwhile, attempts would go on to make our move official.

And that's how ten assorted dogs and I became the first inhabitants of Sha'ar Hagai.

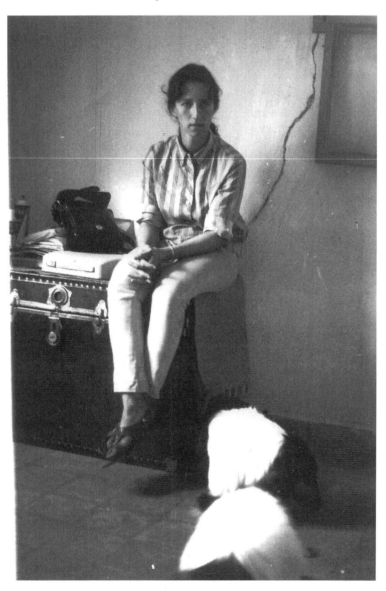

Chapter Five: Pioneering

So, there I was, the sole human inhabitant of Sha'ar Hagai. It was really the first time in my life that I had lived totally alone anywhere. As a city girl, I was accustomed to always having people nearby, but the closest neighbors now were several kilometers away and had no idea that I lived there. There was of course no phone, this being long before the days of cell phones; my only connection with the world was by car.

But surprisingly, I didn't feel lonely. For one thing, I had plenty of dogs to keep me company, and I certainly had plenty to do to keep myself busy.

The first thing to do was to make the house livable, and that was a major project that meant digging out the huge piles of rubble and sheep droppings, and thoroughly scrubbing everything. The house was built of 36-centimeter thick walls of steel-reinforced concrete. The British had built this place to withstand bombings, and it had; there were a few minor cracks in the walls showing where artillery hits had been made during the War of Independence in 1948. The windows were protected with steel bars that were inserted deeply into the walls, and the floor was comprised of gray concrete tiles. There was no electricity, of course, the lines had rotted away years ago. But Dvora was confident that we would soon be connected to power. Meanwhile, I had my first experiences with living by the light of candles and wind lanterns, which were definitely not as romantic as in the movies, but very conducive to an 'early to bed' lifestyle.

Within a few days, I had the place scrubbed and clean, after dragging out innumerable bucketloads of rubble. I installed my meager possessions: my clothes, books, and saddle, a few food supplies that didn't require cooking, and a *sochnut* bed, a metal bed frame with a thin and traditionally striped ticking mattress, named after the *Sochnut*, the

Jewish Agency that provided this as part of the standard new immigrant's kit. I had my dogs to keep me company, but otherwise I was totally isolated—no electricity, no telephone, no neighbors—and soon, I discovered, no water!

Apparently it had been a fluke that there had been water at all; there must have been some water left in the roof tanks, either from the rains of the previous year, or from some historical time in the past when the water pipes had been connected. However, this supply quickly fizzled out after a few days cleaning and residence and I then discovered that there were no water pipes, other than rotted-away remnants from the days of the British, and no connection to any water source. Perhaps my only luck in the situation was that I was never fond of drinking water, being addicted like many Americans to soft drinks, so I was probably saved from countless diseases that could have been conveyed by drinking from the limited water supply I had found.

Fortunately, I did have the use of a car. My parents, tolerant of their rebellious daughter as ever, and hopeful that perhaps I was now going to settle down and start living a normal life, had provided me with the funds to buy a car—my part of the investment in the Sha'ar Hagai Farm, the investment that would make me an equal partner, with the right to live there as well. I had purchased a Volkswagen van, very practical for a kennel vehicle, I thought. Of course, I had never driven a vehicle of that size, and never with a stick shift either, but those were minor problems that I knew could be overcome with practice. I did end up causing several traffic jams in the narrow Jerusalem streets, as the car frequently lurched and died when I tried to change gears. But for now, the major use of the car was bringing my daily water supply. Every day, I filled the car up with 20-liter jerry cans, and drove around to various friends and acquaintances to fill them up. I needed drinking water for the dogs, for washing (I usually showered at someone's house as well, saving water, of course), and for cleaning.

It took some time for anyone to notice that I lived up there on the hillside. One day, after about three weeks at my new home, I heard a car laboriously struggling up the dirt track. When I looked out of my barred windows, I saw that it was a police patrol car. They started to get out of the car to have a look around, when the dogs noticed them, and in a flash charged, barking hysterically. The police officers, not aware that the collies were simply excited to have visitors, leapt for the closest refuge, which happened to be my van, which luckily wasn't locked. It took me a few minutes to reassure them that it was perfectly safe for them to come out again.

They became regular visitors, stopping by for a cup of coffee on their rounds. They were fascinated by the idea of a woman living alone up on the hillside, and the whole idea of a dog kennel seemed very strange to them. Their initial idea had been that we were setting up some sort of house of ill repute in this isolated spot, and truthfully, I am not sure whether they were disappointed to learn that this was not the case.

Another evening, I took a bus to Tel Aviv, which was about an hour and a half from Sha'ar Hagai. Coming home I took a *sherut*, the public taxis that follow the major bus routes, taking as many passengers going in the same direction as they can fit, whether they know each other or not. I asked the driver to stop for me at the entrance to the dirt road. He stopped automatically, and then suddenly noticed where we were.

"What do you want to stop here for?" he asked. "There is nothing here!"

No matter how I tried to explain that I lived there, and that there were indeed houses up on the hillside, he refused to believe it.

"I've been driving this route for 15 years, and I never saw any houses here," he declared. Supported by the other passengers, he refused to let me out of the taxi in the middle of nowhere in the dark of late evening and drove on, letting me off at the next settlement. Everyone was sure they had saved a poor and confused tourist from getting lost in the forest. I had to walk four kilometers to get back home.

But after only a few weeks of total isolation, Israela and Dvora were ready to join me on the farm. Each took over one of the old buildings and began clean-up and repairs. Each woman, of course, was accompanied by another few dogs.

Our first and most important project was to obtain a steady supply of water. There was a limit to how long we could go around collecting jerry cans of water for our daily use. As none of us had the money for hiring the job out, we knew we had to buy water pipes and lay them ourselves. For someone like me, inexperienced in manual labor, digging trenches for water pipes was quite a revelation.

After a few days of serious labor, assisted by a few friends a bit more muscular than we were, the pipes were in and we were ready to have the water turned on. The water line was still not connected to all the houses, but in celebration, we certainly felt that we all deserved a good shower in our own water supply, so a hose pipe was connected to the end of the pipe line, and we took turns showering each other in the relative privacy in the back of the van, away from the prying eyes of our police friends down on the road. The car needed a wash anyway. That was probably one of the most satisfying showers I ever had.

Life was not easy in those days. Living without water and electricity, in isolated and primitive conditions, with very little money, is an adventure when it is for a limited period, but as a permanent lifestyle, the excitement starts to fade. It appeared that all the hopes for quickly getting connected to the electric grid, and to the telephone lines were not about to be realized. I grew accustomed to lighting wind lanterns in the evening, going to bed early and getting up with the sun. After a while, I began to realize that these inconveniences did not bother me as much as I had expected.

Dvora was the most organized of us. She had grown up on a huge ranch in Texas, and spent a good part of her life in all sorts of fascinating adventures in remote parts of the globe, so these conditions were, for her, a piece of cake. She also was well established in Israel, with plenty of furniture and household accessories, and her house soon looked homey and welcoming. She was wonderful at taking the simplest bits of furniture or fabric and turning them into something attractive and welcoming.

Israela, on the other hand, was far from being an ideal homemaker. For her, housekeeping was the minimum effort one needed to expend to be able to find your way through the house without getting lost in the confusion.

I fell rather in the middle. I didn't have very many things to take up space in my house; one trunk's worth doesn't go very far in filling up three rooms. I had very minimal furniture: a bed, a few chairs, an arrangement of bricks and orange crates for shelves, and a camping stove for cooking on, but for the time being it was adequate. It wasn't too hard to keep those limited possessions in reasonable order.

One problem that I quickly found myself coping with was laundry. In my past experience, the dirty laundry was dumped in the laundry basket, disappeared down to the washing machine, and was later returned to my room clean and neatly folded. Now, not only was this system missing the most important part—my mother—but there wasn't even a washing machine: I had to do my laundry by hand. There was, of course, no hot water, but there was a large selection of cold-water detergents, and I began to learn systems of soaking and scrubbing.

Another revelation were the sanitary facilities. My house contained what was known as a 'Turkish toilet.' This consisted of a hole in the floor with a flush tank attached. I found it very difficult to figure out the correct stance—or squat—for making use of this facility. The flush tank itself also seemed to date back to the days of the Turks; it made an astonishing roar when activated and seemed ready to shake itself off the wall, to the point where I frequently found it less intimidating to flush with a bucket of water.

The sewer system was solid. Built by the British, like everything else they had left behind in Israel, it was made to last, and seemed to have been planned to service one of the large boroughs of London. There was a complicated system of manholes and pipes leading off into the *wadi*, or valley, where there was apparently a huge septic tank—of which we didn't know the exact location then. Some of the manholes were large enough to go down into, in case there was a need for doing any work on the system, and even had ladders inside.

In a system that had been left abandoned for twenty years, there were bound to be blockages, so I soon learned all about sewer cleaning. The greatest sewer adventure happened one day when Dvora, home alone, decided to go down into the manhole behind her house with the hosepipe to flush it out. She stripped off her clothes—it was much easier to wash yourself clean than to clean up clothes after a session with the sewer—and climbed down into the manhole in the buff. However, after having completed washing down the pipeline, she discovered that, although it had been no problem going down into the sewer, she couldn't get back up the ladder; she was a tall, large woman, and the space between the rungs and the walls wouldn't let her bend her knees enough to climb up. Dvora was not fit enough to start hauling herself up hand over hand, so she was stuck down there. She knew there was no one around to help, and resigned herself to waiting for one of us to get home. And then, surprise, surprise, she heard the voice of a friend calling her from in front of the house—a male friend, who had chosen just this time to come to visit!

Needless to say, Dvora remained quiet as a mouse until Israela and I got home and were able to help her get up out of the sewer.

Of course, buildings that had been empty as long as ours were bound to have collected other tenants over the years. I soon learned that being squeamish about spiders and other insects that wouldn't have dared set foot in my fastidious mother's domain was totally useless out here. The worst for me were the rats. I had never had experience with rats other than the white variety in the laboratory, but here, the huge field rats felt that they were rightful tenants and we were the intruders. For the most part I only saw a flash of movement in the gloom outside the perimeter of the wind lantern's illumination. I soon got into the habit of sending one of the collies into the room before me, with the command, "Dawn! Rats!" Dawn quickly got into the spirit of the game, dashing in and scouring the room as the rats fled in all directions. Once or twice she even managed to catch one, and then, to my disgust, she ate the beast—making me wonder if this was such a good idea after all.

Even before we built kennels, we took dogs in for boarding and training, as we were all desperate for some kind of income. The primitive conditions of those days would make me cringe today—dogs were kept in empty rooms of all the houses, and were even kept tied outside to convenient trees. Obviously it was urgent to build some proper kennels.

Of course, with money being very short, we couldn't just hire a builder to come and do the work for us; we were barely able to scrape together enough to buy the materials. But one of the things that most impressed me about Israel was the willingness of everyone I met to pitch in and work, even if the job to be done was something totally outside of their experience. So our work crew, composed of other partners in the farm, was extremely varied, including several guys who worked in various white-collar office jobs, our veterinarian, Dvora and Israela, of course, and me, whose only experience with construction work until moving to Israel was passing by a construction site.

The first job was laying a cement floor for the kennel. We had to clean and level the area—done by muscle power, with rakes, shovels and hoes. Then we had to lay down a layer of gravel and pour the cement on top of that. The cement also had to be mixed by hand because we had no possibility of bringing in a machine to do it, both due to the expense, and the fact that the access road was not something that anyone in his right mind would want to drive up with a cement mixer. The work was exhausting and dirty, and I am afraid that my contribution was not major.

42

In the end, though, we had a cement floor, with nice convenient holes left at intervals for the pipes of the kennel framework. In order to leave holes for the pipes, old soft drink bottles were set into the wet cement at the required intervals, and pulled out after the cement dried. Since they were glass, they didn't stick, and left perfect holes in the cement for setting in the poles. My American habit of drinking soft drinks instead of water had come in handy again.

Next we built a framework of pipes that screwed together, and stretched a chain link fence over the whole framework. There were special techniques for this also, making use of a broom handle to stretch the wire to the poles; one of us held it steady while the others tied the wire in place. Finally the doors were made, also out of pipes and chain link fencing, and hung on the hinges that had been welded onto the pipes.

The whole project took days of exhausting labor, but finally, we stood back and looked at our brand new kennel, which was spacious, clean, and just waiting to be populated.

I found that there was nothing more satisfying than standing back to admire the work we had completed with our own hands, especially when we had no idea we could do it.

So now we were ready to officially open the Sha'ar Hagai Kennels for business.

Chapter Six: Four Footed Friends and Others

Although the kennels were really intended for boarding dogs in order to make money to support ourselves, the truth was our own dogs took up a good portion of it. We had managed to collect a number of Canaans as the basis for our intended breeding program.

It is a common observation that people and their dogs are usually similar, often even in appearance and behavior. But I have, from the start, been very attracted to two very different breeds of dog, the collie and the Canaan dog. So which part of me is Canaan and which part is collie? Well, after thinking about it, I am much more like a Canaan—very attached to my own territory, very devoted and loyal to my own 'pack' of friends and family and rather suspicious and shy of strangers; it takes me time to make new friends. But I would LIKE to be more like a collie—beautiful and elegant, friendly, outgoing, loving and loved by all.

Over the years, we have had many dogs, each unique in its own way, but there are always a few that retain a special spot in one's memory. In those early years, we obtained dogs from many sources: strays that appeared to be Canaans, dogs from the Bedouin or wild from the desert, dogs from Professor Menzel or from her breeding, dogs from people who couldn't keep them any longer for one reason or another and thought that we would provide a good solution to the problem. The breed was in the very early stages of development, and there was a wide variation in type. We had the difficult task of deciding which dogs were purebred, and which were close enough to the ideal as described in the standard Professor Menzel had written. The ideal included all the characteristics of the perfect Canaan Dog, from nose to tail tip, putting an emphasis on those qualities most important for survival—a strong and sound body build, agility and correct movement, correct coat as protection against dangers of the environment and enemies, and the correct temperament—suspicious, adaptable, intelligent and quick to learn and react, and extremely loyal. We then did test breedings to see if those dogs were as pure genotypically as they appeared to be phenotypically. It is quite possible for a dog to have certain characteristics that you can see, for example, prick ears—this is the phenotype, the external appearance. But he may also be carrying other factors in his genetic makeup, such as the gene for drop ears, which he may pass on to his offspring—this is the genotype. There were many dogs that spent some time with us, and then were, for one reason or another, eliminated from consideration as breeding stock, and we had to find good homes for them, not an easy task either.

Of the dogs from those days that hold a special place in my memory, the first was Simi, or formally, Laish me Bnei HaBitachon. Simi was from the kennels of Professor Menzel and had been given, as a young puppy, to relatives in Tel Aviv. We first met him when he was about a year and a half old.

Wafi had again come into season, and she was now close to two years of age, old enough to be bred. This would be our first Canaan litter, and the prospect was very exciting. Professor Menzel, or Rudolphina as her friends called her, recommended that we consider breeding her to Simi, so we made contact with the family, and drove down to Tel Aviv.

Simi was a beautiful dog, a perfect example of what we thought a Canaan should be, very masculine and strongly built, cream colored, with lovely small ears and a well-curled tail. He was full of self-confidence, and was thrilled to meet Wafi. To start with, he had no idea of what to do, but after some time playing, his instincts began to take over and the breeding took place.

I did not have very much experience, at this stage, in dog breeding; most of what I knew I had read in books. Simi and Wafi were in what I knew was a 'tie,' or in street terms, 'stuck together.' This was the period when the sperm was being ejaculated into the bitch and, according to the books, could take from ten minutes to half an hour or so. Well, ten minutes passed, and so did half an hour, and the two remained 'stuck' Finally, after over an hour, the breeding concluded. Boy, I thought, if the duration has anything to do with it, Wafi should have ten puppies. That Simi sure must be virile!

Well, Wafi did not have ten puppies, but only two, and both of them were black with white. Shortly after their birth, Simi also became a resident of Sha'ar Hagai.

The story of how he became ours is a perfect example of why living with Canaans is different then other breeds. Simi's owner, a teenaged boy of about fifteen, decided that he wanted to train his dog. There was a training group being held in a nearby park, and the two joined the group. The trainer was a fellow who had spent a number of years in Germany, and very much believed in German training methods. One of the methods that he advocated, and was using in his course, was to agitate the dogs to display aggression, and then to demonstrate the handler's power over the dog by forcing the dog to perform various obedience commands, even when he was in a state of excitement.

Simi decided that the aggressive part of the exercise was very much to his taste, but the obedience was another matter. He began aggressively guarding the territory around his house and soon decided that the public street in front was also part of his territory. He began jumping over the fence and lying in wait for unsuspecting passersby who he then chased off with an excellent example of aggressive display and sometimes with a bite.

Simi's owners were unable to find any way to keep their dog in the yard; one of the endearing qualities of the Canaan is his agility, strength and intelligence, which means that it is hard to find a fence that will hold him in. After Simi bit a number of people, his owners decided that he would have to go back to Professor Menzel, and he was then offered to us. We were, of course, happy to have him; he was a beauty.

Simi settled in very well at Sha'ar Hagai, and, in time, became the first Israel Champion Canaan. One of the conditions, though, for him to receive his championship, was that we agree not to bring him to any more shows. Within a few minutes of arriving at any show, he started to treat even new locations as his territory and began the by now familiar aggressive rituals to protect it from anything on two or four feet.

Simi lived to a good old age and sired many litters. Almost all of the Canaan champions of today go back to Simi, and he remains, in my memory, one of the finest examples of the breed ever.

Dvora and Simi

He always demanded to be treated with respect. The only time I ever had trouble with him was once when I entered his kennel to take out a bitch in season that had been left with him for breeding. What? he seemed to say. Take away HIS bitch? Simi very deliberately walked up to me, looked me in the eye, bit me on the arm hard enough to be sure that I understood but not enough to cause much damage, and then turned his back and walked back to HIS bitch. I got the hint.

Another of the foundation sires of Sha'ar Hagai also had a reputation as an aggressive bastard. Dvora discovered him one day in an army camp—a beautiful red Canaan, very typical, who was being used as a guard dog on the camp perimeter. Dvora asked the commander if she could have him. "Sure, go ahead and take him," the commander answered, laughing to himself. This dog was so aggressive that even the dog handlers on the base couldn't handle him. He was kept permanently tied out and simply brought food and water.

Dvora always had a leash on hand in her car, so she walked over to him, put the leash on, walked off, put him in her car and drove away, leaving the commander and dog handlers staring after her with open mouths. The dog, who we named Patpatan ('Chatterbox,' because he liked to 'talk') was very happy to have 'retired' from army service. Although he was an excellent watchdog, he never caused trouble for the people he knew and who cared for him. But he was never able to tolerate anyone dressed in an army uniform, even people he knew well and loved. Friends on reserves duty dressed in uniform were likely to get a good bite if they were not careful.

Patpatan was also the sire of some lovely puppies. As he got older and ready to retire, a friend of ours who had been a commando and lived in a place where he felt the necessity for a good watchdog begged us to let him have Patpatan; he had fallen in love with him. Patpatan went to live out his last years as a home watchdog, and he and his new master became nearly inseparable.

In those days, we often made trips to Bedouin camps in the desert to look for dogs. The Bedouin kept many dogs, as guards for their camps and for their flocks of sheep and other livestock. It was rare for a Bedouin to have a bitch—they usually kept males. Living close to nature as they did, they were always aware of where the bitches lived and when and where there were puppies. When they needed a new dog, they caught a puppy, and kept it tied up in the camp until it was old enough to work as a guard dog. The Bedouin did not keep dogs for sentimental reasons; their dogs were working animals, and they depended on them to warn of approaching strangers, and to chase off any wild animals or strays that might endanger or prey on the livestock. A dog that did not function as a working animal was not kept, and the Bedouin dog could not expect much in the way of care or affection; he was more likely to have stones thrown at him than to be petted, and his food consisted of scraps and whatever he could scrounge for himself. But if he was a good working dog, he was definitely appreciated, and the Bedouin would not sell him for any price. "He guards my tent and my flock. I need him. Who would do the job if I sold him?" they answered us.

Dvora and I usually made these trips, Dvora being fluent enough in Arabic to communicate. She had enough experience in life dealing with all types of people that she was not to be put off by a few Bedouin. The Bedouin, I am sure, found the situation highly amusing. There we were, two women venturing alone into one of the last bastions of a dominant male society, looking for dogs—one of the most scorned animals in Arab culture. However, Bedouins have very strict customs where guests are concerned, so we were always treated as honored visitors, offered refreshments, and never laughed at, at least not to our faces. We all sat on the floor on beautiful woven carpets and cushions. The Bedouin women were present only to serve; they never sat with us.

Refreshments among the Bedouin first of all consisted of strong sweet tea. I am not a lover of tea; my instant association is of the tea given me by my mother when I was sick in bed as a child, but manners dictated that I drink what I was offered by the Bedouin. At the time I was not aware of the custom they have of immediately refilling your cup when you have emptied it, and found myself drinking cup after cup as Dvora chatted with the men. We were then offered food, which, when we weren't able to find a good excuse, usually consisted of a huge pile of rice on a platter in the middle of the floor, usually yellow in color from saffron, with various sauces and additions, often made of things that I couldn't identify. One was expected to reach out, take a handful of rice, form it into a ball, and eat. It was actually quite tasty. This was followed by coffee—black, thick and bitter. Once again, custom dictated refilling the cups as soon as they were empty. Casual conversation accompanied the meal. On a few occasions, I understand that Dvora was offered several camels if she would sell me to them—as the older woman, she was assumed to be my mother. They apparently liked my green eyes. I doubt that they were serious—it was obvious, looking at me, that I wouldn't be worth much as a worker in a Bedouin camp—they were being polite.

I quickly learned to turn over my cup when I was finished with the first cup of tea or coffee, to save myself from the unending refills. Toilet facilities are not readily available in the desert.

Meanwhile, Dvora discussed dogs with the men. There were many lovely dogs around the camps, but these were not for sale. The men offered to give us puppies if we came back at the right season, or to catch wild dogs for us. At one camp, there was a bitch skulking around the fringes, and they offered to catch her for us. Before we could even react, several of the young men ran off after the poor bitch, who was panic stricken. They chased her for at least half an hour, splitting up and heading her off so that she couldn't escape, and finally flattening her with a hard kick to the hindquarters.

Dvora and I were in shock, but we certainly couldn't show it—the Bedouins felt they were doing us a favor. And so we obtained Zahava. She was a medium-sized golden colored (therefore her name, meaning 'goldie') bitch, with longish coat, a little white trim on chest and feet, and a well-plumed tail. She appeared to be about two years old. We put a collar and lead on her and put her in the car. She was in a state of total shock, and huddled in the corner, not moving.

When we got home, we put her in the kennel with food and water. She lay in a corner, not moving, not reacting to anything, and not looking at us, absolutely catatonic. This continued for several days, and we began to get seriously worried that at this rate, she would die.

And then, after three days, she sat up and looked around. She spotted the food with a look that suggested she had never been given food before and quickly became a dog, rather than a terrified wild animal. She had decided that life could be good if people were willing to feed her, and she was going to enjoy it. She wolfed it down, drank water, and walked over to inspect us. From then on, Zahava began to behave like any dog born into 'civilization.'

She learned incredibly fast. Dvora took her in as a house dog, and within a few days she understood all the rules of being clean in the house, not doing damage, and so on. She also became a wonderful watchdog. However, there was one thing that she could never learn, which was not to steal food; this was too ingrained in her. Her difficult life in the desert had taught her that you never knew what might be available tomorrow, so you had better take advantage of what was around today. Whenever she had a chance, she stole food. What she could, she ate and what was beyond her ability to finish off, she buried in the garden as a reserve for hard times.

Zahava was the only dog I have ever known that was able to steal an entire pot of food off the stove while it was cooking, taking it very carefully by the handle and walking off with it without spilling a drop.

Although a pure Bedouin bitch, Zahava was not of the type that we planned to breed, so in the end we found her a good home in Jerusalem, with a couple who loved her very much, despite her food thefts. She lived to a ripe old age, comfortably fat, and always very protective of her property and people.

We acquired one of our foundation bitches, Sufa (Storm) from the Bedouin in Petra. In this case when the sheikh of one of the tribes with which Dvora was well acquainted, saw how interested we were in the Canaans, he offered to bring us a puppy. Some weeks later, he returned from Jordan (for the Bedouin, borders are insignificant) with a tiny golden puppy, no more than five or six weeks old. Sufa was young, but full of spirit.

She knew from the moment she set foot in Sha'ar Hagai that she was the queen, and so she remained for her whole life. She was a gentle ruler, never looking for trouble, but able to show the other dogs, with a glance, that they had better behave when they were around her. She grew to be a very beautiful and typical Canaan, but was never fond of dog shows, so after a few tries, she was left at home. However, she produced some beautiful puppies that carried on for her in the show ring.

Dvora had, up to now, had a huge influence on my new life in Israel. I had never met anyone like her before in my sheltered Chicago life. She had been born and raised on a ranch in Texas, not the normal environment for a Jewish family. But Dvora was a committed Zionist from a young age, and at the age of sixteen, when the War of Independence broke out in Israel, she decided that she had to help. She managed to get to Israel and participated in the defense of the country in any way she could—like transporting guns by hiding them under her dress. Who would suspect an innocent-looking teenager?

After the war, she returned to the U.S. and went back to school, quickly gaining several degrees in biochemistry—she was highly intelligent and had a photographic memory, remembering everything she had ever read. She married an officer in the U.S. Air Force, who was later lost in a flight that went down over China at the time of the Korean War. Not one to give up easily, she traveled illegally to China to search for him, tragically with no results. She subsequently went to work for the WHO, spending time in Vietnam, a period that ended when her jeep hit a land mine and was blown up, leaving her with a broken back. After a year of hospitalization and rehabilitation, Dvora was ready to return to her active life, and decided the time had come to return to Israel, which she loved and planned to make her permanent home.

She had a variety of jobs in Israel, and published some highly respected research. But the most interesting stories were from her years as the chief biologist and manager of the Jerusalem zoo. One of her projects was to hand raise a lion cub. He lived in her apartment in Jerusalem, and went out in the yard to play like a well-behaved house pet. Her neighbors didn't seem to notice that there was anything unusual; people in those days tended to mind their own business. But as he got bigger and bigger, it began to be obvious that this was an odd sort of pet. One day, Dvora needed a plumber to fix some problems she was having with the pipes. The plumber arrived, and Dvora took him around the back to the yard, where the plumbing connections were. At the gate, the plumber stopped short, looking at Simba the lion.

"I'm not going in there with that lion," he said.

"Lion? Have you ever heard of anyone having a lion in Jerusalem?" Dvora answered. "You've heard of wolf dogs (the commonly used term for German Shepherds in Israel), haven't you?"

"Well, yes."

"Well, this is a lion dog," she explained.

"I'm not afraid of any dog!" the plumber announced, and calmly walked into the yard to take care of the pipes.

Simba finally had to go back to the zoo when he was about a year and a half old, after he hugged Dvora affectionately and broke a few of her ribs.

Another of my favorite stories was the time that she was hand raising an orangutan baby that had been rejected by its mother. It was midwinter and very cold, and Dvora took the baby, which needed warmth and physical contact with its 'mother' to be happy and develop properly, home with her every night.

One morning, when she was ready to leave for work, she found that her car was dead. She bundled the little orang up in baby clothes and a baby blanket to keep it warm, and headed for the bus stop.

As she got on the bus, the driver took a look and said to her, "Sorry, lady, you can't bring an animal like that on this bus."

Dvora, a tall and impressive woman, straightened to her full height and in her most scorching tones replied, "I know my baby isn't beautiful, but you don't have to talk about her like that!"

The driver turned white, and as the other passengers who had heard the exchange told him how ashamed he should be, waved Dvora through on to the bus.

The driver later in the day was talking with some friends and told them, "I did a horrible thing today." He told them the whole story.

Jerusalem was a small town in those days, and everyone knew one another. The friend laughed. "Was she a very tall, large blonde woman? Yes? Well, you've been had—that was Dvora from the zoo, and it *was* a monkey!"

Dvora had, up to now, had a huge influence on my new life in Israel, and it was through her that I met my future husband.

Dvora enjoyed having guests, and she also enjoyed cooking, so Israela and I frequently ate with her at the end of a long day. Dvora also had a proper stove and oven, which was a lot different than trying to cook a meal on a camping gas burner. She had many friends, and most of them were quite interested in seeing this new place of hers, likely wondering what she had gotten herself into this time. So, she often had guests.

One evening when I came down to dinner, her guests were a family, or part of one, at any rate, a man in his early thirties and his two young sons, three and five.

My first thought when I was introduced to Jacques Shiboleth and his children was, "They are so pale!" It was summer, and everyone in Israel looked tan and healthy, but Jacques and his boys looked as if they hadn't been out in the sun for months.

We all had a great time at dinner. Dinner at Dvora's house was always an adventure; she really enjoyed experimenting with all sorts of dishes and with her background as a world traveler, she had plenty of experience with the unusual. Table conversation was lively and ranged over a wide variety of topics. As we ate and conversed, my eyes frequently met Jacques'.

After dinner, the boys were put to bed in Dvora's spare room, and Jacques asked me if I would like to take a walk. It was a beautiful clear night; cool but not cold, with the stars shining brilliantly. One of the great advantages of living outside of the city was being able to see the stars so clearly.

We walked out into the *wadi* and found a convenient rock to sit on. This was the perfect opportunity to find out more about one another.

It turned out that Jacques was Dutch by birth. He and his family had survived the Holocaust, and he had decided that he wanted to live in Israel. He immigrated with his new wife, also a Holocaust survivor, and after completing his studies, he went to work as a diplomat for the Foreign Office. He was now in the process of divorcing his wife, who had been unable to cope with the stress of marriage, children and life in Israel. The children lived with him.

The truth was that the little family, indeed, had little time to spend in the sun. The boys, Joel and Chaim, however, despite being pale, were adorable. They had reddish-blond hair and freckles and charming smiles, and were polite and well behaved. Jacques was a real gentleman, a rare thing those days in Israel, and was educated and loved books and music. It was pretty much love at first sight. We started dating. We often went to concerts. Another favorite for both of us was movies. Jacques loved to cook and was very good at it; his mother who had grown up in Indonesia had taught him not only regular cooking, but cooking Indonesian style, which was exotic and delicious. So I was frequently invited over to his place for dinner. This was an opportunity to get to know the boys better, and after they were in bed, we would sit talking until late at night, about everything and anything—politics and Israel, his ambitions in his job in the Foreign Office, my ambitions with the dogs, and everyday nonsense. As we had no phone, he couldn't call to say hello, but when we met he would make up for it, with flowers or little gifts. We soon began to make plans to marry.

Although we found we had much in common, there was much that was strange about the other for both of us. We both loved culture—reading, concerts, theater, and movies. We both also enjoyed nature and loved spending time away from the city; neither of us had a need to be constantly surrounded by other people. Jacques lived in a location not much less isolated than the farm, in a tiny village in the hills outside of Jerusalem. In the past he had a dog, but had never known anyone before whose household consisted of more dogs than people. And the living conditions at Sha'ar Hagai, which were primitive to say the least, were not what he expected to have to cope with in modern-day Israel.

I, on the other hand, had never thought of starting married life with an instant supply of children. I had been coping with life in Israel under very strange and primitive conditions. To do so with Jacque's family was a new experience that I wasn't really totally prepared for. Instead of being able, at the end of a tiring day, to go to bed with the birds, (birds go to sleep when it gets dark, they don't fly at night, except for owls) now I had to think about making a meal for a family, and going through all the little customs that are part of raising children—preparing their clothes and school snacks for the next day, being sure that they were properly washed and ready for bed, and then to get them settled in bed with a bedtime story. You can be sure that children that are not enthusiastic about washing under normal circumstances are definitely not very cooperative when the water is cold.

I also now had to cope with the problems of laundry for a whole family, all of whom were experts at getting dirty, shopping for four, going to parents' meetings at school, and all the rest of the chores that are part of family life. And all of this was of course without all the modern conveniences that other mothers had—no washing machine, no refrigerator, no vacuum cleaner, and no television. In addition, Jacques could not drive. He had never been able to afford a car so never had learned. So all of the transportation was my responsibility.

My parents also were stunned when they heard the news. A diplomat was good—that was a profession, much more so than working with horses or dogs. But a divorced man with children? Well, anyway, if I got married, then at least someone else would be responsible for dealing with all my crazy whims. When Jacques and my parents met, they immediately liked each other, as was true with his parents and me. Wedding plans were moving forward

Then one day, while visiting at Jacques' place, I started to feel ill. He insisted that I stay overnight in the hopes that in the morning I would feel better. The next morning, although I was still feeling awful, I felt there was no choice—I had to go home to take care of my dogs. Jacques didn't drive or have a car, so there was no other way—I had to drive myself home.

Once home, I dragged myself through the daily routine, and once the dogs were cared for, I collapsed onto my bed. By evening, I had a fever of over 40° C or 104 F, and Dvora, checking in on me, decided that she had better take me to the doctor.

Half delirious, I soon found myself in the hospital. However, although everyone agreed that I was really sick, no one could decide what I had. I was ensconced in a bed in the corridor since the hospital was overcrowded. Through the jumble of delirium-induced thoughts running through my overheated brain, I could hear the doctors trying to decide on a diagnosis. Meanwhile, I developed all sorts of interesting additional symptoms, including a violent rash all over my body.

Finally, after a day or so of this, a little portable computer was brought over, fed in the symptoms, and asked for a diagnosis. The diagnosis was typhus—a disease that was so uncommon in Israel that it had not occurred to anyone that I could have it. It seemed that I had my old friends, the rats, to thank for that.

"We think we know what is wrong with you," the chief doctor told me, surrounded by a flock of interested interns.

Still woozy from the very high fever I had had for the last several days, I was able to rouse myself to ask what they had discovered.

"You have typhus," I was told. "There are not more than one or two cases a year of typhus here in Israel."

"How did I get something like that?" I wondered. So did the doctors.

"Where do you live?"

"We have a dog kennel at Sha'ar Hagai," I answered.

"Aha! Dogs! What other animals do you have there?"

"Well, we have a few cats around."

"What else?"

"There are plenty of rats."

That was obviously what they had been waiting to hear. "Rats! That's the source!"

"But I haven't ever been bitten by a rat or even touched one," I protested.

Apparently it was sufficient that there was rat excrement and urine around, and even possible that it had been passed to me by the dogs touching something that had been touched by the rats. Anyway, that was the way I understood it in my clouded state. I really didn't care. I just wanted to get out of the hospital, and if they could give me a solution for getting rid of the rats, I would be very happy.

The correct treatment was started—massive doses of antibiotics— and I soon felt human again. However, while in the hospital I found myself part of the daily tour for the medical students. Each day a new bunch was brought to my bedside, my symptoms were explained, and I was asked to show my rash to the fledgling doctors. As the rash started to fade as the treatment took effect, one of the 'tour guides' told me,

"Too bad we didn't photograph you while you still had the rash—this was really good for the students."

After a week or so I was fed up with the hospital, the food, the inactivity, and desperately missed home and the dogs; obviously I was ready to be released.

The dogs, though, had prepared a surprise for my homecoming. The collies had been home without me for over a week. Although Israela had fed and let them out, they were resentful at the lack of real attention. So they had looked for pursuits that would break up the boredom of being home alone. This was long before the days of the movie *Home Alone* about the little boy left alone in his house when the family was away—but my collies could have written the script. The most impressive of their activities had been to take all the fruits and vegetables that had been in the basket in the kitchen, and use them for play toys, leaving them well chewed and scattered all over the house— by now, in a very ripe state.

Israela, whose housekeeping skills, as mentioned, were minimal, never even noticed.

My first day home from the hospital was spent housecleaning.

Chapter Seven: Home Improvements

As a typical Jewish American Princess, I had never had to repair anything on my own. As I grew up, if there were any major or minor repairs to be done around the old homestead, all I had to do was use one finger—to dial the telephone and order a repairman. This was considered a perfectly natural state of affairs among our friends. Though there were a few tools around the house—a hammer, pliers, a few screwdrivers—all they were used for was the occasional hanging of a picture or tightening of a handle.

Now I was faced with a house that not only needed repairs, but major remodeling. We couldn't call a repairman to do the job, because we couldn't afford it, and anyway, there was no phone. But, with a wedding coming up, a new family about to move in with me and worst of all, an expected visit by my parents, fixing the place up as much as possible was top priority.

The floor bothered me most about the house. It was made of very old-fashioned gray cement tiles—the sort of thing you might imagine having in a dungeon. I did not relish the idea of living with these tiles indefinitely, and decided that one of the things that our very limited budget would have to stand would be the purchase of PVC floor tiles to glue over the old floor.

So the PVC tiles were duly purchased. Now came the hard part, the work of laying them. Neither Jacques nor I had any experience with this kind of project, but it didn't seem to be too difficult.

The evening after we brought the new tiles out to the farm, Jacques had gone home, with plans for us to work on the floor over the weekend; I felt very restless. I couldn't resist the thought of how nice the floor would look with the new tiles down.

I decided that I would surprise Jacques and finish gluing the tiles to the floor that evening. The next day, after hardening overnight, the floor would be finished and ready.

I cleaned the cement, got out the glue and the PVC tiles, and started work. There were no instructions on the glue container, but I remembered that I had seen contact glue being smeared on both sides of the objects to be glued—in this case, on the floor and on the tiles. I busily spread the glue thickly over the floor and on the back of the tiles and started sticking them in place.

This was easy! Very quickly, half the hallway was done. But as I picked up the storm lantern to move on to the next section, I glanced back at the part I had finished, and noticed that the first tiles I had glued were curling up at the edges.

I went back and pressed them down, holding them down for a minute, but then I saw that the other tiles were also starting to curl up at the edges. This wasn't supposed to happen! Wherever I pressed them down, they would pop up somewhere else. What was I going to do?!

I frantically looked around for things to weigh down the corners of the tiles and opted for some bricks from the yard outside—those worked well. Books were not so good because there had to be several stacked on top of each other to be heavy enough to hold down the tiles. Pots and buckets filled with water worked fine.

By the time I had finished, the hall was filled with all kinds of weights sitting on the corners of the tiles. But whenever I tried to pick one up, the tile underneath would immediately pop up again.

I was in despair. Not only had I not finished the hall floor, but I was sure that I had ruined the part that I had tried to do. I couldn't understand what had gone wrong.

The next morning, things did not look any better. Without the weights, the tiles immediately popped up again. When Jacques finally arrived after work, I was in despair about showing him my handiwork of the day before.

Jacques took the disaster calmly, and decided that the only thing to do would be to go back to ask the advice of the man who had sold him the tiles and the glue. So the next day, I impatiently waited for him to come back with the answers.

The first mistake, it turned out, was that I had tried to glue everything together without waiting. It seemed that contact glue has to partially dry before the two parts will stick together, but I had tried to stick the tiles to the floor immediately—I should have waited about twenty minutes.

Fortunately, according to the man in the shop, there was a solution—if we heated the tiles with an iron, then the glue would stick. Well, that was fine in theory, but how were we supposed to iron the floor, when we had no electricity?

In the end we did manage. Using an antique iron, one of the kinds that were supposed to be filled with hot coals, and heating it on the gas stove, we managed to iron down the floor. Of course, it took many extra hours of work—we had to reheat the iron before every tile as we had no hot coals to put into it and it lost heat very quickly. But eventually the floor was flattened. It did look good, certainly much better than the old gray dungeon floor, but it hadn't been easy.

The next step was to get something to actually put on those new tiles. Jacques had furniture, which was a welcome addition after living for many months with so little of it. Once that was moved in the place started to look like home. We bought a new supply of kerosene lamps, and were ready to set up our household. I was amazed at how easily the boys, Joel and Chaim, took to living under these new and strange conditions. Children are very flexible if you give them the chance.

My parents who arrived a week later were not highly impressed by my living conditions. They had no idea how much better it was then it had been only months before, but decided that now it was Jacques' problem, not theirs.

The wedding was held in an old and venerable hotel in Jerusalem. Fortunately, Jacques was quite efficient at organizing things as I, still a very green new immigrant (it takes years of the Israel experience to begin to understand how to navigate the sea of bureaucracy), had no idea at all how to go about it. It was not a large wedding, as I still didn't know very many people. Jacques' parents arrived from Holland. This was the first time I had met them, and I found them to be lovely, warm and intelligent people who didn't seem to be worried by our primitive living conditions. My parents and little brother were here from the U.S., and the rest of the guests were some additional distant relatives that were living in Israel, and our various friends. I wore a very traditional wedding gown, with my hair done elegantly.

As a basically shy person, and not fond of dressing up, I found it rather an ordeal to be the center of attention for an entire evening, surrounded by many people that were strangers to me, and was glad to escape with my new husband to our one night honeymoon at a fancy

Jerusalem hotel. One night was all we could allow ourselves—children and dogs were waiting at home, and there was no spare money for traveling. But neither of us really was interested in going off on a honeymoon, we were too eager to get on with our new life.

Now as a newly married woman and mother, improving the house was a much greater priority then it had been when it was just me, the dogs and the rats. The next big project we had to look after was to improve the water situation. I had managed so far with the Turkish toilet and without hot water, trying to shower in the middle of the day, when the water was heated by the sun. But with two young children as part of the household, this would not do—we needed a hot water heater and a proper toilet.

The toilet was not a big problem; Jacques managed to install a normal toilet and flush tank in place of the old system. A hot water heater, however, was not as easy.

In Israel, it is common to use solar heaters, which are placed on the roof and have a heating unit that is activated by the sunlight, of which there is plenty. Usually, there is a backup electric heater for those days that there is no sun. However, these heaters were quite expensive, not in the range of our very limited budget, and we still had no electricity. What we were able to afford was a secondhand heater of the sort that had previously been common, especially on kibbutzim. This was a long cylinder, looking rather like a rocket, standing on a metal tripod, with a heating unit underneath that worked on a kerosene drip.

Not only did this contraption look like a rocket, but when lit, it sounded like one too. The kerosene burned with a roar, the cylinder began to shake and rumble, and I was constantly terrified that this thing was going to blow up or take off for the stratosphere before we got any water out of it. Personally, I preferred washing in cold water to lighting the thing. I tried to leave all dealings with the hot water heater to Jacques, but there were times when I had no choice but to go outside, and very gingerly light it. I never did get used to it.

We kept that heater for a few years, and then we moved up one grade to a real luxury, a similar kerosene hot water heater, but this time an indoor one. This saved running outside and behind the house in the pouring rain or cold in order to light the fire. The indoor heater worked, instead of on a kerosene drip, on small brown paper bags full of wood shavings, which were soaked in kerosene and then put into the burner. This unit was no great improvement as far as I was concerned; it made just as much noise and was just as frightening to me as the previous one. Even worse, if this one decided to blow up, it was in the house. It also had a chimney to vent out the fumes, for which we had to make a hole in the ceiling. Some years later, after the heater had become obsolete and we had changed to a real solar water heater, a newspaper reporter came to write an article about the crazy people at Sha'ar Hagai, and found the hole in the ceiling very intriguing. He decided, and wrote in his article, that we had the hole in the ceiling so that we could see the stars while we were bathing.

Living in an old house that has spent many years abandoned means that there is never an end to the things that have to be repaired; you finish one thing and something else pops up. But the major problem that we had with the house, which took us many years to solve, was the roof.

The first year that I had spent in the house was uneventful. The only explanation that I can find for it now was that some twenty odd years of accumulated dirt and leaves on the roof provided a serious layer of insulation. The plaster inside had fallen in many places, but walls and roof were very strong and thick, and other than being ugly, there were no serious defects that I was aware of.

Now, however, we decided to get things cleaned up properly. The roof was cleaned up. We got some professionals in from Abu Gosh, the nearby Arab village, which was traditionally peopled by contractors and builders, to repair the fallen plaster. We were sure that everything was in tiptop shape.

I have always been a blue skies girl. A bright sunny day with blue skies would always give my spirits a lift, while a gray day with rain or snow would immediately give me a head start on a day of depression. I never liked the cold or the rain. My memories of the climate where I grew up in Chicago were of running from the heated house to the heated car to the heated school. Any excess time spent out of doors in the winter meant frozen fingers and toes.

Once, as a college student, I tried skiing, which was a disaster. For one thing, I was not terribly coordinated, and found the skis almost unmanageable. When I finally did manage to get myself together enough to ski down a very mild slope, I realized that I had no idea how to stop, and ended up making a crash stop into a tree at the bottom. Fortunately, at the speed that I was going, it was a minor bump. I was, after that experience, not prepared to try again. I found it very difficult to understand why anyone in his right mind would choose to spend a day out in the piercing damp cold, with frozen nose and other appendages, for the dubious pleasure of trying to slide downhill (after great efforts to get to the top of the hill first) without breaking a leg.

One of the incentives for my coming to Israel was the warm sun, which could be counted on even for much of the winter. And in the worst case, there were a few days of rain, which I could put up with.

And then came the next winter, and we found that the rain inside the house was nearly as bad as the rain outside. There were rooms that could be entered only with an umbrella. All the pots and pans we had were put to use catching the various leaks, and the floor was covered with towels and anything else absorbent enough to soak up the overflow.

It became apparent that the roof was in very bad condition. But having the roof repaired professionally was very expensive—way outside of our limited budget. So the next few years were spent, once again, in a variety of do-it-yourself attempts to dam the flow.

The first problem was to get up on the roof. I have never been particularly athletic, and although I am not afraid of heights, scrambling up a rickety ladder that didn't quite reach far enough and then pulling myself up on the roof was not my idea of fun. Once on the roof, all the supplies had better be on hand, because there was no way that I was about to come down again until I could stay down!

We tried many different methods: cold tar, hot tar, and various synthetic 'miracle' products. We were always highly optimistic until the first heavy rains came, and we heard the first ominous *drip-drip-drip* from various parts of the house. On one of my parents' infrequent visits to see their black-sheep daughter, they arrived at the house to find me stuck on the roof, trying to stretch plastic sheeting over the entire roof, and holding it down around the sides with narrow strips of wood nailed to the walls. This rather imaginative and novel approach was no more successful than the others.

Our winters were spent in a very mobile way since furniture had to be moved according to the location of the leaks. It was not uncommon for one or another of us to wake up in the morning to find part of the bed soaked by a new leak that had started during the night. I soon became hypersensitive to the sound of pots overflowing in the middle of the night and got up to change them. I also awoke to the sound of a new leak in a new place, and had to be ready to start shifting possessions out of the water line.

We heated the house in the winters with a makeshift wood burning stove; this was an ingenious invention of an old metal barrel with a door welded on one end, legs attached to the bottom, and a chimney attached to the top. Because of its size, almost anything—logs, scrap wood, and all sorts of trash—could be used as fuel. We tried to keep it burning to keep at least part of the house reasonably dry and comfortable. The children helped out by collecting pinecones, branches, and scrap wood. There was a leak just over the stove, but the stove, of course, couldn't be moved. Anyway, the drip was evaporated by the heat, and one of the winter's familiar sounds was the *sssss* of the drops of water hitting the stove.

To add to the fun, as a fairly new dog breeder, I also couldn't bear to think of the dogs sitting outside in the rain. True, it didn't seem to bother them much—the collies and the Canaans were rarely seen inside the wooden doghouses we had made for them—but the collies in particular looked so awful when they were dripping wet, with their coats hanging soggily and the rain running off them, that I couldn't leave them outside. So the house was also inundated with wet and muddy dogs, who were happy to look for comfortable sleeping spots as close as possible to the stove. Wet dog is a particularly unique and pungent smell.

There were other results of the leaking roof. The plaster on the ceilings once again began to fall. However, this did not usually happen in the winter. As the roof dried out in the spring after the rains, the plaster loosened more and more until it fell, sometimes in bits and pieces, and sometimes in huge clumps. Fortunately, no one was ever underneath one of these plaster-falls, though we had some close calls. In one case, Jacques had just gotten out of bed to visit the toilet when a huge block of plaster fell onto his pillow. Another time, I was entertaining an elderly friend of my mother's who was visiting. As we sat chatting over coffee, a huge section of ceiling fell into the middle of the room, just between our chairs, scattering dust in all directions.

I just sat and looked at the devastation for a minute, and then excused myself, brought a broom, bucket and dustpan, and cleaned up as well as I could. Then I returned to my coffee. What else was there to do? My guest, however, was so impressed by my 'cool' and my 'pioneering spirit' that she later sent me a check for a thousand dollars (a lot of money for us!) to have the roof repaired.

We finally did manage to have the roof properly repaired. How unbelievable it was to spend the next winter without emptying pots and buckets and shifting the furniture around to find a dry spot. What a pleasure to see the plaster remaining on the ceiling year after year. But still, every year with the first rains, by force of habit, I tour the house, checking for any damp spots on the ceiling.

Over the years, actually, I think there was little involved in household repair or renovation that I didn't attempt. I wasn't really a sworn do-it-yourself type, but I knew that if I didn't do it myself, it wouldn't get done. In fact, I can't think of any household repair task that I really enjoyed—only the results were pleasing. I certainly felt proud of the things that I accomplished after I had done them, but I would have passed on the pride if I could have still used that one finger to call and have someone else do the work.

Next was painting, which I figured would be the simplest of the home repair jobs. After all, how difficult can whitewashing walls be? Well, when you are only 5'2" and even with a ladder can't quite reach the top of the wall, not to mention the ceiling, it can rapidly become difficult indeed. I ended up constructing towers on which to stand—a chair on top of a large crate, with a smaller crate on the chair. All of these constructions were kept, as much as possible, close to the walls where I could, with one hand, support myself against the wall while I painted with the other. When it came to doing the ceiling in the middle of the room, I had to screw up my courage to climb up onto my rickety platform. Usually, I ended up with a satisfactory paint job, but with more paint on me and the floor than on the walls. There were also always at least four or five dogs that were having their turn to be in the house; with the pack getting up into the twenty to thirty range, they couldn't all be inside at once. They always managed, no matter how I tried to keep them out of range, to have their fur decorated by spots and streaks of paint.

The clean up often took longer than the job itself. I have never been able to understand how some people are able to tackle a job like painting, and remain immaculate on their person, and their floors.

Painting doors and windows was even worse—the oil-based paint was awful to get off of hands, clothes, window glass, and floors—one of my most hated jobs was scraping paint splashes off window glass with a razor blade. The paint also stayed sticky for hours and usually ended up with a furry texture from the floating dog hair that seemed attracted to it like a magnet. The smell of turpentine was quite sickening in the confined area of the house, and my hands ended up looking like they had been pickled. The alternative was using gloves, but in those days of 1971-2, work gloves were heavy canvas, and I found it impossible to accomplish anything while wearing them. What an improvement nowadays to have the disposable latex gloves that fit like a second skin.

The wood frames of the windows were old, half-rotten and peeling, and were supposed to be scraped and conditioned first, before painting. I didn't have the patience for that; I wanted fast results. So I just kept painting over them. By the time I finally managed to have all the old windows changed to new ones with aluminum frames, the only thing holding them together were the numerous layers of paint I had slapped on over the years.

Before living at Sha'ar Hagai I didn't know that there were different types of nails, or that only steel nails would penetrate the concrete of our walls. Eventually I found myself wielding, fairly effectively even, hammers, saws and drills.

One of the projects that I was most proud of was the patio. The yard outside the house was basically a mixture of dirt and rubble. There were a few spots that had been planned by the British for gardens, which had been filled with good earth. But the rest was worthless for planting, very unattractive, and a sea of mud in the winter. Jacques and I decided to pave it and make a patio that would be attractive and easy to keep clean.

I knew nothing about laying a patio floor, but how hard could it be? We ordered a truck full of sand, which was to be the base underneath the patio floor, and I drove off to Rehovot to the patio-block factory. We had, at this time, an ancient Willys pickup, which was large enough to load the amount of blocks we needed.

The blocks, made of poured cement, were heavy—they must have weighed at least 12 kilo (25 pounds) each. The Willys was loaded at the factory and I drove off, managing to get a few blocks away, to the middle of the main intersection of Rehovot, before the Willys broke down. With the load, it was too heavy even to be pushed out of the intersection so there I sat, stopping traffic in all directions, surrounded by honking and cursing drivers, until a tow truck managed to drag me over to a garage. In order to repair the car, all the blocks had to be unloaded, and then reloaded after the repair. This time I did manage to get home, but with the cost of the repair and the time spent, it would have been cheaper and quicker to have the blocks delivered.

Now came the hard part. Sha'ar Hagai, being in the Judean hills, was built on terraces on many levels. My house was up about fifty stairs from our little dirt road, where the sand and the blocks had been unloaded. To build a patio, all of the sand and blocks had to be carried up the stairs to the yard.

The procedure was simple—every time anyone, for whatever reason, went down the stairs, they had to carry up either a paving block or a bucket of sand. This went for visitors as well. We also devoted some time everyday to simply carrying sand and blocks up, as many trips as we could manage before exhaustion. It didn't go quickly, but gradually, the sand and the blocks ended up in the yard. It was certainly great for building muscle.

The idea was for Jacques to lay the patio. However, he was away all day at work. I, as usual, had no patience to wait for weekends and vacations to get the job done, so I began the patio myself.

Actually, it wasn't so hard. I had to lay a level bed of sand, and then place the blocks on the sand, seeing that they were set firmly and level with one another. There were two sizes of blocks, one large and six-sided, and one half the size. As there was no way to cut the blocks, the shape of the patio was rather like putting together a puzzle, seeing how the blocks would reasonably fit into the available space in the yard.

It turned out pretty well—maybe not the most level patio ever laid, but I was very proud of it. Jacques' contribution, in the end, other than carrying blocks and sand, was to lay a narrow cement border all around the patio to prevent the sand from trickling out and the blocks from shifting. We must have done a good job—the patio is still holding up today.

Some builders sign their projects in some way or another to leave their mark on the job. This was never necessary for me. Somewhere or other, no matter what sort of job done, you could find my signature—dog paw prints.

Chapter Eight: Motherhood

Several months after Jacques and I were married, I found that I was pregnant.

Adjusting to my new life of being not only a wife but also a mother was not as easy as I had anticipated. If the dogs annoyed me, I could always close them in the kennel, outside, or in another room until my nerves settled; children were different. Although Joel and Chaim were sweet kids, they were boys, and that says everything. Somehow boys seem to be born with a magnet for attracting dirt, and weird life forms—their interest in nature was admirable, but I was not enthusiastic about having cockroaches in jars, earthworms in buckets of earth, or dead lizards in the house. Washing was usually confined to the fingertips. They also had a great fondness for hoarding things for future use; their drawers accumulated piles of candy, matchboxes, pebbles, coins, and parts of unfinished sandwiches, which were usually covered with mold when discovered. Chaim in particular had a talent for driving me up the wall with his eating habits. He could sit at the table for hours, dreaming, and chewing on the same bite of food—especially if it was something he didn't particularly like—until I was ready to scream. If there was ever a kid who believed in chewing every mouthful a hundred times, it was Chaim.

The two of them also had a gift for going out clean in the morning and coming home dirty in torn clothes. This got worse when they were old enough to go to school. Rare was the day when they arrived home with all of their clothes in one piece. It was very lucky for us that we had a number of friends with children a bit older who were less destructive of their clothing, so we had a good supply of hand-me-downs to replace articles that were beyond repair.

I have no doubt that the adjustments of a new home, loss of their old playmates, and the need to learn to live with me (I will be the first to admit that that is far from easy) were difficult for them. It was certainly difficult for me. And now I was pregnant. Of course, I very much wanted a baby, but on the other hand, after the initial taste of being a mother, I wondered what surprises were in store with a new baby.

For the first few weeks after I was sure that I was expecting, I kept it a secret. It turned out, however, when I got around to telling Jacques and the others they already had guessed. Dvora told me that when she noticed me turning green while I was preparing the morning dog food, she guessed that things were not normal. At that stage the dog food was a combination of bread, meat powder and very aromatic cow paunch; dry dog food was a dream of the future in Israel in those days.

Morning sickness was just one of the problems of my pregnancy. Another early effect was sleepiness. It wasn't just a matter of being tired; I found myself falling asleep at every opportunity. We would go to visit friends and after a few minutes conversation, I would nod off in my chair. Falling asleep was one thing, worse was waking up to find myself covered with a blanket after napping for an hour or so while conversation went on all around. We had a season's ticket to the Philharmonic orchestra that year; I heard the beginning of much wonderful music, but rarely stayed awake until the end.

I also suffered periodically from back pains. One day, my back seized up to the point where I simply couldn't straighten up. I was in the middle of caring for the dogs and no one else was around, or due back for hours. And of course we had no telephone—this was 1972, still long before the days of the cellular phones. All I could do was more or less crawl down the stairs to the car, drive a few kilometers to the nearest petrol station, which was also the nearest phone, and call Jacques to come home.

The worst 'side effect' of pregnancy, though, was heartburn, from which I suffered for months. The only thing that helped was milk—I drank enough milk during my pregnancy to have justified buying a cow. Of course, keeping fresh milk without a proper refrigerator was no simple matter, and there were times when I simply had to suffer.

The baby was due in the middle of April, right after Passover. I was not very big —some people were just noticing that I was pregnant.

"Oh, are you starting something?" they would ask.

"No, I'm finishing something," I would answer. I never wore maternity clothes, simply regular clothes a size or two larger.

Passover was at the end of March, and was a time when there were always numerous activities to fill the week when many people were on vacation. One of the planned activities was a big dog show, and I had been asked to judge, having shortly before completed a course and the other qualifications to be a dog judge. I was thrilled because this was a big honor, and there were a large number of dogs entered. I was sure that I would have no problems; I was still feeling quite fit and active.

The Passover Seder at Sha'ar Hagai was a community effort held at Dvora's house on the first night of the vacation week. There was food aplenty, much of it the typical, heavy, traditional Passover cooking. When we finally, quite late, came home to bed, I was feeling quite stuffed and rather uncomfortable.

At about three in the morning, I woke up feeling very uncomfortable. I thought it was indigestion, and cursed myself for eating so much. But after a while, it started to become apparent that this was not indigestion. I woke Jacques to tell him that I thought we had better think about going to the hospital.

"Hey, wake up!"

"Hmmmmmm..."

"Jacques, I feel strange. Wake up!"

"Hmmm...what's the matter?"

"I have stomach pains."

"It was a pretty heavy meal. Should I get you something for indigestion?"

"This isn't indigestion. I know what indigestion feels like and it isn't this."

"Are you sure?" he asked.

"I'm sure it isn't indigestion. It feels different than anything I've had before. Jacques, I think it must be the baby coming!"

"The baby! I'd better call Dvora!"

Since most of my days were spent at home alone taking care of the dogs, I was afraid that I was going to have to drive myself to the hospital when the labor pains began. After all, if I had to drive to the telephone anyway, and seeing that Jacques couldn't drive, oh...I was unbelievably naive in those days. I believed that everything I had seen in the movies or read in popular novels was true and that with some will power, you could get through anything! I was so sure that I was in good condition physically that I hadn't even done a Lamaze course, which was for sedentary women, not for someone who continued riding her horse until the sixth month!

Fortunately, Dvora was available to drive us to the hospital because by the time we got there, there was no doubt that I was having the baby, and it would have been very unlikely, considering how I felt that I would have managed to drive myself.

I was admitted, and went through all the uncomfortable preparations, for which I had not prepared. And then I was left in bed in the ward, to wait.

This child was in no hurry to enter the world. I have never been one to suffer in silence, and hours seemed to go by so slowly as I writhed in pain. Periodically the nurse would come by, check me out, see that there was still time, and go on about her business—sympathy was something for the movies, not for a normal, overcrowded, busy maternity ward, or for a perfectly normal appearing labor.

Finally, after eight hours or so the baby finally seemed to be ready to take a look at the world. I was wheeled into the delivery room—in those days, the father was left to pace in the waiting room—and, after more pain and suffering—stupid, stupid, stupid not to have done the Lamaze course—my daughter was born. My memories of that moment are mixed—relief, joy at seeing this tiny dark haired little girl and an overpowering thirst. For some reason I had never had any doubts that it would be a girl and we had only picked out a name for a girl. All I wanted at this point was to have something to drink, and to go to sleep.

When I awoke after a nap there was another overpowering urge. Not being familiar with hospital procedure, I dragged myself out of bed and to the toilet—what a relief! On my slow and shaky way back to my bed, the nurse came in—and was shocked!

"You aren't supposed to be out of bed—why didn't you call me?" she shrieked. Well, because it had never occurred to me.

We named our daughter Dorcas. Dorcas means gazelle in Greek, and is the name of the gazelle of the Negev desert and was also the name of a character in a book that Jacques and I very much enjoyed. It is a very uncommon name—I have never heard of anyone else in Israel named Dorcas. I thought that a very special child should have a special name.

Of course, I hadn't gotten to that dog show, and Jacques hadn't managed to get hold of anyone to notify them that I wasn't coming to judge. But I did have an excellent excuse for not showing up.

After a few days in the hospital, it was time to bring Dorcas home. Joel and Chaim were waiting eagerly to meet their new sister, and were fascinated by her. But after some time, Chaim came over to me.

"Can I ask you a question?" he asked.

"Sure."

"Well," said Chaim. He was already well versed in biology, having seen dogs and cats breed and give birth. "Does a woman eat the afterbirth when a baby is born like a dog does?"

I was happy to inform him that, although the birth process was indeed similar, this part was not customary for women. I think he was relieved.

Life with a new baby was, well, the only word to describe it is *exhausting*. Dorcas was a very good baby. She didn't wake up frequently during the night, and was a happy and good-natured child. But running the household with a baby, two boisterous youngsters, a pack of dogs, and various and sundry other additions was far from being easy. The dogs accepted Dorcas as another puppy, and were happy to have the chance to inspect her, wash her face, and 'guard' her from all harm—not that anything was threatening her—but they showed me that they were always on the alert.

Quite soon after the birth, my parents came to visit. This was their first grandchild, and they were very eager to see her. Jacques was at home with the baby when I went to pick them up at the hotel to bring them out to meet the new addition to the family. They were very excited and asked a million questions as we drove out to Sha'ar Hagai.

As we walked in the door, Dawn, one of the collie bitches, who was pregnant and due to whelp any day, threw herself across my feet, and glared up at me, as if to say, "Where the hell have you been? I am having my puppies RIGHT NOW and I need you!!"

Thrusting Dorcas into my mother's arms, I said, "Here, meet your granddaughter! Take care of her for a while, will you? I'm having puppies!"

All part of a normal day at Sha'ar Hagai!

Chapter Nine: African Interlude

One of the hazards of being married to a diplomat is the constant possibility of being transferred from country to country. To most people, this is an advantage of the job, and I must admit that in general the idea of travel and of living in foreign countries was inviting. But having just established a more or less orderly and comfortable home, a breeding kennel and boarding business that had acquired a good number of dogs, and with a new baby as well, I was less than joyful when Jacques announced that we were being sent abroad.

Well, maybe at least we were going somewhere where I could show dogs and get ahead with my breeding? No such luck—we were slotted for Malawi, an insignificant little country in the middle of Africa, known for its beautiful scenery and not much else. Certainly not for its doggy activities.

The news left me very depressed, but as we started making plans to go, my natural resilience and curiosity about this new place took over. One thing was sure, I wasn't leaving my dogs behind! Of course, I couldn't take all of them, but three of the collies came with me. I wasn't interested in the opinion of the Foreign Office—no dogs, no me! So crates were built for Degel, Dawn and Julep. We got a long series of nasty vaccinations, one of which left me with a rash for weeks. Then, we started packing for Africa.

Finally, the day of our flight arrived. Jacques and the two boys had flown a week earlier to start getting things organized and I was to follow with the baby, now five months old, and the three dogs.

The flight for Africa left at about one in the morning, and the taxi provided by the foreign office to take us to the airport arrived at ten p.m. The dog boxes were strapped to the roof rack, and Dorcas, the dogs and I along with the foreign office escort piled into the taxi. The driver, staring and scratching his head, seemed to find the whole thing quite mystifying, to come to this unknown and unilluminated hole in the forest in the middle of the night to collect a woman, a baby and three collies.

The dogs had all been given a tranquilizer pill to keep them calm. Julep, however, was not accustomed to all of this, and leaped around like a tornado, trying to see and inspect everything at once. The tranquilizer didn't seem to have had any effect at all, so I gave her another. As we sat waiting to board I fed her more Valium in the hopes of getting to a dose that would calm her down. Finally, after eight pills, I gave up. Julep was indomitable, and would have to travel to Africa as she was.

We were called to board, the dogs were loaded into their crates and taken away, and finally, with only Dorcas to take care of, I could relax. Dorcas was behaving very well because she was tired and wanted to sleep. But as we sat on the plane waiting for takeoff, I could hear barking coming from the cargo hold beneath us; Julep was not yet ready to accept her lot.

The flight was uneventful and we landed in Nairobi in the early afternoon. The flight to Malawi was only the next morning; we would spend the night in a hotel. An Israeli friend living in Nairobi came to meet the plane and take me to the hotel.

First, I asked where the dogs would be unloaded and was told to go to the freight department. But as I was about to leave the passenger arrivals hall, I heard laughter coming from behind me in the vicinity of the baggage carousel, and something told me to go and take a look.

There on the carousel were the three dog crates, riding around and around. Dawn had managed to chew open the corner of her crate and was standing with her head out, watching the people who were watching her.

With the help of my friend, we grabbed the crates, and looked for someone who could tell us where to find the kennel. The Nairobi airport had an animal port, where animals in transit could be kept overnight, and that was what had been arranged for the dogs.

We finally found the kennel and the kennel man, who was very cooperative; he offered to fix the dog box for us before the next morning. Gratefully, I surrendered the dogs into his care, and was taken off to the hotel.

My friend kindly offered to drive around Nairobi a bit to show us the sights, although Dorcas really wasn't very interested. My first glimpse of Africa was fascinating: the profusion of brightly-colored flowers and plant life and the exotically-dressed people were a very different world from any I knew. I felt much better about the prospect of the next three years.

The next morning, bright and early, we were taken back to the airport for the last leg of the flight. No huge jet this time; the Air Malawi plane we were to fly on was a small and rather old-looking propeller plane. But it was a fairly short flight, so I wasn't worried about the comfort.

The kennel man had indeed fixed the crate and the dogs were glad to see me. However, they were not so glad to get back into the crates again, especially not Julep. She was extremely reluctant to cooperate, and there was no more Valium for her. I had a funny feeling about this flight, and as I boarded the plane, I told the stewardess, "When we arrive, please let me stand by when the baggage compartment is opened to unload the dogs."

"Sure, no problem," she assured me.

The flight was smooth although noisy, and finally, there we were, landing in Malawi. As the doors opened and I started to leave the plane, the stewardess came running over to ask me to come down to the baggage compartment. Handing Dorcas to her, I ran after the baggage man.

The compartment door was open and all of the porters, huge and heavily-muscled black men, were lined up ready to start grabbing and unloading. But they were all frozen in place, staring up into the plane's dark belly.

There, poised like a leopard about to leap on its prey, was Julep. She had decided that once in a crate was enough, and had chewed her way out, and thoroughly demolished the crate into a pile of splintered plywood. She had waited for the door to be opened and now she was trying to decide on whom to leap first.

Everyone was very relieved as I called her and put a leash on her. And then, in a procession, me with Julep, the stewardess after me with Dorcas, and the other porters behind with the other dogs, we marched into the arrivals hall.

I didn't find all this too strange, but I had the feeling that this was not the expected behavior for an arriving diplomat's wife. We were speedily rushed through customs and into the car for the trip into town.

Jacques had purchased the car of his predecessor, a luxurious Peugeot sedan. I immediately decided that this would not do; with the dogs and children to think about, we needed a station wagon. Within a few weeks, the Peugeot was gone, and we had acquired a rather elderly but large Cortina station wagon, making us the only diplomats in Malawi to travel in this sort of vehicle. Since it was usually full of dogs as well, this also set us apart from the other diplomats.

We had been provided with a comfortable, nicely furnished house, with a lovely garden, and we had 'inherited' the house servants of our predecessor. I had never even had a regular once-a-week cleaning lady, and now I was supposed to cope with a houseboy, a gardener and a nanny? I was supposed to be able to tell them what to do!

Fortunately, they knew very well what to do on their own. The Malawians are friendly, happy, polite people, and I soon found that I could learn from them how I was supposed to behave. It was rather like living with a Super Mother, but without the guilt: laundry appeared magically, clean and perfectly ironed in my drawers; breakfast, lunch and dinner were ready and waiting for us at the designated hour; and the dishes magically disappeared only to reappear clean and sparkling in the cupboard. If I just left everything to them, the household would have been run efficiently, everything spotless and in its place. This was real luxury! It wasn't as hard to get used to as I had thought it would be.

The dogs had a somewhat different opinion. From the minute they set foot on African soil, they decided they had to protect me from everything African. With no encouragement from me, they did not let the houseboy in the door in the morning until I got out of bed, came downstairs, and opened the door for him. Once he was in, they were perfectly happy to let him feed them and play with them. The Malawians in general seemed to be quite fond of dogs and other animals. Every Saturday all the children from the surrounding villages brought their dogs, tied on bits of string, into town to be dipped in the vet's tank to prevent parasites. Locals not belonging to our household stopped on the corner and looked down the street to make sure that our gate was closed before passing by, because one of the dogs had dashed out one day and grabbed a sack of flour from one poor fellow; the word spread quickly that these were dogs to be wary of. One of the dogs had the habit of grabbing the gardener by the seat of the pants every time he went over to open the gate; we provided him with numerous pairs of new trousers.

The boys went to an English school, a real remnant from the colonial days. They had to wear uniforms, which of course had certain advantages; they did not manage to ruin them as effectively as they ruined 'nice' clothes. The boys looked like real little English gentlemen as they went off each day to school. The greatest advantage was that they became totally fluent in speaking, reading and writing English.

Dorcas, now about seven months old, of course had a nanny. This was something that I found very hard to get accustomed to. Having servants to take care of the house and garden was one thing, but I wasn't enthusiastic about having someone else care for either my dogs or my child. But there was no choice: I was expected to work, and a nanny was essential.

During the period that we were there, there were various threats to Israeli embassies in other parts of the world. The government sent security experts around to check out the living conditions and security status in the embassy and to recommend installation of alarm systems, bars on windows, security doors and so on. When they came to check us out, the dogs met them. Their report stated that our house had no need for extra security measures—"there are some very serious dogs there..."

One of the ways that the Israeli Foreign Office saved money was to insist that junior diplomats' wives work in the embassy. So I was assigned to the job of embassy secretary. I could type in English, and I now had no choice but to learn to type in Hebrew as well.

The job was far from stimulating. A great deal of the correspondence and other dealings of an embassy have nothing to do with diplomacy or state secrets, but with budgets. Whether the ambassador could buy a new sofa, who would accompany the next diplomatic mail bag to South Africa, or who had gotten drunk and made a nasty remark about someone's wife at a cocktail party were all important pieces of correspondence.

Once I learned to read everyone's handwriting, which was far from easy, I think I became a pretty good secretary. The job was certainly good for my Hebrew. But somehow, not all my methods were appreciated, especially my system of filing, which consisted of waiting until there was a good big pile of papers to file. Since it wasn't a task that I enjoyed, I tried to put it off until it was absolutely necessary and then to separate the papers into piles according to subject so that I could file them. There were a great number of subjects, though, and I ended up with piles of papers all over my desk, the chairs, the floor, and halfway down the corridor. This annoyed the ambassador when he had to pick his way through the papers to get to his office. I thought that reaction was rather unreasonable—after all, it didn't happen that often.

I often took one or another of the dogs with me to the embassy during working hours. They were well behaved, usually sleeping quietly under my desk or in front of it. I enjoyed having a dog with me while doing my usual boring work, and it provided extra 'security' for the embassy. Visitors often paused seeing a dog lying there, before continuing through to the ambassador's office.

I have to admit, though, that my dogs were not very well versed in diplomatic protocol. This was not something that would have occurred to me until the day that the ambassador arrived in the office, walked past my desk, stopped and looked down at the dog of the day, who was quietly lying in front of my desk watching him pass by.

"You could at least get up and say hello when I come in!" he said to the dog, "I AM the ambassador!"

Outside of working hours, there was not a great choice of activities. The women of the diplomatic corps spent most of their time shopping. As there was not much available to buy, the shopping often consisted of running around the town markets to see who had the best vegetables and fruits. The vegetables were indeed beautiful, and presented in shining, washed piles that would tempt even the most committed carnivore. There were all kinds of exotic fruits, like mangos and papayas and pineapples, and types of bananas that I had never seen before, which were traditionally cooked or fried. The markets also had a large selection of meats, which hung from hooks along the walls, and numerous types of fish, including little dried fish that the Malawians loved, but whose smell kept me from thinking of tasting them.

Some of the other foods that were popular with the Malawians were also far from tempting to me. They ate a wide variety of insects— an excellent source of protein—apparently quite tasty when cooked in a sauce. But Malawians also had the habit of standing under the streetlights in the evening, catching the large flying ants that were attracted to the light, pulling off their wings, and popping them in their mouths. Every morning, there would be a large pile of wings under the lights.

Even worse, to me, were the cane rats. After the harvest, the Malawians burned the stubble off the cane fields, and stood on the edges ready with *pangas* (a broad-bladed machete) or large clubs. As the huge cane rats fled the fires, they were caught and became supper for the natives. I was never convinced to taste those, either.

There wasn't much to buy in the way of clothing or other 'luxuries,' so most women learned to sew their own clothes, and a good deal of time was spent going around to all the fabric shops looking for bargains. There was an enormous selection of fabrics at excellent prices—multiple tastes were catered to—from the African women who loved bright colored cottons, to the Indians who loved pastel chiffons and delicate silks, to the European women who tried a bit of everything.

As sewing was obviously not only a necessity of life, but also a major topic of conversation at the inevitable cocktail parties and dinners, there was no choice for me but to learn to sew. My first project was a plain long cotton skirt, which I sewed by hand. It took hours of patient and precise stitching—very difficult for me, as neither patience nor precision were among my strong points. I was determined to finish it. Upon completion, it looked rather like a flour sack gathered at the waist. At the time I was so new to the idea of making clothes, I was unaware of the existence of patterns. I did, out of obstinance, wear it once or twice.

However, it was obvious that sewing things by hand could not be a long-term consideration. I bought a very old little sewing machine very cheaply—I think it was one of the earliest models ever made, with a little motor attached later on in its lifetime—and started practicing.

Surprisingly, I found that I enjoyed making clothes. There was a very good choice of patterns available, and I found that I could sit down and in a few hours create a finished garment that even looked good. I began sewing clothes not just for myself but for the whole family. The most fun was making stuffed animal toys for Dorcas.

I even got to the point where I was making cocktail dresses for the various parties we had to go to and the dresses were, amazingly, quite acceptable.

The cocktail parties were quite a trial for someone as shy as I was. My fund of small talk was not very well-developed, and the people one met at these parties were not, for the most part, interested in talking about dogs or horses. There was one American diplomat from foxhunting country who had horses and a pack of hounds; his wife and I had some lovely talks.

The African women, however, made me look like a star of the cocktail circuit. Most of them had little education, although their husbands were university graduates. They also spoke little English. They stood shyly in a corner, dressed in traditional clothes—a Java print wound around the body with a matching cloth turban—looking bored and uncomfortable in the lavish surroundings. I sympathized with them, but my own lack of confidence, as well as the technical problems involved in the language barrier, prevented me from talking to them much.

Jacques and I spent a good deal of our leisure time reading. There was an excellent English bookshop, and the event of the week was going down there to see what new books had arrived. I built up a huge science-fiction collection.

There was a very strict system of censorship in Malawi; the President was puritanical and felt responsible for the morals of his countrymen. Films were censored radically to the point where in the children's movie *Dr. Doolittle*, a perfectly innocent kiss was censored. Magazines were censored; I remember an issue of *Time* magazine where a photo of Henry Kissinger kissing his wife was blacked out. However, for the most part, books were left alone; there was obviously no one there who was interested in plowing through all that reading matter in order to censor it.

There were very strict dress rules as well: women had to wear skirts that more than covered their knees, and were not allowed to appear in public in pants. The rules about above-the-waist dress were less strict— many Malawian women went around at times with their breasts exposed. Men were not allowed to wear bell-bottomed trousers, which were quite fashionable at the time in Europe and in the U.S. The police force carried around tape measures and could stop people on the street to measure whether skirts were long enough and pant legs narrow enough. Tourists could be expelled from the country if they did not dress in accordance with the rules.

As diplomats, we were, of course, expected to attend many national functions. For the most part these were very interesting, involving displays of exciting traditional dance and song. The Malawians loved music, and were outstanding at a capella singing. However, these occasions always included a speech by the Honorable Life President. These speeches usually lasted several hours, and were not in English. The Malawian people were always very enthusiastic, no surprise in an African dictatorship; not showing enthusiasm can be dangerous if it gives any hints of displeasure with the regime. The image that most remains in my mind is that of the women dressed in traditional Java prints stamped with the portrait of the puritanical president's face, molded snuggly to the ample buttocks of his countrywomen as they danced traditional hip-shaking dances in front of the honors stand.

Of course one could not live in Africa without enjoying the scenery. Malawi is an extremely beautiful country, quite mountainous, with plenty of water including streams, waterfalls, and lush semi-tropical vegetation. There is also a wide variety of wildlife and in a place like Malawi, the wildlife does not always keep its distance. Baboons, for instance, were common everywhere except in the center of town. They sat on the roads and tried to stop the cars passing by, asking for handouts. Leopards came into the outskirts of town, looking for some of their favorite delicacies—dog and cat. At night, you could hear the weird hyena voices giggling hysterically to one another.

And of course there were snakes. One evening, as we prepared to go out to a formal dinner, we found our houseboy George, our gardener, and the servants of the neighbors sitting around our back veranda. We had a large freezer on the veranda.

"What's going on?" I asked George.

"There is a snake under the freezer," he stated.

"A snake? What kind!"

"Oh, a mamba," he said, a bit too casually. This was a highly poisonous and very fast snake that was best avoided. The Africans intended to wait for the mamba to come out and then they would get it with a *panga* that they had at the ready.

Well, we figured that they could cope with the situation, and we went on to dinner. Several hours later, we returned home to find them all still sitting on the porch waiting for the snake to come out. As far as we could see, there was no reason for it to come out because underneath the freezer it was warm and dark and protected. It looked to us as though these fellows were prepared to go on sitting on the porch until the cows came home; they didn't seem to have much else to do. But we didn't really want them sitting on the porch all night. So Jacques got a bucket of hot water, told the gardener to get ready, and spilled the water under the freezer. The snake quickly came slithering out to escape the hot water, and was chopped to bits with the *panga*. Our gardener was very proud of his achievement, talking about it for weeks.

Another time one of the Israeli embassy women went to the local bottling factory to return some crates of empty soft drink bottles and to bring home some full ones. She asked the porter there to take the crates out of her car, but after a minute he came back to ask her. "Shall I take the snake out too?" There was a mamba, curled up in the back of the car under the crates.

Malawi presented another challenge: I had to learn to cope with spiders. Everywhere you looked, there were huge black spiders with large bodies and very long and hairy legs making them the size of a dinner plate, commonly known there as 'chicken spiders.' What they had to do with chickens I don't know; I would have believed that these spiders ate them. I was terrified of spiders, and these were the stuff of my worst nightmares. But they were everywhere. If you moved a chair in the house, there was a spider. They were also behind the pictures on the wall and in the cupboards. I finally, after a few months, became totally indifferent to them. Even terror wears down after a while.

Still another wonderful creature that we met in Malawi was the 'chingamalula.' These were centipedes which, if you touched them, left hairs stuck in your flesh that contained some sort of mild poison that was extremely painful and irritating. You never knew where you might run into them; one poor child stepped on one in a swimming pool. And we also soon discovered why every bit of laundry in Malawi was ironed, including underwear. There was a certain sort of fly that laid its eggs in damp laundry. The larva burrowed under your skin and lived there until they were ready to hatch, creating a terrible itching lump. We were sure to carefully iron everything.

But it wasn't as bad as it sounds, and there was wonderful wildlife in the forests and reserves. We took several trips to the nature reserves and saw a fantastic number of animals in their natural habitat. One thing that I was very impressed with as well was the necessity to lock your car inside a steel fence at the nature reserves, otherwise the hyenas would come at night and eat the tires; they loved rubber.

At this point, after about a year in Malawi, I decided that three dogs were not enough. I wanted to be a breeder of collies, and not to wait for three years until we were back in Israel. But Degel had no papers; if I wanted to be a serious breeder, I needed a new stud dog. So, after much correspondence, I purchased a young dog from a well-known breeder in the U.S., and arranged to have him shipped to us in Malawi.

I was very excited as we went to the airport to receive Roddy. There were no direct flights from the U.S. to Malawi—the routing was to England and from there to Malawi. British Airways (then BOAC—British Overseas Airline Company) jet landed, and we waited for the dog to be unloaded. But as the time passed, and no dog appeared, I began to worry. When we checked with the company representative, we were told that there was no dog on the flight, and no one could tell us just where the dog was.

Panic! Calls were made to England and to the U.S., and finally it became clear what had happened. England has always been more concerned about the conditions of animals on planes than those of their human passengers; they had decided in England, when Roddy was being transferred from the U.S.-originating flight to the flight to Africa, that his crate was too small. He was taken off the flight and put in kennel until a new crate could be prepared.

Several days later, on the next flight from England, Roddy finally arrived in a crate that was large enough for two Great Danes to live in comfortably—it was so large that we had to send a truck out to the airport to bring it home. But Roddy was safe and sound, and happy to join the family.

Several months after Roddy's arrival, he had a chance to prove his prowess as a stud, when Julep came into season. The result was four lovely puppies; one female and three males. There was no way that I was not going to keep one of those! So Nova, the female, became a member of the pack.

Nova had a very strong temperament, a fact that she showed from a very young age. She seemed to think that she was a Doberman with long hair. She became the terror of the neighborhood while she was still a puppy—although she never really did anything to anyone, she certainly put on a show as if she was going to. She would run back and forth along the fence barking ferociously, jumping on the fence at times and snapping her teeth. The more nervous the passersby appeared to be, the more enthusiastic she got with her aggressive display. This was fun!

Jacques occasionally traveled to South Africa with the diplomatic mailbag, which had to be accompanied, as the flights from Malawi were not on Israeli planes. In South Africa, the bag was transferred to an El Al flight and didn't have to be accompanied any further. The periodic trip to South Africa was a plum that all the embassy workers enjoyed getting occasionally. Jacques suggested that I come with him on one of these trips and we could spend a weekend in South Africa.

I thought that this was a great idea. But if we were already going to South Africa, then it should be on a weekend when there was a dog show. And then I could enter one of the dogs and take it along!

It is sometimes very hard for people who have not been bitten by the dog show bug to understand the great importance of them. Of course, I have great difficulty understanding what the great importance of soccer is, and can't comprehend how fans could be ready to kill someone who is a supporter of the opposing team. On the other hand, I could certainly consider killing someone whose dog won an unjustified victory over my much more deserving beauty.

Seriously, though, in a way, dog breeding is an art form. Great consideration is put into making all of the decisions involved, weighing the faults and strengths of each dog, and all of its relatives, in the hopes of creating something that is as near to perfection as possible—perfection being the ideal described by the breed standard. Breeding involves creativity and esthetics, and of course, every artist must be able to show off what she creates, which is where the dog shows come in. At a dog show, the breeder has an opportunity to show her best to the world, and, if she is successful and lucky, to gain recognition for what she has produced. Showing dogs becomes just as addictive as any other form of competitive sport.

So Jacques managed to arrange his turn as courier for a weekend when there was a dog show, and I entered Roddy.

The planes to South Africa were small propeller jobs. I notified the airline that we would be taking a dog, a large dog, and they confirmed that it was okay.

We arrived at the airport well in advance of flight time, with Roddy and the crate, though not the huge crate he had arrived in, but a normal sized crate from one of the other dogs. When the check in girl saw Roddy and the crate, however, she looked worried. After going off to check, she returned.

"I'm sorry, but there's no pressurized cargo compartment on this flight that is big enough for the crate. Your dog can't go on this flight."

"So what do you suggest?" I asked, a bit impatiently.

Her suggestion was to either go on a flight via Rhodesia (not possible for us with Israeli diplomatic passports), or to wait for a flight on the next day, in a larger plane. Since the dog show was the next day, this was not possible.

I was furious! I informed the airline people that I had made a reservation for the dog in advance, I had been told that everything was okay, I had to get to South Africa today because tomorrow was the show, and I expected them to find a solution immediately!

In those years, British manners still ruled, and especially when one was faced with a furious diplomat's wife, even if a very junior diplomat. The airline people scurried about trying to find a solution.

"Are you sure you wouldn't like to go tomorrow?" they asked. "It is a much more comfortable plane."

"No, I don't want to fly tomorrow! I have to be at the dog show tomorrow!"

"Well, the dog certainly can't go in the cargo hold on this plane. The flight is full, so we can't even let you have an extra seat for him."

"I expect you to find someplace for him!"

After much thought, they finally came up with a solution.

"We will put your dog in the passenger cabin. His crate will fit in the crew area, where the crew stows their luggage. We'll have them put their cases in the cargo hold today. But you will have to ask the pilot if he is willing to have an animal traveling in the cabin. It is actually against the rules, and he has to approve it."

The pilot was an Englishman nearing the end of his career. His veiny face indicated what his leisure time activities were, and why he was now flying planes in Africa and not in England. He just looked at me as I explained the problem, and then with a world-weary sigh, told me that he didn't care where the dog was, as long as it didn't cause any trouble. I assured him that he wouldn't even know the dog was there.

When we arrived in South Africa, as we were disembarking from the plane, I went over to the porters. "You have to unload my dog," I said.

"Sure," laughed one. "We're unloading everything in the baggage compartment."

"No," I explained, "the dog is in the passenger compartment, not the baggage compartment."

They stared at me in disbelief. I had to reenter the plane with them to show them where Roddy was before they would believe that he had traveled in the cabin.

We stayed in a lovely hotel, and had a great dinner, but I was already very nervous about the show the next day. This was my first serious dog show! I hardly slept that night, and the next morning was unable to eat breakfast. Most of my time was spent running to the bathroom, a result of nerves.

There were a number of collies at the show since they were a popular breed in South Africa. This meant that Roddy would have to show himself off to his best advantage so that the judge could appreciate his quality. This was a problem. Roddy really was a top quality dog but the reason that I had been able to purchase him for an affordable price was that he did not like dog shows. He would enter the ring with his ears back and an expression of disgust on his face.

Over the years that I showed him, I tried all sorts of tricks to try to get him to look as good in the ring as he did when he was running around in the yard. This included starving him for a day and then offering him all sorts of goodies in the ring like smoked chicken, sausages, liver baked with garlic and onion—if he would put his ears up. The smell of these things was enough to make my mouth water, but it didn't always have an effect on him. Nor did having a friend call his name from outside the ring. At one show, I even had a friend run around outside the ring with her bitch that was just coming in season, a fact that Roddy was aware of, but which did not have a tremendous influence on him.

However, on this day, he seemed mellow and agreed to put his ears up, and won Best Dog and his first CC—the much valued "Champion Certificate" of which he needed four at four different shows to win the title of champion. He did not win Best of Breed, however. The judge, it turns out, was a dentist by profession, and felt that Roddy's teeth should be cleaner. "Such a nice dog, too bad about his teeth," was the comment as he gave the BOB prize to a bitch. Ever since then, I have always been very careful to clean my dogs' teeth before any show!

The collie people were quite friendly, and I promised to stay in contact and come again. So the trip, despite the difficult start, was a success. That night, I was able to enjoy dinner. The flight back—on a larger plane—was uneventful.

Now I was experienced in the dog show world, and I was also addicted. The next time we were due a vacation, about six months later, I insisted that we go back to South Africa to do some more shows. This time, Dorcas came with us as well. We were the guests of some doggy friends we had made, and the trip was a success—Roddy got two more CC's. Dorcas, now two and a half, was fascinated by the dog shows, the dogs, and the people. Far from being bored or impatient, she was ready to talk to everyone, pet all the dogs and watch the judging. We had to watch her all the time, as she was likely to wander off to check out things that caught her eye. At one show, as I came out of the ring with the dog, we walked back across the show grounds towards the place where we had been sitting when I suddenly realized that we had left Dorcas at the ringside! I rushed back in a panic to find her sitting happily where we'd left her, chatting with the other spectators and explaining which dogs were the good ones.

Jewish holidays in Africa were usually celebrated by the whole small Israeli community together, but Yom Kippur, the solemn Day of Atonement, was usually spent by each family on its own. There was no synagogue to go to so everyone found his or her own way to communicate with God.

So it was quite a shock when the telephone rang on Yom Kippur in 1973. It was the ambassador telling Jacques that Israel was at war.

The next days and weeks were a period of tremendous tension and worry. Being so far from home, having to depend on news reports and whatever information was sent to the embassy, was nerve wracking. To add to the tension was the fact that all the African countries surrounding Malawi were breaking off their diplomatic relations with Israel and all the Israelis were being sent home. We were unsure if and when the axe would fall, and if we would also be sent home. On the one hand, I wanted to be home, but on the other hand, there was still much I wanted to see and do in Africa.

The President of Malawi, however, had great respect and affection for Israel since it had been the first country to offer medical and agricultural assistance when Malawi became an independent country. He also had no love for the Arabs, and was constantly reminding his people in his speeches that the Arabs were the ones that had sold their ancestors into slavery. So, we remained as a last bastion of Israel in the heart of black Africa.

It took time after the Yom Kippur War for things to return to normal. But life in Malawi was quiet and peaceful, and soon things were back to a typical routine, which meant the boring schedule of typing and filing and the cocktail party circuit.

When I heard about a dog show in Kitwe, Zambia, with an English judge, I decided that I was fed up being a proper diplomat's wife, and that I wanted to go to that show. If Roddy won there, that would make him a champion, and there weren't a lot of other possibilities before we were due to go back to Israel.

However, it was not so easy. This was after the Yom Kippur war. Although Malawi had retained its diplomatic relations with Israel, none of the other black African countries had. Israel no longer had diplomatic relations with Zambia, but as I was still an American citizen, I decided that I would simply renew my American passport, and travel to the show as an American. So, I went to the American embassy, to the consul in charge of passports (who happened to be our foxhunting friend), and requested a renewal of my American passport. No problem!

Next, I had to get a visa to Zambia. So off I went to the Zambian embassy, where the consular officer, who had met me as an Israeli at innumerable cocktail parties, (the diplomatic community in Malawi was rather small—at the time, there were only seven embassies and several consulates) didn't blink at my request for a visa in an American passport.

The plan had been that another Israeli who was employed by the UN would travel with me. But she developed cold feet at the last minute and I was left on my own for 1500 miles of driving through hostile' country to get to a dog show. Despite last minute doubts about the wisdom of the whole idea, my natural stubbornness wouldn't let me back out now. Jacques was certainly not happy about this whole idea. If what I was doing was officially revealed, it could mean not only embarrassment, but the end of his career in the Foreign Office. But he had already discovered, in our relatively short married life, that trying to change my mind when I was set on something was futile. He stayed home with the kids, the dogs were loaded into the car, and I was on my way to Zambia.

The first portion of the road from Lilongwe to the border was a paved highway and despite occasional potholes, it was in a good state of repair. However, this encouraging state of affairs did not continue for long. Soon I came to the section I had been warned about. The pavement ended abruptly and turned into a dirt track. This track carried a good amount of traffic to and from the border, and most of the traffic was heavy trucks and carts, so the dirt surface was full of holes, gullies and tread marks. In places it felt like I was driving over a corrugated washboard. The old Cortina did not have the best springs in the world, and I soon felt like the inside of a cocktail shaker. In addition, it was the dry season, so everything was covered with a thick coating of dust, and every vehicle passing threw up enormous clouds.

The dust hung in the still dry air, making it impossible to see more than a few meters ahead.

Several hours of driving at an average of 30 kph brought me to the Malawi border station. Leaving Malawi presented no problem, but now my first possible obstacle—entering Zambia—faced me.

I parked outside the Zambian border station and entered with all my documents. The first thing I had to do was to enter the car license number in a large logbook. I then had to present my passport. I was worried about how they would react to the diplomatic license plates and the non-diplomatic passport, but no one seemed to notice. The next thing was to present the health certificates of the dogs.

This seemed to be of much greater interest to the border guard. He took the document, a page in length and in three copies, and started to read it carefully. Upon finishing the page, he turned to the second copy and carefully read that. Finally he read the last copy, took his official stamp and *bang!bang!bang!* stamped all three copies. Despite it being clearly marked at the bottom that one copy was to be returned to the dog owner, one copy to be sent to the local veterinary station and one copy sent to the main office in Lusaka, he handed me all the copies and waved me back to my car. I was now in Zambia.

The highways in Zambia were marvelous and the speed limit was 120 kph. One of the reasons that there were no speed problems was that there were very few cars on the highway. The scenery was lovely, but unlike Malawi with its dense population, here there were no roadside villages and not a soul to be seen for hundreds of kilometers. It was very easy to imagine all kinds of wildlife watching from behind the trees, as well as perhaps a few Africans. There were no petrol stations between the border and Lusaka. I had been warned of this and had a few jerry cans of petrol with me. But this meant that there were also no rest stops with toilets, something a pampered American is not accustomed to. There was no choice but to stop at the side of the road and duck behind a tree, with my imagination conjuring invisible eyes staring from behind each tree.

The drive was planned to take a day and a half. The first night I spent on the farm of some friends who we had met in Malawi and who some months before had moved to Zambia. It was fun seeing them again, getting a good meal and a hot shower to wash off the dust of the road. The next morning, refreshed, I was ready to continue to the Copper Belt. This was the far end of Zambia, where the famous copper mines were, and the largest town there was Kitwe, the venue of the show.

It was a holiday weekend, the Easter weekend to be exact, and as I drove off on my way that Saturday morning, I had no idea of the Zambian holiday custom I was about to encounter. It seemed that, to increase revenues, on holidays the Zambian police force placed their troopers at intervals on the highway with the instructions to do safety checks to all passing cars. These safety checks included rocking the car back and forth to test the brakes to see if they held and other similar little tricks. For safety violations, the drivers were fined on the spot. The troopers could go off duty after they had collected a certain quota in fines.

I ran into the first roadblock about twenty kilometers after leaving the farm of our friends. Several two-and-a-half-meter tall police officers with submachine guns slung casually over their shoulders stalked around examining the car. The dogs did not approve of this inspection and started barking hysterically. One thing that my friends had warned me about was that if the dogs annoyed a policeman there, he was just as likely to shoot them as not, so I frantically tried to persuade them that I didn't need to be protected and would be much happier if they would shut up. Meanwhile the police had finished their inspection. Deciding that one of my tires was too worn down, I was fined and sent on. About twenty kilometers later, I ran into another roadblock. Again several black Schwarzeneggers submitted me to an inspection. But this group also had an officer present.

He walked around the car staring, and then asked me, "What is that license plate?" Uh-oh, I thought. How was I going to explain a diplomatic plate and a non-diplomatic passport? I had visions of ending up in a Zambian jail, the cause of an international diplomatic incident.

"It's a Malawi number," I answered.

The answer seemed to be acceptable, and anyway, the officer was now distracted by the report of his inspection crew. Once again it was the tire. I had visions of being fined every 20 kilometers between Lusaka and Kitwe until I ran out of money. On a holiday weekend, there was certainly no chance of buying a new tire. Having already passed beyond panic, I decided that there was nothing to do except to ask for help.

"Look, sir," I said, "I have a spare tire, but I can't change it myself. Maybe you nice policeman can help me?"

And sure enough, they did. At an order from the officer, the policemen effortlessly changed my tire. Gratefully, I was on the road again.

The next few roadblocks were passed uneventfully. They even started to recognize the CD plates and pass me through with a salute. It seemed that my troubles were over.

Then, as I comfortably skimmed along at the posted speed limit of 100 kph, I suddenly came to a road sign for 70kph. Fifty meters further was another sign bringing the speed limit down to 50, and twenty meters after that, another sign for 30 kph. Five meters past that was a town, consisting of two shacks and a gas pump, and, of course, a policeman was waiting to catch the speeders and—what else?—to fine them on the spot.

Finally, without any more adventures, I arrived in Kitwe. It was noon, and the first day of the show, the obedience competitions, were to be held that afternoon.

I drove back and forth down the main street of Kitwe, looking for a sign as to where the show was being held. I presumed that a public event, like a dog show, would be signposted for the public. But not only were there no signposts, there also didn't appear to be many people. The streets were bare of pedestrians, and there were few cars to be seen. I didn't know what to do. Not only was I due to compete with the dogs in the obedience trials, but I had to meet the people who were putting me up for the night there. I had no other way of getting in touch with them.

There was a petrol station open in the center of town, and I pulled in to ask directions. The station owner, a well-dressed Zambian, was the only one there. He had no idea about a dog show or where such a thing might be held.

I was in despair. I was tired and stressed from coping with the police blockades, and felt lost and friendless. I didn't know anyone and had nowhere to go. What could I do?

I started to cry. The poor gas station owner stared at me in horror as if wondering what he was going to do with this crazy white lady sitting in her car in the middle of his gas station bawling.

"Look, lady, don't cry, I'll help you!" he exclaimed. He jumped into his own car and signaled me to follow him, and in procession we started to drive through the streets of Kitwe, stopping every now and then when he saw someone he thought it worthwhile to ask.

Finally, we arrived at the local fairgrounds—a logical place for a dog show to be held. And sure enough—the dog show was indeed there. My guide pointed at the people and dogs milling around, turned his car and zoomed away, not even waiting to give me a chance to thank him for his consideration.

What a relief it was to be in the familiar surroundings of a dog show, and with other people around. I was quickly found by my hosts, who helped me to get settled and ready for the competition.

Nova was the first to compete in the beginner's trials and as I could have expected of a puppy in totally new surroundings and after a long and stressful car ride, she was a total disaster. But, by this time, after all the stress of the morning, I found myself totally calm, or maybe 'burned out' would have been a better term. Julep's turn came, and she did every exercise with style, ultimately coming out the winner of her class, not a very common achievement for a collie. In good spirits again, we went home with our hosts to a very welcome hot shower, meal, some dog talk and a good night's sleep.

The next day was the conformation judging, where the dogs were judged not for their performance but for their beauty. I was, as always, nervous before the show, especially because the judge was English and I didn't know what she would think of my collies. The other exhibitors were almost all British ex-pats living in Africa, and the breeds were mostly breeds that were popular in Britain and had been imported. There were some dogs of very high quality there as well as far as I could see.

Finally it was time for the collie judging, and I couldn't believe it when Nova won the puppy class, Julep the open bitch class and Roddy the open dog class and Best of Breed. Impressive trophies accompanied these titles.

At the end of the day was the Best in Show judging and the various interbreed challenge classes. Again, I couldn't believe it when Nova won Best Puppy in Show, Julep Best Bred by Exhibitor in show, and Roddy, finally, Best in Show! I was euphoric! It didn't even matter that all these enormous and impressive trophies were revolving trophies that couldn't be taken out of the country, and the only thing we would have to show of them were the photographs we took.

The next day, however, the euphoria lessened as I considered the drive home. I was planning to do it in one day, and now all I wanted was to safely get out of Zambia and back to Malawi. Hopefully, now that the holiday weekend was over, we would manage to get home with no more mishaps.

Indeed, the drive went well. There were no police to be seen, no speed traps, no safety checks. There was very little traffic, and as I had equipped myself with a jerry can of petrol, I didn't have to worry about the lack of petrol stations on the way. All I prayed for now was for my old and beat up Cortina to hold up until we were back over the border.

Finally I reached the border station. We easily left Zambia, crossed the border, and now were at the Malawi station. The official there took my passport and started to check, and then said to me, "But where is your entry visa to Malawi?" Entry visa? But I had left Malawi only three days ago! I explained that to the official, and that this was a new passport, and the original entry visa was in my old passport. He thought about that for a while, and then requested identification. I had my Malawi Diplomatic Corps identification card with me, which I handed him. He looked at the card, listing me as belonging to the Israel Diplomatic Corps, looked at my American passport, handed them back to me with the admonition that I have my visa transferred to my new passport, and let us through.

We were home! Almost. There was still the road back to Lilongwe with the potholes and dust, but at least I was back in Malawi.

Another few hours and I was truly home, exhausted and exhilarated, telling Jacques all my adventures. Only afterward did the true craziness of what I had done penetrate—1500 miles alone in the African bush, through a country that didn't have diplomatic relations with us, to go to a dog show. But I had done it!

Jacques was very pleased with my victories, but I think he was even more pleased that I had gotten away with the whole thing without getting 'caught.'

The only real disappointment was that, other than the family, there was hardly anyone that I could tell about it; the whole trip would have to remain a secret, at least until we had left Africa.

Soon enough, the end of our tour of duty came. I had very mixed feelings about it, for although there had been many things that were frustrating and boring, there had been a lot that was fascinating. Plus, the world of breeding and dog showing was much better developed in South Africa than it was in Israel.

So, I decided to take advantage of things while I had a chance. I decided to leave Malawi a few months before Jacques was free to go, and spend them in South Africa. I had friends I could stay with, and I could do the South African show circuit before I left for Israel. So, Dorcas and I and the dogs packed up and left for South Africa.

We stayed with a friend we had made there, an elderly lady who was a longtime breeder of collies, shelties and bearded collies. She had quite a large kennel and a large number of dogs, so having a few more around for a few weeks didn't make much difference. Dorcas, who was just over three, was also a very well-behaved little girl and rather precocious for her age. She had spent very little time with children of her own age, rather mostly had been either with her elder brothers or with adults, and was quite capable of carrying on a serious conversation. Of course, sometimes her ease with adults was not beneficial as the time when we had a Malawian government minister over for dinner. He was a Zulu, a huge man of very dark complexion, and a booming voice. He was apparently a chief in his tribe, and wore a pure ivory bracelet about two inches wide as a badge of his position. His position in the government was just as important. This all did not impress Dorcas. When he came into the house, she looked up at him—a long way up, as she was a tiny little thing—and asked in a clear voice, "Why are you so fat?" If the floor could have swallowed me up, I would have been happy! Fortunately, he loved children, as most of the Malawians seemed to, and had a good sense of humor as well.

As we were spending a few weeks in South Africa this time, we had a chance to see things that were not only related to dogs. We explored Johannesburg, saw a gold mine, and other typical tourist occupations. We also met a number of people and visited at their homes.

I enjoyed South Africa tremendously—the people were very friendly and open, the standard of living was high, and it was not expensive. But there was still a vague uncomfortable feeling I couldn't shake and eventually I realized what it was. This was 1975, the period when Apartheid was still in effect. I realized that, wherever you went, you saw only white people unless you were being served in some way by a black. The black areas—toilets, drinking fountains, transportation — were all well concealed from the public eye. After we had been to a few dog shows, I realized that there were no blacks there unless they were groundskeepers or serving refreshments. At one show, I discovered that there was a black dog owner—but he was not allowed to show his own dog. He had to hire a white handler. Having grown up in America, spent several years in the liberal and accepting atmosphere of Israel, and then getting to know the wonderful Malawians who were kind, friendly and open people, the situation in South Africa felt strange, unnatural and slightly ominous. In the dog world as I had known it up to now, no one was really interested in what your ethnic or religious background was, what you looked like, or what your politics were—they were only interested in your dogs. I had made dog friends in many countries from many backgrounds, and we always had plenty in common to talk about. Despite the great life style, South Africa did not seem to me to be the kind of place I would care to live in long term.

We traveled to several dog shows, in various parts of the country like Durban and Pietermaritzburg. I was fascinated by the differences, from the rather barren plains to the lush almost tropical vegetation of the coast.

Dorcas had her first opportunities to show her prowess as a dog handler at these shows. As I was showing all three of the collies, often two or three of them would have to come back into the ring for the Best of Breed competition. Since I was only one person, Dorcas would come in with one of them as the handler.

"Just hold the leash and do what I do," I told her. She proved to be very competent, showing much better than some of the adults competing. This was probably the first time that there was a three-year-old dog handler in the ring in South Africa.

But all good things come to an end, and it was time to go home. Jacques and the boys would shortly join us back in Israel. The dogs again were loaded in their crates, we said a sad and possibly permanent goodbye to the good friends we had made in South Africa—I didn't know if or when we would have another chance to visit Africa—and we took off for home.

The flight was uneventful, but it was long and tiring, and I was looking forward to getting home. Dvora was coming to get us with a small pickup truck so that there would be room for the dogs and the crates. We touched down at Ben Gurion airport late, close to midnight.

In the arrivals hall, I collected the dogs, and was trying to figure out how I would manage to get Dorcas, our luggage, the dogs, and the crates out through customs to where we were being met, when I was approached by a customs official.

"You can't leave with those dogs," he said. "They have to go into quarantine."

I was tired, and this was the last straw. There was no way that I was going to allow my dogs, cared for and vaccinated, to be thrown into the quarantine kennels, which was where they kept all the stray, sick and vicious dogs of the area. I refused. And of course the officials refused to let me take the dogs out of the airport. We were at a standoff.

I decided that the only thing to do was a sit-down strike. I was going to stay there in the airport with the dogs until they decided to let us all go home. Dvora was waiting, and I sent Dorcas and the luggage and dog crates home with her, and I sat down in the arrivals hall with the three dogs, Roddy, Nova and Julep, on leash with me. Degel and the two cats we had picked up while we were in Malawi were coming back with Jacques and the boys.

Every now and then as I sat there with the dogs, some official or other came by and asked me who I was and what I was doing there, and I explained that I was not leaving the airport without my dogs. I began to feel a lot of sympathy for my cause among the airport workers as the night passed.

In the morning, Dvora went to consult with the veterinary in charge, and got permission to take the dogs home and keep them in home quarantine. She came back to the airport to pick up the dogs and me with the proper documents. The officer at the airport was relieved to have a chance to get rid of me—airport workers had begun to drive him crazy, coming by and asking him, "Why is she still here? Why don't you let her go home?" He was glad to tell me to get out of there and to be sure to keep my dogs at home in quarantine. Triumphant, we left the arrivals hall. We were back in Israel. Our African interlude was over.

Chapter Ten: Home Again, Home Again

At home at Sha'ar Hagai we all had to go through another major adjustment. Three years of having electricity, a telephone, house servants, a gardener, and the life-style of a diplomat had been easy to get accustomed to. Now we were back without electricity, without a phone, and anything that needed to be done had to be done with our own hands. Instead of finding clean clothes ironed and waiting in the cupboards in the morning, now I had to do the scrubbing myself. And without electricity, there was no ironing, not that I really wanted to complain about that! When Dorcas was born, for those first months before we left for Africa, I had had to wash her nappies by boiling them on the gas range in a huge iron pot. I thanked heaven that now she was 'housetrained,' and at least I was free of the nappies, although just to have a hot shower we often had to heat pots of water on the stove. I had to start cooking again, washing dishes and cleaning the house. Jacques and the kids helped and everyone had their jobs and responsibilities but still I wished we had brought at least George, the houseboy, home with us!

There were a lot of new dogs too. Dvora and Israela had been busy while I was away, both in breeding and in collecting dogs from the desert, the Bedouin, and similar sources. The boarding kennel was doing pretty well also; there was plenty of work for me in the kennels.

We had to get the house in shape again. After standing empty for three years, or periodically being inhabited by temporary workers, it was not in great shape. We now had a bit more in the way of furniture, having brought some things back with us from Africa, so we started making it into a comfortable place to live.

It took some weeks for all the household goods that we had sent back from Africa to arrive, so we spent the time painting and repairing.

The walls were whitewashed, and the house started to look clean and welcoming.

The children were still quite small; Dorcas was only three and a half, Chaim was eight and Joel was ten. Since there was no electricity we left a kerosene lantern burning low as a nightlight. One evening soon after our return, we were all down at Dvora's for dinner—we all often ate together, everyone providing some part of the meal. When it was bedtime for the children, we returned up to the house, and opened the door on a cloud of greasy black smoke and terrible kerosene fumes.

The lantern had begun to smoke and as we were not around to adjust the wick, the house was filled with the smoke and fumes.

We quickly extinguished the lantern, opened all the doors and windows, and aired everything out. But a layer of greasy black soot had been left all over every surface, including the freshly-painted walls. Counter tops, tables, and utensils could be washed but getting the soot off the walls was impossible. The whole house had to be repainted, and it took four or five layers of paint to reasonably cover the soot—and even after that I was sure that there was still a gray shadow under the paint; it was not the pristine white it had been before.

There were other experiences as a result of our do-it-yourself efforts. Friends who had installed a new kitchen gave us a large kitchen cupboard as a gift. It was very difficult to hang it on the kitchen wall—the wall was cement and it was hard to get fixtures in. But finally, with our mutual effort, Jacques and I were able to lift it into position and into place on the wall. Our possessions had arrived from Africa, and we carefully placed all of our dishes (not fine china, but a nice set), glassware, and so on, in the new cupboard. We were very pleased with our efforts and with the fact that all had arrived from Africa without breaking.

A few days later, Jacques and I were in the kitchen, with several of the dogs standing around our feet hoping for handouts. Suddenly, without warning, the cupboard began to slide down the wall, ending with a huge crash on the floor against the door. Its doors had burst open scattering china and glassware all over the floor. We were trapped in the kitchen until we could empty the cupboard and move it away from the door.

The dogs—Julep, Nova, and Wafi the Canaan—stood pressed against our legs looking at the mess and trying to make themselves as small and invisible as possible, lest more cupboards be thrown on them from above, or lest Jacques and I decide that they were responsible.

A major portion of the china and glassware did, amazingly enough, survive—but the perfect record of the shipping from Africa was definitely smashed.

Knowing that we would be returning to no electricity, we had purchased a few things in Africa that would run on alternative power sources. As both Jacques and I were music lovers, we bought a battery-operated record player and had accumulated a nice collection of records. We also had purchased a freezer that operated on kerosene.

We already had a kerosene-operated refrigerator that we got just before we left for Africa. It was a very old model fridge that had been converted to work on power provided by a small kerosene burner; such models could be found occasionally in Arab villages where there was no electricity as yet. It worked quite effectively as long as the tank was kept full of kerosene and the wick was kept clean and trimmed. One of the daily housekeeping tasks was taking care of the refrigerator. We felt that now we would be living in luxury—not only a fridge, but a freezer!

F.F., as the freezer became known (short for "fucking freezer"), had operated very well in Africa. We were looking forward to being able to store things, and even having ice cream.

But F.F. apparently did not approve of its change in location. It refused to work. We tried everything—cleaning it, changing parts, leaving it lit, leaving it unlit, banging the pipes, standing it upside down and sideways; this was supposed to get the coolant flowing and free it of air bubbles if there were any. But nothing helped. We lit it and checked every few minutes to see if it was even slightly cold but no luck. We even, at considerable expense, called in a refrigeration expert to come and check it out. But F.F. never worked again. It remained a dead white elephant standing in a corner of the porch, until we finally gave up and had it hauled away.

Joel and Chaim adjusted easily to being back at home. They had gone to an English school in Malawi and were now totally fluent in

English, but they also remembered all their Hebrew, so had no trouble returning to school. Dorcas, however, had spoken only English in Malawi. Her nanny, of course, spoke no Hebrew, and we spoke mostly English with her. She was entered in nursery school, but it took her several months to adjust. Being as stubborn as her mother, for several months she refused to speak at all in the nursery school. Then one day, apparently deciding that she knew Hebrew well enough, she calmly joined the group and started chatting away in a totally natural way. She had no more adjustment problems.

However, she did live a fairly isolated life. Most of the time that she was not in school, she spent at home, whether with me or with her brothers, and with the animals. I did not always have transportation available, and although I tried to take her to see her friends and have her friends come to visit whenever possible, the possibilities were limited. We didn't always have a lot of time for keeping an active little girl occupied, so she had to learn to fend for herself. This had some rather odd results.

As could be expected, Dorcas learned to use her imagination to invent games to keep herself busy, and seeing as how she lived with so many animals, the animals became her role models. One of her favorite games was to pick up a pine branch, tie it to a piece of string and then tie the string around her waist, creating a 'tail.' Then she galloped around the *wadi* playing horse. Or she ran back and forth on the terrace in front of the house with the dogs, 'barking' at visitors or passersby, and not understanding why people thought it odd—if the dogs could do it, why couldn't she? Visitors didn't realize that when she came up to them and asked if she had 'a good coat,' she didn't mean an article of apparel, but rather her hair.

She also, understandably, became a real dog expert at a very young age. One day I arrived home to find that some people had arrived with a bitch to be bred to one of our stud dogs, and Dorcas, with her four-year-old superiority, had taken charge. She was standing there directing them in what to do; "You'd better stand with the bitch on the step there—she is a little small..." as they stood there with mouths open in shock. Or another time, when we took one of our bitches to be bred, she watched from the side as the dog made unsuccessful attempts to consummate the mating, and commented, "Our dogs do it better!"

It was good to be home, but life wasn't easy. The Yom Kippur War had left the country in a state of depression, both emotionally and economically. It was not at all easy to make a living—prices and expenses were high, even for the minimal things we required. The kennel was doing reasonably well, but we had a lot of our own dogs and a lot of expenses. Canaan dogs, as much as they were my passion, were not a commodity in demand. The breeds that were popular were those that were imported and served as a status symbol. There was little interest in 'things Israeli,' especially a dog commonly known as an 'Arab dog.'

I was told by friends that the Afghan hound, sold for high prices all over the world, was considered a street dog in its home country and wandered the villages stray and uncared for. This was no great comfort—we were hardly able to give puppies away as a gift, not to mention selling them for a decent price. But, on the other hand, we were not willing to give up trying to preserve and establish a breeding base for this breed that, for many reasons, we felt deserved to be preserved. However, all these dogs ate a lot, and our income was not enough to live and raise a family on.

Jacques was back at a desk job in the Foreign Office, but was not very happy there; he didn't feel he had much chance for advancement. It was time to look for something new to do.

Chapter Eleven: Hi-ho, Savta!

I have heard it said that most pre- and teenage girls have a tendency to be horse crazy. In this, I was no exception. As a child I dreamed of having a horse, entered every contest that offered a pony as a prize, and read all the books available on the subject—I bet most don't know that the *Black Stallion* appeared in a whole series of books.

When I was sneaking away from summer camp in the morning before the other campers were awake to go riding, my knowledge of the subject was only theoretical from those books. But, naive as I was, I was sure that I could keep that hidden from the stable owners by throwing around some good horsey terms. They were probably very amused by my self-expressed expertise as I jounced along on my horse hanging on to the saddle and mane for dear life. But I was in heaven!

The only 'serious' boyfriend I had in high school was a fellow who was willing to take me on dates to the riding stable in Lincoln Park, where we could rent horses and trot along the bridle paths with the 'high society' of Chicago. In university, I was thrilled to discover that one of the choices for the required Physical Education requirement was the riding club. I managed to hold my own with the kids who had, more or less, grown up on horseback. Although I was far from the best in the class, I didn't fall off and I even managed to learn to jump, despite being regularly assigned the most passive horse in the stable. While other horses ran at the jumps and had to be held back, my horse languidly jogged along, his feet dragging in the soft earth of the ring. Following all the teacher's shouted instructions, I squeezed and kicked and collected and all the rest but none of this seemed to be even noticed by the horse, which jogged along in the direction of the jump and sort of skipped over it, hardly lifting his legs at all. Only someone as horse crazy as I was could find any excitement in this activity.

In Israel, I discovered that very few people knew much more than I did. Riding in Israel was still on the level that it must have been on in the Wild West—if you could get on a horse, get him to do what you wanted, and not fall off, then you knew how to ride. In comparison to most, I was a real expert because I actually knew something about the finer points of the sport.

During the first year I was in Israel, I managed to get a job at a riding stable just outside of Tel Aviv. The stable owner had been in the British Cavalry and had become an institution in Israel. He had even been a member of the Camel Corps, which was much harder than riding horses, for sure. I was thrilled to get the job, which involved grooming, feeding, and mucking out the horses, and if I proved myself, taking people out to ride.

I was determined to become a good rider and practiced at every opportunity, including grabbing a horse to ride bareback when I was sent to bring the horses in from grazing out in the field. Still no great athlete, I ran into major problems trying to get up on the horse—I never did manage any of those flying leaps onto the horse's back like you see in the movies. I had to grab the horse, put a halter on it, and wander around looking for a convenient rock or fence that I could climb on, hoping that the horse would agree to stand still alongside it long enough for me to clamber on. I did become pretty proficient at this, though, and certainly improved my control over the horses.

I soon was considered good enough to take people out for trail rides, and to be sent out to exercise the horses. This was a mixed blessing—the horses that needed to be exercised were the more difficult ones that couldn't ordinarily be rented to casual riders for trail rides or lessons. If there were a few days of rain, or other reasons why these horses were confined to the stable, they could be pretty frisky when they were taken out. I learned this the hard way when I was sent out to exercise one of the stable's 'race' horses.

Horse racing in Israel at that time, and actually still even now, was a rather disorganized event. It consisted of anyone who felt that he had a fast horse showing up at a designated location and running hell-for-leather until one horse was declared the winner. There were no organized racetracks, no official organization running things, no betting, not much in the way of rules; it was really a very casual affair.

My boss was fond of these races and kept a few horses to run in them. These horses were not among those that I could exercise so he exercised them. The horse that I was expected to exercise was a boarder belonging to a friend of the boss. This horse was a small bay with a white star, named, with the usual originality, *Kochav*, which is Hebrew for star. And he was a bastard.

There had been about a week of heavy rain and the horses were full of energy. I was told to take Kochav out and trot him for a while to work off some of his excess energy, but Kochav had other ideas. As soon as we were out in the open, he took hold of the bit in his teeth, yes, it is true that horses can do such things, and he bolted at a full racing speed

126

for the other side of town. There was no way that I could stop him. Following all the rules of good riding, I started turning him in a circle so that I could slow him down. Okay, Kochav thought, if she wants to turn, we WILL turn! And he turned sharply to the right, directly under a low hanging tree branch.

I saw the branch coming, but there was no time to do anything, and it was too low to duck under. The branch and I connected solidly, right on the level of my forehead. Fortunately, I seem to have a pretty hard head, and though I was dumped unceremoniously in the mud and ended up with a cut across the forehead and a headache, there was little damage beyond that.

But there was no way I was going to let that horse win, or let anyone know what had happened! He headed back to the stable and so did I. I caught him and remounted and took him out again, and this time I held him so short he could hardly move—but I did get him exercised!

I finally did prove myself as a horsewoman sufficiently to be awarded the greatest prize of all—the chance to exercise my boss's own prize racehorse. Negev was a gorgeous white Arabian stallion that had won many races. I was allowed to ride him in the riding school ring, and was warned to simply walk and trot him calmly.

How proud I was to be riding on this magnificent horse! I really felt on top of the world. My Canaan, Sheikh, also wanted to join in the fun, and ran into the ring and began to run along with us, close to Negev's hooves.

I was a bit worried that Sheikh might get kicked or stepped on, so I leaned forward on Negev's neck to see where Sheikh was and warn him to move back.

Instantly, Negev leaped forward like a racehorse! No one warned me that the signal for him to start running with all his speed and strength in a race was for the jockey to lean forward. I grabbed his neck and hung on for dear life, as he raced around the small yard. Not only did I have to cope with the speed, but also with the turns as he ran around and around and around.

Gradually, my wits returned enough for me to realize that if I didn't want to fall off, I would have to stop him, and if I wanted to stop him, I would have to sit up and take control of the reins. As I sat up, Negev began to slow down—just as he had been trained to do—and soon I had him back to a comfortable walk. I had stayed on him! And I would never forget the feelings of power and speed.

Life as a stable girl, however, after a while began to pale. I was ready for some new adventures. So when I was offered the opportunity of going down to Eilat to work with the horses in a movie being made there, I didn't hesitate. This was before the beginning of Sha'ar Hagai, during my first year in Israel in 1968. I packed up my meager possessions and Sheikh, and was off to Eilat.

Israel at that time was one of the favored locations for making Westerns, along with Italy. A number of the so-called 'spaghetti Westerns' were actually made in the southern desert of Israel, where the landscape was similar to that of the American west and the labor was cheap. Eilat itself was pretty much a frontier town, with one stoplight, some housing developments, the harbor, and a gorgeous beach that was still mostly undiscovered by tourists.

The movie company had built an entire Western town up in the mountains at the outskirts of Eilat, and it really looked as if it belonged there. There was a herd of about 50 horses, and my job was to help take care of them, and keep them fed, watered, groomed, and saddled and ready for filming. I also was to be an extra in the film, riding when they needed a lot of riders in a group.

The idea of being in the movies was thrilling and glamorous, but reality was a bit different. The job was hard work, long hours, and hot!

I felt sorry for the horses, which were expected to gallop around in that heat. The actors and crew had a union, but the horses didn't!

I was also too naive to realize that the director and crew were only interested in what would look good on camera. We were given things to do that, looking back on them now, were totally insane. "Take that horse, go to the top of that steep mountain over there, and when we give you the signal, gallop down at full speed—and try not to make too much dust!" But I actually managed to accomplish the assignments, a source of pride to me and certainly something that raised me a notch in the esteem of my fellow 'horsemen.'

When Jacques and I married, his wedding gift to me was a horse. We had discovered a horse for sale in Abu Gosh, the Arab village not far from us. She was a gray mare, not a pure Arabian, but Arab type, fairly young and quite spirited. When we came to see her, the family patriarch who was selling her looked at me skeptically, and told Jacques (he wouldn't talk to a woman, after all) that he didn't think that she was suitable for me. Women didn't ride horses like that!

Well, as you can imagine, that got my dander up! I told them that I wanted to try her out, had them put a bridle on her, and, boosted by Jacques (I still was no good at jumping up on to a horse's back), jumped on to her bareback and trotted off.

We took a short turn around the village, during which the mare demonstrated that she was quite well-trained, with smooth gait, but had a lot of spirit. I rode back and dismounted. The patriarch looked at me, and then told Jacques that he guessed that we could buy this horse after all.

I named her Shachaf (Seagull), and had many hours of pleasure riding through the hills around Sha'ar Hagai. She was a lovely mare, and we got along beautifully. I continued riding until the sixth month of my pregnancy.

When we left for Africa, Shachaf was left at the farm. Although no one other than me was 'horsey,' they figured that they would be able to take care of one horse while I was away. But this was not to be—Shachaf was stolen and I never saw her again.

I really missed having a horse when we got back from Africa, but there was no way that our budget would allow the purchase of a new horse, certainly not of the type I wanted. But sometimes things do work out.

First a fellow for whom I had worked for a few months several years before contacted me. He was a Frenchman who had been running a riding stable not far from Sha'ar Hagai and I had helped him out in the early days. He had now decided to leave Israel, not an uncommon decision, I was to discover, among those who tried to make a living working with animals. He wanted to give me a horse!

The horse he gave me was an old white mare called Savta (Grandma). When I say old, I mean old—she was about 25 or so. This was obviously the reason he was willing to give her to me; no one was interested in buying a horse of that age, and he wanted her to have a good home. But Savta didn't look or act like an old horse. She was quite Arab in looks, with a lovely head, and pure white coat—she was really quite beautiful, especially when she was moving. She would step out like a youngster, neck arched, pulling at the reins and ready to go, and when you gave her the chance, she loved to run, and had plenty of endurance. I was glad to have her—she was a horse that I could really enjoy.

And now that we had one horse it began to rain horses. Two acquaintances of Jacques' in the Foreign Office had horses that they had been keeping in Claude's stable, and now that he was leaving, they were looking for a new arrangement. Could they board their horses with us?

Sure, why not—the income was welcome and covered the costs of keeping our own horse. So our stable expanded to include two well-trained geldings, Mig and Tiran. The names were very typical of the times—Mig, of course, was the Russian fighter plane and Tiran was for the Straits of Tiran.

After a few months of boarding the geldings, one of their owners approached us with a proposition. He liked the care his horse was getting, but what was lacking was a riding ring for working with the horse and possibly doing some jumping when he didn't feel like riding out in the hills. There was no place at Sha'ar Hagai where there was enough flat land for a ring, but he was interested in opening a small riding stable not far from us. The idea was to take over a stable that had failed due to poor management and lack of professionalism, and to re-establish. He would invest in improvements and the purchase of some additional horses, and I and other members of Sha'ar Hagai would run the place and give riding lessons.

Everyone at Sha'ar Hagai was enthusiastic about the idea. I certainly was! Jacques felt that this was an opportunity for him to leave the Foreign Office—he would take over the kennel work in my place, and would start doing the course for tourist guides. He decided this would be a superior profession to diplomacy. We also had a few new additions to the Sha'ar Hagai population, who were very much in favor of the plan and would be working with me at the stable—Americans both, there was Esti, who had just completed Army service and loved animals and riding, and Sally, a long time friend of Dvora's who had separated from her husband and was looking for something to do. She had grown up on a ranch and had competed in horse shows, and probably knew more about horses than any of us.

The stable was located only about ten minutes away from the farm by car. It was behind a gas station and restaurant complex. The owner of the complex had decided that having a stable there would be a good idea—it would attract more customers, and parents could sit in the restaurant eating while their children were riding. Basically, this was a good idea. There was only one major mistake in this thinking—this was the Jerusalem area. Everyone knows that Jerusalemites are not eager to spend money, and certainly not on such suspect pursuits as riding horses. What would have been a huge success in Tel Aviv was here struggling to barely cover expenses.

However, we were sure, with our usual cockeyed optimism, that we could turn things around and make a success out of the place.

The stable itself and the riding ring were quite adequate. But the horses were a collection of some of the most miserable specimens of horseflesh I had yet seen. We would have to get some new horses if we wanted to run a proper stable.

Our budget was very limited. Of course, there was Savta, Tiran and Mig, who were transferred to the new stable. And soon, after inspecting various possibilities offered by the horse dealers, we had a few more—no great beauties, but enough to open the stable for business.

A few deserve mention. First there was Massoud. He was a rather elderly gelding, actually a very good-looking horse of Arab type, or rather, he would have been if he hadn't had a permanently sour expression. Obviously life had not been good to poor old Massoud, and he had few hopes for the future. His immediate response to anyone coming near was to lay his ears back, bare his teeth, and glare as if to say, "Don't you dare get any closer!" If you took your eye off of him, he was likely to bite as well. He also hated being saddled, and when he saw the saddle coming, hunched his back and turned with a threatening face, ready to attack. The only way to saddle him was to tie him short so that he couldn't turn his head around. Once you were on him, he was actually quite a pleasant ride and quite reliable for children—he never acted up under saddle or tried to run away. But although we treated him very well and tried to gain his confidence and affection, he was never able to overcome the memories he had of whatever had happened to him in the past—he remained forever suspicious of the intentions of humankind.

The absolute opposite of Massoud was Jerry. Jerry was a young gelding about three years old when we got him. He was a pinto, with very attractive brown and white markings, and a stocky build. He was a very sweet horse that loved to be petted, fed tidbits, and socialized with. Pintos were at this time still quite rare in Israel, so Jerry with his friendly temperament and special color was very popular. He was also as lazy as the day was long. When being ridden he ambled along in no hurry for anything. If his rider was sufficiently experienced, he could be prodded into a clumsy trot or even a heavy-footed canter, but given the chance, he would immediately revert back to his favorite gait, a slow amble. On trail rides, he trailed along at the end of the line, falling further and further back. The children coming for lessons initially fought over who got to ride Jerry, but after a few experiences riding him, they fought to see who could avoid riding Jerry. However, because of this he was a very useful horse. Any riding stable certainly has its share of the show-off type— "Yeah, sure I know how to ride—give me a horse that can really go!" Israel has more than its quota of this sort. So Jerry became the mount of these types. As he was such a good looking horse, they were pleased with him, and by the time they found out that they couldn't get him to move—well, it was too late. After all, they had bragged about what good riders they were! Once in a while I was challenged by one of them as to why I had given them such a lazy horse. Since I knew Jerry and his habits intimately, and knew just what worked with him, it was no problem for me to mount him for a few minutes and gallop him around the ring to show the complaining customer that the horse did know how to run. And after all, "You said you know how to ride!"

The opposite of Jerry in this respect was Haldiyeh. She was a little Bedouin mare, hardly larger than a pony, with a prominent belly that made her look as if she was permanently pregnant. She was really an ugly little thing—but when she was under saddle, that was a different story. Haldiyeh loved to run. She had two gaits—standing still and full out gallop. She was very popular.

Another horse very useful in such circumstances was Lady, a large bay mare, quite young and usually very amenable. However, she had a very interesting reaction to anyone who thought that just whamming her with their feet would get her to move. In this instance, she walked backwards. The harder they kicked, the more persistent she was in backing up. Trying to turn her didn't help. It was not uncommon for me to continue on with the rest of the group on a trail ride, as Lady backed off in the other direction, impervious to her embarrassed rider.

We had high hopes for the little stable, and although we couldn't afford any of the high priced, 'fancy' horses that were beginning to be seen in the country—thoroughbreds, Hannoverians, Quarter horses, and such—we decided that we would do the maximum possible with the ones we had. There were a few horse shows a year in the country, which included competitions in dressage, show jumping and cross country jumping. We decided that we would train the horses and try to get to a level where we could compete.

My background in this was minimal, but I couldn't let anyone know that—I was supposed to be the expert. I ordered a bunch of books and became well-versed in theory and terminology. I have always been good at giving the impression that I know what I am doing, even if I don't, because I know when to keep my mouth shut. I absorbed all I could from all available sources, including from the experience that Esti and Sally had, and we began training the horses.

We had one major stroke of luck. A fellow came to work for us who was really an expert. He was a South African who had spent most of his life working with horses, and had even been a professional jockey and had competed in dressage and jumping. He had worked in one of the large and classy stables in the Tel Aviv area, but had gotten fed up with them. I guess he figured that life would be easier with us at Sha'ar Hagai. I never really knew exactly why he joined us, but I was certainly grateful. Moshe soon became a good friend; as nutty as the rest of us, he fit in very well.

Under Moshe's instruction, we did manage to get a few of the horses up to competition level—a very novice level, perhaps, but then the whole country was still on that level. My special mount was Haldiyeh. With Moshe's help, I taught her to jump. She was a whiz and nothing frightened her. Just turn her head towards anything and ask her to jump it, and she did, at high speed. I had never been really comfortable doing things on horseback at high speed but I felt very confident on Haldiyeh. I think perhaps it was because she was so small that it wasn't very far to the ground even if I did fall off. Moshe even persuaded me to do cross-country jumping, the idea of which had been terrifying. Just to think of galloping across country at full speed and jumping over obstacles! But Moshe said I could do it, and I was still trusting enough to believe things like that. And I found that I could do it—and it was absolutely thrilling!

One day Moshe announced we were ready to enter a competition. There was a three-day event at one of the fancy stables, and we would take a few of the horses. We weren't likely to win anything, but we could at least show that we were a part of the horse world.

My main memory of that event was the cross-country competition. Haldiyeh, as ever, was ready to run. She took off from the starting line like a bat out of hell, with me fighting to keep her enough under control to turn her into the right jumps at the right time. In the background I heard the announcer over the loudspeaker describing the ride:

"The rider is now fighting to turn the mare into the jump, yes, she has managed! And they are over that one and the rider is fighting to slow the mare down for the approach to the next jump..."

135

And then there was one jump that both Haldiyeh and I miscalculated, and Haldiyeh hit it and fell, and I, of course, went over her head. But, well trained by Moshe, I landed still holding the reins.

We both got up, found that we were uninjured if a bit bruised. The worst had happened and I had survived it! So, gathering the reins, I remounted, and we finished the course, including the jump that had stopped us. Haldiyeh was perfectly willing to pick up where she had left off and race on.

We didn't win anything, though from the scores it appeared that if we had not had that fall, we might have placed. But that was much less important than the pride and satisfaction I felt. I had taken an untrained little Bedouin horse and trained and ridden her under terrifying circumstances, and we had held our own among all the expensive imported jumpers and high society riders. I will never forget that feeling!

Running a riding stable was, of course, composed in small part of exciting things like competitions and training horses, and in large part of daily drudge work—cleaning stables, grooming horses, giving lessons and taking out trail rides. Some of our customers were really lovely people; they worked hard to improve their riding, were very fond of the horses and were considerate of them, and it was fun working with them. But there were many who were only interested in making an impression on friends and had no interest in the effect their antics might have on the horses. I was really fond of all of our horses, and felt really sorry for them when those types were riding them.

Dorcas attended a kindergarten not very far from the stable. I often did not have a car available to pick her up after school, so I rode over and picked her up on horseback and brought her back, riding double with me, to the stable where she spent the afternoons. She was quite a competent rider already at the age of six or seven, and loved spending the time with me at the stable. She also gained a lot of prestige with her classmates since none of them had ever heard of someone being picked up on horseback before.

I also rode over to the local grocery store to do my shopping, bringing my parcels back in saddlebags. Savta was the horse of choice for these expeditions—she was fast but not hard to control, and she could be tied outside the store without any fear of problems. The nearest grocery was only a few minutes ride away from the stable but it was in an ultra-orthodox community. It was quite an attraction there to show up with a horse.

Every good stable has to have a few dogs as well, so we brought a few of the Canaans out to live at the stable. Two of them lived in the stable with the horses, where they could discourage anyone with ideas of horse theft. One bitch, called Vesta, was kept in the office-storage room, where all the equipment was stored. She was a very aggressive bitch with a very high-pitched and penetrating bark, and looked very ferocious—we were not worried about anyone trying to break in while she was there.

Then there was You-you. He was a little black and white furry dog, almost like a little Border collie, who showed up one day out of nowhere. He started to follow me around and, when we were ready to go home, he tried to follow me on to the bus. This would not do! I locked him in the office for the night—and from then on, he was the stable dog. He was a very brave little fellow, willing to do anything to earn his keep. His name evolved out of us calling him, "Hey, you! Come over here!"

Sometimes, one or another of the collies came with me to the stables as well. Andy in particular enjoyed accompanying me. Apparently the horses awoke her dormant herding dog instincts. She tried to collect the horses when we turned them loose in the yard, nipping at their heels, and, when that didn't work, grabbing them by the tails and swinging. I was always sure that she was going to get a good kick—but she was fast, and it never happened.

One day Andy disappeared, and after an hour or so returned with a sheep. Bedouins with their flocks sometimes passed through looking for grazing—Andy had apparently discovered one of these, and had managed to steal a sheep from the flock. Having good herding instincts was great but the Bedouins did not look kindly on anyone stealing their sheep! I quickly closed Andy in the office and chased the sheep away, hoping it would find its way back to the flock. Sheep? What sheep? I never saw a sheep!

The horses may never have kicked Andy but I was not so lucky. We had one horse at the stable named Vered who was a very beautiful Arab-thoroughbred cross about three years old. She had been purchased by a rather well-off family as a bar-mitzvah present for their young son who was learning to ride, and she was being boarded with us. It turned out that her temperament was as bad as she was beautiful.

Vered was afraid of everything, and when she was scared she reared, kicked, bucked, and refused to move. The youngster was not able to handle her, and we were left with a young and energetic horse on our hands that was not getting nearly enough exercise.

When the weather was rainy, in the winter, not many people came to ride. We turned the horses loose to run around in the yard to work off their excess energy. One winter's day, several of the horses, including Vered, were loose. I came into the yard with the intention of putting them in and letting out some of the others. Vered, as I approached her, whirled around and planted a good solid kick right in my stomach.

I doubled up, unable to breathe. After a few moments, I got my breath back, and, angry and sore, was ready to get back to work.

"Oh no," said Esti and Sally, "You have to go to the emergency service to be checked out."

"I'm fine!" I protested.

But they were adamant—even if I was fine, if something should turn out to be wrong, for the insurance coverage I had to be examined.

So off I went to town, to the emergency service. I was dressed in my usual shabby work clothes, and had nothing with me except a bit of small change for bus fare, but I anticipated a quick check up.

I explained to the staff what had happened, and the doctor began to poke and prod.

"Does that hurt?" Of course it hurt—I had just been kicked by a horse!

"I'm afraid there's danger of damage to your spleen. You must go to the hospital to be checked out," he said. "We'll call you a taxi."

"No taxi," I protested, "I don't have enough cash for a taxi. I'll take a bus." I was sure I could manage to escape and go home.

"Well, then we'll send you in an ambulance," the doctor offered. I was bundled off in an ambulance with a note explaining the urgency of the matter.

In the crowded emergency room, I stood in line for an hour, waiting for someone to look at my note. Finally my turn came. The nurse took the note, looked at it, turned pale and said, "Oh my god! You shouldn't be standing there! You should be lying down!"

She rushed me into a cubicle and put me to bed, ignoring my protests that I felt fine. The spleen was a very tricky organ, she told me, and damage to the spleen could quickly become critical. I was examined, and an intern was instructed to stay in my vicinity and check my pulse every five minutes to be sure that my blood pressure wasn't dropping—a sure sign of a rupture and internal bleeding. I was to be admitted to the hospital and would have to be under observation until they were sure there was no danger of that happening.

I managed to get word to the stable that I was not going to be home for a while ("It's your fault—you made me go to the doctor!") before I was wheeled up to the ward and connected up to an infusion. I was not allowed to eat or drink, in case I had to be rushed to surgery, and my blood pressure was still being checked every five minutes.

At this point an X-ray was ordered. I was wheeled in a wheelchair over to the roentgen department—and there I was parked in the hallway alone for 45 minutes until someone came around to X-ray me. Apparently, no one dies while waiting for an X-ray.

After two days of this, I was going crazy. Yes, my belly was sore— but that was quite reasonable after a kick in that region. I was hungry, and I wanted to go home!

That was the day when a social work student came around doing a survey. She was checking out reasons that people were hospitalized. She had a whole long questionnaire, with questions about parents—did they smoke, drink, have a history of any of fifty diseases or health conditions, and more, and questions about me—did I smoke, drink, take drugs, drink coffee, drink tea, have a history of this, that or the other—answers no, no, no, no, no. "Well, what are you here for?" she asked.

"I was kicked by a horse," I answered. She looked stumped—this didn't fit into any of her categories.

Finally, I was released with a warning that I had to come back for a checkup in a week, or they would send the police after me—they had certainly gotten my number! I didn't dare not show up for the examination, but was then given a clean bill of health—my spleen appeared fine and I was not about to die just yet.

When we took over the stable, there was one little 'bonus' that went with it—a camel. The previous owners had decided that since the gas station-restaurant complex was a rest stop for many tourist buses, it would be good business to have a camel and take photos of tourists on its back.

Camels are nasty creatures; I had enough experience with them to know that. This was a fairly young female, though, and for a camel, she was quite good tempered. She was often fed all sorts of sweets by passing children and tourists, so she felt that people were good things. However, she was definitely not interested in cooperating by giving camel rides to strangers.

I named her Yaniki, because her natural Afro and patrician nose reminded me of a friend—and started training her to lie down and get up, the primary commands that a camel must know. Very aware of the propensity of camels to bite and kick when they were angry, I was very careful to stay out of range of feet and teeth, although it was impossible to stay completely out of range since camels, like llamas, can spit when they are annoyed.

Fortunately, after a few protracted sessions, Yaniki conceded that I was the boss, and followed my commands. I even managed to ride her. This was a very weird feeling, totally different from that of riding a horse, and something that I decided that I could do without.

Now it was time to try our prowess on the tourists. I saddled Yaniki with the traditional Bedouin equipment, I dressed in a long Bedouin dress, and we stood out in front of the gas station waiting for tourists.

Tourists came and tourists went, and many came over to pat Yaniki, feed her sweets, and take photos of her, but no one was interested in shelling out a dollar to ride on her.

After a few tries at this 'terrific business opportunity,' Yaniki was retired from the tourist business and spent her time in the shade out behind the stable, begging treats from anyone passing by.

The stable was fairly successful as far as having customers but financially, we were not doing very well. Inflation in Israel was very,

very high. Feed for the animals, equipment, and all other expenses were growing at an unbelievable pace, but we were not able to raise the prices for riding at a comparable pace—no one was willing to pay that much for the luxury of riding, certainly not the Jerusalem area population. So the decision was finally made that the stable would have to be closed after only four years in operation.

Several of the horses—Mig, Savta, and Haldiyeh—came back to Sha'ar Hagai with us while the others were sold. I felt especially bad about old Massoud. Who knew what his lot in life would be now, just when he was starting to trust people, perhaps for the first time in his life. It was quite heartbreaking for us, but there was no other choice. It was time to move on to new pastures, hopefully greener ones.

Chapter Twelve: Gainful Employment

Running a kennel is not easy. As with all forms of work that involve animal care, the work is hard, physical and often dirty. Running a boarding and breeding kennel has an additional disadvantage; as well as having to care for the animals, you also have to deal with the customers in all their variations.

Most of the customers, both those that came to buy puppies or dogs, or those that came to board or train their dogs, were pleasant and reasonable. But there were those that expected more than was reasonable, who felt that we should be on call to serve them twenty-four hours a day including Saturday and holidays; in short, any time that it was convenient for them to and from the airport. I will never forget the couple that showed up at ten o clock at night on Passover when we were in the middle of the Pesach seder to leave their dog in boarding. "But you are a service," was their excuse. "You should be available all the time."

Many of the dogs were terribly spoiled. I love dogs, but I don't believe that they should run your life. It is amazing the things some people will put up with from their dogs—things they would never allow their children to get away with. The dogs would arrive for boarding with a two-week supply of cooked steak fillet, as that was all they were willing to eat at home. Or we would get dogs that barked and howled incessantly as they had never been left alone before. The worst of those was a pair of Norwegian Buhunds, belonging to a United Nations family. These two started barking the moment they arrived and never stopped for three weeks until they went home—day and night, twenty four hours a day. The only break was when they stopped to eat for a few minutes a day—they had no food problems, their appetites were excellent! They had totally lost their voices by the time they went home, but continued barking anyway. Their owners were not concerned about it when they came to pick them up; they were used to it.

Another tough customer was a little dog that had his owners so well trained they never left him alone. This meant that, although they were cultured and intelligent people, they could never go to a movie or a concert, or eat out in a restaurant, as dogs were not allowed there. If they tried to leave him home, or in the car, he howled and screamed and destroyed everything he could get a hold of. Being in boarding was a shock to this little dog, especially since for the first time his tricks didn't work. Once he discovered that howling was a waste of time and there was nothing in the kennel he could destroy he became a model resident. Of course, as soon as he went home, he reverted to his old behavior, which worked fine on his owners.

Everyone who breeds or cares for animals has bad times as well as good, times of having to deal with sickness or injury, and having to deal with death. The serious breeders have the hardest times. People with a pet bitch that they breed to the neighbor's dog seem to always have a healthy litter of puppies with no complications, no diseases and no problems, while the serious breeders who are trying to produce high quality puppies free of genetic problems have bitches that miss, dogs that don't breed, litters of one, and epidemics of various sorts. We were no exception to this rule; despite all precautions, we had difficult times when we had to cope with real heartbreak.

The first time was an epidemic of distemper that broke out in young dogs and puppies, despite the fact that they had been vaccinated. There is no cure for distemper, an insidious virus that attacks the nervous system. We did everything possible to give the dogs supportive treatment. Dvora was a trained biochemist so we even tried some radical treatments. One such treatment involved drawing blood from distemper-immune adult dogs, after which Dvora separated out the serum and injected it into the sick puppies in an attempt to provide some support to their immune system. Most of the puppies did not make it. I had two extremely promising young collie bitches that I planned to keep for breeding and showing. Despite being vaccinated, they contracted distemper. I sat next to them as they sank into a coma, trying to stimulate them with massage. I was unsuccessful at reviving them as they sank deeper towards death. I couldn't accept that they would die when I was fighting so hard to keep them alive.

Some years later, we went through several epidemics of parvovirus, a new and terrible disease that attacked puppies. The Canaans were particularly susceptible perhaps because this was a new disease, something that in their long history they had never been exposed to before, and for which they had no defenses. The corridor of the house became a hospital ward, with dog crates lining the walls, sick puppies in each crate. The vet came daily to change the infusions, but we spent most of the day caring for the puppies, changing newspapers to keep them clean, and mostly talking to them and petting them to try to give them the will to fight. Few of the puppies survived, though they did fight and some of them held on for long days.

Dogs, under the best of circumstances, have such a short life span. We have had to say goodbye to many dear friends over the years, and it never becomes easy. People think that because I have a lot of dogs, I must not get particularly attached to them, but this is so far from the truth! I still miss so many of them, those that lived a full long life span of fifteen or more years, and those that, for one reason or another, had their lives cut short. I am not at all a religious person, and I cannot say that I believe in the existence of a God, but if there is an afterlife, for me it will be heaven only if all my dogs are waiting for me there.

Anyone who tells you that you can make money working with dogs is a liar, especially if it involves living in Israel. Over the years I worked at many additional jobs to make enough money to feed the family, both two-legged and four-legged.

Probably the best job that I had was working as a research technician in animal behavior research at Tel Aviv University. This involved the best of all worlds—working at a respectable job that satisfied everyone including my parents, earning a decent salary, and doing something that was fun and interesting with people I enjoyed. And what a relief for my parents to be able to tell people that I was working in a university!

The first projects I worked on were with birds. We had several projects going at the same time, and they were all quite fascinating. Projects with animals, even with such animals as birds, which are not considered to be especially intelligent, are always challenging, as the personalities of the individual animals are always an unpredictable factor, and behavior can always be influenced by things we may not have considered in planning the project.

We worked with several different sorts of birds, investigating their behavior and their learning ability. We took a flock of homing pigeons, for instance, out to various locations, released them, and then investigated their homing abilities. We researched the learning capabilities of a group of crows and ravens who turned out to be quite clever. One raven even learned to talk and spent the day yelling, "Telephone! Telephone!" and enjoyed watching us run to answer.

We had another project with seagulls in which the eggs of a certain species of seagull were imported, and we incubated them and hand raised the chicks. Preparing half-digested fish to feed to these ugly little creatures five or six times a day was no great joy, but as they grew and began to look and act like seagulls, the project became much more fun. Although these gulls were hand-raised and supposedly imprinted on their handlers, apparently no one had explained the meaning of this to them. After preliminary training in a large flight cage, we took them down to the beach and released them, expecting them to respond and come back to a call. But gradually, over the months, one after another of them decided that the call of freedom was too strong to deny and took off over the sea. The persistent mental image I have of this project is of my boss running along the beach after a defecting seagull, trying to persuade it to stop and come back.

At a later stage we also did a project with dogs, trying out some varied training methods. Some of my dogs were participants in this project, including Yitzhar the Canaan, and later Fizzie the Border collie, who was quite a star. This project was great fun and very interesting.

However, in Israel, all research projects are ultimately dependent on funding, which was very hard to come by. Although professionally our projects were quite successful, practically they did not bring any money in. Thus the day came that the projects were cancelled, as was my job with the university.

There were some additional problems involved. After ten years of marriage, Jacques and I had divorced, after a number of years of developing problems. I know that most people were sure that it was because of the dogs and other animals—but this wasn't true. Jacques liked the dogs and loved the lifestyle. The problem was simple incompatibility: Jacques, having survived the concentration camps as a small child, had learned that survival was a matter of not pushing yourself forward, but rather of making yourself invisible. He was content to drift along in life, taking what ever came along, but not trying to control events. He didn't have a lot of drive or ambition. All he really wanted was to go to work every day, do what he was expected to, earn enough to support the family, and come home in the evening and enjoy his home. For him, the best things in life were to sit reading or listening to music in the evenings with the children quietly doing their homework, and once in a while to go to a movie or a concert. He liked the dogs and other animals, and liked 'country life,' but I think he could have been content anywhere, as long as he had peace and quiet.

I was different. I had goals in life and plans of getting ahead. I was also young, only thirty-five, not very experienced in life, stubborn, and intolerant, and was unable to understand Jacques' passivity. I had a great need to prove myself, not only to others but to myself as well, and this was primarily expressed through the dogs—I wanted to compete and I wanted to win. I can't say I was a very good wife or a very good mother, and now, with the advantage of retrospect, I know I could have done better. With what I have learned over the years, things probably would have been different, but we can't go back.

So, Jacques and I came to the decision to separate. The boys, of course, went with Jacques to an apartment in Jerusalem. Dorcas stayed with me. I was left with a ten year-old daughter to support, as well as running the household and caring for a pack of dogs and other animals.

The job that I now found was working for the Israeli safari park, which was located in Ramat Gan. I was very enthusiastic about this job because I was sure that it would be great fun to work with all sorts of wild animals. However, the job at the Safari required me to start work at seven in the morning and was an hour's drive away from home.

I began my day at four a.m., fed the dogs, cleaned the kennels and cared for the other animals, which I finished at about five-thirty. Then I rushed back in to sweep out the house, did some minimal housework, prepared breakfast, awakened Dorcas and got her ready to go to school, prepared her lunch, and then rushed off to work. Dorcas caught the bus to school. I finished work at about three, rushed home to be there when Dorcas got home from school, did whatever chores were left around the house, cared for the animals, made us dinner and then collapsed in exhaustion when Dorcas went off to bed.

Despite all the difficulties, the job was fun. I was in charge of the petting zoo, which had ponies, exotic sheep and goats, donkeys, rabbits, geese, and more. As I was experienced in animal training, I was also given special projects. The zoo had just acquired a young male Bactrian camel from Germany and I was in charge of training him. Hans, as he was called, was quite young and quite frisky. I taught him to walk on a halter and took him walking around through the zoo. Every few steps, out of high spirits and the energy of youth, he would give a few hops or leaps in the air, rather similar to the way a bucking horse hops, with stiff legs. Camels are also capable of kicking in all directions, simultaneously, I think. I knew he meant no harm and was just having fun but the zoo visitors stayed well back as did the other zoo workers. No one else was willing to take Hans out.

I also was in charge of a hand-raised green Macaw called Koko. I took him out of his cage when I got to work in the morning and he spent the rest of the day riding around on my shoulder. He became very attached to me and I to him. Parrots, when they become attached to someone, can be rather aggressive to anyone else, and the bite of a parrot can be very painful! Koko was not willing for anyone else to handle him: I was his person. That meant that he also shared all my meals. Whenever I tried to eat anything, he was there, leaning forward and grabbing bites. His favorite was ice cream—we licked ice cream cones together —which he ate with his very strong and mobile tongue. He also walked around on the table in the keeper's room when we were having our lunch break, helping himself to appetizing bits from everyone's lunch. No one really had the nerve to try and chase him away. Just one look from those glaring eyes, with the head hunched down and feathers puffed up into attack position, was enough to convince anyone to share.

I also learned never to wear shirts with buttons, unless I had something else underneath. Koko could, in a flash, reach down and with his strong beak snip all the buttons off my shirt as if he were cracking sunflower seeds.

I got to know many of the zoo animals intimately—their habits, behavior, what they liked to eat, how they cared for their young and more. I often brought Dorcas with me when she had days off from school. She loved coming and had a natural gift of getting along with animals. Plus the crew was very fond of her. She was very mature for her age, always wanted to help, and never made a nuisance of herself, and she knew *a lot* about animals.

However, a good deal of the work was hard physical labor. I had to clean all the pens in the children's zoo daily, carry food and water, and so on. I began to suffer from serious back pains. The schedule of getting up at four in the morning and working through was taking its toll as well. I finally decided that I would have to leave the job.

I was sorry to say goodbye to the Safari crew, but most of all I was sorry to say goodbye to Hans and Koko. I knew that Hans would now be confined to his pen—no one else cared to take him out walking; they were all afraid of him. And Koko would also now remain in his cage. It was very sad for me to realize that the lives of these animals would change because I was leaving the job.

There was another major change that came about at this time–Sha'ar Hagai entered the modern world. Finally, all the bureaucratic problems were overcome, and we got electricity and a telephone after seventeen years of being without. Of course, once all the paperwork was taken care of, it became clear that the actual installation of the phone and electric lines was no problem at all, and not even as expensive as we had expected. It could have been done years before.

There were only three things that I wanted, and quickly managed to acquire, old and second-hand though they were—a washing machine, a refrigerator, and a television. A born American is, after all, a born American.

It was very strange to be able to come home and turn on the lights instead of lighting lanterns. It was weird to suddenly be getting phone calls. It was a pleasure to be able to do laundry, though! It was amazing how quickly we became accustomed to the new luxuries, and how the first winter, when there were electricity blackouts (not rare in Israel, where no one seemed to believe that there would ever really be rain or storms so why be prepared for them) we were ready to complain.

But it really wasn't such a great difference. Life at Sha'ar Hagai went on pretty much the same—a bit easier, perhaps, but we were not in a position to start living a life of luxury—and I, for one, really wasn't that interested.

Chapter Thirteen: More Four-Footed Friends

We had always had cats on the farm. I liked cats; their sleek and elegant beauty and their stunning way of moving appealed to my artist's eye, though I was always much more a dog person than a cat person. Dorcas, on the other hand, really loved cats: her first word, embarrassing for a doggy family, was "cat." Her first sentence was "No, don't bite!" Before I married Jacques, I had a pair of Siamese kittens, and always after that there were a few cats around. It was good for the dogs, I felt, to grow up with cats around—that way they wouldn't turn into cat chasers and wouldn't be distracted if they were working and a cat strolled by. We also found over the years that there was absolutely no method of rodent control superior to a simple cat. Since there were always plenty of rodents around, we had to have several cats to keep the vicinity clear.

There were, of course, a few cats that stood out from the rest. The first was 'Fichsa' and she was a calico cat. I had always loved that color, and when Lenny, our resident shepherd and beatnik, asked me if I wanted one, I eagerly said yes. I came over to his place to pick her up and bring her home, and asked him what her name was. 'Fichsa,' he said (the meaning of the name is just what it sounds like, a middle eastern form of ick, or just disgusting.) When I asked him why he called her by such a disgusting name, he just said, "You'll see!"

Fichsa quickly took charge of everything. She came and went as she pleased; no one could keep her in when she wanted to go out or keep her out when she wanted in. Tearing the screens off the windows was child's play for her. Any foodstuffs that were not under lock and key were fair game and the dogs learned to gulp down their food to keep her from chasing them away from their dishes. She was also a superb hunter, bringing home samples so that we could see how effective she was.

Then, one evening, as Dvora sat quietly at home with her dogs, a fox walked into her house. It was immediately apparent that the fox was not well—its appearance and behavior were totally abnormal, something that was easily apparent to someone as experienced and knowledgeable with wild animals as she was. Rabies is endemic in Israel, and was particularly prevalent in the fox population.

Acting quickly, she locked her dogs in another room, trapped the fox in the house, and called for assistance from the Nature Reserves people. The warden quickly arrived and put down the fox, taking the body off for inspection.

Of course the fox had rabies. That should have been the end of it—it hadn't touched anyone, animal or human. But Dvora had acted in full accordance with the law, and therefore we suffered the consequences. We were declared in quarantine.

To start with, the veterinary services that were in charge wanted to destroy all the dogs and other animals on the farm. Of course, there was no way we were going to put up with this—over our dead bodies was pretty much the language of our answer. Instead all animals had to be kept closed up, and no animal was allowed in or out until the veterinary services decided that it was safe. It didn't matter that all of our dogs were vaccinated, or that we had dogs in boarding that were due to go home. There was no one to talk to; those were the rules, and we had to accept them. Another beautiful example of bureaucracy in Israel.

To make sure that we followed the rules, a list was made up of all the animals and the area vet was assigned to come out to the farm once or twice a week to make sure that all animals were present and accounted for, alive and healthy.

The dogs were no problem; they were either in kennel or in the house. Boarding dogs' owners were, of course, quite upset—they wanted their dogs home. And it was a major blow to the income of the kennels, as we were unable to accept new customers, and didn't know when the quarantine would be lifted. It also meant we couldn't attend any upcoming dog shows. But we were resigned to the situation.

The major problem was Fichsa. There was no way that that cat could be kept closed up anywhere. I tried to keep her closed up in the house, but she tore the screens out of the windows, leapt on us when we entered the house in order to dash out the door— anything she could think of to be free. I had to have her on hand and closed in when the vet came to count animals.

The whole family became trained in Fichsa-trapping. Fortunately, we were able to convince the vet that he had to tell us in advance what day he was coming, so that we would be at home. After all, we lived out of town and had much to do, and no telephone, and... On the day that the vet was due to come to inspect, everyone had a station—a door, window, or whatever.

Fichsa's food was put out—we always offered her something especially tempting that day—and when she came in to eat, immediately all doors and windows were closed and Fichsa was trapped in the house. She was then, over ferocious protests, locked in a dog crate, with the result of various scratches and wounds to the anatomy of whoever was assigned to grab her, and there she stayed until after the veterinary inspection.

The vet, poor man, did not enjoy any of this. It was the middle of the extremely hot summer, and he had to walk up and down the row of kennels, counting dogs and trying to figure out if they were sick or just hot. I was very tempted to quote to him that, "Only mad dogs, Englishman, and council vets go out in the noonday sun."

One of the others on the farm suggested that I dress up in my riding boots and breeches and carry my crop and tell him the next time he came that he should get on with things quickly, I was in a hurry—I was going fox hunting.

The instant he had counted all the animals, including cats, and driven off in his car, Fichsa was released, and went tearing off to the forest. Fortunately, she was not clever enough to figure out that this happened regularly—she kept coming home for food. I don't know what I would have done if there had been a day that she didn't appear!

Finally the veterinary services revoked the quarantine and the animals were free to come and go again. I am sure that it was in part due to the constant phone calls of one of our clients, whose dog was in boarding. He wanted his dog home and called the veterinary services daily, announcing, "This is Professor Einstein," true, not THE professor Einstein, but it was indeed his name and title. "When do I get my dog back?" What a relief it was to all of us and to Fichsa.

Another memorable cat was Calico. She, obviously, was also a calico cat, and quite a beauty. She was very calm and sweet, the total opposite of Fichsa, and I was very fond of her. She was also very prolific, having litters of five or six kittens twice a year. Her litters were fascinating—every kitten seemed a fragment of her—she had black kittens, orange kittens, white kittens, but never calico or mixed color kittens.

Calico was a very devoted mother, and she felt that it was necessary for every well-educated kitten to know how to hunt. So she provided hunting lessons. These lessons always took place, of course, in the middle of the night. I would suddenly wake up to crashing and banging, and find Calico sitting on the side while her kittens tore around the house after a half dead rat or mouse that she had brought in and released for them to catch.

Sending her kittens off to new homes did not end her attempts at education. She continued bringing rats home, but released them and called the dogs—in the same calling tone that she had used for her kittens—to come and chase the rat. The dogs found this quite a lot of fun. I didn't. It was not my idea of amusement to spend half the night chasing a scared rat around the room with a broom until I was able to get it out the door. Calico would look at me in disgust for I was spoiling the fun and wasting a perfectly good rat.

Then there was the raccoon. Dvora, in her capacity as manager of the Jerusalem Zoo, was sometimes faced with the problem of abandoned animals that had to be hand raised or that couldn't be safely left with their mothers. When she asked me if I was interested in raising a raccoon cub, I was thrilled. The mother raccoon had previously killed her entire litter—not an uncommon occurrence in the artificial conditions of a zoo—and the population of raccoons was more than the zoo wanted.

I was always ready to take on another animal. Having grown up in the city, I was not familiar with these little animals; all I knew was what I had read about them, usually in books or novels about hunting dogs, or what I had seen in Walt Disney-type movies. They seemed to be very sweet little animals.

At this time, Dawn, the collie, was nursing a litter of only two puppies, and we decided to try to foster the baby raccoon on the bitch. It would certainly be easier and healthier than trying to hand feed the baby. Collies are usually very accommodating. Dawn, after inspecting this weird creature, decided that it was a baby, after all, and adopted it.

As the strange little creature grew, I am sure that Dawn began to have her doubts about the situation. Ricky, as the raccoon was named, grew much faster than the collie puppies, and was a very demanding baby. Dawn could take a break and get away from her own puppies—but not from Ricky. Ricky gripped her neck and hung on like a little monkey. She was very demanding, chittering and screeching for attention. If we tried to leave her closed in the house or out of it, she climbed up the screen door, screeching for attention: "Hey! Here I am! You forgot me!"

Ricky was very affectionate, loving to cuddle up and be petted, to go to sleep curled up in a convenient lap or curled up next to a convenient dog. But she was also a highly curious little beast, and had to inspect everything. Because of her hands–raccoons have almost human hands—her inspections were very thorough. What could be picked up, she picked up, turned over, smelled, tasted, manipulated, tried to open, closed, or took apart, and then the object was dunked in the nearest water source.

This was usually the dogs' water dish, where the object was thoroughly turned, manipulated and scrubbed. Many items did not survive this regime, ending as a pulpy mass in or near the water. If the object was too large to be lifted, this did not prevent Ricky from doing her best to inspect it.

This included opening cupboards and drawers and pulling out anything that was movable, such as books out of bookcases, or fruits out of the fruit bin; anything was fair game for Ricky.

Another habit she developed was climbing up the drainpipe to one of the roofs—for some reason she especially liked Dvora's roof—and then standing there screaming for someone to come and get her down. At first, we were very concerned, because that roof was high and she was a little animal. Someone would immediately run off to find a ladder, climb up, collect Ricky and bring her down, whereupon she would often promptly run up on to the roof again. After being manipulated in this way for some time, we finally decided that if she could get up on the roof herself, she could also get down, which proved to be true. When Ricky saw that no one was about to climb up for her, she quite easily shinnied down the drainpipe just as she had gotten up it.

It wasn't only our houses that suffered Ricky's ravages. She was totally unafraid of any of the people or dogs on the farm, and felt that any door or window left open was an invitation for her to enter. The neighbors didn't always agree.

One of the inhabitants of the farm in those early days was a young fellow who was a photographer by profession. It is really hard to say what it was that attracted Hezi to Sha'ar Hagai. The black sheep of a family of Torah scholars, his vocation was photography and his avocation was girls. In his mid twenties, he was already divorced twice and we never saw him more then once with the same female.

Maybe he was attracted by the idea of a 'rustic idyll' in the forest, with the birds singing, the flowers growing, and all sorts of sweet little animals frolicking. At any rate, he claimed that he really liked dogs. He took over one of the upper houses, and started in on improvements.

Hezi put a lot into fixing up his apartment. He installed electrical wiring in the walls for that time when the electricity would be connected. He put in a picture window. He replastered the walls in a stucco finish. Furniture was minimal, but, as we soon saw from his lifestyle, more than that wasn't necessary. All that seemed to really be necessary was a bed. We didn't see much of Hezi—he seemed to mostly come rolling in late at night, usually accompanied, although his companion was rarely the same one twice, and he disappeared again sometime in the morning.

Sha'ar Hagai by moonlight is a very attractive picture with the bright rocks and deep shadows of the *wadi*, the houses silver and looking clean and new, and the canopy of stars overhead. I am sure that Hezi would have been happy and successful continuing his romantic idyll, but there were a few things that he didn't realize about living out in the country.

First of all there was Ricky. Ricky was a pretty well grown raccoon by now, and she liked to stay out at night and prowl around. Ricky had no qualms about inspecting anything that caught her attention.

Apparently one night Hezi caught her attention with his late return. No sooner had he and his evening's companion made themselves comfortable and gotten down to action than Ricky made her appearance through the window. She apparently found the whole scene fascinating and decided to participate.

With some difficulty, Hezi managed to get her out of the house and to calm down his ladylove. But from subsequent reports, no sooner had they gotten back into the mood, when a piercing shriek echoed through the hills, quickly followed by slammed doors and a car engine revving up, as Hezi's Volkswagen beetle chugged rapidly down the hill.

Apparently in the midst of a tender scene, the poor girl had glanced around and found a scorpion calmly staring back.

Hezi shortly after decided that maybe Sha'ar Hagai was not exactly what he was looking for and moved out.

Raccoons mature at about a year, and as she approached maturity, we began to see some changes in Ricky's behavior. She had always been very attached to the dogs, apparently thinking of herself as a dog. Now she began to behave in a dominant way, even chasing the dogs away from their own food dishes. She threatened and even bit them if they didn't give in to her demands.

With us, she also began to behave in a similar way. It was impossible to take something away from her or to pick her up to put her out of the house—the procedure became to use a broom to push her out the door when she began doing damage. The bite of a raccoon is not pleasant—they have strong jaws and sharp teeth, capable of opening the shells of shellfish, one of their favorite foods. I was not interested in that sort of confrontation.

She was still sweet and affectionate—but only when she wanted to be.

One of the neighbors had decided to raise chickens. He had brought a flock of fifteen Speckled Sussex hens and a rooster, intending to have fresh eggs, and perhaps occasionally a chicken dinner. These chickens were not common in Israel—they were huge, about three or four kilos each, speckled black and white. He kept them in a large pen in his yard.

The chickens began to disappear, one every night. Our neighbor was, understandably, very disturbed—as were we. What was going on? We soon found out.

Ricky had discovered the chickens, and this had apparently awakened her hunting instincts. Every night she crept into the neighbor's yard and stole another chicken, which she carried off into the woods. We spotted her one night—it was hard to believe that she could carry a chicken that weighed more than she did and was considerably bigger—but she did. And all was done in silence.

The decision was made that Ricky would have to return to the zoo: she was becoming dangerous. For years, whenever we went to the zoo, we passed by her cage to say hello. It was doubtful that she remembered us, but she was plump and content, washing everything she could pick up in her little pool of water.

One day Dvora came home with another tiny baby—a little gazelle that had been orphaned and picked up by the Nature Reserves

Authority warden. Bambi was only a few days old and had to be bottle-raised. He took to the bottle very well, and soon was strong and active, romping around. The bottle, however, was not enough for his strong drive to nurse, and soon he settled on Dvora's old German shepherd bitch, Cora, as the object of his affection.

Cora was a one-person dog, totally devoted to Dvora and ferocious in the protection of her person and property. But she was a soft touch when it came to babies. Although she had no milk, she was willing to tolerate Bambi's attempts to suckle and he followed her around everywhere, greedily grabbing for a nipple whenever she stood still. It became a common sight around the farm: Dvora, followed by Cora, followed by Bambi. At first, while Bambi was small, it didn't seem too strange to see this tiny fawn enthusiastically sucking away, but as he grew, rapidly becoming bigger than Cora, the sight of this creature stooping and bending so that he could reach the bitch's nipples was hysterical.

Bambi felt totally comfortable everywhere on the farm. The dogs all knew him and he was totally unafraid of them, and he wandered around, in and out of our houses, looking for a tidbit or a pat. But as he approached maturity, we had to make a decision about what to do with him. A mature male gazelle really couldn't be allowed to go on living as a pet—various natural urges would start to be felt, and he could even become dangerous. He was entitled to live a life with his own kind in the forest.

So Dvora began taking him out to the forest to areas where she knew there were groups of gazelles and leaving him for longer and longer periods, until finally he managed to integrate into one of the groups. We missed him—he had been a lovely and affectionate pet—but we knew he was all right. Every now and then we saw tracks showing that a large gazelle had, during the night, wandered through the farm. No dogs had barked, and we knew that no other gazelle would dare come so close to human habitation and dogs. Obviously, Bambi was coming to visit.

Then there was Shusha. One day, someone called up and asked me if I wanted to buy a fox. "Not particularly," was my answer. A week or so later, I was called again. Would I be willing to take a fox for free?

The situation was that this person had managed to capture a very young baby fox, and deciding that it would be a nice and unique pet, took it home and bottle raised it. Foxes have a very strong body odor, so this little animal was kept in a small, dark shed in the yard. But foxes are also very clever, and as she grew, she began to find ways to escape from the shed. As he lived on a moshav, there were plenty of chickens and such around, of extreme interest to a little vixen looking for things to do.

Shusha, as she was called, was very friendly and totally unafraid of people and dogs, so there was no chance of releasing her back into the wild. And if she remained on the moshav, there was no doubt that one day soon her life would end either by an annoyed farmer's shotgun, or by poisoning.

Dorcas thought that a fox would be a super pet, so I agreed—we would take her.

My first sight of her was a shock. She was very thin and had almost no hair. Although she had not been purposely mistreated, no one was quite sure what her nutritional requirements were, and keeping her closed in a dark shed all the time without exposure to sunlight, had resulted in a serious vitamin deficiency. However, despite her poor physical condition, she was very friendly.

Dorcas decided that Shusha would live in her room. One day was enough to change her idea about this. Foxes are like quicksilver—very active, curious, and fast. She investigated everything in the room, which also meant tasting things and trying to tear them apart. She was also almost impossible to catch, being quite capable of climbing up on, darting under, or jumping over almost everything in the room. Shusha's very pungent and woodsy body odor in Dorcas's small closed room, quickly became very unpleasant.

There was no chance of setting her free on the farm, either. As she was not afraid of dogs or of humans, she believed that everyone was a friend and only existed to provide food and fun for her. We were also located too close to the main highway, and I had no desire for her to end up a road-kill casualty.

Fortunately, a good friend of ours had a few days free and volunteered to help build a cage for Shusha. This was a major project: it had to be big enough so that there was plenty of room for her to run around, high enough for me to stand in when I went in to take care of her, and secure enough, including being fully roofed, so that a mouse would have had a hard time getting in or out. Foxes don't have a reputation for cleverness for nothing; they are quick and sly, and can get through holes and spaces that you wouldn't believe.

Shusha seemed to be quite content in her new home and, being exposed to fresh air and sunshine and a healthy diet, she soon began to look good. She loved playing with the dogs. She learned to walk on leash very quickly, and we let her run around with our dogs on a long rope. She was incredibly friendly and loved to be petted by anyone who came by. She was always very sweet and never tried to bite although we knew from her chicken-killing days in the past that her instincts were merely dormant.

However, keeping an animal like her confined to a cage alone for most of the time was not something that we really felt was a good permanent solution. After some time we found a much better place for Shusha—she went to live in an animal corner on a kibbutz, where there were already several other foxes. She was integrated into the group and lived a happy life, even though in captivity. Dorcas was quite pleased with the new arrangements; she had quickly realized that a fox was not meant to be a house pet. But it is very sad when people interfere with nature by catching baby animals that would be best off left to grow up as nature intended.

There were a number of other odd animals that passed through Sha'ar Hagai over the years, for a few days or weeks. It was always fascinating caring for them and learning their various quirks. Like the baby ibex, for instance. Ibex is the species of wild goat that is native to Israel. They are about the size of the domestic goats we are familiar with, but are brown with white markings and some black shading. What are most impressive are their huge curved horns, which sweep back and are very effective weapons when necessary. Ibex babies can be caught only when they are a few hours old—after that, these little mountain goats are too quick and agile as they leap away up the crags where no one but another goat can follow. The Nature Reserves Authority wanted to relocate some ibex, and managed to capture nine newborn babies, but these babies had to be bottle fed. It was decided that for the first week, until they were strong enough to be transferred to a new reserve, Dvora would hand feed them.

So one day she arrived home with nine baby ibex in her car. They were adorable! We put different colored ribbons on their necks so that it would be possible to identify who had eaten—they had terrific appetites and each one appeared ready to finish off all nine bottles if it had a chance. We fed them and closed them in Dvora's bedroom, where they were safe from dogs, cats, and whatever. They were still very small, and since they had full bellies, they would surely go to sleep now.

A few hours later, it was time for another feed. We went into the bedroom to get the babies, but there was not one ibex in sight! Where could they be? We searched all over, under the bed, in the closet—nothing!

Finally, Dvora sat down and started to think rationally about ibex. Ibex were mountain goats that liked to climb..., so we looked up, and sure enough, there they were! Dvora's house had very high ceilings, at least two and a half meters high, and she had a massive, old-fashioned bookcase in a corner of the bedroom, crammed full of books, and nearly reaching the ceiling. There on the top shelf, lying comfortably in a row with only their noses showing over the edge, were nine baby ibex.

How they got up there was anyone's guess, but mountain goats are mountain goats. For the week or so that they resided on the farm, Dvora was liable to find them anywhere in the house, as long as it was high up.

After a week of pampering, the ibex were very strong and active and there was no question that they would be able to survive in more natural conditions. Dvora took them to the nature reserve they were intended for, where they were introduced to the outdoor life they would be leading from now on. The wardens there would continue bottle feeding them until they were old enough to completely feed themselves, but they could now play in natural surroundings. It was somewhat of a relief; although they were adorable and quite friendly, taking care of them was quite time consuming. It was much better for little ibexes to be leaping up and down rocky hillsides than book cases and kitchen cabinets.

I have always liked owls. I love their expression, and have for years collected figurines of owls. So when I had the opportunity through my job at Tel Aviv University to hand-raise some owl babies, I was thrilled.

The university had a center for the rehabilitation of wild birds that had been injured or displaced. It was not uncommon for owls to be brought in. They did have a tendency to get into trouble in agricultural areas. When some barn owl eggs were discovered in a field and brought in, I thought it would be fun to hatch them and raise them, and then to set them free.

The owl eggs were hatched in the incubator at the university zoo, and then I brought them home to Sha'ar Hagai. I now had three tiny, ugly nestlings to care for. Caring for chicks of this sort is not easy. First of all, they have to be kept warm, but not too warm, as they can easily dehydrate and die. In nature, they would be fed on partially digested food provided by their parents—I had to do the work instead.

The hatchlings were meat eaters. I had to take baby mice, raised in the zoo for the purpose of feeding the various small carnivores, kill them, skin them, chop them into tiny pieces, and treat them with a special enzyme that partially digested the meat to the consistency that the babies could eat. It was very important for them to receive the entire mouse as the calcium in the bones and the vitamins and minerals in the internal organs were essential to the proper development of the little owls. But not the skin; the skin was indigestible for owls and these babies were too small to be able to vomit up the indigestible bits as adults do, so I had to be very careful to skin them thoroughly.

I did not at all enjoy the food preparation, but I had no choice—this was what the babies needed to survive. I did enjoy seeing them grow and develop, and turn from ugly and naked little chicks to beautiful white and beige barn owls.

The owls became quite attached to me, and happily sat on my shoulder or arm—not pleasant in the summer when I wore short-sleeved clothes, as they had long and strong talons. When they began to fly at about two months of age, I fixed up a roosting box for them outside on the porch, on the top of an old storage cupboard next to the door. They slept there during the day, and in the evening when I called them, they flew down to my arm, and I took them out to the *wadi* to give them some flying practice. As they became confident, they would start flying around on their own, swooping down to grab their food out of my hand when I held it up for them.

By this point they had graduated to eating baby chicks I received frozen from the university zoo. No more need for food preparation! I kept a supply in the freezer and thawed each day's portion.

Most of my friends and acquaintances were animal people and never thought twice about things like chicks in the freezer. But one day a new acquaintance came to dinner and offered to help out in the kitchen. Moshe was a doctor who I had met through friends and he decided that my lifestyle sounded fascinating. He invited himself out to the farm to see it for himself. It was obvious he had no real idea of life on a farm, as he showed up in an elegant suit and tie. Dinner went well enough. The dogs were left in the other room so that they would not beg for handouts. But now it was owl feeding time and without thinking about it, I took a few chicks out of the freezer to defrost.

His expression was indescribable. Without even trying to make excuses, he fled, and we never heard from him again. Well, after all, who needs that kind of friend?

Anyone familiar with barn owls knows that they make a sort of hissing noise. Whenever anyone came to the door, the owls, roosting inside their box and not visible to whomever was below, hissed loudly, startling a number of visitors who feared the sound to be the hiss of a snake.

Eventually, when they were about four or five months old, the owls started flying away more and more, and coming home less and less to eat. Obviously, they were learning to hunt on their own. Finally, they stopped returning. I was happy to think of them free and back in nature where they belonged.

Dorcas wasn't just a spectator to all these adventures. She always showed a great affinity for animals of all sorts. One would have thought that all the animals surrounding her were too much, but this was not so. She had guinea pigs, mice, and rabbits as well. She is the only person I know who was successful in raising an orphaned baby mouse from birth, hand feeding it a drop of milk at a time from a medicine dropper. She also hand-raised a baby rabbit that was discovered abandoned by its mother. The little rabbit had apparently been at least several days without food or water when it was discovered; Dorcas managed to save it and raise it. It was named *Ness* (Miracle) and followed her around the house like a puppy. It was house trained—the only rabbit I have known that learned to use a cat litter box with total reliability. It slept in bed with Dorcas at night, and was one of her most beloved pets.

Of all the animals we've had at Sha'ar Hagai, Baba the Hyena was unique. There aren't many people who can tell you they've raised and lived with a hyena and probably even fewer who would say they enjoyed it. But all animals can teach you something, and Baba was certainly no exception. You will hear all about her later.

Chapter Fourteen: Some of Those Dogs

Despite all the other animals that resided at Sha'ar Hagai over the years, the dogs always occupied the center of life on the farm. There were many over the years, but there were always a few special ones.

The Canaans are fascinating dogs. Being so close to the wild, their behavior was quite different than that of other breeds of dog, and each one, aside from that, was very much an individual. The Canaans were very much Israeli in temperament—very territorial and possessive, suspicious of strangers or strange things, intelligent, and very independent. And you couldn't force them to do anything without first persuading them that it was worth their while.

My first Canaan, Wafi, was a great introduction into the characteristics of the breed. Born in the U.S., from one of the first litters whelped there, she spent her first year living with me in New York City, a lifestyle that really wasn't to her taste. She was not interested in making friends with the masses of people she saw every day, and was oppressed by the tall buildings all around that kept her from seeing the sky. When we walked down the street, she looked up, as if she thought all these brick towers around her were about to fall on our heads. She was only happy when we went to the park and she could run free on the grass, with only trees and shrubs around.

Wafi became the first Canaan Dog to 'return' to her homeland of Israel, and seemed to instantly feel at home. She loved Sha'ar Hagai— the space, the forests around, without tall buildings or people. But Wafi was really at her best when she had puppies. She was totally devoted to them, ready to nurse them indefinitely and to clean up after them. And, like any good mother, she felt that she was responsible for the education of her youngsters. Unfortunately, her idea of education what not quite what we thought was necessary or convenient for a puppy to know.

The first item on her agenda was 'escaping'—how to get out of fences, enclosures, or anything that was used to try and keep Canaan puppies from the freedom that they certainly deserved. I spent hours in ambush, watching the puppy pen where Wafi's puppies were confined, just to see where they would escape from this time. Wafi sat outside the fence analyzing the situation; walked around and around the pen making up her mind and then called the puppies and showed them some new way to go over, under or through the fence. I frantically tried to block off the new escape route to no avail because the next day, they were out again.

Canaan puppies are real Houdinis; I have never seen any other puppies, at five weeks of age, climb up a meter and a half fence by getting in behind the dog house, and using it to support their backs as they climbed up the wire like a cat.

The second item on Wafi's curriculum was 'survival' which is obviously very important for Canaan puppies. After springing them from their 'prison,' Wafi trotted off into the forest with the puppies after her. Some time later, sometimes even several hours, Wafi reappeared alone. She sat down on the porch facing the forest and calmly waited. Eventually, her puppies appeared out of the forest and she ran over to greet them, tail wagging, to give them all a thorough grooming. Wafi let her puppies use their developing instincts to find their way home.

Wafi's great-granddaughter, Hava, was also a special pet. Dorcas chose her from the litter when she was a very small puppy and decided that she would be her own personal pet. So, Hava grew up as a privileged housedog, sleeping in bed, and being pampered. Hava eventually arrived at the age suitable for breeding and Dorcas was thrilled by the idea of Hava having puppies. The only question was who would get to be the lucky father?

We were always on the outlook for new breeding stock. The Bedouin had many lovely dogs, but it was a real problem trying to get anything from them. We did get puppies on several occasions, but few of them grew up to be exactly what we were looking for. It is very hard to look at a five or six week-old puppy and to know for sure what it will be like as an adult, and in those days I was far less experienced at it then I would be later on.

After several years of breeding with the dogs we had available, we realized we really needed to bring in some new blood in order to keep the Canaan dogs healthy, and as close as possible to how they originally were in the wild. Almost every other breed is quite inbred, which contributes so much to the health problems seen in purebred dogs. This philosophy is something we have come back to again and again with the Canaans, and is part of why they are such special dogs.

So, in order to increase the gene pool and bring in some of that new blood, we came up with a new idea—to travel down to the desert with a bitch in season and breed her to the best Bedouin male we could find.

The bitch selected for this great experiment was Hava. When she came in season, I got in touch with a friend of ours who lived in Arad, a city in the south. Marvin, a dog man himself, was a biology teacher and had been the chief biologist of the southern region for the Israel Nature Reserves Authority. He knew the Bedouin well and was very familiar with all the roads and tracks in the area.

I looked forward to the trip. This time I was on my own, without Dvora there to guide me. It was winter, and in our area it was cloudy, cold and rainy. I looked forward to the warm desert sun. The drive took about two hours, and what a difference it is driving south, away from the busy traffic of the Tel Aviv/Jerusalem area! The roads may not have been as good, but in 1984 you could drive along sometimes rarely seeing another car.

It was sunny in Arad, but there were clouds moving up and it was not very warm. Oh well, so much for enjoying the desert sun!

We took the road out of Arad in the direction of Massada, the famous mountaintop fortress used by King Herod as a luxury residence in the years 37-4 BCE. It was captured by a group of Jewish rebels in 66 CE during the revolt against the conquering Romans and was held by them for a long period against the Roman centurions. In the end, the

Jewish zealots chose to commit suicide rather than being captured and becoming slaves to the Romans.

Massada has only two approaches, both very difficult ascents, which is one of the reasons why it was such an impregnable fortress. We, however, were on the side of Massada without access to the fortress on top. The road was almost untraveled except for Bedouin returning to their camps. There was absolutely nothing there at this time of year—December—not even a blade of grass or the slightest touch of greenery among barren hillside covered with loose rocks. Everything was gray and brown until we came over a rise and suddenly found a concealed Bedouin camp.

The Bedouin in this area still lived in tents in very traditional style, not in the tin shantytowns that had begun to spring up in much of the south. However, the area was so barren that the Bedouin had trouble finding enough feed for their flocks, and many of the adult men of the tribes worked in Arad as watchmen or in construction work, with a good portion of their earnings going to buy feed for the sheep and goats. To the Bedouin their traditions were very important, and even though keeping their livestock was sometimes not profitable, they were not willing to give up this way of life. Even in the shantytowns we had often seen the traditional tent pitched in the yard outside of the government-provided housing, with the house being used in part as a shelter for the animals. For the most part, we found only teenagers and children in the camps; the women usually stayed out of sight.

The only redeeming part of this bleak landscape, which in its own harsh and unforgiving way is very beautiful, was the sight of the Dead Sea through the hills. Our sole reminder that we were in the modern world was the apartment buildings of Arad in the distance.

There were many dogs when we arrived; all the Bedouin camps had at least three or four, but several of them were out with the flocks.

The Bedouin mentioned that there was a lot of trouble with predatory wolves, and that the dogs were very necessary to protect the flocks.

We saw a number of very good-looking dogs, but none were exactly what I wanted. Most of them had cut ears because the Bedouin felt that it made the dogs more alert and less vulnerable in fights. It was impossible to tell if these dogs had standing ears or not. Standing ears are very important for a proper Canaan, and I didn't want to add any wrong genes to our pool.

We decided to drive to the other side of Arad, near the garbage dump, to look for more dogs.

The Bedouin are not generous with the food they provide for their dogs, and expect them to take care of themselves: therefore, garbage dumps are favored haunts of Bedouin dogs, since they must eke out their diet scavenging and hunting. It was common to find numbers of Bedouin dogs checking out the pickings there.

As we drove in to the dump, we spotted three dogs—a beautiful black and white bitch, a cream colored dog with a longish coat, and a magnificent red and white male of ideal type. The latter was the one! We stopped and I started to pull Hava out of the car, but the dogs didn't wait to see what was happening—they trotted off across the desert.

The great chase began. We tried to find tracks going in the direction of the dogs; in most places, a track through the desert was where one set of tire tracks, usually of a Bedouin pickup truck, had at some previous time passed. We spotted the dogs again and tried to get ahead of them. I figured that if I could get in front of them with Hava, maybe they would stop to check her out. We drove ahead of them and I took Hava out on a lead. No such luck. The bitch paused to bark at us but then they all ran on and I ran too, chasing them with Hava. She didn't understand what the purpose of this chase was either; she would have preferred to stop and check out all the strange and fascinating smells.

Suddenly, I came to the top of a rise, and there below me was a Bedouin camp. This was the goal of the dogs—they had settled down in the center of the camp.

I left it up to Marvin, who had caught up to me in the jeep, to try to explain to the Bedouin why anyone should bother bringing a bitch to breed to one of their dogs. They found this a very strange idea, but had no objections—it certainly provided a break in the day-to-day routine. The male, however, was another story. Bedouin dogs manage their sex life very much on their own, and this dog was very suspicious of strangers appearing with a bitch in season and expecting him to do something about it in front of an audience. When he finally became interested enough to come over and inspect Hava, she clearly showed that she was not about to carry on with a total stranger! She flattened her ears and glared at him with her teeth exposed in a threatening snarl.

It was getting towards dark and it was bitterly cold and windy; so much for the sunny, warm desert! But there was nothing to do but wait for the dogs to get acquainted; they went through the entire routine of sniffing, playing, testing dominance, chasing away other interested dogs before finally getting down to business. The breeding took place successfully, and then the tie lasted for forty-five minutes. Highly successful from a breeder's standpoint, but I feared I would freeze to death before they finished.

While we waited, the Bedouin boys told us that they had had a lot of trouble with wolves, and that the year before their dogs had killed a wolf that had come into the camp and stolen a lamb. They also had had the mother and father of our stud, both of whom, they said, were excellent dogs, the sire red and bigger than his son, the dam cream colored. However, the Nature Reserves people had killed the dogs during a rabies control crackdown, which had been very upsetting to the tribe. The story of the wolf showed that these people valued their dogs. They now made sure to keep all their dogs vaccinated against rabies and to keep the vaccination certificates on hand.

By the time the breeding was completed it was pitch dark. Finding our way out of the desert was an experience since tracks that are hardly visible during the day are totally invisible at night. All there was to guide us was the lights of Arad in the distance and Marvin's familiarity with the desert. Every now and then there was the flash of the eyes of some animal—fox, jackal or even wolf—caught in the headlights of the car.

The two-hour drive home felt much longer than the drive down, but I had a successful day behind me. The result, after two months, was a lovely litter of five puppies—all male.

Dorcas was 'grandmother' for these puppies, since Hava was hers. When the time came for them to go to new homes, it was obvious that one would stay with us. Dorcas chose a red boy she named Yitzhar.

Yitzhar grew into a very impressive dog. While some of the Canaans had very sweet faces and expressions, Yitz had a wolfish look—no one could look at him and mistake the fact that he was close to the wild. But he was extremely affectionate to us and very protective. He also was a good working dog, and very willing to learn. Like most Canaans, though, he had a mind of his own. Repetitive exercises bored him, and he clearly showed that he was fed up. There were also a few things that he considered beneath his dignity, like retrieving. If sent to retrieve a dumbbell, he walked out to the spot where the dumbbell lay, sniffed it, looked at me with disgust and peed on the dumbbell before walking away.

Yitzhar became a champion, an experienced European traveler, and also a movie star. My days in the entertainment industry were not over after ATF and the spaghetti westerns. Later it would be the Canaans' turn to shine.

The most famous of the Canaans was Sirpad me Sha'ar Hagai or, as his friends knew him, Solo. His mother was a lovely and sweet-natured bitch, brown and white in color, called Sheba. Her official name was Ayn HaArava me Sha'ar Hagai, which is Hebrew for desert spring. As the Canaans were the only breed of dog that was native to Israel, we tried to name all of them with Hebrew names. She was the first female champion of the breed. She had had a number of litters, with some lovely puppies, but she was getting to retirement age. From about eight years of age, bitches are retired from the duties of motherhood, and are allowed to retire to the task of grandmother/advisor to the younger dogs. This was to be her last litter. The sire was a handsome black dog with white trim called Shimshon. He hated dog shows and so we left him at home, but he was a wonderful producer and had sired some super youngsters.

The eagerly-awaited litter consisted of exactly one puppy. One of the 'joys' of being a dog breeder is that you never know what you are going to get! But what a puppy! Immediately nicknamed Solo for obvious reasons, he was very pale cream in color, so close to white that the only reason we knew he was not really white was that he had a barely visible white blaze and white feet. His eyes and nose were black and he had a marvelous sweet expression. His tail curled over his back, his coat was thick and plush—in short, he was as close to an ideal Canaan Dog as any we had ever seen, including his outstanding grandsire Simi.

There was never any thought of selling Solo: he was a 'keeper.' We planned to start showing him as soon as he was old enough. However, there was one problem. Solo got carsick. He only needed to LOOK at a car to start drooling, and riding in one was a disaster. He, the car, and anyone in his vicinity ended up soaked. He also invariably vomited, and always at the end of the trip. It didn't matter if we took him for a ride of five minutes or two hours; a minute before we were about to stop, whoops! Nothing seemed to have any positive effect—not fasting, motion sickness pills or open windows.

Solo did eventually get accustomed to riding in the car, but it took many months of daily drives and daily car washes. He learned to like riding in the car, but many of his descendents have the same tendency to motion sickness.

Dorcas showed Solo at his first show. He was just old enough to compete in the Open Class, where he could start accumulating CACs towards his championship. His major competitor was Lapid, Hava's brother, a lovely dog that was somewhat older and more mature than Solo. Lapid was the winner that day, and Solo was second. Dorcas was very disappointed; she was sure that Solo was the better dog by far.

That was the last time that Solo was defeated until at the age of ten he was Best of Opposite Sex to his daughter who was Best of Breed. He was in many shows, both in Israel and in Europe, and was always the Best of Breed winner. His calm temperament, quality, showiness, and exquisite expression won him many admirers. He gained many titles including : Israel Champion, Netherlands Champion, International Champion, World Winner five times, Bundessieger, Europasieger, and many more.

Being a show dog was only one facet of his life. At home, he was king—not because of his prowess in the show ring, but because he behaved like one. Solo was never a dog that looked for fights, and he was never aggressive to people. Other dogs backed down from him with little more than a glance. He was never a troublemaker, but if he felt that something was important he took matters into his own hands. When there was a bitch in season in the kennel, Solo was an unchallenged expert at making holes in the fences to get to her. There were times when he went down the row of kennels, making holes from one pen to another, through five or six pens until he got to the bitch. On the way, he put every male he met into the corner, with the minimum force necessary; we found a row of males cowering in the back of their kennels, some of them with a few bites here or there, while Solo cavorted with his bitch totally unscathed.

Solo was quite famous; he appeared many times on TV and in the newspaper, due to his many wins, and was featured in dog magazines all over the world. As he got older, he stayed at home in 'retirement,' but was always thrilled at the opportunity to get out and show off. He was a very affectionate dog, but always in a quiet and gentle manner.

Solo died at the age of fourteen, comparatively young for a Canaan; many Canaans reach ages of sixteen or seventeen and we even know of some who passed their twentieth birthday. He had been in perfect health, and then one day he went off his feed and started to act rather apathetic. I made an appointment to take him in to the vet the next day to do some tests, but the next morning I found him dead, curled up in his bed, as though asleep. I had anticipated more years of his companionship and never imagined that I would lose him so suddenly and so soon.

He is buried under a lemon tree that looks out over the *wadi*. He lives on in all his many descendents—there is hardly a Canaan in Israel and even in most of the world today that doesn't trace back to Solo.

Zaaka was quite a different story. Her sire was a grandson of Simi, Dardar me Sha'ar Hagai, or Danny, a lovely dog who, after finishing his championship in Israel, was exported to become one of the first Canaans in South Africa. Her mother, Petra HaMuvcheret, better known at home as Poppy, astonished us all by whelping a litter of thirteen puppies, the one and only time we have ever known of a litter of this size among Canaans. As can be imagined, we were all involved in raising this litter. Some of the puppies were put on a foster mother, and we had to bottle feed them all with supplements to assist the poor overworked mother and 'auntie.' But, amazingly—a testimonial to the hardiness of the Canaans—all the puppies survived. Zaaka was our pick of this litter.

Zaaka was a large cream-colored bitch, and an excellent example of the breed. However, from a very early age she showed herself to be a real scrapper. She was out to prove to everyone that she was top dog, and no other bitch was about to stand in her way! She loved a good fight, and was not at all put off by the possibility of gaining a few scars here or there.

Because of her temperament I decided that it would be good for Zaaka to be obedience trained so we could control her, but it turned out that she was a very good obedience dog; she learned quickly and loved working. We went regularly to the training club where she became one of the regulars in demonstrations that the club put on.

Zaaka was the perfect dog to illustrate the difference between a working Canaan and a working German shepherd or similar breed. For example, one day we went to a new location, a large open field. We did some distance control exercises, in which we left all the dogs at a stay, walked about fifty meters away from them, and then, one by one, the handlers called their dogs.

One by one, all the German Shepherds, Dobermans, and other breeds came streaking to their handlers when called. Then it was Zaaka's turn. I called her and she started running towards me in perfect form.

However, there was a huge rock standing in the middle of the field. As Zaaka neared the rock, she slowed down, walked over to it, sniffed it, circled it entirely, sniffing all the way, and then, after completing the circuit of the rock, continued running towards me, completing the exercise with a stylish sit. After all, she was not some dumb shepherd. One never knew if something dangerous might not be hiding behind that rock! One didn't pass such things without checking them out!

As Zaaka got older, she became a house pet, deciding that it was worthwhile to tolerate other dogs for the privilege of sleeping on the bed. She died at the age of nearly seventeen, a champion herself and the mother of a number of champion offspring who have been very influential in the breed.

Of Zaaka's daughters, the one most like her was Chami. Chami resembled her mother not only in appearance, but also in personality; she had the same dominant temperament, love of a good scrap, and quick intelligence. She also was a smiler. When you talked to her, she answered with a wide grin. Chami quickly made her mark in the show ring because as well as being good looking, she was also very showy and swaggered around, clearly expecting everyone to look at her in admiration. But aside from that, Chami was quite a good obedience dog, enjoying learning and enjoying showing off what she knew.

Chami and I went once a week to the training club; it was always more fun to get together with others and practice together than to do things alone. Aside from the usual obedience exercises, the club offered classes towards the title of "Schutzhund," a German working title that included high level obedience, tracking and protection work. One day, while we were at the club, the instructor decided to try introducing some dogs to the protection work. The beginning phase of this was to agitate the dogs and see if they reacted aggressively.

All of the inexperienced dogs and handlers were placed in a large circle. I joined in with Chami to see how she would react. The instructor stood in the center of the circle with an old sack, and started flapping the sack in a threatening way at the dogs, going around the circle from dog to dog. Each dog in turn had a chance to react and was expected to lunge forward and try to grab the sack that was being flapped in his face. This was very exciting! All the dogs that were not being flapped at also began jumping around, barking hysterically and snarling at the instructor.

All except Chami. She sat calmly next to my leg, very alert, watching all the commotion, but not reacting.

Soon it was our turn. The instructor, seeing that Chami was sitting quietly, decided that she wasn't going to react, and sauntered over to her in a careless manner and started to flap the sack at her.

Instantly, Chami's teeth were bared, and she lunged. But she did not lunge at the flapping sack. She headed over the sack at the instructor's arm. Up until now, she hadn't seen any reason to react—but now she was being threatened. This had become personal. Now she had a reason to attack. Fortunately, the instructor had quick reactions and managed to avoid Chami's snapping teeth. But he had learned never to underestimate a Canaan.

Barry was a perfect example of another common characteristic of the Canaans—stubbornness. He was a good-looking dog, white with brown spots, and showed promise for the show ring, but we had too many males already, and it was decided to sell him to a good home. The mother of a good friend of mine, an elderly woman who lived alone, was looking for a dog that would serve both as a companion and watchdog, but that wouldn't be too big and strong for her to handle. Barry seemed to be perfect.

I agreed to keep Barry in the house for a few weeks and house train him since this was difficult for Mrs. Cohen to do. But in the end, it turned out that Barry lived in my house for several months when Mrs. Cohen fell down and broke her hip, and couldn't take a new dog until she was back on her feet.

Finally, the day came when Barry was to go to his new home. He had become very attached to me, which was natural as he had been living in the house as my pet, but he was only ten months old, and I expected that after a few days of depression, he would settle into his new home. Mrs. Cohen was prepared to make every necessary effort to help him settle in. He looked at me in misery when I left him in his new home, but I was sure that soon he would discover that it was very worthwhile to be the only dog.

After four or five days, Mrs. Cohen called. Barry was still very depressed—he wouldn't eat or drink, and spent his time huddled in a corner, going out only when she dragged him out on leash, and otherwise not moving. I gave her some suggestions of how to behave with him, and told her that he would surely begin to settle in. Several more days passed, and Barry's behavior had not changed. He still refused to eat or drink and didn't move. Mrs. Cohen dripped water down his throat with a spoon and tried to put food in his mouth, which he promptly spat out. She was quite frantic. I once again encouraged her, and told her that he couldn't possibly hold out much longer.

But hold out he did. After twelve days of fasting, Mrs. Cohen broke. "Come and take the dog back," she begged. "If he stays here, he will die!"

I drove out to pick Barry up. As I walked into the house, he looked up from his bed in the corner, saw that it was me, got up, walked over to the door, and looked at me. "What are you waiting for?" he seemed to be saying. "Let's go home!"

Weak and hardly able to stand on his feet, he climbed into the car and we drove home. As we walked into the yard, his tail came up, he ran over to the water dish, drank, and then turned around, ran to the gate which was still open, bit the neighbor who was standing outside watching (he had never liked him anyway!), and then settled down to eat. Barry was home.

Then of course there were the collies. I had always wanted to have collies, from the time when, as a child, I had read *Lassie Come Home* and the books of Albert Payson Terhune. I admired the beauty, intelligence, gentleness and devotion of the breed, and once I began living with them, found that they did suit me very well. Collies and Canaans are very different from one another, but I have found that both of them are essential parts of my life—apparently each one suits a different side of my own personality.

The most special of the collies, for me, was Julep. She was the puppy I chose to keep from the first litter born to me, the first registered under my own kennel name. Julep and I were an inseparable team. She was very intelligent, learned quickly, and was ready to do anything; she did obedience, tracking, herding, and was a devoted guard of my possessions and of me.

That description makes her sound as if she was a paragon, an angel of the dog world. That was not quite true; Julep had a mind of her own, which was exemplified by her performances in obedience. Julep and I competed in obedience trials during the period that we were in

189

Africa, and she achieved the highest level of competition, the "C" trials. This included some very difficult exercises such as scent discrimination (choosing an object with the judge's scent out of a number of other identical objects, some with 'decoy' scents), and send-away (where the dog was sent away from the handler in a straight line to a distance of about 30 meters, where, on command, he had to stop and lie down in a small marked area). When she wanted to, Julep could do all the exercises perfectly.

As an example, we competed in the obedience trial at the Goldfields Kennel Club show in South Africa. This was the biggest and most important show of the year and there were thousands of dogs and spectators. The obedience trial was held on the second day of the show, in a ring that had hosted conformation judging the day before and therefore was flooded with smells of dogs and people. Despite the difficulty Julep responded like a champ to the challenge. She was one of only four dogs that succeeded in doing the scent exercise. However, on another day, in much easier conditions, she went out to do the scent exercise, looked back at me with a look that was the canine equivalent of a shrug of the shoulders, and chose the wrong object—deliberately, I am sure.

She hated the send-away exercise and wanted to be with me. She didn't understand why I was sending her away, so she often made her opinion of this exercise clear to all. One day when I sent her away, she ran forward, stopped at the designated spot, looked back at me, and calmly walked out of the ring as if to say, "You wanted me to go away? Well, I am going!" On another very hot day when the ring was in the glaring sun, she simply walked away, turned towards the judges' table, crawled underneath and lay down in the shade, saying, "You may want to mess around in the sun, but not me!"

Julep spent her whole life waiting to save me from danger. She was always on alert, ready and devoted. There never was an opportunity to save me, but dogs never give up or get discouraged; until the day she died, she was still certain that the time would come when she could save me from something!

Julep died of cancer at the age of nine. The disease attacked suddenly and rapidly, and we hardly realized that she was ill before she was gone. I was devastated. I couldn't face it and for the first time, I ran away. I went off to stay with some friends living in the north for a few days. I was unable to cope with the other people and animals at Sha'ar Hagai until I had time to come to terms with the loss of Julep.

Other dogs can never fill the hole made by the loss of a special friend. Each friend has its own place in one's life, and while there are places for many, the holes from the loss of each one remain as part of the fabric of life.

Prise was also a very special friend. He was a big golden collie, very successful in the show ring who became a champion easily. He was also a marvelous working dog, willing to learn anything. He even appeared in television commercials and in a children's play of *Lassie Come Home*. He was a very gentle dog by nature so when in one of the scenes of the play he was supposed to 'attack' the 'villain' this was very hard for him to do; the actor playing the villain was a friend of his, as was just about everyone he met. He didn't want to even pretend to bite him.

However, like Julep, he too was ready to 'save' me if the opportunity arose. One day we were at the training club when I was asked to help.

"Could you do us a favor? I want to agitate this ridgeback to see how she reacts, and need someone to handle her."

"Sure, no problem."

"You just have to hold her leash while I tease her, I want to see how she reacts when I make threatening moves."

So I left Prise at the side of the field in a down-stay—he was very obedient and would stay for a half hour or more without moving—and took the leash of the other dog.

The instructor came towards me, waving his arms in a threatening way and flapping a sack at me, to try and get a reaction from the dog I was handling. Suddenly I saw a golden streak fly through the air past my shoulder in the direction of the instructor. It was Prise! He had seen that I was being threatened and he was on his way to defend me.

I immediately screamed, "Prise, no!" Prise, in mid-air, turned his head aside just as he was about to grab the instructor's arm, and immediately returned to me on command. He was very disappointed; at last he had had a chance to save me, and I had spoiled everything.

My most famous collie was Prise's grandson, Glory. Glory came out of a litter of ten puppies and was outstanding from the day he was born. He became a highly successful show dog, winning the titles of Israel Champion, International Champion, and World Winner. He also was a very successful sire, having many offspring that became Champions and International Champions.

Glory was also a very gentle dog and very dignified, but he was also the leader of the pack. He never really fought with anyone, but somehow he managed to convey to the others that he was the boss. He was totally uninterested in obedience or such. All he wanted out of life was to love and be loved in return. He was a world-traveler who went with me to dog shows in the U.S. and Europe, taking it all in stride. He spent a year with a friend of mine in Poland entertaining the ladies. My friend fell in love with him and was sorry to send him back, but I was only willing to do without him for one year.

Glory lived to be fourteen, a good age for a collie. He was healthy and active until the end. One day he went to sleep and never woke up, but he lives on in his descendents; most of my collies trace back to him.

Canaans and collies are still my first loves; but I have always been the lover of animals and ever curious, so there have been other dogs over the years. In my travels I saw Border Collies at work in various places. They were marvelous working dogs, considered to be the most intelligent breed. I decided I would like to have one. A friend of mine in England, a collie breeder, also had a Border Collie bitch and she had puppies. I ordered a little female from her.

Fizzie was four months old when she arrived from England, and her name fit her perfectly. She was from a line of sheep-working dogs, and spent all her time looking for something to work at. Her first project was cat herding. I had three cats living in the house at the time, an elderly Siamese female and her two half-grown kittens. Fizzie spotted them the minute she came into the house, locked onto them with her sheepdog stare, and spent all her spare time, whenever she wasn't being given something more serious to do by me, trying to herd them. She would stand frozen, staring at them, waiting for them to move; the instant they moved she circled them to keep them in a nice orderly group, and tried to move them around. If the cats split up into different directions, she tried to collect them back together again. The ideal for Fizzie was to 'pen' them—have them all sitting together on an easy chair in the living room—and then to keep them there with her penetrating gaze. The cats thought that this was very boring and ignored her, but Fizzie never got discouraged or gave up. Border Collies are persistent.

Another project Fizzie set for herself was to keep other dogs away from me. She decided that I belonged to her, and no other dog had the right to approach. This was, of course, unacceptable, and Fizzie quickly learned that she had to tolerate my other dogs. But a strange dog was another matter. When we went to the training club, or anywhere else where there were other dogs, Fizzie leapt at these adversaries in a black and white streak, snarling. More than once she grabbed a poor dog by the scruff and threw it over even if it was twice her size, accompanied by sound effects that gave the impression that she was about to commit murder. This was all sound and fury—the 'victim' never received as much as a scratch; however, it was rare for a dog to approach more than once after being subject to her aggression. This was one behavior pattern that no matter how hard I tried, I was never able to change.

She was a marvelous worker, doing all sorts of shows and demonstrations with me. She also found many projects to keep herself occupied at home—collecting all the shoes in the house in a pile on my bed, taking all the stones out of the potted plants and piling them in the center of the carpet in the living room. Life with Fizzie was never dull! She died of cancer at the age of seven, leaving another unfillable hole in my life.

I first become acquainted with the Shiba Inu breed in Sweden, where I saw them at a dog show. I was fascinated because they looked like miniature red Canaans. When I met the breed again at a show in Ireland, I decided that I had to have one. I had never been very interested in small dogs, but these seemed to be big dogs in a small package. I always had between twenty and thirty dogs around, but little dogs were different. The collies and Canaans could not sit on my lap. The Shibas, despite being big in attitude, were small enough to fit on my lap.

My first Shiba was Kito. I brought him back from Ireland when he was two and a half months old. From the day I met him as a small puppy, he was a dignified Japanese gentleman who took everything in his stride. He had a typically inscrutable expression and other characteristics that are generally attributed to the Japanese: he was extremely clean, quiet, dignified, and expected to be treated with respect. He was, for example, very affectionate and enjoyed being petted, but he did not like being picked up, held on a lap, or hugged around the neck.

Kito became a part of a show I was doing in schools and community centers, a real contrast to the hyperactive Border Collies that were his teammates in the demonstrations. Notice the plural, Border Collies; once I had one, it was inevitable I would keep a few more around in the pack. Kito's particular part of the show was to bark on command, responding to an almost invisible hand signal I gave. The audience was invited to ask him questions and he answered by barking, and I 'interpreted' his answers. I was amazed at the questions that people asked him—about politics, economics, current events— apparently his wise expression persuaded people that he knew what he was talking about. He probably knew as much as many of the people who usually answer such questions.

Kito is an old man now, and as dignified as ever. He retired to be the companion of a friend of mine who fell in love with him, and last I heard, the two were still enjoying an orderly and dignified life.

Chapter Fifteen: The Witch and Others

Um Fathi was the only witch I ever knew personally.

Many cultures still have their respected witches, those who are knowledgeable about native plants and the many things they can be used for, the powers of natural objects like special stones, shells, and other found objects, and can prepare spells and charms for the benefit of their devoted clients. Village Arabs still strongly believed in the powers of these witches, and Um Fathi was known to be one. Dvora had acquired her somehow after the Six-Day War; she was at the time living in Beit Hanina on the outskirts of Jerusalem in the direction of Ramallah. As one of the first and only Jews living there, Dvora found it impossible to refuse to give a job to this poor old woman with a family to support.

It turned out that Um Fathi was not so old and was in fact the same age, more or less, as Dvora—in the mid forties—but she looked like she was at least eighty. She was wrinkled with skin the texture of well-cured camel hide, her teeth were snaggled and sparse, her hair looked like a prime spot for birds to nest in, and her eyes looked in different directions at the same time. Um Fathi dressed like a typical Arab peasant, in several layers of dresses, skirts, and blouses over trousers, and always kept her head covered. She was the sole support of her family. Her son had been killed in the war, and she was supporting his wife and small children. Her own teenage daughter was in trade school, and there were several other children of various ages as well. Of course, her husband did not come into consideration. Abu Fathi, who looked about twenty years older and probably was, spent his time doddering around after his hardworking wife, sitting in the shade and supervising.

Um Fathi worked as a housemaid and laundress for Dvora one or two days a week. When Dvora moved to Sha'ar Hagai, Um Fathi was loathe to give up the job—aside from making a nice salary, she had become very fond of Dvora and was teaching her Arabic. So she agreed to come out once or twice a week to the farm and continue working. I thought this would be a great opportunity—for the first time in my independent life, I could join the ranks of the affluent that had a cleaning lady and laundress. So I agreed to take Um Fathi to work for me one day a week as well. Little did I know what I was getting into.

Um Fathi had a unique method of housecleaning. This consisted of taking buckets of water and violently flinging them around the floor. One of my jobs before she came each week, just for the sake of preserving my personal effects, was to make sure there was nothing on the floor. She then took the floor mop and swept everything out the door into the yard. Of course, this made a lot of mud, which subsequently was tracked into the house by all people and animals coming in, but that wasn't her concern.

Her method of doing the laundry was even more interesting. This required preparation including rolling up her trousers and sleeves and tying her skirts around her waist. She had already removed her shoes— she never worked with shoes on. Once she was stripped for action she threw all the laundry into the bathtub, poured soap powder liberally over it, turned on the water full force, and climbed into the bathtub to knead the clothes with her feet and hands. This method was said to be effective with grapes, but was not terribly effective with clothes.

One of the main reasons she liked to come to work at Sha'ar Hagai was because it gave her a chance to collect tools of her witchcraft. After finishing the housework, she went out into the *wadi* and collected enormous bundles of local plants, like the zatar, oregano, salvia, and all kinds of things that grew wild in the vicinity. From all of these, and from who knew what other ingredients, Um Fathi made up charms that she sold to a large clientele of villagers, and according to Dvora, had a very good reputation as a witch in the villages surrounding her home.

She was not beyond trying to influence things on her own either. Several times Dvora found a bundle of herbs hidden under her mattress—a fertility charm, apparently. Who knew where else she hid her little tokens for what she felt we were lacking.

The dogs hated her. She looked and smelled very strange, and her behavior was certainly out of the ordinary, so I had to keep the dogs closed up when she came to work. But she never seemed to be very concerned about them. Perhaps she felt that her witchcraft was enough protection.

Eventually, we had to give up the privilege of Um Fathi's services. She found that the time and effort of getting out to us on the bus was a problem, especially as it was not uncommon for her to sit at the bus stop and watch several buses pass her by before one would stop for her. She found other clients in Beit Hanina, closer to home, among the class of people who welcomed having a cleaning lady. Little did they know what was in store for them.

Since she left us, I have done my own cleaning. I don't know if I could survive another like her.

Sha'ar Hagai was organized more or less as a cooperative. Everyone had their own house and their own possessions, and most of the members had outside jobs and incomes; Dvora, for instance, worked for the Nature Reserves Authority, and Ofer worked in his family's business. But everyone pitched in to help out with farm jobs and projects. Theoretically, everyone also had the right to share in farm profits, but for the most part we actually shared in covering the farm's debts.

To join, everyone had to agree on a new potential member. With such a small group living so closely together, we all had to be able to get along together.

There were, over the years, a number of people, some of them rather strange, that passed through Sha'ar Hagai. Our lifestyle was distinctive enough to attract attention. Dvora also tended to attract a following, rather like a local sort of Guru. Some of these people were highly respected and intelligent, and some were simply weird. One who stands out in my memory is the political activist who used to show up and go wandering through the *wadi* in the nude. Exactly why, I can't really say.

There were those who visited, those who worked for a while, and those who became addicted and stayed.

While we were in Africa, there were various employees, but none of them lasted for very long. The boarding kennel was quite busy and we had a lot of dogs of our own as well, and as we were usually involved in additional schemes to try and increase the income of the farm, there was often work available.

The most memorable of the employees we had was Dorit. She was in her early twenties, from a good Jerusalem family, and attractive and intelligent. But if ever anyone was justifiably described as an "airhead," it was she —head in the clouds, feet not touching the ground.

Dorit was perfectly willing to do the work she was assigned, and she loved the dogs and other animals, but sometimes you had the feeling that words simply didn't get through to her, and that logical thinking was an unknown concept.

As an example, one day I told her that one of the dogs was too fat and would have to go on a diet. At this point, most of the dogs were being fed twice a day, so I told her to feed this particular dog only once a day with a smaller quantity of food. A few days later, I came down to the kennel and found that the dog that was not to be fed had a food dish in with him.

"Dorit," I said, "You weren't supposed to feed that dog in the mornings."

"I didn't feed him," she answered. "I gave him an empty dish so he wouldn't feel left out."

On another occasion, while I was trying to groom a boarder that was not at all cooperative, I asked Dorit, "Do you have a muzzle around?"

"No," she replied, "but I have a hammer." I didn't care to follow that train of logic any further.

One day a new fellow showed up with Dorit. He had met her on the bus, was attracted to her, and came out with her to see where she worked. Dorit didn't stay much longer, nor did her relationship with the fellow, Ofer, last. But Ofer became fascinated with Sha'ar Hagai and decided to stay.

Ofer, also a nice Jerusalem boy from a good family, lived at Sha'ar Hagai for many years. He was tall and strong, great at working with his hands, was willing to take on any project, from repairing kennels, to weeding, to cleaning the sewers, and did everything well and with style. He loved the dogs and was always willing to come along and provide more hands at a dog show. Lapid, the Canaan, was his house pet and companion.

After a number of years at the farm, Ofer married and brought his new wife to live there as well. Chava also fit right in, and they had three children while living on in the community. Even 'normal' people had a place at Sha'ar Hagai! But finally, due to family considerations, they moved to a nearby town. But Ofer still makes himself available for special projects, when necessary.

One Yom Kippur afternoon, the dogs started barking hysterically—not usual for Yom Kippur when there is no traffic and everything is usually silent. The cause turned out to be a rider on horseback, who had suddenly appeared, accompanied by a Rottweiler bitch. He had a weathered face, a bushy red beard, and was dressed in sort of modernized wild-west garb. His horse was a tall and nervous gray, prancing and uncomfortable about the strange dogs. This was our first sight of Jesse.

Jesse had gotten a job as a forest ranger in the forests around us. He was now looking for a place in the area where he could live and keep his horse, and he had decided that our farm would be ideal.

At the time there was an empty flat on the farm, and everyone agreed that it would be possible to let Jesse use it. There was also some empty stall space for his horse. In exchange, he could help out with work around the farm.

Jesse turned out to be just as strange as he looked. He had many tales to tell—we were never sure which of them were true, maybe all or maybe none, but they were certainly fascinating. Although Danish by birth, he claimed to have been in the French Foreign Legion, and told us about his various adventures in remote parts of the world. He claimed to have been a sergeant major in the army, and this we certainly believed since even his horse stood to attention when he was around.

One day he was cleaning out the stables. We had some chickens running around the farm at the time that served a very positive function; they ate insects, including fleas and ticks, and fly larva. One chicken, however, decided to look for something tastier to eat, wandered into the stable and started eating some of the grain Jesse had put out for his horse.

That made Jesse mad! No one steals his horse's feed! Fixing the chicken with a baleful stare, he gave a yell at the top of his lungs in real sergeant major style, "Get out of there!"

The chicken leaped up into the air, flipped over, fell on its back with its feet in the air, stone dead. Jesse had killed it with one yell! He was around for quite a while, until one day he disappeared as suddenly as he had appeared, never to be seen around Sha'ar Hagai again.

Chapter Sixteen: Gardening

Before I came to Israel, I was a city girl. Although we had a house, none of us in the family were avid gardeners. We had someone come around once a week to mow the lawn and trim the hedges and occasionally we made an attempt to plant a few flowers. Not with huge success, I might add.

Sha'ar Hagai, however, was all country. There was forest all around us as well as fields with a plethora of wild flowers in spring and summer. Once we had cleared out all the weeds and overgrowth from around the houses, we were left with bare earth. Obviously, something had to be done.

Dvora was very fond of gardening and having grown up on a farm, was very knowledgeable about growing things, much more than could be said for me. Basically, I copied what she did and began to plant the same flowers and shrubbery. Somehow, they didn't look the same in my garden as in Dvora's, though. But gradually, I learned something about gardening.

The primary thing I learned was that gardens and dogs do not really go together. The average dog loves to dig a nice hole in the middle of the cool, damp flower bed with the nice, soft, well-cultivated soil, and to lie there on a hot summer's day. Plucking flowers and leaves off of plants is also a highly amusing pastime, especially for puppies. I discovered that even rose bushes, with their vicious thorns, were no deterrent—I would find dogs chewing happily on the woody branches, ignoring the thorns.

I decided to find something that would survive the dogs—a cactus garden! I had seen a gorgeous cactus garden in a kibbutz, with a huge variety of cacti, of all sizes and shapes, some of them absolutely huge.

They are fascinating plants, and their flowers are always most beautiful, even though they often last only one day. So I started collecting cacti from various people and places and planting them in front of the house.

One advantage of the cactus is that you can take just about any little piece, stick it in the soil and it grows. Soon I had quite a large and impressive cactus garden and the dogs did not go into it to play or dig. Success! I was even able to plant a few other plants, such as African daisies and violets, among the cactuses.

But as it became bigger and more developed, I discovered that maybe this wasn't such a great idea. For one thing, it was almost impossible to weed, and of course the weeds loved to grow among the cacti. If I tried to get in to weed, I would end up looking and feeling like a pincushion. The propensity of the cactus to spread out, with every branch that broke off and fell to the ground taking root and growing into another menacing bit of vegetation quickly turned the whole well-planned garden into a vicious jungle. And cacti do not sit by passively and let you prune them—they attack back. Somehow, I would end up full of spines in places that I was sure had never touched a cactus. For a week after a session of cactus pruning, I would go around unable to pick anything up because of the spines left in my hands, and involuntarily wincing as some bit of clothing pressed against a thorn that I hadn't even known was there.

Finally, as the cacti started to spread their spiky arms towards the path and the entrance to the house, there was no choice but to cut them down. That was a major project, requiring layers of heavy clothing through which the spines managed to penetrate anyway, and heavy-duty spades, hoes, pitchforks and such. By the end of the day, the cactus garden was history, but the spines left in our hands, arms, and legs kept the memory fresh for days.

Well, if cacti weren't a solution, I could put up fences, I thought. Other parts of the garden that had not been invaded by the cacti, but had several things growing, like roses, carnations, margaritas, calendula, irises, were fenced off. Now, it doesn't do much good to have a garden if you have to put up a fence that hides the whole thing. So, I could only put up a symbolic wire fence, about half a meter high.

The dogs loved it—it was great fun to jump over. And in the heat of the summer, the nice cool earth of the well-watered garden was the best place to dig holes to lie in.

Well, if I couldn't have a garden, at least I would have a lawn, I decided. That was in the days before all of the modern conveniences such as pre-prepared lawn squares that you put together like floor tiles, water, and there you have it. Those were the days when you had to prepare the ground, get runners of grass from someone who had a lawn that they had trimmed, plant the runners in rows, and hope that they grew, spread out, filled in the spaces and became a lawn.

Dvora, of course, had quite a nice a lawn, and she was willing to provide runners. I prepared a little patch of ground, and took out all the stones, which was not easy in the Judean hills where the stones seem to multiply much more successfully than anything else. I raked and smoothed it, and planted the grass in several rows. The whole lawn was maybe a square meter—Dvora didn't have much spare grass to give me—but it was a start.

Of course, a lawn requires care, and one of the major tasks was cutting it periodically. I did not have a lawn mower; it didn't seem worthwhile to have one for a square meter of grass. So once a week I got out on the lawn with my sewing scissors and cut the grass. I found it very relaxing, actually—anyone who is really uptight can't help but calm down after an hour or so on hands and knees in the summer sunlight, cutting grass with a sewing scissors.

There was one period—a short one, I will admit—when I was pretty affluent. I had a good deal of work, and was away from home quite a lot. So I decided to pay for a gardener.

My garden at this point was a total disaster. I was ashamed for the gardener to even see it. I could see in his eyes as he looked around that he didn't consider me a fit person to have a garden. I was very apologetic and explained that the dogs now had another yard to run in, and I would keep them out of the garden, but I did want him to plant things that were hardy and could survive almost anything. Backing down from his caustic glance, I told him that I would leave the garden in his hands entirely.

Within a few weeks, the garden was totally unrecognizable. He had done a wonderful job, I will admit, but the whole garden was full of small, delicate flowers with tiny, fragile blooms that you had to look for with a magnifying glass. My taste tended to run in the direction of huge masses of bright, cheerful, colorful flowers covering everything in a riot of happiness, not this subdued and ladylike garden in pastel shades. Oh well, I thought, this is certainly better than no garden at all, or the disaster that I had before!

The garden did last for some months under the loving care of my gardener—until my work fortunes changed and my budget had to be revised, sans gardener. When I was at home the dogs were at home with me, and it was so much easier to open the door and let them out than to take them around to the dog yard. Soon the pastel English garden was only a memory. Now I could throw down some flower seeds and try to have the kind of garden I liked—dogs permitting! Strong and hardy flowers like zinnias, marigolds, and geraniums survived and bloomed and were much more suited to my temperament and tastes.

Since money was always scarce, but there was plenty of empty land around, one of the things I tried was growing vegetables. Flowers weren't successful, but I was certain that vegetables would be simpler. This would be a worthy addition to our diet—fresh vegetables, bursting with vitamins. Growing vegetables was pleasing to my mental image of myself as a pioneering type.

I quickly learned that this was far from easy; in fact, it was a lot of hard work. To start with, the earth had to be properly prepared—dug up, hoed, weeded, raked, fertilized. I vigorously attacked the weeds, which were well rooted in ground that hadn't been turned for at least thirty years, possibly since biblical times. I must admit that once it was turned, the earth didn't look very promising. Rather than rich and loamy as I had anticipated, it was hard, dry and crumbly, full of stones, and even when raked and watered had the consistency of mixed builder's rubble. Well, if it grew weeds, then it should grow vegetables. And if Dvora could grow vegetables, then so could I!

The seeds had to be carefully planted in well-spaced rows. After some days of careful watering, the seedlings sprouted, and then had to be thinned so that the plants would have room to grow. Of course, once the seedlings were growing so were the weeds, which were much stronger and faster growing than my poor little vegetables. I have never understood how in the carrot plot, there would suddenly be all sorts of weeds looking ridiculously similar to carrots—weeds I had never seen before! While in the tomato plot there were weeds looking like tomatoes. How did they know where to grow? How did they get there?

Actually, some things did sprout. Tomatoes, being fairly close weeds themselves, came up nicely. Experience over the years taught me that tomatoes will grow pretty much anywhere that a seed falls, providing they have water. Their favorite place, and the one that produces the most gorgeous, juicy, succulent fruit is in the sewage runoff. A few cucumbers came up, and a few eggplants and peppers. Eggplants are fun to watch grow—you can really see why they are called eggplants. The baby eggplants are round and white and really look like eggs, only turning purple as they mature.

My greatest success was with lettuce. As with all my other crops, I liberally scattered seeds in the trench, expecting the minimal percentage of success that I had with other things. I don't know how many lettuce seeds there are in one packet—maybe a million, and I think that every single one of them grew; masses and masses of lettuce sprouted. Being a new gardener, I couldn't imagine thinning my tender plants and letting the thinned out ones just die, so I replanted them. Every lettuce sprout took. I gave presents of lettuce to everyone I knew, to every customer that came to buy a puppy, put a dog in boarding, or ask directions. The lettuce started to go to seed and to replant itself in more places. I still have lettuce coming up here and there in gardens around the farm, after generations that have reseeded themselves from my original crop.

Tomatoes, cucumbers and carrots provided a crop sufficient for a few salads. When I sat down to figure out just how much, in terms of work and manpower these vegetables had cost, I could have bought five times as much in the market for less.

Then there was the year of the squash. The first year, almost nothing came up. All my little seedlings that had started out so well—corn, beans, and peppers—started to wither when they got to a few centimeters high. I had no idea what was wrong. They had plenty of water and I weeded assiduously. But not the squash! I threw a few zucchini seeds in a barren little patch of ground behind the kennel, where there was drainage from the daily washing of the kennel. I never really bothered to check on what was growing, but after a few weeks, I noticed that there were huge vines climbing up the kennel fence. When I went back to check, I found zucchini, with no exaggeration, the size of baseball bats but much thicker. And there were huge quantities of them! Obviously the kennel drainage had provided fantastic nutrients!

For several months, everyone who showed up at Sha'ar Hagai left with a bag of giant zucchini. Customers who brought their dogs in for boarding got a bonus of giant zucchini. We ate zucchini, pickled zucchini, did everything one could think of doing with zucchini.

I never planted zucchini again.

Chapter Seventeen: War

I had never experienced war in Israel. I first came to Israel in 1967, just after the Six-Day War, and experienced all the feelings of euphoria of the victory without any of the tensions or stress of the war itself. That was a period when the Israelis felt invincible, and everyone caught the mood.

During the Yom-Kippur War, I was in Africa. Although I felt the tensions, and spent my days glued to the news reports and the telex machine, and although there was plenty of worry involved in our position in Africa, still my family and I were one step removed from the actual fact of the fighting.

I did not experience the years of the War of Attrition firsthand, although I was at home in Israel for this period. I had no children in the army, and few friends or acquaintances that actually were serving in the frontlines, so again, everything I experienced was through news reports. For most of this period we were without electricity, so I didn't watch television news. Reading accounts in the newspapers is no more effective than reading a good war novel: it is hard to take it personally. And since I had never done army service, having immigrated to Israel when I was already over the age of draft, I really had no experience to make war real to me.

The Gulf War was something else, however; this conflict affected everyone in Israel, not just those who were in the army or called up for reserves.

Dorcas was at this time in the Navy. In Israel, both men and women go into the armed services at the age of eighteen; men serve for three years and women for two. She had decided that this was the branch of the service that most suited her—she liked the opportunities they offered, and she especially liked the uniform. She did look super in her spiffy whites. The job she chose was radar operator, so she was stationed on dry land most of the time as well. She didn't spend much time at home; she and her boyfriend (soon-to-be husband), a really great guy called Tzvika who I adored, had rented a small house in a moshav nearby, and most of her leave time was spent there with him.

Living with her boyfriend had another advantage aside from the most obvious; she was able to take her personal dog Shachmat with her. Tzvika was able to care for him when she wasn't at home, and he was there waiting for her whenever she was on leave. And, at the same time, Shachmat was able to guard the place when there was no one home. He was soon joined by his daughter Mickie, a lovely little bitch who was sold to an American diplomatic family and returned to us when she was a year old. When Tzvika and Dorcas saw her, they immediately fell in love with her and decided that Shachmat would love having company. And he did!

Dorcas had always said while growing up that when she was living on her own, she would not have a lot of dogs—one would be enough. Despite her good intentions, heredity was apparently stronger and her dog population gradually grew and grew.

As the situation in the Gulf escalated, tension in the country built up. There were endless discussions in the newspapers, radio and TV of the military capabilities of Saddam Hussein. There were constant speculations on whether we would be involved, whether Israel would be attacked, and if so, with what weapons. The greatest fear of everyone was the fear of chemical warfare, insidious and lethal. All Israelis were issued gas masks and were instructed to keep them close at hand in case of need. Instructions were broadcast over and over of how to insulate a room against the penetration of gases and other chemical materials. All windows had to be covered with thick sheets of plastic, taped around thoroughly on all sides with a special sort of heavy duty, extra-wide masking tape. Doors were to be insulated with damp towels or rags wedged into all cracks and spaces.

I didn't really believe that anything would happen. I found it hard to believe that even Saddam Hussein was crazy enough to take on the military power of the United States and add to his problems by getting Israel involved as well. And of course, if I did want to take all of this seriously, then what about the dogs and other animals? I couldn't bring them all into the house into a protected room. There was certainly no way I could provide them with gas masks or a protected environment.

On the other hand, Sha'ar Hagai was pretty isolated (as far as any place in Israel is isolated) from other settlements. What were the chances that a missile would, of all places, land on Sha'ar Hagai? Not very high, I thought.

Then one night I was awakened from a sound sleep by the telephone. It was Tzvika. Israel was being attacked with Scud missiles, the alert had been sounded, and all citizens had been instructed to close themselves in their protected room with gas masks on. Dorcas was on duty, and had asked Tzvika to be sure that I knew—the closest air raid siren was some distance away, and she knew that I was not likely to hear it.

In a state of shock, I got out the brown cardboard box with the gas mask, opened it, pulled out the mask and put it on. It was a horrible feeling—I felt as if I was going to choke. The dogs looked at me as if I had gone mad and went back to sleep. I turned on the TV to see what was happening.

Israel had indeed been attacked, missiles had fallen, and we were requested to remain masked and closed in until further notice. There was nothing to do but sit there with a gas mask on, watching the TV reports and waiting for further instructions. After what seemed like an eternity, but was actually only a few hours, the all-clear was broadcast, and the gas mask came off.

The first attack was very scary. In the next days, as the attacks continued, many Israelis took off from their homes in the center of the country for places they considered to be safer. In many cases, to our disgust, they left their pets, dogs and cats, to roam the streets and fend for themselves. This, to me, was inconceivable—how could they leave their pets behind?

Since I was a pragmatic person, I immediately decided that Sha'ar Hagai was very unlikely to be a prime target for missiles. The gas mask had been a very unpleasant experience, and I didn't intend to make use of it again. It was available in its little brown carton, and like all Israelis, for the duration of the war I carried it around with me wherever I went, but I never put it on again.

The same went for the 'safe' room. As there was no way that I could provide a safe room for all the dogs and other animals, and as I really felt fairly confident that no bombs were going to fall on us, I decided that whatever fate was in store for the dogs, I would share it. I had two girls, just after their army service, working for me at the time and they prepared a sealed room and dashed off into it whenever there was an alert, as I stayed in the living room, watching television, and waiting for the all clear.

Not everyone abandoned his or her animals. There were many people that tried to find ways of protecting them, and of course there were those who took advantage of this, to the point of marketing gas masks for dogs and cats. People would call me up in a state of panic asking me what to do, and what I was doing with my dogs, and all I could answer was that no, I didn't have gas masks for the dogs, and that we would all die together.

There was one thing that annoyed me during this period, perhaps unjustifiably, as there were really only good intentions involved, but regardless I was unable to accept it. A Canaan Dog breeder in the U.S. called me several days after Israel had become a target for Iraqi missiles, and told me that she had found a few other people to join her, and they were interested in paying the airfare to bring the Canaans over to the U.S. until the end of the war. They proposed to take care of them and then after the war, providing that Israel still existed, return them. I politely turned down the offer, although inside I felt that, at a time when Israel might be fighting for its very existence, I really didn't feel justified in shipping some dogs off to the U.S. so that they could survive. As I had already said, my dogs and I would either survive together or we would die together.

Even though Sha'ar Hagai was considered, under normal circumstances, to be a fairly isolated place, Israel is a small country. If I were standing out of doors, I could hear the Scud missiles hit in the Tel Aviv area. There was a Patriot anti-missile battery located apparently somewhere on the other side of the mountains from us, and the houses shook and all the windows rattled whenever the missiles were fired off. I was especially tense with Dorcas being in active military service. She was in what was considered a fairly safe location, but under the circumstances, no place in Israel was safe.

The dogs felt the tension in the air and of course, with their more sensitive hearing, reacted to the sirens and sounds of missiles. It was especially traumatic for some of the young dogs, who were exposed to the tensions but on the other hand, were not well socialized. Under these war circumstances there were no dog shows, and as we all tried to stay at home and off the highway as much as possible, there was no chance to take the youngsters out to various places to meet new people and see new things. Many dogs remained traumatized for the rest of their lives by their experiences during those weeks, always a bit nervous and jumpy in regard to new sounds and people.

Most of our life revolved around the television in those days. Broadcasts were on for twenty-four hours a day to keep people up to date on what was happening; no doubt to keep the children (and the adults too, actually) occupied; and to provide a cure for insomnia (one wonders where they found some of the things they were broadcasting). There were new media heroes, the greatest being Nachman Shai, the spokesman for the Defense Department, who broadcast the all-clear each time we were under attack.

When the announcement that the war was over came there was a great feeling of relief and joy but also doubt. As always, in Israel the number one occupation of everyone is criticism—everything is analyzed, discussed, criticized, and for every two people discussing something there are usually at least three opinions. But the bottom line was we all still have our little brown cardboard boxes with the gas masks packed away in a cupboard in a corner of the house, just in case.

Chapter Eighteen: Sheep

I suppose you could say that the sheep were my fault.

I had collie puppies for sale. When a moshavnik showed up to see them, and told me that he wanted a collie to train to work with his flock of sheep, I was thrilled. And then when he told me that, well, he didn't really have the cash, but would I be willing to trade, how could I pass up an opportunity to have one of my collies become a real working sheep dog? What was so bad, anyway, about having a few sheep on the farm?

So Tweedledee and Tweedledum arrived, two purebred Merino lambs. They were adorable. There is nothing as cute as a little lamb. There is also nothing as dumb. Probably one of the major reasons for the high intelligence bred into the sheepherding breeds of dog is that the shepherd would go nuts with no companionship but sheep. Since my only experience with sheep to date had been painting twenty of them different colors for a TV commercial on woolen carpets, I still had a lot to learn.

Since it was spring, and there was a lot of grass out on the hillsides around the place, we decided that the lambs would do well out on pasture. For a few days, we took them out a few yards away from the fence and let them eat under supervision. It appeared that they had grasped the idea. They seemed to be ready to come home as the dusk approached. So Tweedledee was provided with a bell on his collar so that we could find them if they were hidden behind bushes, and we turned them out on their own.

For a few days, things went fine. The lambs happily browsed in the nearby fields and at dusk wandered back home, waiting to be put in their pen for the night. But then one evening we realized the sheep hadn't come home. Panic! Two defenseless lambs on their own in the wilds of the *wadi* at night was not good. Grabbing storm lanterns and flashlights, we ran out to scour the hills.

Tweedledee and Tweedledum were standing with their heads against the fence about five meters from the gate. Had they turned and walked a bit, they could have come in as usual. But that was beyond the imagination of a sheep. If you walk into a fence, well, then you can't walk any farther, right?

The next day, being a glutton for punishment, I let them out again. All was well. But a few days later, once again, the dark came but no sheep. Once again, the search party went out.

Climbing up a rocky hillside in the pitch dark—there was no moon—with only a wind lantern for light is no great pleasure. I can imagine what it must have looked like from the highway below to see those spots of light moving jerkily up and down the mountain; lucky that the sound couldn't be heard at that distance. But despite clambering up, down and around for what seemed like hours, calling, and baa-ing, there was no response and finally we gave up. I was sure that was the end of the lambs. Something would surely come in the night and get them. I was up at dawn, climbing the mountain to look for any signs.

Lo and behold, there on the hillside under an enormous pine tree that we must have passed in the vicinity of at least twenty times during the night, huddled Tweedledum and Tweedledee. They stood pressed against one another, one facing east and one facing west, waiting for the daylight, so petrified and so stupid that they hadn't moved enough, even when we passed them making *baa* sounds, to ring the bell.

That should have been enough to teach me. Tweedledum and Tweedledee were disposed of to a friend with a herd of goats and sheep, and I figured that was that. My collies had to suppress their sheepherding tendencies and devote themselves to something else. Unfortunately, I seem to be hard to teach sometimes.

At the time we had a resident beatnik, or flower child, or whatever it was that was in fashion just then. Lenny had spent most of his life, about twenty years at this point, wandering from place to place, working at whatever came up just long enough to get together enough to eat on, and then pushing on to greener pastures, or maybe pinker clouds. He turned up at the farm one day when I was desperately in need of someone to shoe my horse. He had been hanging around one of the local riding stables for some time, and one of the skills he had picked up in his travels was horseshoeing. The farm appealed to him, and he hung around more and more. As well as being proficient at horseshoeing, he did beautiful leatherwork. However, all this didn't really interest him. His true life's ambition, he confided, was to be a shepherd.

In no time, we found ourselves with a herd of twenty Awasi sheep and Lenny as the official shepherd.

Awasi sheep, also known as fat-tailed sheep for obvious reasons, were native to the area. They were the type of sheep the Bedouin kept and while not more intelligent than any of their other relatives, were hardy and adapted well to the climate. The Bedouin raised them very successfully, keeping them out on pasture and using the wool, the milk, and eventually the meat as well. The idea was to get the sheep out to pasture at first light, so that they could have a number of hours of good grazing before the day became too hot. The sheep then rested in the shade during the heat of day, and in the afternoon grazed again until dusk, when they were brought in for the night. Being a native breed, they did not suffer much from the heat and needed to drink only once a day.

In theory this was all fine. However, after a short time we discovered that Lenny had a few problems, one of which was getting up in the morning. Rare was the day that he saw the sunrise or that the sheep saw pasture in the early morning. Some time in mid-morning he managed to struggle out with the herd. This effort was so exhausting that most of the rest of the day he spent resting under a tree while the sheep wandered at random searching out tasty morsels to graze on.

One day, Lenny awoke from his afternoon snooze in the shade to find heavy clouds overhead and no sheep. After searching up and down the hillsides, he wandered home at dusk to tell us that he had somehow misplaced twenty sheep.

There wasn't much point in looking for them in the dark. The next morning, surprisingly unable to sleep, Lenny got up and continued his search in a steady drizzle. No luck. Towards the late afternoon, he came to see me with the suggestion that I try to track the sheep with one of the dogs.

One of the collies, Nova, had had some tracking training; however, she had been trained to work on human scents and not on animals, and she hadn't done any tracking at all for quite a long while. It had also been raining all day, and the track was nearly twenty-four hours old. This made me very doubtful of the chances for success. Lenny, however, was insistent, so I figured it was worth a try.

Nova was happy to see her tracking harness; although she hadn't worked for a long time, she remembered and was eager to go. I picked a tuft of wool off the fence where it had caught as a sheep went by, gave it to her to smell, and started her from where Lenny had lost track of his flock. Nova seemed to pick up the scent and led me through the woods and down the fire path in the direction of the highway.

At the edge of the highway, she plunged into a tangled thicket of bushes. Peering in after her, I saw nothing but brambles—certainly nothing resembling twenty sheep. Thinking that she must be mistaken, I called her out and started her again at the beginning of the track. She once again tracked straight to the bramble thicket, crawled in and

219

refused to budge. Without great enthusiasm but without much choice, I crawled in after her. There under the bushes was a deep pit, so overgrown it could hardly be seen, and there in the pit, so tangled that it couldn't move, was a sheep. When Lenny and I tried to get it out, it became clear why it was so tangled—the poor creature had all four feet tied together.

It became clear what had happened. There was known to be a group of rustlers around. They must have seen an irresistible opportunity, herded the sheep down to the highway, tied them, and loaded them on a truck during the night. One rebel had managed to get managed to get away and they apparently hadn't felt it was worth trying to get her out of the brambles.

So now we were left with one sheep, a collie that had proven that she was a great tracker, and one very contrite shepherd.

That should have been the end of it. Anyone reasonable would have learned her lesson, but then Ginzberg showed up.

I have never considered myself unusually perceptive or a great judge of people at first sight. My first sight of Ginzberg, however, set all my nerve endings screaming, "Stay clear! Stay clear!"

He was a very well-dressed businessman, obviously prosperous. He appeared in a very expensive new car with his expensive new girlfriend in tow. He was articulate and well mannered, and I couldn't stand him. I had a terrible feeling that he was a crook, maybe not literally, but certainly in attitude. Oh no, everyone reassured me, Ginzberg is perfectly respectable and has a great proposition for us.

The proposition was that he would invest money in buying a herd of sheep, and we would provide the place, the labor and the professional expertise. We would split the profits, which were to come from the sale of milk and sheep cheese, wool, and lambs.

The plan was to keep the sheep out on pasture. This way, feeding them would be cheap and the venture would be profitable. Lenny, the penitent, was to be the shepherd again and he swore that he had learned his lesson.

My irrational feelings of distrust didn't have much influence on anyone. Ginzberg and Dvora began looking for a suitable herd to buy. Soon a Bedouin flock was found for sale. The sheep, according to Dvora, were in good condition and the price was right. The deal was made and Ginzberg and the rest of us became the possessors of 101 supposedly prime Awasi sheep.

The flock consisted of 99 ewes and two rams. One was a young fellow of about six months of age that the Bedouin had praised to the skies and then charged double for after we had persuaded him to sell. The other ram was fully mature with a nice spread of horns and a good knowledge of his purpose in life. We immediately named him Ginzberg as there was something about the look in his eye.

Things started off well enough. The sheep went out to pasture in the early morning and came home in the evening. However, keeping track of one hundred sheep is not quite the same as twenty.

One afternoon, while taking care of the dogs, I glanced down towards the highway and saw about thirty sheep casually wandering down the road and making straight for the center strip, full of wild flowers and ancient olive trees and designated as a nature reserve.

Now at this particular time, one of the main jobs that Dvora was doing for the Nature Reserves Authority was keeping the Bedouin from pasturing their sheep in the nature reserves, which was very tempting to them, as the vegetation there was much lusher than in other places. One of the Bedouin who got up in the morning, or so went his story to the judge, found that his flock had disappeared. After hours of hunting them, where would he find them but in the nature reserve. Of course, just as he found them and was about to herd them home, who should come along but the ranger. Of course his donkeys were there with him as well—how could he go hunting for his sheep and leave his donkeys wandering alone? So it would not have been very pleasant if someone in the know had driven past and seen Dvora's sheep pasturing in our local nature reserve, even if it was no more than a traffic island. Galloping down the hill, I managed to round up the sheep and drive them home.

Several hours later, Lenny came wandering back with the flock. Hadn't he noticed that he was missing some sheep, I asked. Well, no, he said, he hadn't tried to count them and there seemed to be plenty of sheep there.

Unfortunately, after the first flush of ambition, Lenny showed signs of returning to his former lazy habits. The only thing to do was to divide up the task of taking the sheep out to pasture, everyone having his own days to do it. I quite enjoyed it. The weather was lovely, especially early in the morning before the heat of day built up. I took one or two of the collies for company, determined that they would prove they still had sheep herding instincts. Book in hand, I took the flock out. The idea was to head them in a particular direction, sit down on a rock where I had a good view of the field in the direction that they were moving, and read for a while as they grazed their way along to the next field. Before they got out of sight, I got up and followed them, found another rock, and repeated the process. I had to be careful not to get too absorbed in my book, or they could easily disappear. Awasi are not like the fat and placid European sheep that graze contentedly in one field for hours; they are walkers, grabbing a mouthful and moving on looking for something better.

The system seemed to be working quite well, when suddenly one morning we found one old ewe dead in the sheep pen. A few days later, there was another. The vet examined the bodies and the rest of the flock and made his diagnosis. It seemed that one of the common wild plants in our area was an anise-like plant that the sheep found very tasty. However, this plant was a natural anticoagulant. Quantities collected in the sheep's bodies from what they ate, until finally the sheep died of internal hemorrhaging from the slightest blow—and sheep are always bumping and banging each other. The consensus was that the sheep could no longer be taken out to pasture but had to be fed in their pen on hay and grain. Some of the flock had to have veterinary treatment as they were suffering from the effects of this plant, and there were a few who could not be saved.

The collies were very disappointed. They had enjoyed being sheep dogs. I felt that this was a great time to get out of the sheep business; after all, it was too expensive to keep the sheep in and feed them without any pasture. Oh no, everyone answered, we could still make a good profit from the milk and the wool and the lambs.

Milking sheep is quite different from milking a cow or a goat. A highly productive sheep gives about one liter of milk, while others don't give more than a few squirts. The milk, however, is very thick and rich. Sheep are also milked from behind, apparently because their teats face that way; however, many sheep tend not to be very mannerly about the procedure. They don't usually kick, but a lot of them seem to feel that a touch behind is a request for something other than milk; if you are milking a sheep you have to be very quick about getting the pan out of the way if the little beastie starts to squat. The pan has to be covered with several layers of cheesecloth—the heavy wool and tremendous fatty tails pick up a lot of burrs, straw, sticks, and less mentionable items which have a perverse tendency to fall off just as you are milking.

There was an additional hazard; Ginzburg the ram enjoyed stalking around viewing the proceedings. Apparently, the temptation when he saw someone's exposed bottom stooped over the milking pail was too much to withstand, resulting in spilled milk and the milker face down in the mud.

There was plenty of mud, too. The rains had begun and the wet ground was quickly churned into a bog by the flock of sheep. Rain or shine, there was no choice; the sheep had to be milked. We sank to our ankles in mud. The sheep sank even further and their wool was caked with it. We muttered under our breaths at the injustice of it all, until finally one day, at the peak of frustration, one of the other guys snarled at Lenny, "Hey captain, your sheep are sinking!"

As the breeding season approached, the milk production went down, and finally we got to stop milking. However, these sheep were not to be allowed to breed as nature had intended. Modern methods dictated using hormones to bring the sheep into season, so that they could be bred within a limited period of time and then all would lamb within a few weeks. The hormone treatment meant catching the ewes and inserting little hormone soaked sponges that would then cause the ewe to come in season. Of course this treatment was quite expensive, but was supposed to be infallible.

The ewes duly came into season and Ginzburg and his young friend were kept busy. Far from tiring Ginzburg out enough to make him amenable to being handled, it now really became a matter of agility to get into the sheep pen, do whatever had to be done, and get out again without coming into reach of his horns. Now it was a matter of waiting for all those lovely and profitable lambs. Meanwhile, the sheep happily stayed in their pen and ate and ate and ate since they were, after all, pregnant.

Lambing season arrived. For five months we had been looking forward to the fruits of our labor, and now we couldn't wait for the sweet little things to arrive. All the ewes must be pregnant, after their hormone treatments!

One problem with some of the ruminants is that, because of their digestive arrangement, it is sometimes hard to tell if that bulge is stomach or baby. The sheep looked pregnant, but as the due dates arrived, nothing happened.

The final score was three lambs, one born dead, one that was too weak to live, and one strong and lively female.

The vet didn't really have any definitive answer about the breeding failure—maybe the sheep were too old, maybe they were not healthy enough. Whatever the reason, there were no more lambs and of course, no profit.

That was the last straw—not for us, as I am sure that everyone would have felt it was worthwhile continuing for another season to make up our losses—but Ginzberg wanted out. One day he showed up with a truck, loaded his sheep and drove them off to market. He was left with the cash, and we were left with our professional expertise.

That should have been the end of the story. But there was a postscript. One day we were delivered with an invitation to court; Ginzberg was suing us for 'loss of expected profits' with his sheep.

I was ready to believe that the sheep jinx would continue and that we would have to pay Ginzberg for all the lambs that were never born. The judge, however, a man of reason, took one look at the file and threw the case out of court.

We never saw Ginzberg again.

Chapter Nineteen: Goosey, Goosey, Gander...

In the post-Africa days, we were continually on the search for new sources of income. The cost of living was going up all the time, and raising three children was not cheap. Dorcas was already in nursery school, which was another added expense.

One day Dvora brought home three geese. These, she explained, were the best alarm system in existence. They were very territorial, made plenty of noise when a stranger appeared, and they would eat all the weeds in the garden and along the roadside. They were also very clever birds.

Everything she said was true. The geese, two females and a male, were indeed marvelous 'watchdogs,' honking loudly when anyone approached 'their' territory. Their territory quickly expanded from Dvora's yard to the entire farm, aside from my yard, which was fenced and full of dogs. The geese paraded around as if they owned the place—and there is nothing as proud-looking as a goose. The dogs learned to beware because not only did the geese make plenty of noise, they were not averse to charging with snapping beaks extended and wings flapping when they felt challenged. And the bite of a goose or a blow from its large and strong wing was painful! Dorcas was very suspicious of these creatures, and did not like to go anywhere near them when she was not accompanied by someone big who could protect her

All in all, though, the geese did appear to be quite intelligent and interesting birds. So when Dvora suggested that maybe we could make some money by raising geese, it seemed to be a good idea.

Israel had a fairly successful industry of raising geese for pate de foie gras. I had only a vague idea of how it was done; I knew that the geese were fed quantities of food to develop a huge liver, but I had never seen it done and we were not to be involved in that. We were going to raise geese from the day they hatched until they were three months old, of a sufficient size and weight to be marketed.

Two of the houses on the farm were unoccupied, so it was decided to turn them into brooders for the geese. The floor was covered with a thick layer of sawdust, which we bought from carpentry shops, and this would provide insulation for the baby geese and absorb their droppings. It would also be fairly easy to clean up. We planned to have three groups of geese—the newly hatched, one-month-olds, and two-month-olds, the latter of which would be marketed when they got to three months of age. The first two batches would be kept indoors with heating, and the two month-olds, which had already grown their feathers, would be kept in outdoor pens. Dvora and Jacques were very ambitious—each group would have five hundred geese. So we would have one thousand five hundred geese around when we were in full swing.

One thousand five hundred geese is rather different than three. The first batch of five hundred arrived: they were absolutely gorgeous little golden fluff balls. They were also very delicate and stupid as the day is long. Geese may be intelligent birds when they are raised as individuals but in a group, they are dumb. We often found the babies sitting in their waterers, and half a centimeter of water was enough for them to get soaked in and to die of exposure. Or they crowded close to the heaters and died of suffocation. Or they trampled each other trying to get to the food dishes.

The older geese didn't prove to be any more intelligent. Julep became our official goose-herder. We had prepared some outdoor yards for the geese, fenced in with chicken wire of about fifty centimeters in height since the geese didn't fly or jump over things. However, we soon found that they had a very odd behavior pattern. Once they had been inside a fence, they believed it to still be there even after it was taken down. We took down a side of the fence to move them to another pen, and they refused to cross the line where the fence had been, stopping dead and turning and stampeding the other way. All of Julep's efforts to head them off were useless; they ignored her and simply moved around her like water around a rock. The only way we could get them to cross the line eventually was to grab a few of the geese, toss them over to the other side of the line, and then, when they saw their friends safely on the other side, they crossed over with Julep urging them on from behind.

Cleaning up was not the easy job we had anticipated, either. We discovered that the phrase "loose as a goose" was based on fact. We also discovered that there was not much we could do with the huge quantity of soiled sawdust that we accumulated. There was only a limited need for mulch on the farm.

Feeding the geese involved dragging around fifty kilo sacks of feed. Jacques really developed muscles during this period. Those geese ate! They were always hungry. We also fed them grass that we would go out to cut, but a few hours worth of hacking away with a scythe provided about ten minutes worth of food for the flock.

When marketing day came, we had to catch the five hundred three month-old geese and pack them into shipping boxes. Geese are quite fast, especially when they think you are after them. It took hours of running after the geese in the dust before we got them all crated. Everyone participated—kids, Jacques, Dvora and I. It was a sort of rodeo, Sha'ar Hagai style.

We hoped we would at least make a lot of money from this project. Well, no such luck! The bottom sort of fell out of the goose market and we were stuck with one thousand, five hundred hungry geese, with the price of the feed having climbed to unprecedented heights. We had a talent for getting into a branch of business just when it was about to become unprofitable.

When the goose project came to an end I don't think anyone was sorry. Better to stick to a few nice geese as watchdogs and to forget about commercial quantities! I think the only one who was sorry was Julep, since she had enjoyed being a goose herder.

Chapter Twenty: Wheels

Americans take cars for granted; just about every American who wants one has a car. I had my first car when I was sixteen, a brand new Pontiac Tempest, which was a present for my high school graduation and meant to help persuade me to stay at home and go to a university nearby. It was an effective bribe.

In Israel, things were different. Cars were a luxury when I came to the country; only people with a lot of money were mobile, or people who required a car for their work. Buying and keeping a car was very expensive, so the rest of us traveled by bus.

I missed having a car, and once we were planning to move out to Sha'ar Hagai, it seemed that it would be almost impossible if we didn't have a vehicle. An appeal home brought results; my ever-indulgent parents provided me with two-thousand dollars as my portion of the investment in establishing the farm. I used this money to buy a car. The car would be in my name, as I could buy it with a reduction in taxes as part of my immigrant's rights, which was a considerable saving.

We farm members bought a Volkswagen commercial van, which was both in our range financially and ideal for our purposes. But it would take a few weeks for the car to arrive, so meanwhile, I was provided with a rental, a Beetle with stick shift.

My first few days with that bug were an experience. I had never driven a stick shift car and wherever I tried to go, I created traffic jams as I got stuck trying to start, stop, or shift gears. By the end of the first few days I was a nervous wreck, but I had begun to master the gearshift. Before I had a chance to truly get comfortable with the bug, the van arrived, and I was learning to drive a new car again.

I had never driven anything as large as the van, and it took me a while to feel comfortable. As I started to feel more comfortable, though, I began to notice that I seemed to be attracting a lot of attention. I soon realized that since in Israel in those days, women did not drive vans or trucks or such, people found me a strange sight, barely peeking up from behind the steering wheel.

Keeping the car running was another problem. Trying to start a new business wasn't as economically viable as we hoped, and we found ourselves short on occasion. It was always possible to go and bum a meal from someone, but it wasn't so easy to bum petrol for the car. At one point, we ended up picking lemons off the tree growing by the farm's entrance road and selling them to the local shop to get together enough money for a tank of petrol.

Mostly, though, having the car was a pleasure, until we were sent off to Africa and had to sell it. Oh well, we thought, surely in Africa we will be able to make enough money to buy a new and better car when we get back. We were naive then, not well educated in the ways of living in Israel.

In most countries, your first car is a cheap, fifth-hand jalopy. With time and some level of success, subsequent cars are better ones. Somehow in Israel, there seems to be some sort of reverse factor involved. First cars were new and tax free, because of immigrant's rights. After that, as the prices went up, the quality seemed to go down.

The only car we were able to afford when we came back was an ancient Willys truck. It must have been about twenty years old, and looked every day of its age. But it was tough, and the engine was good, we were promised by the seller, who told us that he had cared for it over the years with more love than he had given his children. It was painted blue for good luck.

Good luck was the one thing this truck seemed to be lacking, but the fact that I have come to be considered a good and cool-nerved driver is due to that vehicle. Every day there was a new adventure. One day the gear shift lever came off in my hand as I was trying to change gears on the upgrade to Jerusalem. Another day, the hood flew open in my face, blocking my vision as I drove down the highway. Another time, right after passing the yearly safety inspection, relieved that that ordeal was over for another year, the brakes suddenly stopped working on the downgrade. I managed to stop the car at the bottom of the hill by using the handbrakes—with a police car right behind me watching my every move.

Eventually, the Willys gave up the ghost. At the bottom of our entrance road, it died totally; the battery was dead, and the truck couldn't be moved anywhere. At this point we couldn't afford a new battery, and besides, we had our doubts as to whether it was worth putting any more money into the old wreck. So we left it sitting there at the entrance to the farm.

Some days later, the Willys disappeared. This was mystifying, as we knew very well that it couldn't be started. Anyway we thought, this would save us the problems of getting rid of it. But just as a matter of good form, we decided to report the theft to the police.

We all went over to the Beit Shemesh police station, and lo and behold!, there in the station yard, was the Willys. What was it doing there? Well, the police patrols had seen it sitting in our entrance for several days, decided that it looked suspicious, and came and towed it away. "Well," I said, "since it can't be driven, and you stole it and towed it away, then you can tow it back."

Once the Willys was towed back, it sat alongside the road for some months until we finally found someone who was willing to buy it for parts. (I still wonder what parts were still usable in that thing). It was rather sad to see it go, though; that little truck was history. Well, now I had no vehicle and no money, so I came up with the great idea to learn to ride a motorcycle. I could get an old motorcycle very cheaply, and the upkeep wasn't expensive, and then I would be mobile again. So I started taking motorcycle lessons.

At first, the lessons went fairly well. It is true that I had not ridden a bicycle since I was a child and had a tendency to sit on the motorcycle as if it were a horse, which is not a very successful technique, but I thought I was beginning to get the hang of it.

One day, one of our current neighbors, Yossi, a real motorcycle expert, offered to take me to practice on his fancy cross-country motorcycle. He proposed taking me up the forestry trails in the mountains around the farm, which had very nice dirt tracks, where I could practice without worrying about traffic. That sounded like a great idea, so off we went.

Soon I found myself zooming along the forest trails, with Yossi sitting behind me, relaxed and half-asleep. Suddenly, the motorcycle seemed to realize that a novice was driving, and took control—or at least that was how it felt to me. The bike seemed to leap forward and I couldn't do anything to slow it down or turn it aside. Directly ahead was the edge of the dirt track, and a hundred meters or so beyond, straight down the side of the mountain.

Before I knew what was happening, I found myself in a heap on the very edge of the trail with the motorcycle hanging half over the edge, and Yossi holding on for dear life, not quite sure what had happened. We were caught by a tree branch just as we were about to go over the edge, looking straight down at where we might have ended up.

That was the end of my nerve and my motorcycle lessons.

My next brilliant idea was to get a riksha. No, not a Chinese vehicle, but a three-wheeler with a Vespa engine and a small closed cab. It also had a closed compartment behind for carrying things.

This was also a very cheap vehicle, and I didn't have to have a special license or any special skills to drive it. However, it did have its drawbacks. The first was that the maximum speed it could go, in optimal conditions and on the downgrade, was 40 kph. Thus, it took me about two hours to get to Tel Aviv in it, and at this time I was working at Tel Aviv University and traveling back and forth every day.

The second drawback was that it had no radio. I really like to have a radio in the car when I am driving despite whatever gibberish might be on, because it helps to keep me alert. In this case, since I was spending long hours in the riksha getting to and from Tel Aviv, it was disappointing not having a radio. There was only one thing to do; I started singing to myself. My repertoire was not so hot, but at least trying to think of new songs kept me alert.

It quickly became apparent, however, that the riksha was not built for long-distance travel; it started breaking down regularly as we got to the beginning of the hills approaching the farm. I would get out, hitch a ride to the farm, catch my other neighbor, Ofer, who had a truck; he would come back with me, tie a piece of rope to the riksha and tow us home. These, I must admit, were some of the most terrifying rides I have ever taken—I had to sit in the riksha to steer, as it swayed from side to side at the end of a piece of rope.

No one seemed to be able to discover what the problem was; apparently the riksha was allergic to hills. So there was no choice but to dispose of that vehicle as well. That was not easy either, as there was certainly no market for such a vehicle. In the end, the riksha was abandoned to the junk dealers. I can't say that I was really sorry to see it go.

Being without a vehicle was no solution to my problems. At this time, I was still working in Tel Aviv at the University. So once again, I was faced by the problem of finding something reliable that I could afford to commute in.

The solution was a Subaru station wagon. It was a 1976 Subaru station wagon, faded and far from elegant, but it was in my price range and it ran. It was big enough for the dogs, and for the baby hyena that I was raising as one of my projects for the university. Quickly, it became even more decrepit in appearance—the hyena was fond of chewing everything in reach, and this included the door handles and the knob of the gear shift lever—but the engine was sound, and the car was reliable. The mechanic I used for the regular service and repairs also rapidly learned that I needed very quick service; otherwise he might be stuck indefinitely with me and my hyena waiting around his garage.

I became quite fond of that old car. So you can imagine how upset I was one evening to come out of a movie in Jerusalem to discover that it was no longer where it had been parked. My old wreck had been stolen! It was hard to imagine who would want to steal it, but facts were facts. I immediately reported it to the police and the next morning to my insurance company. However, just to be sure, I also hired a company that was expert in finding stolen vehicles. I had to have my car back; I couldn't get along without it!

A month and more went by and despite my constant pestering of the police and the car-finding company, there was no news. After six weeks I could put in my claim to the insurance company. I was already trying to figure out what else I could buy with the payment I would get from the insurance.

A few days before the six-week limit, I got a phone call from the police—in Haifa! My car was there in the police lot. It had been there since the day after it had been stolen. Apparently someone had needed a quick ride to Haifa, had stolen the car, driven up to Haifa, and left it abandoned in the street, where the next day it was towed away by the police. "Why haven't you come to get your car?" the police questioned. "Don't you want it?"

Well, I had my car back, even if without explanations of why it had taken the police almost six weeks to notice that it was in their possession. But that was not the end of the story.

A year and a half later, the car license renewal was due, but I hadn't gotten the renewal form in the mail. I had to go down to the vehicle licensing office to get the form. After giving the clerk the details of the car, I was told, "I can't give you the form for re-licensing. That vehicle is stolen!"

I was speechless. When I got my breath back I asked, "What do you mean?"

"That car is listed in our records as stolen. You have to bring us verification from the police that it is yours."

"But it was stolen from me! I'm the one who reported it to the police! And the police returned it to me!"

"Well, that may be true, but you still need the verification. According to the records, it is still stolen. There are procedures to follow, after all."

So I had to go into town to the main police station. The guard at the gate asked me what I wanted. "I need a letter that my car isn't stolen," I replied.

"What?!"

After a short explanation, he sent me to the right department, where I went through the whole explanation again. Sure enough, when they punched it all through the computer, my car came up still listed as stolen. All right, they would change it, they said, and give me the letter for the licensing office.

"Just one more question," I added. "If my car has been listed on the police records for the last year and a half as stolen, and if I have been driving all over the country in it all this time, why haven't you managed to find it?"

Silence. I took my letter and left.

After several years of hard and faithful service, the time came to sell the Subaru and look for something a bit younger and better. The Subaru still valiantly attempted to do all that was asked of it, but it was getting tired, and you could see the highway through the rust holes in the floor. Amazingly enough, I managed to find someone in even worse financial condition that was willing to buy it, and for several years I would still see the old thing on the highway passing by.

After some searching, the next vehicle to join the family was a small, secondhand Talbot van. The Talbot was a cheap car, but it was known to have a good engine, although the body wasn't anything special. It was also roomy enough for dogs and all kinds of other things.

The Talbot was indeed a strong and reliable little car, and I used it well for several years. The height of its service was my trip to Europe with the little van loaded to capacity with dogs, people and equipment, doing 10,000 kilometers in a month's time, and going up and down mountains with almost no complaint.

Eventually, the time had come to sell the Talbot. I was due to get a new job, which would provide me with a company car. I was ecstatic; we would finally be able to get a little ahead. I could sell my well-running Talbot for a decent price and I would have a company car to replace it.

As if the little car knew I was about to abandon it, it started to lose power, struggle up the hills from Tel Aviv to home—nothing compared to the hills that it had always zoomed up in fourth gear—to overheat, and complain of general malaise. I was hoping to sell it and have a bit of money on the side for a change, to use to pay off some other bills. There was even someone who was interested in buying the little car. And then, as if in spite, a few days before the sale was due to go through, the car simply refused to move anymore. After having it towed up to the garage in Jerusalem, the verdict was that the engine was shot.

I did sell the car but for a minimal price minus the cost of a new engine. It was sold to a neighbor, and is still a real little workhorse, and may well go on for many more years, though I have to admit that I haven't seen it around for a while. I, however, had moved up in the world. I got a job as a representative for a dog food company, and I had the use of a company car.

The car I was provided with was a 1989 Subaru pickup, a car that was only 2 years old, and although I started out with a secondhand one, after some months of work for the company, I was provided with a brand new one. What a pleasure, having a new car! It was not the most comfortable vehicle in the world to drive, especially not when it was loaded but who was complaining? I spent many hours in my job on the road, and that car became like my home away from home. It was also roomy enough to fit in a number of dogs on weekends if there was a dog show or such.

Israel is infamous for being one of the countries in the world with the highest percentage of traffic accidents, and worst drivers. The lexicon of the average Israeli driver does not include the words 'patience' or 'courtesy.' Driving is like entering a free-for-all, without ever being sure that you will get to the finish line.

I had been driving since I was sixteen, and always considered myself a good driver. I never was nervous about being on the highway. I had also never been involved in an accident.

One late Thursday afternoon, I was peacefully driving home. The Subaru was very heavily loaded; there were two dog shows over the coming weekend for which my company was providing sponsorship. Traffic was fairly heavy, but nothing out of the ordinary.

Suddenly, in the rearview mirror, I saw a car coming up behind me really fast. Just before crashing into me from behind, it swerved sharply into the passing lane and zoomed past. But then, instead of passing, the driver, a bearded young *yeshiva bocher* (a student at a Rabbinical seminary), tried to cut in front of me and then lost control of his car, which then made a half circle and came directly at me!

There was no way to get out of the way. An instant after I saw this car coming head on at me, it had crashed hard into my car on the left front. This threw my car into a wild spin towards the right, and the margin of the highway, which at this spot was about ten meters above the fields at roadside.

I managed to turn the car away from the margin, but this threw it into a wild spin in the other direction, towards the cement wall that was the road divider. Again I managed to turn the car away from a direct collision, but this time it was too much for the overloaded Subaru, which rolled over, spun around twice on its side, leaving smashed windshield glass and dog food scattered in its wake, and then rolled over once more, ending up on its wheels in the middle of the highway. The poor car was rather like an old war-horse after a major battle, panting, steaming and wounded, but still on its feet.

My major memories of the experience were of the world turning over, and the thought going through my mind as I turned upside down, held in place by my seat belt, "How am I going to get out of here?"

I was totally shaken as I managed to climb out of the car after it had settled on its four tires once again. Debris was scattered up and down the highway—my purse, along with some of the other contents of the car, were a few hundred meters down the road; a passing driver who stopped to see if I was all right was kind enough to bring it to me. It was obvious that the Subaru was going nowhere soon, other than by way of a tow truck.

The other driver, however, who had caused all this, was not even scratched and his car was only dented on the front fender.

I started trying to pull myself together. An inspection showed that everything seemed to be in place on my aching body and nothing appeared to be broken or seriously damaged. A policeman stopped to ask how I was; when he saw that I was functioning and not in imminent danger of bleeding to death or otherwise complicating the situation, he drove on; there are so many accidents that the police get involved only if there is some sort of serious injury to those involved. Property damage doesn't concern them.

I borrowed a cell-phone from a passing motorist and called the company. Somehow, I made myself clear enough for the guy in charge of the company vehicles to understand that he would have to come and rescue me.

About half an hour later, he arrived with another pickup truck and a tow truck. Everything that was salvageable was loaded on the pick-up, and my car was towed away. I was given the new pick-up. "Can you drive?" he asked.

Well, I figured it was like riding a horse—if you were thrown, you had to get back on and ride again. So I drove home—only seven kilometers—but it took me a long time, as I drove along at about 20 kilometers an hour, hugging the margin.

The next day I felt much worse, and much worse than that the day after. The result of that adventure was some months of dealing with doctors, examinations, and treatments. Worse, I lost my pleasure in driving; I still cringe inside when a car starts speeding up behind me or passes me close on the side, and I try to drive as little as is necessary. The Subaru was repaired, but I never wanted to drive it again. Soon after the accident, I stopped working for the company. The next car I bought was a little compact, low to the ground and very stable.

The other driver, as far as I know, never even got a traffic ticket.

Chapter Twenty-One: Show Biz

In Israel, I didn't entirely forsake my former 'profession' of 'show biz' animals. Opportunities did present themselves for occasional work in ads or films, especially since here there were no established professionals in the field as far as working with animals went; I was as much of a professional as anyone else they could find.

This kind of work, for some reason, seemed to go in cycles. There would be entire years when there was nothing, and then, within a few months, we would get several requests for dogs in the theater and the movies all at once.

The work was usually fun as long as one didn't depend on it to earn a living. The more often I had the opportunity of working in the field, the surer I was that if I had to do it all the time I would go crazy.

One of the busiest show-biz cycles I worked started with the request from a Jerusalem theater to train a dog for them to appear in an Ibsen play, *Little Eyolph*. The dog was in one critical scene; it was to be hidden in a large handbag belonging to one of the characters, and at the appropriate moment, to stick its head out for a moment, and then to disappear back into the bag. Sounds easy? Hah!

The dog chosen for stardom came from the local SPCA, and was one of the ugliest dogs I have had the pleasure of knowing. She was a very small mixed terrier, black with a bit of gray, with scruffy hair and ears that were all over the place. She was also totally un-housebroken and thoroughly disobedient, with a terrier's typical energy. The idea of this little beast sitting inside a closed handbag for ten minutes without moving was hard to imagine.

Mopsy, as she was called, was an immediate hit with the cast, and they decided that she should live in the theater. However, after one day's experience of cleaning up after her, the plan was changed. She would live with me, and I would bring her to the theater for rehearsals and then after that, I would come down with her for each performance.

She did learn quickly, especially when motivated by edible rewards. I soon had her staying inside the handbag, putting her head out on cue. She even began behaving in the house, although she still loved opportunities to escape and go garbage hunting.

Now her part had to be coordinated into the rest of the play. This was not so easy. The actress who would be carrying the handbag loved Mopsy, but was totally incapable of disciplining her. Mopsy quickly learned that most of the cast were soft touches for cookies; she would arrive in the theater and go dancing around from one to another, begging in all imaginable ways, and usually getting what she wanted. I would put Mopsy into the bag, but from the moment it was handed to the actress, anything could happen. Mopsy might start squirming around, or she might jump out entirely, and the actress was not capable of stopping her.

Finally, after a serious heart-to-heart talk with the actress, we managed to get the situation under control. Mopsy learned that she would not be allowed out of the bag, and became a real trooper, performing her part beautifully, but there were occasional rebellions, of course. For example, there was the performance when she decided that sticking her head out was not enough, so she got out of the bag entirely. The actress coped beautifully, managing to remember to say all her lines while she was stuffing Mopsy back in the bag.

Mopsy developed the syndrome that I have seen in a lot of performing animals—they really love their work, and get very depressed on days when there is no performance. On off days, Mopsy sat around the house, depressed and unhappy, all the time hoping that I would get out the handbag and call her to go to the theater.

When the run of the play was over, Mopsy remained unemployed. But she had developed so many friendships with cast and visitors that it was not hard to find her a home with a lot of attention to make up for not being a star any more. Last I heard of her, she was nursing a litter of puppies, even uglier than she was.

I had hardly finished with Mopsy when we got another casting call—a producer of children's theater was doing a revival of *Lassie Come Home* and needed a trained collie for the part. It was Prize's turn to become a star. He was already very well trained, and quickly learned to do all the little tricks required for his part. He really was the star of this show, and appeared on stage almost the entire hour plus of the performance, very efficiently following my commands from offstage.

This was a traveling show that went all over the country and played in theaters, community centers, and all sorts of other places. Conditions were often very difficult, but wherever we went, the audience, mostly children and some parents, loved Prize, and many tried to come around backstage to pet him after the show. Prize was very tolerant of all the attention, sitting there with a long-suffering expression on his face while children surrounded him on all sides, petting and kissing him.

Prize, however, expected to be treated as a professional on stage, which the other actors learned. One of his important scenes was with an actor who played an artist. The artist left his paintbrush on a stump, and Prize's part was to come sneaking out, pick up the brush, and carry it away while the artist was not looking. Then, when the artist began frantically looking everywhere for his brush, Prize would sneak back and replace the brush on the stump.

This was not an easy task to train him to do, but I got it accomplished in a clever way. Prize had had no trouble learning to go and get the brush—that was a simple retrieve. However, putting the brush back was more difficult, as he had to learn to put it back precisely in the same spot he had taken it from. This was accomplished by having the actor put a little piece of sausage on the stump, while he was looking for the missing brush. Prize would come over to the stump, put down the brush, take his reward of sausage, and happily trot offstage.

Sometimes actors do forget their lines for a moment, and one day our actor forgot to put the sausage in its place. Prize trotted out with the brush in his mouth, got to the stump, looked around and found no sausage. He analyzed the situation and calmly trotted offstage with the brush in his mouth. No pay, no work!

The scene with the brush stood Prize in good stead when he was 'hired' to do a TV commercial for government medallions. These were medals issued periodically by the government in commemoration of various things. Prize had to take the box with the medallion off a table and present it to the actress playing the mother of the family. This presented no problem for him. Filming this commercial, however, which in the end was about thirty seconds screen time, took twelve hours. Prize, however, stood up well under the pressure, which was more than could be said for the poor children in the scene, or Dorcas who was handling him in this job.

Another of our canine stars, Dum-Dum, was even longer suffering. Dum-Dum belonged to a popular children's television series, the stars of which were a singing group who also traveled around the country making live appearances. He was another rescuee from the SPCA, another small terrier, but an extremely attractive little fellow, with long silky wheaten coat, a curly tail, and pricked ears. He was also particularly clever and willing to learn anything. Unfortunately his abilities were never really taken advantage of, perhaps for fear that he would steal the show. But even so, he was very popular. At personal appearances, almost as many children ran after him, screaming "Dum-Dum! Dum-Dum!" as ran after the stars of the show.

There was only one problem: Dum-Dum hated children. We never knew what happened to him in the past to cause this, but although he was very friendly to everyone over about fourteen years-old, for anyone under that age, his reaction was growling and snapping. Every time we appeared in public, I firmly grasped the little fellow's head under my arm, one hand firmly holding his mouth shut, as he growled and snarled under his breath. Of course, all the petting children never knew; we couldn't spoil his public image.

As this was a show that traveled all over the country and did live performances, there were times that we would have to stay overnight in a hotel. Israeli hotels for the most part are definitely not enthusiastic about pets, and some of them suggested that Dum-Dum sleep in the car. No way! Dum-Dum was one of the stars, a member of the crew, and we insisted that he sleep in the hotel room. We always won in the end.

Things became a bit more difficult when a new edition of the show was prepared that included two more dogs—a miniature pinscher and a Saint Bernard. Usually I would bring them to the theatre in my own car. But on long trips, I preferred not to drive and traveled in the crew's van. I did so primarily because I had the Subaru, a very old car by that time with no air conditioning, and in the heat of the summer, I wanted the dogs to be in an air-conditioned car so that they would be fresh for the performance. Fitting all of us into the van was an experience. Dona, the St. Bernard, pretty much took up an entire seat on her own, and despite the fact that the van was air-conditioned, she still panted on the trip, usually resulting in a small puddle. She was not popular with the driver of the van, who prided himself on a spotless vehicle.

We were even less popular in the hotels this time. Letting Dum-Dum stay in the room was one thing, but letting all three was another. And it certainly was a sight to see me, early morning and evening, walking these three together around the hotel district of Tiberius or wherever.

Dum-Dum has been living with one of the members of the group for a number of years. He is quite an old dog now, and though he still appears, it is mostly just to come up on stage for a bow. I am sorry when I see him that his 'career' never went any further; he could have been a real star!

The Canaans were not left out when it came to show biz—actually, my most major projects involved them. The first to have a 'major role' was Ami. Ami was born at Sha'ar Hagai. He was a very bold dominant puppy with a strong temperament. He had to be separated from his littermates at quite a young age, as he grabbed and shook them to prove his superiority. He was sold as a puppy to a friend who wanted him as a watchdog for his stable of Arabian horses. When Ami was about a year old, he was returned; he was not working well enough. I found this hard to understand knowing him as a puppy. Back at Sha'ar Hagai, he again showed great self-confidence and a strong tendency to dominance. Ami knew he was king.

We had a number of males and decided that we would sell Ami again if a suitable owner appeared. He was, by now, functioning marvelously as a watchdog. We decided that he had been highly insulted by his previous owner and was ready to prove him wrong. A family showed up looking for a good family dog that would also be a watch dog, and did not want to start with a puppy. I warned them that Ami was a very dominant dog.

"That's fine," said the father, "I have lots of experience with all kinds of dogs. We won't have any problems." So Ami went off to his new home.

One month later, quite late at night, there was a knock on the door, and there stood Ami's new owner with Ami. "Take him!" was all he said.

The story slowly was revealed. At the start, Ami was absolutely wonderful. He guarded the house, was affectionate to the family, and was perfectly behaved. But as he started to become comfortable in his new surroundings, things began to change. He started to guard his food dish; when he was eating, no one could approach him. After a few days, while he was eating, no one could come into the room. He decided that one of the easy chairs in the salon was his and no one else was allowed to sit there. He then decided that the entire salon was his, and no one was allowed in or out without his 'permission.' When he started to take possession of the bedrooms as well, that was the end.

So Ami stayed at Sha'ar Hagai. I put him through a course of obedience training and started to show him as well, and at this point he was well on his way to becoming a champion. So when I was approached by a film company looking for a dog that would look like a "natural dog of the last century," and could also look aggressive in one scene, Ami seemed right.

The project was a television film based on a story by one of the classical Jewish writers. Basically, the story was about a peddler who meets a witch in his travels and falls in love with her, and then he kills her in the end to save his own life. This witch did not have a cat as her familiar, but a dog that accompanied her everywhere and guarded her home. Ami was ideal.

Ami really enjoyed all the attention that he got on the set. When he was with me, and outside of his own territory, he was calm, friendly and very obedient. Most of what was required of him in the film was very simple. Primarily, he just had to be present with the witch and accompany her from place to place. The one big scene for him was yet to come in which he had to 'attack' the peddler when he first showed up and tried to approach the witch's house.

Time for the big scene arrived. Ami was tied to the front porch of the witch's house and had to bark, snarl, and lunge at the peddler as he approached. The crew kept asking me how I would get Ami to do it—they knew him as a friendly, calm and amenable dog. "Don't worry," I said.

There was one crewmember who had been consistently driving me crazy. He worked with props and scenery. Part of his job was to take care of the animals—some chickens, rabbits and such on the set to give it a country atmosphere. He was sure that he was a huge expert on animals, including dogs, and was constantly chatting away at me and pestering Ami.

As we prepared the attack scene, I called this guy over and told him I needed his help. He was thrilled.

"Stand behind the camera," I told him. "When I tell you to, raise your arm in a threatening gesture."

As the "Action!" call came, I signaled to the fellow and he raised his arm.

This, of course, was all that Ami needed. He saw the lifted arm and immediately lunged forward to the end of his chain, barking, snarling, and ferociously baring his teeth. All of the crew leaped backward in shock.

The lights over Ami's head needed adjusting, but the lighting man, who had only a few minutes before been fussing over him, refused to get near until I moved Ami away.

The scene was filmed very successfully. Every time our now reluctant 'animal expert' lifted his arm, Ami responded perfectly. After the scene, Ami returned to being his calm and friendly self with one exception. Every time he spotted our 'animal expert' friend, he growled and bared his teeth—a Canaan doesn't forget his enemies! For the rest of the filming, we didn't have to worry about being bothered; this particular crewmember stayed a good distance away!

The next production we were involved in was a big feature film, *The Dreamers*, an Israeli production, but with a few big Hollywood stars as well—the one that made the most impression in Israel was Kelly McGillis. *The Dreamers* was a story of an early part of Israel's history, and there was one scene where a pack of dogs was required to run forward barking at intruders approaching an Arab village. The dogs, of course, had to look authentic, and of course, there is no more authentic dog than the Canaan.

The first step was to prepare a pack of four or five dogs that would be willing to work together, not so easy with Canaans who can be quite aggressive to other dogs. I managed this, basically by getting the dogs to understand that I was the pack leader and I would kill any dog that dared to make trouble!

People often have difficulties making their dog understand that they are the pack leaders. This is not a matter of shouting at them, grabbing them or smacking them. In fact, it is a matter of using the correct body language. Dogs within a group do not often fight and bite each other to decide who is boss; it would not be beneficial to the pack to have injured members. Often it is enough for the top dog just to give a sideways glance at another pack member to show his dominance. For me it was the same. These dogs had known me from the day they were born, and we spoke the same language: it was enough for me to show them through body posture and facial expressions that I was in charge.

Once this was accomplished, the next step was to train the dogs to run forward and bark at the intruders. We made regular trips and spent time at the filming location so that the dogs would start feeling that this was their territory. One of the actors who was to play one of the 'intruders' also started working with me, teasing the dogs so that they would dislike him enough to bark and run at him when they saw him, but not enough that they would really attack him.

Finally filming day came. The scene was filmed, but the director decided to film two versions, one with the dogs, and another version without.

When the film was released, I was invited to the premiere. I eagerly awaited the dogs' big scene, but it never appeared on screen. The director had decided to use the second version. What a disappointment! However, at the end of the film, in the credits, appeared "Dogs provided by Sha'ar Hagai Kennels." Those invisible dogs are really rare.

The biggest film project that I was involved in was an American movie made in Israel in 1987 called *The Beast of War*. It had a real Hollywood cast: Steven Bauer, Jason Patric, and George Dzundza. The story was about the war in Afghanistan, and as at the time filming a movie in Afghanistan was not highly recommended, it was decided that Israel was similar enough in terrain and modern enough in facilities to be an excellent substitute.

The script had a number of scenes that involved a pack of jackals or wild dogs. The film company soon discovered, on their arrival in Israel, that a pack of trained jackals was not readily available (surprise, surprise!) However, it was suggested to them, by someone highly intelligent I am sure, that a pack of Canaans might just suit the purpose.

I was contacted and requested to bring one of the Canaans to an audition in one of the fanciest hotels in Tel Aviv. The hoteliers were not enthusiastic when I showed up in the lobby with a dog. But film companies spend a lot of money in hotels like that, and we were allowed up to the director's room so he could see the dog.

I had brought Yitzhar with me, since he was the wildest appearing of the dogs. Yitzhar had a very penetrating and wolf-like stare that could be very discomforting. The director was indeed impressed and I was hired to provide a pack of five dogs to work in the movie.

This was not a simple task. Again as in the last movie, getting five Canaans to work together, off lead, and in some scenes from a long distance, without them deciding to have a free for all in the middle, was not easy. The pack consisted of three bitches and two dogs, all of which were already obedience trained, and which, fortunately for me, already had experience working together from the previous movie we had done. So after a short refresher course of who was the boss, we were able to get down to business.

The actions that were required of the dogs were not easy. The story involved a Russian tank crew that gets lost in the Afghanistan desert, and the dogs track them. There was even an attack scene involved. This was of course the hardest to train the dogs to do, as Canaans are not the type of dog to attack without a good reason. I knew that I would not get the dogs to really attack on command, and I had no desire, really, to encourage the dogs to bite. I decided that the best way to accomplish this scene was with food. I explained to the film company just what equipment I needed for the training, and they promised to provide it.

One evening late, Dorcas and I arrived home from an evening out, and, to our horror, found a man's body lying on the porch in front of the door. After the first shock, on closer inspection we found that it was a human-sized dummy (at least six feet tall) dressed in a Russian army uniform, exact in every detail down to the boots. This was to train the dogs.

The method was simple. In the film, the dogs were meant to jump up and attack a man who was left tied out on a huge rock. So, I tied the dummy up on a terrace of about the right height, and started to hide tasty pieces of sausage in its clothes and boots. The dogs quickly learned that they would find treats if they starting searching the dummy and they quickly learned to do this with great enthusiasm, leaping up on the dummy and competing with each other to find the sausage. As I hid the treats inside the clothes and boots, and inside pockets, they learned that they would have to grab, pull, and even tear the clothes to obtain their goal. On camera, I knew, this food digging would look like a real attack. As the dogs were competing with each other, they also growled and snarled, which made it all look very authentic.

Finally, rehearsals were over and the time had come for filming. The movie was being made near Eilat, and we stayed on location. The scenes with the dogs were expected to take about a week to film.

The location was out in the desert. For the Canaans, it was like coming home; they immediately felt perfectly comfortable. It was very hot already in May, with the temperatures already close to the summer maximum. This didn't bother the dogs. As we sat around waiting for our scenes, they dug themselves deep holes under the scrubby bushes in the vicinity and lay there comfortably sheltered from the heat and glare. Being Canaans, they also very quickly took possession of the territory, and would not allow other crew members to approach 'their' bushes.

The dogs, of course, were physically in very good condition with thick shiny coats since most of them had a career in the dog show ring. The director felt that they looked too good for the role; they needed make-up! The movie's make-up expert was not enthusiastic about the idea; she had worked on all kinds of actors, but never on a dog! However, she had no choice, and the dogs ended up with all sorts of brown and black powder rubbed into their coats to make them look scruffy. The filming went well. I was very proud of the dogs' performance.

Of course, there were some difficult scenes. One was the opening scene of the film, a close up that showed the dogs sleeping on a ledge in the desert with the sun coming up. Suddenly, one dog lifts his head and alerts, and then the others also come alert. This was very difficult for several reasons.

First of all, I had to train the dogs to 'sleep,' or in other words, to lie flat and still with their eyes closed. They had to do this even though all the crew and cameras were only a foot or two away. Another difficulty was to get only one dog to raise his head first, while the others remained "sleeping." And the scene had to be shot exactly at sunrise so there was no possibility for numerous retakes. The dogs performed like troopers and I was tremendously proud of them!

In another difficult scene, I left the dogs with a few of the crewmembers, and I was taken about a kilometer or so away across the desert. The dogs were let free and I whistled to them, and they came running to me. The scene beautifully pictured a wild pack running across the wilderness.

Inevitably, the dogs, like any actors, had their moments of temperament. It was very hot, the workdays were long, and sometimes the dogs got fed up. One day, while waiting for a shot to be set up, the two males, Yitzhar and Tiggy, lost patience and decided to have a go at each other. As I tried to separate them, the bitches, inspired by the boys, decided to join in. Trying to separate five dogs on your own just doesn't work! I called to the crewmembers standing around to come and help. None of them was willing to get near that snarling mass. Finally, I just waded in, grabbed a dog, lifted it out, grabbed a crewmember, told him, "Hold on to this dog!" and went back to grab another, in the same way. In a few minutes, everything was again calm. The dogs felt better because they had worked the edge off of their nerves, and no one had been hurt. The crewmembers were not in such good shape, however; it took them a few days to get over the trauma, and I seemed to have gone up in their esteem for being ready to wade into the battle.

On another day, when I was off the set for a few hours, one of the dogs got loose, took possession, and wouldn't let anyone into 'his' part of the location. For several hours, everyone had to detour around that area, until I got back and called him off.

Finally, we got to the final scene with the dogs, which was by far the most difficult. This was the 'attack' scene. In this scene, the 'hero' of the film is left staked out on a rock in the desert by his fellow soldiers, and the pack of wild dogs, who had been tracking them throughout the movie, find him and start to attack. The hero manages to save himself by rolling a grenade into the midst of the pack, which explodes and demolishes the dogs.

As is obvious from this description, this scene was not likely to be something the dogs would enjoy doing. Of course, the 'explosion' of the grenade was simply a harmless smoke bomb. But I knew that the dogs would not at all appreciate having even a harmless smoke bomb exploding at their feet, and I had warned the director that this had better be the last scene the dogs were expected to do, because after this, they would not have fond memories of the set or the people involved. I also warned him that they had better get it right on the first take, as there was no chance that the dogs would agree to participate in a retake.

Everything was set up. The scene was being played by a stuntman since the star was not about to expose himself to the chance of being bitten by accident. The stuntman was rather nervous as well. He asked me if I was sure that the dogs wouldn't really bite, and I assured him that he was safe. He took up his position on the rock, and I planted sausage in his boots, pockets, and other parts of his clothing.

The dogs hadn't been fed that day, so that they would be really eager to get the sausage. We did a rehearsal, and everything went beautifully. The filming began. The scene was filmed several times, from different angles, with the explosion being the last shot. The dogs performed beautifully in the first shots, running up to the rock, leaping up and grabbing the sausage out of the actor's clothing and boots, which on screen really looked as if they were attacking him.

And then the time came for the last shot. The smoke bomb was set in place, the cameras rolled, the dogs were released, and BOOM!

The dogs, as one, turned and ran, heading for the distant hills. No one was going to get another chance to set off a bomb under their feet! I whistled frantically, and gradually, four of them turned back and returned to their familiar resting holes under the scrub. But the fifth, one of the bitches, Hava, continued running like a small brown streak of lightning, until she disappeared into the hills.

As this was the last shot on this location, the crew was all packed up now and ready to go home. There was a van waiting for me to take the dogs and me home. Our job was finished.

"What are you going to do now?" the driver asked me.

"Wait," I said.

The other vehicles drove off on their way home. After an hour or so, the site was abandoned except for me, the dogs, and the driver, who was not at all happy about the situation. We all sat there quietly as the sun disappeared behind the mountains. As the dusk thickened, there was a noise from the direction of the van, which was parked with the door open. There sat Hava in the van, ready to go home. Now that everyone had gone and she was sure no one would set off any more bombs, she was ready to come back.

Well, that had been an interesting experience, but I was glad that it was over. Or, I thought it was over.

About a week later, I got a phone call from the director. The shots of the attack had been damaged in the developing laboratory and were unusable. The scene would have to be shot again. Would I be willing to come down again with the dogs for a few days?

"You must be crazy!" was my first response. "These dogs are not stupid—they are not going to be willing to get anywhere near the spot where you blew them up!" But this was a critical scene in the movie.

"You have to do it for us." He pleaded. "This is one of the most important scenes in the film!"

"But I really don't think the dogs will perform," I answered.

"We'll pay you time and a half if you are just willing to come down and try," he said. "No, we'll pay you double!" This was very convincing.

"Well, okay, I'll try it," I answered, "but I certainly can't guarantee that you'll get the scene you want."

So once again the dogs and I arrived down in the desert. The dogs were definitely unhappy about the idea; the location had very unpleasant associations for them. However, I had not fed them for a day, and they were hungry, and when I got out those tasty little pieces of sausage, they started to show more interest in the idea.

Canaans are very much dogs with minds of their own, and cannot usually be 'bought' by food. However, among the five, there was one bitch, Terra, who was a true chow hound willing to do anything for a tidbit, and now she was hungry. Two of the others were also willing to consider approaching the spot in order to get their treats. The last two, true Canaans through and through, were very suspicious of the whole thing, and hung back on the fringe of the group, not willing to come up to the rock where terrible things had happened.

I informed the director that this was about as good as it would get. I also warned him that this time, there was one take only and after that, he didn't have a chance in hell of ever getting any of these dogs anywhere near this location again.

The take was a success, though in my opinion it was not as good as the first one that had been ruined by the lab. The dogs took off, but by now, having been through the whole thing before, didn't run far.

I waited eagerly for the movie to be released. I wanted to see the results of all this hard work. But *The Beasts of War* was not a great success in the U.S., and never got to the movie theatres in Israel. Finally, after a few years, it came out on video, and I managed to get a copy. I thought it was a pretty good movie, actually, and I was really proud of the dogs. They looked great on screen! All of the several weeks of work, of course, came down to a few minutes of screen time—but I was proud of it!

There was another period of a few years that I spent running around giving my own live stage show with a few of the dogs. It started as a promotional deal for a pet food company that I was working for. I went around doing a show in shopping centers, and passed out food samples and flyers after the performance. But the show turned out to be quite successful, and I continued to do it as an educational program for schools, community centers, summer camps and so on, as well as in the shopping malls.

The idea behind the show was to present the dog to the public as a friend and helpmate of people, with friendly dogs doing amusing things. I began the show by showing large posters of various breeds of dog doing useful things such as herding, hunting, police work, pulling a sled, and so on. Then I asked the children to tell me what we had to do for our dogs so that they could work for us. Of course, the answers were feeding, vaccinating, playing with them, grooming, and TRAINING! And from that introduction I went on to show them what a dog could be trained to do.

The dogs in this show were my two Border Collies, Fizzie and Bounce, and my Shiba Inu, Kito. Fizzie and Bounce loved working, though Fizzie hated it when cameras were pointed at her, at which point she would slink through her exercises. Kito put up with it, but one couldn't say that he was highly enthusiastic. But he was such a rare breed and so attractive that it was worth putting up with his moods. Bounce was highly enthusiastic about everything.

We started off with a demonstration of obedience on and off lead. This was usually done by Fizzie, and after the standard exercises, we finished off with a bit of flash, with Fizzie weaving between my legs as I walked. Then we got on to more advanced things, like retrieving. The Border collies were both maniacs about retrieving, but since the idea was to get the audience involved, I requested audience participation. I got two children up on stage and told them that we were going to have a competition. I threw a ball and one of the dogs ran to fetch it. At the same time one of the kids threw a ball and his friend ran to fetch it. Obviously, a dog ran faster than a child did; the outcome was quite clear. The Border collie streaked across the stage after the ball, and sometimes even tried to pick up both balls at once.

"Well, that wasn't very good, was it?" I said. "But I'm going to give you kids a second chance. Do you want to try again?"

"Yes, yes, we do, we do!" was the invariable reply.

"We are going to do things a bit differently this time," I told them. I walked over the far end of the stage, put two medium sized plastic bowls upside down on the floor, and under each one I put a ball.

"What you have to do now is to run to the bowl when I tell you, pick it up, and bring back the ball."

I gave the signal, and child and dog went running at full speed to the bowls. Obviously, it was much easier for the child to pick up the bowl and get the ball and come running back to me, very pleased at winning this time.

"Why do you think that the dog lost the race this time?" I asked the audience. "Because people have hands and can do things that dogs can't do."

But don't think that the border collies didn't put up a good fight, Bounce in particular. Bounce, when sent after the ball, streaked across the stage, came to a skidding stop at his bowl while slamming it with his front feet. Usually, the bowl went flying and he grabbed the ball. Sometimes the ball went flying as well and he chased it all over the stage or into the audience. Sometimes the bowl just slid along the floor, and then he kept it bouncing with his front feet until he finally got it turned over. His antics were so amazing that sometimes the kids competing forgot what they were doing and stopped dead to watch.

We then went on to demonstrate things that dogs can do better than people such as jumping, where the dogs jumped over various obstacles including a few kneeling children. We also did scent discrimination exercises in which a dog chose one object with a particular scent out of a number of identical objects.

But the trick that mystified everyone was our 'telepathy' trick. Here, Fizzie was the star. She waited offstage while I explained to the audience that she was telepathic. I collected three small items—a watch, key ring, or such—from the audience and place them on the stage.

"Okay, now choose one of these objects," I asked the audience. I then covered the objects with large plastic funnels so that they couldn't be seen. I called Fizzie in.

"Okay kids, now concentrate your thoughts on the object you chose." I sent Fizzie, and she went over and lifted the funnel that was over the object the audience was thinking about.

This was a tremendous success and no one, including several dog trainers, managed to figure out how it was done. I was begged to reveal the secret, but all I would say was that Fizzie was really telepathic. Of course, the truth was that this was just another scent discrimination exercise; Fizzie chose the funnel that had a particular scent on it, regardless of the object underneath. I was always careful to put that particular funnel over the chosen object.

The finale of the show was Kito. Kito was my 'talking dog' who answered questions by barking. Of course, Kito was not performing for free; he barked when I signaled to him, and he only did it if he got treats. But the signal was a subtle one, and many people never realized that I was signaling him. I explained to the audience that he 'spoke' with a Japanese accent and was hard to understand, so I 'translated' what he said. The audience was allowed to ask him questions, and sometimes it was amazing what he was asked, like who would win in the next government elections! I always wondered if Kito's answers had any influence on how the questioner was going to vote.

At one point, when Fizzie was in season and had to stay home, I decided to substitute one of the Canaans. Shachmat was Dorcas' personal pet. She had fallen in love with him, the one male in a litter of two, the day he was born. His flashy markings won her heart; he was shiny black with very symmetrical white markings—collar, feet, chest, tail tip and blaze on his face. He had a wonderful personality; he was happy and outgoing, full of self confidence, and very devoted. He was her constant companion, and proved to be a great show dog. He loved the show ring—what could be better than having everyone looking at him! He would prance around with the attitude "I am without doubt the best!" and the judges usually believed him. He quickly became a champion, and in a few trips abroad, gained additional wins, including the title of World Winner.

But he was more than a show dog. He loved to learn things, and Dorcas trained him for a variety of dog sports—obedience, agility, pulling a cart as well as some popular tricks like jumping through hoops. She sometimes put on shows with him at various doggy events, and he loved it—so much applause and attention!

Since Shachmat was very well-trained and had even won a few obedience competitions, I decided he would be the perfect dog to take Fizzie's place. He was thrilled with the idea of coming along, rather than staying at home all day. The first few times, he performed beautifully, enjoying being out in public and getting applause and attention again. But after a few days, he began to realize that he had to do the same exercises every time. This was boring! Being well-trained, he didn't refuse to work, but he developed his own method of working—in slow motion. He followed all the commands precisely, but very slowly, one foot at a time, sitting inch by slow inch; he even managed to jump obstacles in slow motion! I was relieved when Fizzie got back to work and Shachmat returned to his boring days at home.

Shachmat did continue to get chances to appear at shows and other events, continuing to win even as a venerable old gentleman. But life at home was not boring anymore; with the birth of my grandchildren, Shachmat became the chief guardian and babysitter, a job that he enjoyed tremendously, having infinite patience for these 'puppies'. He died at the age of fifteen, dearly loved and missed by the whole family.

Chapter Twenty-Two: Traveling

I had, over the years, done a fair amount of traveling, and most of it with dogs. I had already experienced travel by ship and by plane, and coped with Africa. I had been to England to pick up a new puppy and had delivered a puppy to a buyer in Holland. But now, I decided, it was time to hit the European dog show circuit.

To promote the Canaan Dogs, and to promote my name as a breeder as well, the dogs would have to be seen outside of Israel. There were so very few of them as yet in Europe. Financially it wasn't viable for me to travel to many dog shows, but every year in Europe there were a few prestigious shows. The most prestigious was the World Dog Show, held every year in a different country, which awarded the winning dog of every breed the title "World Champion." In 1985, the World Show was being held in Holland, and I decided to attend it and show several Canaans.

The dogs I took were Solo, Chami, and Chami's little sister, Rani, who would be in Junior Class. Chami and Rani, like many siblings, hated each other; I had to keep them well away from one another. This was not easy, as I was traveling alone and had only two hands to hold onto three dogs. As I waited in the airport to board the plane), I held Solo and Chami short in one hand, and Rani in the other, and prayed that they would not decide to start a family scrap right there. The airline company felt that they were being very humane by allowing me to keep all the dogs with me until the last minute, instead of putting them in the crates and taking them away to cargo. Fortunately, discipline prevailed and we didn't air our family grievances in the airport.

Violette met me in Amsterdam. She was the woman I had delivered the puppy to, which was the first Canaan to live in Holland, and she was very interested in the breed. She had become a friend, and I was going to stay with her.

I had never been to a show of this size before. It was huge! There were thousands of dogs of hundreds of breeds being shown. The show was divided into four days, and even though not all the dogs were there on the same day, the size of it was still awesome.

We arrived with the Canaans on the day they were to be judged and found our ring. Each dog was assigned a box where it was kept throughout the day, except when he was in the ring to be judged, so that the spectators would be able to see them. Many people stopped to look at the Canaans and asked questions. Since it was such a rare breed, few people knew what they were.

When time came to enter the ring, I was petrified. Solo went in first, and won the CACIB and World Winner title. Then it was time for the bitches. First was Rani. She was only about a year old and didn't have much experience in shows, so this whole situation was very strange for her. I took her off the bench into the ring, and Rani decided that this was walk time. She immediately squatted and peed in front of the judge.

I was mortified! The judge, however, was a dog breeder himself and didn't take it too seriously. After the ring crew cleaned up, he judged Rani and awarded her the Junior World Winner title. Chami, who behaved in a much more dignified manner, was the World Winner bitch.

At the end of the day, Solo, who was the Best of Breed, appeared in the main ring for the group competition, where he was not considered for an instant—I doubt that the judge of the group even knew what breed he was. But that did not dampen my spirits. I was ecstatic! The trip was a success!

Solo and Rani stayed in Holland with Violette; I agreed that she could have them for a year to produce a litter. In exchange for that, she would show them at more shows in Holland.

The next year, I was determined to do the World show again. But I was more ambitious. I planned to go to the U.S.—for the first time in about fifteen years—to see my family, accompanied by Dorcas, who was now thirteen. The plan was to take two collies, Glory and Jason, show them at the Collie Club of America Specialty show, visit the family, and come back through Europe. Dorcas would go on home to Israel, and I would stop off in Europe, pick up Solo and Rani, meet some friends, and go to a few shows with the four dogs, including the World Show in Austria.

Our visit to the U.S. was fun. To start with, we stayed with my brother and family in New Jersey. My brother Michael was everything my parents could have wanted. He was an actuary, working his way up the ladder very successfully in the company where he worked, married to a lovely, intelligent and attractive Jewish girl who efficiently managed a traditional Jewish household. They had three beautiful daughters, ages two to eight.

I had never met my nieces before. They were adorable. Tova, eight, was a bit shy but very self possessed, a real little lady. Rachel, six, was a darling petite blond who was curious about everything and always ready to express her opinion. Chani, the baby, was always smiling and was a real little rascal. My nieces had never really met a dog before, and having two of them as houseguests for a few days was a new and exciting experience for them. It was funny to watch the dogs and the girls interact in the back yard, as the girls learned that they could play with the dogs. Their initial fear of the unknown turned to budding affection which Glory and Jason were happy to return.

We then visited my parents in Florida. Aside from not having seen them for some time, I had never been to their new condo in Tamarack.

Florida was a huge shock to me. It was an entire state of old people, with all services and everything geared to the elderly, but these were elderly that intended to stay young at heart to the end! It was very strange and hard to adjust to seeing entire communities made up entirely of retirees, with no young people or children other than occasional visitors.

Dorcas and I had a chance to spend a few very enjoyable days at Disney World. We especially enjoyed the Epcott Center, with all the fascinating rides and exhibits that also taught so many amazing facts. Dorcas was not very daring and didn't like all the wild rides like roller coasters. At Epcott, things were more moderate and were highly entertaining. I think I enjoyed it even more than Dorcas. We ran around seeing some of the other Florida sights, of course, like the seaquarium shows, the trained parrots at Parrot Jungle, and the Miami Zoo, where the two of us rode on an elephant.

As no pets were allowed in my parents' condo, the dogs spent a few days in a nearby boarding kennel, which was as luxurious as the rest of the Florida facilities.

Dorcas stayed with her grandparents, and I flew off to Chicago to the Collie Club of America Specialty Show. I was quite overwhelmed by hundreds of gorgeous collies, and an elaborate venue—the ballroom of a luxury hotel! Needless to say, my two youngsters did not achieve a great victory, as I had dreamed of happening. But despite that, the experience was worthwhile.

Then it was time to return to Europe. Dorcas continued on to Israel, and I got off the plane in Holland with the two dogs. Violette was going to meet me with the Solo and Rani at the airport, and we were to go on together to the first show, in Germany.

I disembarked, collected luggage and dogs, and waited, but Violette did not appear. After waiting for a few hours, I tried to call her, but somehow was unable to get through. I then tried to call the friends we were supposed to stay with in Germany—again, unsuccessfully. Finally, I discovered that I was dialing wrong—I had no previous experience dealing with area codes and leaving off zeros or adding them on and such that one must do to make a long distance call in Europe. Having discovered the method, I managed to call Violette, and discovered that she was not coming. Her son was ill, and she couldn't leave him.

What could I do? Well, there was no choice really. I had to rent a car, drive up to Violette's place which was a few hours north of Amsterdam, pick up the dogs, and drive back to Germany.

I got to Violette's in the early evening. It was another five hours or so to get to Cologne where my German friends lived. Violette apologized for the change in plans, and invited me to spend the night, but I had to get to Germany for the first show. So, with the four dogs, crates, and luggage all packed into the tiny hatchback, all I could afford to rent, we set off for Germany.

I have discovered that somehow, the time that it is supposed to take to get somewhere and the time it actually takes have little relationship one to another. I should have gotten to Cologne by about nine in the evening, but there were a lot of road works on the highway, and I got on the wrong road, which was much slower. By the time I got into the city, it was after midnight.

I didn't know my way around Cologne. I had been there once, and I had a map and a vague idea of where my friends lived, but didn't really know how to get there. I also had no German money, so I couldn't even stop at a public phone or go into a bar, the only thing still open at that time of night, to call my friends for instructions. After driving around and around for a while, I was getting desperate. I was exhausted; it had been over twenty-four hours since I had gotten any sleep. What was I to do?

Then I spotted a sign–*Polizei*. A police station. They would have to help me! I parked in front of the door and stumbled out of the car.

The police officers were having a quiet cup of coffee when I dragged myself in, exhausted and in wrinkled clothes covered in dog hair. Through the glass door, they could see the heavily-loaded little car with four dog heads peering out.

I managed to explain in my very limited German that I was looking for my friends' house. They called and told my friends—already rather frantic with worry—that I was safe and sound in the police station and that they would bring me over.

As we were getting ready to leave, the officer in charge asked me why I had come to the police station. "Well," I said, "the police are supposed to help people, aren't they?" The officer looked at me in surprise and muttered that he wished the Germans thought that was the case...

The rest of the trip was relatively uneventful, although I was forever after referred to as "Myrna and her traveling Circus" by my German friends. We did well at the dog shows, and Solo once again won the title of World Winner in Austria. But I was certainly glad when we all set foot on Israeli soil once again.

The next time I traveled was in 1989 and the plan was even more ambitious. Two friends and I planned to rent a camper in Holland and travel around for a month to four dog shows. It would be comparatively cheap, as the camper would provide both our transportation and our living facilities. We would be able to stop wherever we wanted. We could also cook our own food, and wouldn't have to spend money in restaurants.

One of the friends, Zipporet, had very good connections with the airline and arranged for us to fly on a cargo flight, which saved us a lot of money on the fares of the dogs.

We met at the airport. I traveled with only one Canaan this time, Yitzhar, and with two miniature pinschers that we were showing for another friend. Motti joined us with his Doberman bitch, and Zipporet took two of her Great Danes. We also took a Viszla and a Weimaraner, which we were handling for other people.

The time came to board, and then we were notified that we could travel on this flight with the dogs, but no one was going to load them for us—we would have to do it ourselves. We trudged out to the runway with the dogs and crates, and found that there wasn't even a hydraulic lift. We had to climb up the stairs with all the crates and the dogs and load them in the proper compartment.

Loading the Great Danes in particular was an adventure! I was glad that at least two of the dogs were miniature pinschers. By the time all this was managed we were totally exhausted.

Cargo flights are not luxurious, but there was a mattress spread out on the floor behind the seats for off-duty crewmembers to rest on. I immediately took it over and slept until landing.

In Holland we picked up the camper. It looked rather old and decrepit to me, but it was also pretty cheap. Fitting everything in was not easy, but we managed. Finally, we set the crates up on the beds, and left the floor space for the Great Danes. I didn't even think of where we were going to sleep.

I was the driver. I had never driven anything like this before and found the feeling of this unwieldy vehicle very unsettling. But I managed to get on the highway in the direction of Germany. Our first show was in Budapest.

Finally starting to feel comfortable driving, I picked up speed on the Autobahn, and we were making good time, when suddenly there was a big bang from the upper level of the camper. We pulled over to the margin of the highway as soon as there was a possibility, and got out to examine what had happened.

There was a bunk over the cabin, as well as in the back of the camper. The window of the bunk had blown out and was lost somewhere behind us on the highway.

There was nothing to be done. We stopped at a petrol station, bought some masking tape and plastic sheeting and taped the plastic over the window. It was not a great solution, and frequently blew out, causing us to stop and retape it, but it kept the cold wind out.

There were no more major problems, and we managed to get to Budapest safely. However, the trip was hard. Buddy, the Viszla, was not accustomed to be in a crate; he was a pampered house pet and he spent the entire day barking at the top of his lungs. The Doberman bitch was also very spoiled and spent the days sitting on her master's lap, for otherwise she whined. The Great Danes were very aggressive to other dogs, so they had to be taken out separately and kept a good distance away while we exercised the others. Only Yitzhar took it all in his stride, staying calm and well behaved.

There were other difficulties. Motti was very slow about getting up in the morning, and it took him longer to shower and shave than it took both Zipporet and me together. I fidgeted in impatience to get on the road as he was still poking around in the shower stall. And Zipporet was very fond of shopping.

But we got to the show in Budapest, where we soon discovered that no one there spoke any of our languages—only Hungarian. There was no one to give us directions, instructions, or anything—we had to figure everything out for ourselves. We dashed from ring to ring, trying to figure out who was being judged when. Somehow, we managed to figure most things out correctly. In the middle of the day, there was also a huge cloudburst—and the show, of course, was outdoors. I was really glad I wasn't showing any collies that year! A wet collie looks rather like a greyhound dressed in a wet floor mop, and takes hours and hours to dry.

The judging of the Vizsla, a Hungarian breed, was the most interesting. There were many Vizslas at the show. The judge had us all walk around and around the ring—not at the normal show ring pace, which is a trot—at a slow amble. Meanwhile the judge was busy talking to friends at ringside. We kept on walking—this went on for at least an hour. Finally, he decided that we had walked enough, and he judged the dogs. The purpose behind this never became clear to me.

After the show, we did a bit of sightseeing in Budapest and had some excellent meals. Then we were on our way to the next show, in Austria.

Hungary was still under a communist regime, and we were stopped at the Austrian border. It was already dark and we were tired and eager to get to our next stop.

We stopped at the barricade and one of the border guards came out of the booth and walked around the camper, looking inside. As he came up to the driver's side, he looked at us and ordered, "*Raus!*" in a stern tone.

I knew a bit of German, having taken it as my required language in university. "He wants us to get out of the car," I informed my companions.

We climbed out of the camper, disheveled from a day of driving.

The guard began to give us instructions in rapid German, accompanied by waves of his hand in the direction of the camper.

I was able to catch only a few words, which seemed to be "all dogs." "Sir," I said politely in English, "we don't know German. Do you speak English?"

"*Alles* dogs, out from auto," was his reply. He was not broadcasting feelings of friendliness.

We looked at each other in bewilderment, but decided that it would not be a good idea to start to argue. We began to take the dogs out, everyone taking a few and standing a good distance from the others. The miniature pinschers we took out in their crate—we were not willing to take a chance of them escaping and running off on the Austrian-Hungarian border.

The guard did not seem to be satisfied. Meanwhile, the other guard who had remained in the booth came out to see what was going on.

"*Alles*, out von auto!" he ordered us.

Alles? Everything? It became apparent that he wanted us to unload all our luggage, dog crates and supplies. He intended to do a thorough search of the camper.

We had no choice but to start dragging everything out to the roadside. Managing to empty the camper while still holding the dogs required a lot of complicated maneuvering. While we were doing this, the door to the living area of the camper fell off; we found that one of the hinges was broken. While we struggled to get it back on, the guards stood by watching and smoking. At this time of night, there was very little traffic on this road, and we were providing a pleasant evening's entertainment.

Finally, everything was out of the camper. The guards climbed in and searched, opening every cupboard and storage space, looking under the mattresses, and then opening our luggage for a look there too. I have no doubt that they were very disappointed not to find any contraband, only clothes and dog food.

"Where you going?" we were asked.

"To a dog show," I answered.

"*Wass ist* dog show?"

"*Hundeaustellung*," I answered. This was one of my more recently acquired German terms. I pulled out the catalog of the show we were heading for.

"*Hundeaustellung* for big dogs. These are babies," he said, pointing to the mini pinschers. "Sie ist Mama." He pointed to the Doberman bitch. "*Vorboten* to sell babies von Hungary in Austria!"

Apparently he had decided that we were smuggling Doberman puppies into Austria to sell.

"No, not babies!" I exclaimed, searching frantically through my bag to find the health certificates with the birth dates of the mini-pins.

He carefully scrutinized the documents of all the dogs, consulted with his partner, and finally, reluctantly, told us that we could go.

As quickly as possible, before he could think of anything more to ask, we loaded everything up, jerry rigged a rope to keep the broken door on the camper and tied shut, and crossed the border. It had only taken about three hours.

A broken door and a window were obviously omens. Too bad I didn't realize at the time what the next problem would be.

Austria was clean and well organized as ever. The only thing that surprised me there was the judging of the Weimaraner, which is a popular breed of Austrian origin. The judge, dressed in hunting attire, entered the ring where we all stood with the dogs, and went up to each dog and made threatening gestures and loud noises. The dog I was handling was well trained and well behaved, but he reacted with a growl and a lunge forward when threatened by this funny looking stranger. I grabbed him short and told him to stop—this was absolutely forbidden behavior in shows! "Oh no, leave him," said one of the other competitors. "That is how he is supposed to behave!"

From Austria we moved on to Trieste, Italy, where we arrived two days before the show. We had not received the entry tickets in the mail before we left Israel, so Zipporet and I went to the kennel club office to pick them up. Zipporet had lived in Italy for a while, and she told me that we should get dressed nicely. "In Italy it always helps if women look good!" She had plenty of attractive clothes with her, and with her bright blonde hair and careful makeup, she looked very fashionable. I managed to look neat.

An elderly Italian gentleman was in charge of the kennel club office. We explained our purpose for visiting. He looked up the records and informed us that our entries had never arrived and we couldn't show the dogs.

This was devastating; we had come all this way for nothing!

"Can't you do anything at all?" we asked.

"I am very sorry," he answered politely. "The catalog is already printed and we cannot admit any dog that is not in the catalog. This is an FCI rule." The FCI, of course, was the Federacion Cynologique Internationale, which was responsible for all international dog shows.

"There must be some way! We have come so far, and the trip has been so difficult!"

"Sorry, madam, nothing can be done."

There was nothing left to do but to take emergency measures. We both started to cry.

The poor little man was totally flustered. "Oh no, do not cry! Please do not cry! It is not so terrible!'

We were getting a reaction—obviously this was not the time to stop crying.

The little man, an Italian gentleman through and through, pulled out his handkerchief and handed it to us.

"*Please*, stop. I will find something to help you. Just wait."

We sat in his office as he made a number of phone calls. Zipporet knew some Italian, but was unable to understand his rapid fire talk. After a few moments, he turned to us with a smile.

"You can come to the show," he said. "We make a special page of the catalog for your dogs, and will put it into every catalog. This way, it will be okay!"

This was amazing—for the club to go to so much trouble just to accommodate a few foreign exhibitors. We couldn't thank him enough.

We got our entry tickets, and had a very pleasant and successful show, with several of the dogs winning high honors.

At the end of the show we had to drive back to Holland.

As we drove towards Milan we started having engine trouble. There was no choice but to stop at a garage and have some repairs done. We were almost out of money and had to borrow some cash from a friend who was stationed in the Israeli consulate. After a lost day, we were back on the road, hopefully on our way home.

We got as far as Frankfurt. Suddenly, as we drove along, Zipporet, who was riding in the back of the camper, started to scream at me, "Stop! Stop!" I quickly pulled over to the side and looked back, to see a cloud of black smoke coming out from under the camper! We were on fire!!!

The fire was not serious–but the engine was burned out. We could go no further in the vehicle. We called the road service people and were towed to another garage, from which we called the people who rented us the camper. They would come to get us, they said.

The next day they arrived in a pickup truck. They tied a rope to the camper, loaded us all back in, and headed for Holland, dragging us after.

That was the most nerve wracking trip I have ever experienced. Motti sat behind the wheel (my nerves wouldn't allow me to drive any more) trying to keep the camper from fishtailing all over the highway as they towed us down the Autobahn at high speed in the direction of Holland.

Even carrying dogs and crates up the stairs of the plane was a relief—I was definitely ready to get home!

We were not entirely without successes, though: Yitzhar had gained titles and CACIBs at every show, and the pinschers also had been very successful. However, I think that the primary results of this particular trip were frazzled nerves.

For those involved, dog breeding is as highly competitive as football or horse racing. It is not merely a hobby, but an obsession. Breeders attempt to breed the finest possible dogs and come closest to the standard of perfection that exists for each pure breed. Proof of the quality comes at the dog shows, where each dog is judged and rated by experts. Of course, for me, in the clutches of an obsession, (and apparently a tendency to masochism), the few dog shows a year held in Israel were not enough. I was ready again travel to Europe and participate in the tough and highly competitive world of European dog shows. This time, I was experienced, and it would certainly all be better organized.

The next year's trip was to be the most ambitious yet. Due to the high expense of traveling with dogs—the cost of flying only one dog back and forth to Europe would have cost as much as my own ticket—the only way I could afford to travel was to take my own car, the little Simca van, by boat and to drive the rest of the way. So plans were made to take two of the Canaans (once again Solo and his daughter Ofrah) and two collies (two of Glory's children, Flame and Oz) to four European shows, in Austria, Germany, Denmark and Belgium. A friend, Moshe, decided to join us with his Groenendael bitch: better known perhaps as a Belgian Sheepdog. She was a large black, furry dog, elegant in appearance, extremely alert, and a bit nervy, her pricked ears constantly swiveling to seek any sounds. Three more dogs were added: two Samoyeds—big hairy white bears with sparkling black eyes and enough energy for ten—and a Gos d'Atura, a shaggy brown floor mop of a dog with a curtain of hair covering her eyes. The handling fees for these dogs helped to cover expenses. To save money we planned to camp out, so we equipped ourselves with a tent and cooking gear.

May 28 was the departure date. Everything was loaded into the car, despite the popular opinion of my fellow travelers that we would never manage. The car sank lower and lower on its overloaded springs, but we got everything aboard. The dogs had the back of the van. They had two levels; one across the seats—where we had set up two large traveling crates, in which some of the dogs traveled—and the rest in the space underneath the seats and the crates. Sundries were crammed into cracks and crannies all around. The rest of our equipment such as tent, cooking gear, clothing and dog food was tied on the roof rack. With doubts as to whether we would get there, we set off for Haifa to catch the boat.

I had traveled by ship before, but never with eight dogs. The ship was a passenger ferry, equipped to handle passengers wanting to cross over to Greece with their cars. The cabins were comfortable but not luxurious and there were plenty of basic facilities and some extras—a restaurant, snack bar, swimming pool (about the size of a decorative fishpond) and even a mini-casino—to keep the passengers comfortable for the three-day trip. The crew seemed unable to believe their eyes when we drove aboard. I asked where we were supposed to put the dogs. No one seemed to know or, in the rush and confusion of loading the ship, to care. Finally, the officer in charge informed me that I could put the dogs on the 'monkey deck.' One look at his forbidding expression and I refrained from asking where the hell the monkey deck was. Finally, one of the crewmembers took pity on me and offered to show me. Leaving Moshe with the car and the dogs, I disappeared into the ship after the crewman.

We climbed three long, steep, and very narrow staircases, and came out on a bare and windswept deck. This apparently was the monkey deck. Was this where I should put the dogs? Dogs?! The crewman knew nothing about dogs, but this was the monkey deck. As far as he was concerned, I could do whatever I wanted on it.

Ships of this size do not have elevators. The only way to get the dogs and equipment up to the monkey deck was up the three long narrow flights of stairs—past the reception, past the crew quarters, and out to the deck. By the time Moshe and I had been up and down the stairs twice, each time with a dog and a folding crate to serve as the dog's kennel, we had attracted a good deal of attention from passenger and crew. As we staggered up the stairs for the fourth time, they seemed disappointed to hear that the circus was over and no more dogs were coming up.

The dogs were set up very comfortably on their private deck; even deck passengers were not allowed to sleep there. Each had his own crate to sleep in, with an enormous canvas stretched over them all to provide shade and a windbreak. Once they were settled, we collapsed from exhaustion. It was a relief to know that we had three nights and two days on the ship to relax before the reverse trek back to the car.

The days on the ship passed very enjoyably. The weather was beautiful, accommodations were quite comfortable, and crew and passengers, once they had discovered that the dogs did not cause problems, were friendly and interested. They asked us many questions about where we were going and what we intended to do. The infamous monkey deck was just outside the communications room, and we had some nice chats with captain and crew. The crewmen also told us about their own dogs. In Greece (this was a Greek ship and the crew were almost all Greeks), the popular dogs were the hunting breeds. One crewman said he was very proud of his "German Tractor." It took me until the trip back to discover that he meant a German "drahthaar"—a wirehaired pointer.

The dogs quickly adjusted to their new living conditions and seemed comfortable. There was, however, one problem. All of these dogs were accustomed to living as house dogs, and the idea of 'doing their business' on the wooden-floored deck didn't seem right to them. For the entire first day, not one of them would do anything. By the second day, most of them, out of lack of choice, realized that they had to use the deck, and once one started, the others followed suit. Flame, my collie bitch, found it impossible to overcome her inhibitions. As time passed, I wondered if she would hold out for three whole days. Finally, on the third day, she couldn't hold out any longer and a river flowed from her!

We arrived in Piraeus on Wednesday morning. With the good wishes of the crew, who watched as we dragged down the stairs everything we had dragged up, we loaded the car and drove on to dry land—the last ones off the ship. This was in a way an advantage, as by this time everyone else had gone through customs and passport control and we didn't have to wait in line. The only thing that really interested the Greek customs people was the documentation of the car, so we were soon out on the busy streets of Piraeus, maps spread out on our knees, heading north.

Greece is a beautiful country, similar in appearance to parts of Israel, but with gorgeous, clean, unpolluted and uncrowded beaches—at least at this time of year before the start of the tourist season. As we drove further north, the landscape became more rugged and hilly. People were friendly and helpful wherever we stopped, and were fascinated by the dogs. Purebred dogs were not very common in Greece and there was no kennel club. However, hunting dogs were used, and there was even a local Greek hunting breed. The Samoyeds, which were different from any dog a Greek had ever seen, fascinated people especially.

That evening we stopped for the night in a campground along the coast not far from Saloniki, and set up our tent for the first time. We unloaded the dogs and set up their compound—crates for sleeping, covered with a canvas, tied to the surrounding trees as protection from the weather. Again we collected an audience. We answered questions about the dogs, where we were going, where we came from, and so on. As most of the campers were German, my kindergarten level German got a good workout, but I managed to communicate.

There was even one man who started asking for advice on health problems of his own dog; he assumed that because I had so many dogs, I must have the answers to all dog ailments.

Camping is very popular in Europe, and there are lovely campgrounds with excellent facilities everywhere that are clean and orderly; many of them have shops, washing machines, and so on. People travel in a great variety of luxurious vehicles—campers, caravans, vans, tents—and they are for the most part friendly and interested in meeting new people.

Here the campground was located on the beach, so we took the dogs for a good long run to work out the kinks of three days on the ship. Then we were all ready for bed.

In the middle of the night, I awoke to crashing thunder, lightning, winds, and pouring rain. A true Israeli, I had never even thought about the possibility of rain in the middle of the summer, and we hadn't put the rain cover on the tent. There was nothing to do but go out and fight the winds to get the cover on, before everything got soaked.

The next day after an early start, we crossed into Yugoslavia on our way to the first dog show, which was held in Austria. The first surprise was at the border where we had to change money. In Yugoslavia in 1989, one dollar was worth more than 16,000 dinars. At the bank, I was handed a stack of bills like you would see in an old gangster movie after a bank robbery. We just collapsed in laughter. In Yugoslavia, the prices were very low, but trying to calculate things was quite an experience. The Yugoslavs didn't seem to manage it any better.

The atmosphere in Yugoslavia was very different than that in non-Eastern bloc countries. Things were shabby and there seemed to be little pride in the appearance of property. People were not well dressed, and seemed less interested, less animated, and less friendly. But apparently the Yugoslavs made up for whatever adventure was lacking in their lives by their driving.

Driving in Yugoslavia was an experience. The roads were only two lanes and not in the best repair. The route we took was the major highway from Greece to Austria as well as the major trucking route. Long rows of trucks went past in both directions, moving at a maximum of 60 kph. Passing was impossible for me. The Yugoslavs, however, had a little game of passing between the lanes. Driver after driver in their tiny sardine-tin imitations of European economy cars zoomed along on the white line in the center of the highway while enormous trucks roared along inches away on both sides. It was hard to believe that all the way through Yugoslavia we saw only one accident.

Everything was of course government controlled, and all along the highway were large complexes of motels, gas stations, restaurants, campgrounds, all open twenty-four hours a day. The most prominent were the duty-free shops, which seemed to be the major business of Yugoslavia; every gas station, snack bar or even grocery shop had a duty-free shop attached to it.

Although all day we had seen numerous campgrounds and motels, as the evening approached and we wanted to stop, there was not one site to be seen. We drove on and on with no sign of a legal place to stop, and feared that we'd have to keep on driving all night or until we ran out of petrol—a real possibility. Finally we found a place. The campground was well kept up, although the toilets were 'Turkish style' and the mosquitoes were the size of Boeing 707s. It was quite cheap.

The next day we had to get to Austria, and the plan was to get there as early as possible, so as to have the afternoon to start preparing the dogs for the show the following day. But now we headed into really mountainous areas. This was the part of the trip that really had me worried from the start, about how well my little car would do climbing real mountains with such a heavy load. Just to add some spice to the situation, the weather had changed to on and off showers. The scenery, however, was magnificent. Even though a good part of the climbing was done at about 40 kph, there was plenty to look at—mountains, valleys, forests, rivers, waterfalls, and picturesque villages. The car took it all in stride and we made steady progress.

At the last gas station before the border, we stopped to fill up. The price of petrol in Yugoslavia was significantly less than in Austria. As we were ready to go on, we discovered that we had a flat tire. There was no way to change it but to start unloading the car so that we could jack it up. As dogs and equipment piled up alongside, we gathered our typical interested audience. People stopped to ask if we were having trouble, but no one offered to help. Fortunately, we managed to change the tire without unloading everything.

A few kilometers later we reached the border after a few very steep climbs and several tunnels. The mountainous parts of Europe are peppered with tunnels, and they are certainly convenient, saving some very difficult climbs. But there are places where you start feeling that you are under ground more than above it and I started feeling claustrophobic.

The Austrian border was at the end of one of these long tunnels. As we came out into the daylight, the border guard awaited. He didn't know what to make of all the dogs and seemed to think that we were smuggling them out of Yugoslavia. He asked many questions, which my German was inadequate to answer. He had no idea that the next day there was to be an international dog show a few kilometers away. Telling me to park, he took me into the station, where another guard had heard of the dog show, checked the papers, and decided that everything was in order. By now all the guards had become interested; they wanted to see the dogs. I trooped out of the guard station with four border police after me. They crowded around the car asking questions. Moshe looked a bit worried until I reassured him that it was just friendly interest. One of the guards had owned a Groenendael and wanted Moshe to take his bitch out of the car so that he could see her.

As all this was going on in friendly good spirits, I glanced back and saw a line up of cars from the border post back into the tunnel from Yugoslavia, all waiting quietly and patiently for the border police to finish playing with our dogs. Finally, playtime was over; we loaded back into the car and crossed over into Austria.

We found a beautiful campground on the shore of a scenic lake about half an hour's drive from the dog show grounds. The only drawback was the continuing rain. I was dressed in a sweater and my winter jacket; the Austrians and Germans at the campground, enjoying their early summer holiday, were in shorts and t-shirts. The manager of the campground was nowhere around either; the other campers told us to just move in and eventually, maybe the next day, he would show up.

The next day was the first day of the show and we had to prepare the dogs. Showing longhaired breeds like the collies, and especially the snow white Samoyeds, requires a lot of grooming and preparation, and a tent is far from the ideal grooming parlor. There was no alternative; I had to groom them outside, despite the weather. I set up a grooming table—one of the crates with a board across the top—and during short pauses in the rain, I set to work.

Under the circumstances, it was impossible to wash the Samoyeds, although they were rather dirty after a week's travel. To get them white again, I had to powder them thoroughly with a dry cleaning powder and brush it out. As clouds of powder drifted over my head, I found that all of our neighbors in the campgrounds were standing outside their caravans fascinated by the display.

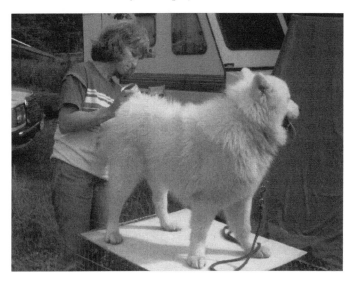

People walking by on the road that passed the campground fence also began to stop to watch. With an air of doing something perfectly normal, I continued grooming. A few people did ask what we were doing and I explained that we were showing the dogs the next day. All wished us the best of luck.

I enjoyed dog shows in Austria. They were always very well organized, people were for the most part very polite, and there were always wonderful trophies. This show was no exception. Of course, as in any show, there were the questionable moments, as when one of the judges left the ring in the middle of judging to go over and show her own dog in another ring; she did not win. But overall, we were received very well, and there was a great deal of interest from the spectators, especially in the Canaan Dogs. Before the trip, I hadn't been sure what to expect, especially in countries like Germany and Austria where other Israelis had run into problems of anti-Israeli attitudes. We, however, had no problems. The dog world tends to be very non-political; dog show people are mainly interested in dogs. When people heard that we were from Israel they responded with interest and friendliness.

After two days of showing, we returned to the campground with five enormous and impressive trophies, including one for the best pair in show, won by the collies, and another awarded to us by the local kennel club—a huge trophy to honor us for having come the longest distance to the show. They had announced proudly over the loudspeakers to the applause of the crowd that the Israel Canaan Dogs had indeed come all the way from Israel.

At the campground we set all the trophies out on the 'grooming table.' At the sight of all the booty, our neighbors came running to congratulate us, hear the story of the show, and celebrate our victories with a bottle of wine.

The next few days had us leisurely driving toward Frankfurt, the site of the next show. There we were due to meet Iris, my Dutch friend who would accompany us to the rest of the shows, and as well to pick up Dorcas, who was flying to Frankfurt to join us for ten days. The weather was better, even sunny, the scenery was lovely, and there was plenty of time to stop and let the dogs run around and relax.

We spent an afternoon visiting a collie breeder friend of mine near Frankfurt, who was speechless when she saw how we were traveling, and then we met Iris. She had come with her own car, a little Simca van just like mine, but painted a bright kelly green. It had been a postal van in Holland. Now we could unload some of the dogs and equipment to her car, and take some of the burden off of mine. We decided to find a good campground in the Frankfurt vicinity, where we could stay for the next few days, and to get settled in before Dorcas arrived the next day.

Imagine our surprise as we traveled from campground to campground only to be turned away because they were full up and anyway, no dogs were allowed. This was the first time we had ever had such a problem, or met such an attitude regarding the dogs. Everything in this area was also much more expensive than in other places we had camped. Finally, after a whole day of driving around searching, we found a place willing to take us for one night, with an extra charge per dog. Having little choice, we spent the night there. As the guests at this campground all seemed to be transient workers, mostly Turkish, we were glad to have the dogs, and glad to leave early the next morning.

The next day was also spent in searching, and following maps and directions. Each campground that turned us down recommended some other place that turned us down and recommended another...and so on. Iris led us in her car down all sorts of confusing, winding narrow roads and through numerous villages too small to appear on the map. I was amazed at how well she found her way around. Only later did I learn that she had a compass in her car. Finally we did find a pleasant campground forty minutes away from the show site. Not only did they have no objections to our dogs, there were many other dogs in residence. Our immediate neighbors were a young Yugoslav couple working in Germany who had a friendly little Kleinspitz that immediately came running over to inspect us. We got the tent set up and the dogs settled in just in time for me to dash to the airport to pick up Dorcas.

Dorcas had her own problems as well. The girl who was taking care of the kennels while we were away had disappeared for two days with a new boyfriend. Dorcas had been on the verge of notifying the police and canceling her flight, when Natalie reappeared; she had simply never thought to notify anyone that she was going to be away for two days since no one had ever cared before.

It turned out that all of our breeds were being judged on the second day of this show, so aside from once again thoroughly grooming everyone, there was time available for sightseeing in Frankfurt. Fortunately at this campground there was a hose available where we could wash the dogs that needed it, so I didn't have to resort to the powder again. I was amazed at how little traffic there seemed to be for such a big city. Prices of things in shops also were considerably lower than back home. The weather was beautiful, so we walked around the mall in the city center, full of strolling people and street performers of all sorts.

Although Germany had a reputation for organization and precision, the dog shows there were a different matter. The time schedule was a joke, the benches where the dogs were supposed to be kept were impossible to find, and the ring organization, noise level and confusion were indescribably bad.

Some of the stewards were downright impolite. No one there was impressed or interested that we had come from Israel.

The Germans are also very stingy with prizes: there were no trophies, unless the individual breed clubs had provided them. Winners received only a certificate. Each participant did get a souvenir, though, a picture book of Frankfurt. At the end of the day, we had eight identical books of Frankfurt to take home. We did, however, collect four CACIBs—two for the Canaans, one for the Groenendael, and one for the Gos d'Atura. We were not very impressed by the quality of the dogs at this show. There were a few excellent dogs but many more mediocre ones. Entries were large, with a wide variation in type in many breeds.

The next day we were up early to start for Denmark. Our plans were to get to our camping place near Copenhagen by evening where we would spend the next week in the same campground—what luxury!

It took us about fourteen hours to get there, which included an hour on the ferry from Germany to Denmark, a very lavish ferry indeed. However, in northern Europe in the summer there is full daylight until about eleven p.m., so we arrived and settled in at the campground before dark.

The campground was in a lovely location just a few minutes walk from the sea and on the edge of a large forest with many paths where we could walk the dogs. We chose a camping spot just on the edge of the forest, and every day the dogs got a chance to run for several hours. The hedgehogs in the forest fascinated them—and maybe other things we didn't see.

The week before the show was quite a restful time, which we spent sightseeing in Copenhagen and Tivoli. It was a welcome change to be able to stay in the same place, to do some laundry and have time to hang it out to dry; these were the little comforts of home.

The 1989 World Dog Show of Copenhagen was divided into three days of judging. The entries were enormous; there were about 10,000 dogs altogether of several hundred different breeds. There were even large entries in many of the rare breeds, when normally it was unusual to see more than one or two at a show. But what was most impressive was the overall outstanding quality of the dogs. I was really impressed by the high standard of the dogs in the ring. Titles won in this show were well deserved.

The show was held in the Bella Centre, a massive and fairly new convention hall on the outskirts of Copenhagen. The organization was super, but there were some unexpected problems. The indoor rings were very large, but the floor was very slippery. The show management had therefore laid carpet runways, rather like you might expect to see in a fashion show, for the dogs to be gaited on; however, not all the dogs were enthusiastic about being moved on this narrow strip of carpet. There were also many rings outdoors. Here there were also problems with the floor—the weather was unexpectedly beautiful, with shining sun and high temperatures (for Denmark, anyway), and the rings were all in the sun. The pavement heated up and the dogs trotted around as if they were crossing a bed of hot coals. Although the show management hosed down the floors to try and cool them off, it was not enough to keep the dogs comfortable. In this, our Israeli dogs had a bit of an advantage because they were used to the heat.

Our dogs were once again due to be exhibited on the same day. Early that morning, I took the dogs out for a good run to stretch their legs and relax them before the hard day ahead. Taking the two collies and the two Canaans, I followed the forest paths I had become familiar with. My mind wandered as I thought of the show and daydreamed of fantastic victories.

Suddenly, I realized that the part of the trail we were walking down did not look familiar. We came to a crossroads that also looked strange, and of course there were no signposts on a forest trail. Soon I found myself wandering up and down various paths at random, with no idea of where I was. I was lost in a Danish forest when I had to get to a dog show! I was starting to feel quite panicky—the time was getting short, and we had to get back to the showground. What was I going to do? I walked faster and faster, but still had no idea where I was. Even the dogs were getting tired. I began to feel really panicked. How long would I have to wander around in the forest before I met someone or found my way out?

Then I heard a familiar sound: the sea! If I could get to the beach, I could then figure out where I was. I rushed in the direction of the sound and came out on a hillside above the beach. One look around and I knew where I was. Orienting myself, I started rushing back in the direction of the campgrounds, the dogs panting after me.

How happy I was to see the gate of the campground, and everyone else standing around the cars waiting for me to show up.

"Where the hell were you?"

Totally out of breath and barely able to speak, I answered, "I just wanted to give the dogs a good run before the show." I was never going to admit to any more than that!

All the dogs did respectably, but our stars were the Canaans. Solo gained his fourth World Winner title and his young daughter won the title as well. The Gos D'Atura, however, found herself competing for the first time against other dogs of her breed, including some of the top from Spain and Portugal, and this time she was rated only very good and not excellent. Well, you can't win them all.

The group and best in show judging was put on with a real flair, with music, national costumes, trumpets, light shows, obedience and agility demonstrations. We were left with a feeling of having really seen something special, both from the standpoint of dogs and of showmanship. Then it was time to get organized for our next move. My daughter was to fly back to Israel the next day, and we were to continue on to Holland, on our way to Belgium and the last show on the agenda. .

My daughter's flight left Copenhagen in the late afternoon, so it was late by the time we got on the road to Holland. We had planned to spend the night at the house of a good friend of mine in the north of Holland, but by the time we crossed the border, it was two o'clock in the morning. Although my friend did habitually keep very late hours, I decided that this was really too late to appear on her doorstep, so we stopped by the roadside, unloaded dogs and sleeping bags, and managed to get a few hours of sleep without being rained on. In the morning, we discovered that we had gone to sleep less that a half-hour's drive from my friend's house.

We spent the next few days visiting friends and dog people of interest in Holland. The most noteworthy people we met were a young couple who bred Groenendaels in the south of Holland. They lived in a very old and very ramshackle farmhouse on the outskirts of a small town. There were about forty dogs, divided into a number of groups. Each group had its own room in the house; there was a group of five in the living room, another few in the kitchen, another group lived in the laundry room, and one group had the kennel runs out back. Most of the day and a good part of the night were spent letting one group out to run in the fields, and then after an hour or so, changing to another group, and so on.

The people were very friendly and hospitable, and invited us to stay with them for a few days. Their life style was rather mystifying. The toilet, for instance, had to be flushed with a bucket of water. As there were several rather aggressive Groenendaels who lived in the corridor outside the toilet, I was very hesitant to use it at all. Then, the shower was also out of use, since one of the twenty or so cats of the household had taken it over to raise her family. Meals were catch as catch can, and often came straight from the nearby chips shop. But they had very good dogs. Some people will sacrifice a lot for the sake of breeding.

The next show was in Belgium, in a beautiful part of the country close to the Holland and Luxembourg borders. This was a new show, the first year it was being held, and in addition to being international, it was also a country fair, with a cat show, stock exhibitions, demonstrations of hunting and herding dogs, and innumerable other features. The dog show was held in an enormous stockyard building. The weather was gorgeous: sunny and hot. Unfortunately, in Europe they never count on sunny weather, so all rings were inside, packed between the benches where the dogs had to be kept.

There were many dogs, many rings, and also many spectators. As the morning went on, it became stiflingly hot in the building, and pushing through the crowds to get to the rings was exhausting. Of course, all of our breeds were scheduled to be judged in different rings at the same time. I tried to explain in French to the ring secretary that I had to be in several rings at the same time. French was all that most of the officials spoke. My French is much less fluent than my German, so you can imagine the results.

The judging did not go according to the time schedule and I spent the day running from ring to ring to see who had to be shown where when. Somehow we did manage to get all the dogs into their respective rings in time to be judged, though in some cases it was pure luck. But at the end of the day, with all of us in a state of total exhaustion, we had very satisfactory results. The Canaans had each won a CACIB, as had the Samoyed bitch, and the collie bitch had a Reserve CACIB.

I am often asked by non-doggy people if there is at least a monetary prize when we do manage to win. No, I have to answer, we are doing it only for the honor.

Well, that was it for the shows. Now we had to get back to the boat and home. We said goodbye to Iris after the show; she was returning to Holland with the collie bitch and the Groenendael bitch that were to be bred and then sent back. But everything else was loaded back into our one little car and we were on the way. We had three and a half days to cross Belgium, Germany, Austria, Yugoslavia and Greece to get to the boat on time.

The first day on the road we seemed to be driving without getting anywhere. Road signs were difficult to follow, roadwork was ongoing, some of the roads on the map didn't even seem to exist, and we drove in circles. Finally, we managed to get on to the right autobahn and ended up near Munich for the night.

As we settled into the campground in exhaustion (already a natural state of affairs for us), one of our neighbors came over to ask about the dogs. When he heard that we were from Israel, he beamed proudly, and let flow a flood of excited German; I felt I was drowning as I tried to pick enough out of the flow to understand what he was saying.

Apparently he was a Jehovah's Witness whose greatest dream in life was to visit Israel. He couldn't believe that we had actually come all the way from Israel—and in that car! and with all those dogs! and so on. He called his friends over to introduce to us, and all in all, it was a great public relations success for Israel. I won't be surprised if one day, when his dream comes true, he comes knocking on my door. He gave us a large stack of Watchtower magazines, the publication of the Jehovah's Witnesses. In German, of course.

The next day, we drove out of Germany, across the corner of Austria and into Yugoslavia. As usual, it was raining. Mountain driving with a heavily loaded car is not much fun in the rain.

When we arrived at the Yugoslav border station, we expected to be able to cross quickly. After all, we still had the visa we had been granted when we passed through on our way north from Greece. This bit of cardboard was marked as being good for thirty days, and we were still within the time limit.

The border guard took a look at it, glared at me, and asked where our visa was. In a state of confusion, I replied that when we had crossed Yugoslavia from the other direction, we had been given to understand that this was a visa. With a pitying look expressing that it was hard to believe that I could be so stupid, I was ordered to park the car and go inside.

The border station was empty. I stood by the desk and waited, but no one appeared. Finally, after about fifteen minutes, I went over to the next counter—currency exchange—to ask where the visa clerk was. With a gesture, the clerk pointed at the border guard who had sent me inside. He was sitting in his booth carrying on an animated conversation with one of the other guards. I returned to the counter to wait. Some time later, he entered, scowled at me, gave me another slip of cardboard that was identical to the first one he had confiscated, charged the visa fee again, and sent us on our way.

We decided to play smart this time and go through Yugoslavia by a scenic route, thereby avoiding all the problems of truck traffic. The route on the map was somewhat longer, but was marked as being a good road and very scenic. Without all the trucks, we were sure we could make good time.

Well, it was very scenic, spectacular, in fact. The road wound along the coast, revealing mountains and gorgeous seascapes, off-shore islands, beaches and picturesque towns. It was also absolutely impossible to travel more than 60 kph on this road, and that was only when we were lucky enough to strike one of the rare straight stretches. I was really impressed by the great beauty of the country, but also by the rapidly dwindling amount of time we had left to catch the boat home. That day we drove until eleven at night and then stopped at a motel. In Yugoslavia, tourist facilities are open twenty-four hours a day; they don't want to take any chances of missing out on foreign currency. When we checked the map, we were discouraged by the distance we had covered that day; we still had a long way to go and only one and a half days left until the ship sailed.

I wanted to get an early start the next morning and the motel manager assured us that we could check out at six a.m. However, we found at six that he hadn't yet received the updated currency exchange rates. These apparently changed every day, thus making the price of the accommodations variable. Finally, after an hour of calculations with a calculator, pencil, and head scratching, he managed to work out what we owed and we got on our way.

We drove steadily through the day, with only short stops to give the dogs a break. But by late afternoon we were still a good distance from the Greek border, and we still had all of Greece to cross. There was no choice but to keep on driving through the night.

On the map, we saw a road that looked as if it could provide a short cut, saving us a good distance of driving along the coast. According to the map, it was a good secondary road.

My advice to all travelers is that Yugoslavia is a wonderful and inexpensive country to visit with spectacular scenery, but only if you are not in a hurry to get anywhere. Never take secondary roads unless you have lots of time, a jeep, and don't suffer from fear of heights. The good secondary road turned out to be a one-lane road, which after the first few kilometers—where it was in good repair—was full of potholes. The road climbed up the mountains in an endless series of hairpin turns. Just the thought of meeting another car was terrifying. However, we soon realized that there wasn't much chance of that. There was no railing at the margin of the road, only a few rocks here and there. As we climbed higher and higher, the view was absolutely incredible; the mountains and the sea, with tiny villages below and islands offshore, were all bathed in the glow of the setting sun. It was the type of view you get from an ascending aircraft but not quite so enjoyable when viewed from my laboring little car climbing up a mountain in the uninhabited wilds of Yugoslavia.

We finally reached the top, which seemed to be thousands of meters high. And what was on the other side? Of course! Another mountain. The road wound down into a valley and then climbed up again even higher.

I had the feeling that this short cut might be the worst mistake of the trip. We started down and near the bottom of the valley passed a village consisting of three houses and several cows, with the population, including the cows, staring at us in total astonishment. They didn't get much traffic through there and certainly nothing like us.

Several mountains and villages later, as it was getting dark, we got back to the main road. Civilization! Even Yugoslavian civilization was a welcome relief.

Main roads in Yugoslavia are two lanes; that was about the only improvement. It was by now very dark, and had started to rain. We had no choice but to go on driving through the night. When I looked at the distance on the map that we still had to cover by four the next afternoon, when we had to board the ship, I began to feel quite uneasy.

Probably the darkness was to our benefit. I think that if I had been able to clearly see the road we were driving on, I never would have been able to do it. It wound along the edge of the mountains, frequently cutting through in long tunnels, and from what we could see, followed the edge of an abyss. As it got later and later at night, traffic became very infrequent, not that there was ever much on this road. Mostly there were trucks and buses, traveling at a speed I never would have dreamed of trying on those roads. There were some villages along the road, but all were dark and silent. I found the signposts along the way very difficult to follow; the spelling of the same place could be very different on different signs, and some signs appeared to be in Greek letters and some in Cyrillic. I had visions of wandering by mistake into Albania—the border was nearby—and never being seen again.

Just to make matters worse, the radio died. When I drive, I always like to have the radio on; it keeps me alert. During this trip we had heard everything from Greek folk music to Turkish pop to German spirituals, but as long as there was something it was all right for me. But then the radio just quit, which was a real blow. My companion Moshe was not much help; he spent most of the driving time sleeping soundly.

Even though I tried to keep him awake to talk to me, he kept dropping off after a few minutes of conversation.

It was a long night but by morning, we were back on the main highway of Yugoslavia that we had so scorned at the start of the trip, on our way to the Greek border. How happy we were to be back with the familiar trucks and traffic after a long, rainy and solitary night.

We were now able to pick up speed. At about eight in the morning we crossed the border in Greece with no problems other than having to wait in line for some time. And then we were back on the good Greek highways, ready for the last sprint for the boat.

Exhaustion does funny things. I sang to myself to the rhythm of the car wheels, which seemed to be singing different songs to me. While not as good as a radio, singing gave me something to occupy my mind. We stopped only to fill the gas tank and to take the dogs out for short walks. The poor dogs behaved very well during these two crazy days.

We made it! At just about four in the afternoon, the listed embarkation time, we were in Piraeus at the port. After a half-hour or so of running back and forth to police and customs and so on, we were ready to board. I was so glad to see that ship! Even knowing that we still had to drag all the dogs and equipment up to the top deck, it was a welcome sight.

Our friends on the crew recognized us immediately, ran over to the car to say hello and asked how we had done. They moved us to the front of the line to board. This time, we were better organized and they were cooperative, and the unloading went quickly. The crew was proud to hear of the victories of their four-legged passengers.

We and the dogs needed the next two and a half days of rest in the sun. The other passengers were very interested to hear of our odyssey. By the time we reached Haifa, we were rested and ready for the last effort.

For the last time, we dragged dogs and crates down the stairs and loaded everything into the car. Passing through customs to get back into Israel, even though we had nothing to declare (our budget on this trip had definitely not allowed for shopping), took over three hours, which was longer than the total time at all the other borders we had crossed. We certainly were home!

Chapter Twenty-Three: Courage

Bounce's name was a definition of his spirit; he never seemed to have all four feet on the ground. He was a Border Collie from a line of splendid working dogs, and from the day he stepped out of his crate at the airport on his arrival from Italy at the age of four months, his life was a pageant of activity, enthusiasm, curiosity, and joy. He was not content on the way home to sit in the back of the car like a dog; rather he insisted on sitting on the front seat, so that he could watch my every move and at the same time see everything going on through the window.

His name was quickly decided upon after watching his enthusiastic leaps into the air; nothing else would have suited him. He became my constant companion.

Like all Border Collies, he learned everything very quickly and was always eager to do new things. Of course, some of the things that he found to do were not very desirable, such as chewing holes in the wall-to-wall carpet. But by the time he was one year old, he already appeared as a performer in educational programs I led in schools and community centers. He did everything with incomparable gusto and joy. He was very popular with the school children; he tirelessly fetched anything they wanted to throw for him, and loved to play games with them, always, however, taking care to be very gentle despite his speed.

We also began visiting an institution for the handicapped several times a month. Bounce didn't need any explanations of what it meant to be handicapped; he quickly understood that these people, confined to clumsy wheelchairs, were limited in their abilities to play with him. He began, on his own, to deliver his toys to the hands of the physically limited, in some cases even jumping up and setting his ball down on the tray of the wheelchair, well in reach of the hands of the person. Even I was stunned by the brilliance of his perceptions, not to mention the astonishment of the nurses and staff. From week to week, we saw an improvement in many of the patients who practiced in order to be able to throw the ball more effectively for Bounce to fetch.

Then one day, when Bounce was two and a half, I noticed a slight twitch in one of his hind legs. At first, I thought that he must have banged it or otherwise injured himself. He seemed to be perfectly fine otherwise, in great spirits, and with his usual good appetite.

But after a few days, I noticed that the twitch had become slightly more pronounced. Worried, I took him to the vet.

After a thorough examination, my vet decided that there was some sort of neurological problem, and prescribed some medication that was intended to relax him and cause healing. However, there was no improvement and the twitch became more pronounced. Even when Bounce rested the leg twitched incessantly, and sometimes, while sleeping, Bounce moaned in time to the movements of his leg. He began to develop sores on his leg and foot from the constant rubbing against the floor. I brought home a special basket with a soft cushion for him, to try and prevent the chafing, but the sores continued to develop.

The next step was to take him to the veterinary hospital for further examination. The diagnosis was distemper. The doctors in the hospital could see in my eyes how much I loved this dog, and did not want to give the worst prognosis. They prescribed Phenobarbital, and explained that there was a chance that the disease would stop progressing and remain as a single twitch, pronounced and obvious, but something that Bounce and I could learn to live with. But how was it possible? I asked, Bounce has been vaccinated! There was no answer for that either.

Bounce, of course, had no conception of being sick. His spirits were as high as ever, and he ignored the twitch in his leg, running and jumping as he had done before, and ignoring the instability that caused him sometimes to stumble. It was only when he was asleep that I heard the soft moans under his breath, in rhythm with his twitching foot.

As the days went by, the twitch slowly became more and more pronounced, and I began to see a slight twitch in his second hind leg as well. I was in despair. What could I do? But I was not prepared to give up. Bounce didn't know what giving up was, and I could do no less. I decided to consult a veterinarian friend who dealt in homeopathic treatment.

I can't say that homeopathy is more effective than conventional medicine, but it has one great advantage—a homeopath never gives up. If one treatment doesn't work there is always another. I desperately needed to know that we could continue to try, and perhaps find something to stop the insidious progress of the disease. Bounce wanted as much to live as I wanted him to.

If this was a novel, then a miracle would have occurred, the disease would have been cured, and Bounce would have lived a happy life. But the disease, despite everything we tried, continued to progress in real life. The twitch spread until all of his legs were affected, and he was hardly able to control his hind legs at all. I had to carry him out of doors to do his business, but once he was out on the grass, he made a supreme effort to stand and keep himself clean. He followed me all the time with his eyes, and tried with all his strength to get on his feet and come after me. Stumbling and falling, he never gave up, always getting up to try again, picking up his toys to try and bring them to me so I could throw them for him to fetch, as in the past. My heart broke as I watched.

He developed friction sores on all his legs and feet, which I kept bandaged and padded as best I could. His appetite became very poor, but I tried to find things that would tempt him to eat.

In our consultations, both the vet and I were very aware of the deterioration of Bounce's condition. But when she saw how alert he was, how hard he tried to function, how much he wanted to live, she, as I, did not have the heart to come to a decision to "put him out of his misery."

Bounce was only a dog. Therefore, he never knew how to feel sorry for himself, to complain, or to look for pity. He only knew that he had to try ever harder to do the things he had been bred for—to be a loving companion and to serve his beloved master. All he knew was to face life with courage, and when the end came he faced death in the same way.

After months of attempted treatment, when Bounce could no longer get up at all, I knew it was the end. He wouldn't eat. I had to face the fact that there was no point in continuing his suffering.

I had hardly slept or eaten myself for days. That morning, as I woke up and looked at him lying on his thick cushions next to my bed, I was sure that he was gone. But as I got up and knelt beside him, he lifted his head one last time, licked my hand, and died.

Chapter Twenty-Four: The Wet Finger of God

I was at work in Tel Aviv when I was called to the phone. Tzvika, my son-in-law, his voice sounding shaken, was on the line with the terrifying announcement,

"There is a forest fire all around the farm. We have been evacuated, and I'm afraid that everything is gone!"

There was no time or possibility for more talking—all he could tell me is that he, Dorcas, and my infant granddaughter, Bar, were safe, but that he had no idea what the situation was at home.

Within minutes, I was in the car, on the way home. It was just after noon of a typical early July day, exceedingly hot, as it had been for the last few days, but nothing appeared out of the ordinary—not until I approached Latrun, about seven kilometers from home, and saw the huge black cloud of smoke covering the sky ahead of me, in the direction of home. I began hearing reports on the radio of a major forest fire burning out of control from Sha'ar Hagai in the direction of Shoresh—the next village beyond us! That meant that my home was in the middle of it!

As I approached the Sha'ar Hagai junction—only two kilometers from there to home—I ran into a huge traffic jam. All traffic was at a standstill. Always very law abiding, this time I drove like I have never driven before, weaving from lane to lane around the standing cars, zooming down the road margins on both sides, anything I could think of to get to the end of the traffic jam and beyond, to get home!

At the Sha'ar Hagai junction, there was a police barricade, which was the reason for the traffic backup. No cars were being allowed through, and nothing was coming through in the other direction from

Jerusalem either. As I stopped next to the police cars blocking the road and looked ahead, I saw why. The forest ahead was a wall of flames and smoke as far as I could see on both sides of the entrance to the *wadi*, and ahead as well. The fire had jumped the wide four-lane highway, and driven on its way by the wild *khamsin* wind of the unseasonably hot day, raged through the beautiful but summer-dry pine forest,. The pines were not burning, but exploding into flames, and the dry pinecones were catching on fire, bursting, and scattering the flames even further.

I begged the police at the barricade to let me through.

"I have to get through! My house is there, only two kilometers. I don't know where my daughter is, and we have a lot of animals. My dogs will die if I can't get there!" I begged.

"I understand, but we just can't let you go. Look at how strongly it is burning! We can't let anyone through," the police officer in charge explained.

Tears in my eyes, I protested, "My dogs depend on me! I can't abandon them there! I have to go on!"

"Human life is more important that the life of animals. I am sorry, I know how painful it is, but we can't let you go. We can't let you risk your own life. As soon as it is safe enough, we will let you go."

I stood helplessly next to the police cars, listening to the reports coming through on the police radio. The fire was totally out of control and raging onwards, driven by the unceasing wind. Settlements were being evacuated. Shoresh, the settlement beyond us, was burning. Neve Ilan was being evacuated and homes there were burning. Fire trucks roared through from all parts of the country, from Hadera, Netanya, and Haifa. Helicopters passed overhead with enormous containers of water to be poured on the flames from the sky.

I kept begging the police to let me through, and they kept refusing. They tried to help, offering me water to drink, and a slice of a watermelon that they had. The weather was extremely hot—it turned out to be the hottest day in years, or some such statistic—but I never felt it. I couldn't think of anything except the dogs, depending on me for everything, and abandoned there, alone and unprotected. One of my greatest fears was that some good Samaritan, from the fire fighting crews, would decide to help them by opening the gates, turning my dogs loose to run in a panic into the burning forest.

I sat by the roadside and cried—for the dogs, which were surely dead, at my failure to do anything to help them, in frustration and futility, at seeing my whole life go up in smoke. I didn't know what I would do.

There were many little dramas going on around me. People who were annoyed at the traffic jam came up and yelled at the police with no comprehension of what was going on. A band due to appear at a very important wedding that evening in Neve Ilan were desperately trying to find out what was going on, although from what I heard on the police radio, there was certainly not going to be any wedding in Neve Ilan that evening! News crews of all sorts were coming and going, interviewing people, and photographing everything.

After about three hours, except for a few occasional flare-ups the flames were no longer visible. I spotted a police car coming up to the barricade from the direction of the fire, and discovered that it was the car of the officer in charge of the barricade. I ran after him, and once again pleaded to be allowed to go to the farm.

After hearing from the other police about my vigil at the barricade, and consulting over the radio, he agreed to take me in his car, with the warning that I was not to get out of the car, no matter what, without his permission. I would have agreed to anything just to get home. I jumped into the squad car, and we started into the *wadi*.

Around us was desolation and destruction. Everything was black and smoking; here and there flames still crackled. The beautiful forest was charcoal, with occasional green branches, or an entire tree that by some miracle had been skipped over by the flames. It was hard to breathe; a pall of acrid smoke and heat hung over everything.

We came to the dirt road entry to the farm and turned in. At the entrance, there were a few green trees, sheltered by the bulk of the water pumping station behind them. In the entrance, the police officer stopped the car and turned to me.

"You know that what you see up there may be very hard and even horrible," he said.

"I know," I replied, "but I have to go up there." After seeing all the destruction around me, I was sure that all I would find were blackened corpses.

At the top of the road, I was astonished to find that Dorcas, my daughter and Tzvika, my son-in-law, had gotten there before me. They had been evacuated to the other side of the fire, had taken the baby to Tzvika's mother in Jerusalem and managed to get back from the other side, just minutes before me. A fire truck and crew were there too, checking things out, as well as Tzvika's father Moshe, who was in the civil guard and on duty, and, another surprise, our friend Ofer, who had come from Mevasseret just beyond the range of the fire.

As I got out of the squad car, Dorcas, Tzvika, Moshe and Ofer all yelled down to me, "The dogs are all right!"

I couldn't believe it. I ran down to the kennel first. The lock on the gate was broken. I later found out that Ofer had broken in to check on the dogs. The trees, tall grass and weeds behind the kennel and around the sides were burned and black but the kennels themselves were untouched; the wooden doghouses were whole and unscorched, and the dogs were all right! They were covered with soot, but happy to see me, and without harm. Even the litter of two-week-old puppies was fine.

I ran upstairs. The dogs were all running loose in the yard and looked unharmed. Kito, the Shiba Inu, was very stressed. The Border collies, running like maniacs as usual, were scratched up but otherwise looking well. I let them and Kito into the house, and started counting heads.

All the collies were accounted for and looked fine. Poor old Twinkle, at twelve years old, was a bit shaky on her legs, but seemed to be all right otherwise, and the others, aside from being dirty, looked unharmed. The young Canaans also looked unharmed, but were frightened and stressed. But one was missing—the four-month-old puppy who was due to go to a new home in a few days. She hadn't come to greet me. I looked around the yard, in the pens, and in the boxes but there was no sign of her.

Finally, I found her on the porch at the side of the house, flattened to the ground, and pressed against the door of the house, afraid to move, afraid to answer my calls, but unhurt. Everyone was all right!

I entered the house. During all the time I waited to get past the barricade, I never once thought about the house and its contents burning, and now, when I entered the house, containing everything that I possessed in this world (and that not being very much, either), it was the first that I realized that everything could have been lost.

But there was absolutely no damage. There was a bit of ash that had blown in through the windows, but the house wasn't even particularly dirty!

Dorcas was the heroine of the day. She had been at home alone and without a car when she noticed the haze of smoke in the direction of the road. She telephoned the fire department that was already in action and approaching. When she saw the smoke clouds coming in the direction of the farm at high speed, she grabbed the garden hose and began to wet down everything she could. She let the dogs out of the kennel next to the house and opened the gate to the garden where there was a damp green lawn, and tried to soak them all with water. She tried to fight the flames that she could now see approaching the fences, but finally was forced by the heat, flames and suffocating smoke, to flee down to the road, where she was evacuated by the police who were clearing the area. She carried in her arms with her one little Shiba bitch—the only dog she could manage to take with her. Tzvika arrived with their car to pick her up and wanted to go up to the farm to take some more dogs with him, but the police wouldn't allow it. From the road, they saw the flames burning fiercely along the fence line.

"When I got here," Ofer told us, "everything was totally silent. I can't remember it ever being so absolutely quiet here. No cars on the road, no dogs barking, nothing! Just a bit of crackling here and there from branches that were still burning. I broke the lock on the kennel gate and went in, sure that all the dogs were dead and everything burned down. But the dogs were all sitting there, pressed against the far wall of the kennel, as far as possible from the fire, not moving or barking, just sitting there."

"They must have been frozen in panic," I said.

"Well, they got over it pretty quickly. When they saw me coming, they got up, shook themselves off, looked around and saw there was no more fire, and started to bark at me."

The flames had reached the wall of the kennel, but wooden dog houses inside the kennel, not more than a meter or two from the flames, were undamaged. The dogs upstairs in the yard of the house were filthy and covered with mud and soot, but were also unharmed. Dorcas and Tzvika arrived and immediately wet everything down to prevent the flames from flaring up again, and then I arrived.

Everything around us was desolate. Where there had been a beautiful forest, there was only blackness now. The heat had been so intense that a large heavy-duty plastic shipping box that had stood outside the gate was not melted but actually vaporized; only a small pile of ash remained. The fire had burned everything up to the gate of the house, up to the fence around the kennels, but had not crossed the fence line, before continuing on. In the midst of the black desert of ash, the garden of the house still remained green and flowering.

Why? Perhaps because I had always been scrupulous about keeping the dogs' yards clean of thorns and weeds. Perhaps because we had tried to grow decent lawns and nice gardens, which were kept green and watered, even in the height of the long, dry summer. Certainly Dorcas' efforts to protect the dogs and the property had helped. And perhaps, as was so well expressed by a good friend, because God laid his wet finger on the farm.

Fifteen years have passed since the fire. The dogs, animals that are very capable of adapting, quickly returned to the norms of daily life. But I am sure that deep within, there will always remain a scar caused by the terror of that day. The hillsides around us have been cleared and replanted. But it will be many years before I can walk the dogs again through a beautiful green forest.

Chapter Twenty-Five: Baba

There are a lot of ways of attracting attention in this world. Not having ever been one of those girls who stops traffic simply by walking down the street, I managed to find an even more effective method—walking around town with a hyena on leash.

By the time of Baba's arrival, Sha'ar Hagai was a well-established kennel, specializing in breeding the Canaan Dog, the native breed of Israel, and my own first love, collies. We also had horses, cats, chickens, ducks, goats and rabbits.

I had also managed by this time to become more or less respectable. I worked as a research technician in animal behavior at Tel Aviv University, which my mother accepted.

At the time, I worked with birds. Although I do like birds (actually, I can't think of any type of animal that I don't like), my major interest has always been in mammals. After about a year of chasing crows and seagulls that were tired of cooperating, I looked for something more challenging.

What could be more challenging than raising a hyena cub? I pestered my boss until he agreed that it would indeed be a wonderful idea to do a behavioral study on a hand-raised hyena. The only problem was obtaining one.

Chapter Twenty-Six: Why a Hyena?

There are several different types of hyena, but one thing that they all have in common is their bad reputation. The spotted hyena, the largest and most aggressive member of the family, found on the plains of Africa, is a source of deep primitive fear among the native tribes-people. The animal's weird laughing noises, its crazy giggle, makes you feel like laughing back in terror. Its slinking nocturnal movements are considered proof that it is under the control of supernatural powers.

In Africa, where witchcraft is a common practice, the hyena plays an important role in folklore, perhaps more than any other animal. People known to be witches ride hyenas at night—that is why hyenas have sloping backs—casting their spells accompanied by mad laughter. Not only do witches ride hyenas, but they also keep them as house familiars and live on hyena milk and hyena 'butter' the yellowish excretion that the animals use to scent mark their territory. Hyena butter is also said to be used to fuel the witches' torches.

According to African lore, a man can protect himself and his cattle from the evil influence of witches by feeding the cattle pieces of ground up dried hyena skin, genitals or heart, and by smearing these substances into small cuts in his own arm. This defense is not without risks, for if one kills a hyena, one can expect the revenge of the owner-witch.

The deep fear of the hyena displayed by the Africans is in some measure justified, as the African hyena has been known to attack a defenseless child or adult sleeping unprotected outside the village perimeters. But in addition to its evil persona, the hyena plays another role in the fables African mothers tell their children; the hyena is the butt of the story, the greedy, loutish beast that ends up being tortured or beaten or killed.

Folk stories about hyenas in the Middle East are no less derogatory, despite the fact that the type of hyena found there is much smaller and less aggressive than his spotted African cousin. The striped hyena, widespread throughout the Middle East and most of Africa, especially North Africa, is absolutely terrifying to the Arab population; indeed, to all of middle-eastern or eastern cultural backgrounds. Most of these people, however, unlike the African natives, have never even seen a hyena, yet they seem to have a mental image of a ten-foot tall beast with eyes of fire and jaws of steel.

For the Arabs, the hyena is the mother of the devil. She cries at night like a lost child to lure her unsuspecting victims into her cave so that she can then devour them. If you step in her urine, you are lost; you become hypnotized and must follow her.

According to folk legend, which has become widespread belief in Africa, the hyena can change its sex at will, a handy trick. In fact, there is very little difference in the appearance of the external sex organs of the male and female spotted hyena and it is very difficult to discriminate between them. What is interesting is that in the Middle Eastern species, in which the external sexual differences are much more apparent, the belief that hyenas can change their sex is also prevalent.

Bedouin women are said to have a great fondness for these tales of terror about hyenas, and have learned to make good use of them. If a woman disappears for an hour or two and her husband wants to know where she has been, she can always say, "You see, I met this hyena and she hypnotized me and dragged me off to her cave and it was just a miracle that I escaped!"

The truth of the matter is rather different, at least regarding the striped hyena, the only one of the four types of hyena that is native to Israel. The striped hyena is a fearful and fairly inoffensive animal. As Bodenheimer, the great zoologist, noted as early as 1835, "When attacked by men, the hyena makes use of its terrible jaws only when it is cornered and has no opportunity to escape. It is shy and nocturnal in its habits." No fire breather—far from luring you into his cave, he is much more likely to head for the hills himself should he meet you face to face in the dark of the night.

The striped hyena, unlike his aggressive African cousin, lives primarily from scavenging the remains of the prey of other predators. Man, the most wasteful creature of all, with his omnipresent garbage dumps, provides plenty of food for the hyena, who also supplements his diet happily with fruits and vegetables stolen from the fields, insects, and any birds or small animals that are ill, weak, or stupid enough to fall into his mouth. The striped hyena has no well-developed techniques of hunting.

Smaller than his African spotted cousin, he stands about 70 cm. high at the shoulder and weighs about forty kilograms. Although there can be a fairly wide variation in size and weight, the hyena is a tremendously powerful animal and a possessor of the most powerful jaws in the animal kingdom. He has extremely strong teeth, which are long and rather blunt, very muscular and well-developed neck and forequarters, but on the other hand, a comparatively weak and less developed rear assembly.

The great power of his jaws and forequarters, of course, are for the purpose of demolishing bones and other remains that other carnivores are incapable of handling. His sloping back is meant to help him when he lifts up a hunk of carcass to drag off to his den. His digestive system seems to be made of cast iron, considering that he is known to be fond of chewing up such interesting tidbits as old rubber tires.

The hyena occupies a very important niche in nature—that of cleaning up the waste of other animals and of man: in the Ethiopian village of Harrare, hyenas are the official street cleaners, wandering through the streets unmolested and unmolesting, keeping things neat and tidy. In spite of this positive role, its eating of carrion and its unappreciated habit of digging up insufficiently covered graves in the desert—something, incidentally, that dogs and wolves also do if given the opportunity, have made the poor hyena a thoroughly despised creature, considered unclean, smelly, and disgusting by the general population. Not having the charm of lions, tigers, wolves and the other more charismatic carnivores, comparatively little study and research has been done on the hyena,.

Even the name of the hyena in the Hebrew language, *tzavua* is derogatory. The word apparently comes from the same base word as *tzeva*—color—that refers to his varied colors or stripes. But the name in Hebrew also has the meaning of hypocrite—which also relates to the idea of colors, as in changing one's color. All I can answer to the people who ask if a *tzavua* is *tzavua* is that I haven't known any animal hypocrites, only human ones.

An example of the typical attitude toward hyenas is the Arab family that visited the Jerusalem zoo. Father, mother, and five children came up to the hyena cage and stood there for some time looking at the animals that did not conform to their preconception of what a hyena should look like. Finally the family patriarch came up with a satisfactory explanation: "This isn't one of ours; this is a Jewish hyena."

These attitudes fascinated me. An animal couldn't be evil as the stories claimed. On the other hand, Hans Kruuk, the well known researcher of hyenas, wrote: "After all this (superstition) it comes as a surprise that hyenas make such nice pets—somewhat rough and boisterous but very affectionate and intelligent, somewhat in general character between a dog and a cat." James Michener, in his book *Covenant* refers to a pet hyena kept by one of the pioneers in South Africa. I knew that I wanted a hyena. It seemed like a real challenge to raise and develop a relationship with such a powerful and superstition-shrouded creature, and to discover what the truth was behind all the strange beliefs.

The next problem was from where to get one. In the wild, hyenas' dens are very well hidden. The cubs develop slowly and are not usually observed outside of the den until they are several months old, which is already too old to develop the imprint necessary for the human-hyena bond that I wanted. I wanted my hyena to relate to me as a substitute mother, leader, and example for her own developing self-image. I wanted to raise the cub so that it would be totally dependent and attached to me. My idea was to see if a hyena, raised from a very young age and exposed to people, cars, other animals, and all sorts of strange and changing circumstances, could learn to overcome some of the natural suspicion and fearfulness of the species. I wanted to see how well the animal would adjust to such a lifestyle, how it would relate to me, and to what extent, if any, it could be trained and 'domesticated.'

A cub from the wild would have been too old for such an experiment, even had it been possible to obtain one; the hyena is, like all wild animals in Israel, protected, and the Israel Nature Reserves Authority is very fierce in its protection of its wild charges. So, my cub would have to be born in captivity.

There were no young hyenas born in the Tel Aviv University zoo that year. The safari park wardens were not interested in the idea, and anyway, their cubs were too old.

There was a litter in the Haifa zoo, however, about five weeks old. The cubs had been taken from their mother at birth, out of fear that she would kill them, which was not an uncommon problem with zoo animals living under unnatural conditions. They were being hand raised. I knew one of these cubs would be perfect for me. After much negotiation, the zoo authorities finally agreed that I could have one.

I was ecstatic! I was getting a hyena! Now all I had to do was to make arrangements to go to Haifa and pick it up and the sooner the better.

317

Chapter Twenty-Seven: Bringing Baba Home

One of the advantages of working on a research project that is based primarily on fieldwork, aside from the great advantage of being able to spend my entire day outdoors and not in an office, was being provided with a jeep. Jeeps carry great status in Israel, since with the high cost of petrol, there weren't many private individuals who could afford to run them; those who could generally drove Mercedes.

Not being one of the affluent Israeli car owners, it was reassuring to know that the jeep was available for emergencies like traveling to Haifa to pick up a hyena.

The evening before we were due to make the trip to Haifa, my coworker Ilan and I were doing field work not far from Sha'ar Hagai. Ilan offered to drop me off at home before driving back to the university. Great, I thought, that would save a lot of bus travel time.

As we drove up the dirt road to the kennel (actually, calling it a road is much more than it deserves, but then this was a jeep), we heard a loud clunk and the jeep listed noticeably sideways. A spring had broken on one of the front wheels. There was no alternative; Ilan had to return to the university by bus, and I had to wait in the morning for the tow truck to come and haul the jeep away.

By the time I finally got to Tel Aviv the next day, it was eleven a.m. The logical thing to do, of course, would have been to postpone the trip to Haifa for another day when the jeep was again available. But I didn't feel much like behaving logically; I wanted my hyena baby. So I set out for Haifa by bus.

Getting there was no problem, but I was worried about getting there in time. The trip from the university to the Haifa zoo, with the best of luck, was over two hours by public transportation. By the time I left Tel Aviv it was after twelve, and the zoo was scheduled to close at three. Haifa is a city that is built on a good-sized hill (by Israeli standards, it is even a mountain), and the zoo is at the top. In order to get there on time, I took a taxi from the Central Bus Station at the bottom up Mt. Carmel to the vicinity of the zoo. I ran through the lovely park surrounding the zoo and by two-thirty I stood panting at the gates.

I was on tenterhooks while the zoo manager sat explaining to me the care and feeding of baby hyenas. I could hardly absorb what he said; I just wanted to see her. Finally, my little hyena was brought in.

She was a tiny ball of gray fluff, no larger than a good-sized kitten. Her baby fur was very soft, with none of the harshness it would develop as she grew older, and it was very symmetrically marked with neat black stripes on back, sides and legs.

She still had no teeth, but had enormous jet-black eyes, full of expression that ranged from sleepy softness to pure devilishness. I could never understand how people were able to look her in the face and say she had no expression; to me, from the start, this animal's expressions were as varied and as easy to distinguish as those of a dog and were just as meaningful. Her ears were enormous and stood erect like antennae, swiveling around at every sound.

But her most outstanding feature was her voice. The sound she produced, very loud in proportion to her size, was something I was totally unprepared for. It was like a combination of a croak, a wail, and a clearing of the throat, or maybe like a rusty door hinge being sandpapered. I had no idea what it meant, not having yet become fluent in hyena language, but I was sure it didn't mean that she was happy. Since I was supposed to be the university-trained expert in animal behavior, I didn't want to ask Danny, the zoo manager, what her howl meant, but as I sat trying to hold her still as she squirmed about in my hands, protesting very vocally all the time, I wondered just how easy it was going to be to take her home on the bus.

In my rush to come and get the little beast, having been counting on the jeep, I had come without any box to carry her in. I had a large soft pouch bag that I had thought she would curl up in, but having now met my little hyena, I realized that her activity level was much greater than I had anticipated. It was unlikely that she was going to sleep quietly in my bag all the way home.

The first step of the journey was to take a local city bus down from the top of the Carmel to the port where the intercity transportation is located. I stood at the bus stop waiting with my hyena firmly clenched against me, trying to muffle her weird noises. People gave me strange looks as the sounds continued, but like most sophisticated city dwellers, they were not about to ask questions. When the bus arrived, however, the driver was very interested. He offered to adopt my 'puppy' if I didn't really want it. Ha, I thought, you should only know.

The vocalization continued. I worried that it would go on for the next three hours until we got home. This baby was not the least bit interested in quietly going to sleep in my lap. She tried to climb in all directions. Her contortions, and mine, were highly entertaining to the other passengers. Heads turned to watch. One fellow got up from his seat and walked over to me.

"Excuse me," he said, "but isn't that a hyena?" After a moment's hesitation, while the bus driver glanced reproachfully at me over his shoulder, I answered in the affirmative.

"I knew I recognized that voice," he commented. He went on to explain that he had a friend just outside of Haifa, a former warden for the Nature Reserves Authority, who had raised three hyenas in his backyard as pets. Once having heard that distinctive hyena voice, who could fail to recognize it? I took down his name and phone number because it would certainly be of interest to get in touch with him and get some tips on raising hyenas.

When we arrived at the intercity bus station for the next stage of the journey, I decided to take a *sherut*, a communal taxi. I knew it would be faster than the bus, and probably more comfortable. There would also be fewer passengers to cope with since such a taxi only takes seven people plus the driver.

As I crossed the road to the taxi station, a car came to a skidding stop opposite me when the driver caught sight of me. I ignored the mini traffic jam I had unwittingly caused and asked the taxi dispatcher to order me a seat to Tel Aviv. After clarifying what the animal in my arms was, he called over the radio to one of his taxis to "save a seat for a passenger here at the station with a hyena." The driver's answer was unprintable.

The taxi arrived. The driver looked over at me, and said to his dispatcher in disbelief, "You were serious!" I climbed in, settling into the furthest back corner of the taxi to keep the baby away from as many of the other passengers as possible. Most of them were fairly blasé. After a few rather scornful glances, they settled down for the trip.

The passenger sitting next to me, however, seemed to fascinate my little hyena. She sniffed up and down his arm and licked him. A well-dressed man in his thirties, he was very tolerant.

"She likes the taste of blood," he commented.

Blood?!! Apparently my expression indicated the need for an explanation; he was a surgeon, he said, and had just come from a day in the operating room. The explanation was not very reassuring.

There was a heavenly period of peace while the cub slept on my lap, lulled by the motion of the car. When she awoke, she reacted just as I, the expert in puppy raising, should have anticipated: she peed. It was a copious quantity for such a small animal, and, of course, was right in my lap. I sat with a poker face, hoping that none of the other passengers, and especially the driver, would notice, as my jeans soaked it up. Fortunately, as is common in public taxis, everyone was asleep but me, and the driver couldn't see me hunched down in the back corner. I had a roll of toilet paper in my bag, standard equipment for traveling with animals. Surreptitiously I pulled it out and tried to soak up the flood. My jeans were more effective. Jeans are highly absorbent; however, they are certainly not very comfortable when wet.

We finally arrived in Tel Aviv. The hyena, refreshed by her nap, was in good spirits, but mine, like my pants, were rather dampened. I tied my sweater around my waist to hide the embarrassing stain and headed for the next taxi, to Jerusalem.

Taxis to Jerusalem tend to be crammed with very respectable and highly religious folk—women always immaculately dressed in hats and dresses of expensive-looking materials and men in long dark coats, long bushy beards, and often wearing lovely furry hats. Under the best of circumstances, these people do not tend to be fond of animals. As I approached the queue with my strange beast, again vocally protesting all this traveling, and with a rather interesting aroma hanging in the air around us, the crowd looked on the verge of rebellion.

Luck was with me, however; one of the drivers waiting to fill his taxi knew my animals and me, although the hyena stunned him for a minute, and he gave me a seat in his cab, despite the disapproving glares of the beards already inside. It was obvious that the driver was no great sympathizer with the ultra-orthodox, and found the whole situation very funny. I didn't find it so funny. I was rather tired and very wet, but the hyena, full of fresh energy, spent the trip squealing and trying to climb out of my lap to inspect the weird-smelling hairy people with the furry hats.

Finally, our stop came. Wet, smelly, and exhausted, I climbed out of the taxi to introduce my hyena to her new home.

Chapter Twenty-Eight: Baby Baba

Introducing a hyena to a house full of other animals was a very interesting experience. It is true that most of my animals, having lived with me for some time, were trained to expect anything. On various occasions they had shared their living quarters with goat kids, lambs, raccoon cubs, and owls, to mention a few. But I expected that a hyena would definitely be a surprise to them. This little animal must have a very strange and wild smell to a dog or cat.

The collie bitches inspected the little creature very carefully from all sides and decided that whatever it was, it was definitely a baby, and immediately started cleaning its bottom. The males, of course, were excluded from this happy pastime, and walked off grumpily; babies were no business of theirs. The cat took one good look, glared at me and seemed to say, "Well, if it leaves me alone, I'll leave it alone!" and stalked off, tail high.

The first and most important thing to do to make the baby a member of the family was to give her a name. This was very difficult and took a lot of thought. Finally, Dorcas, ten years old at the time, suggested 'Babayaga.' This was the name of the witch in a children's story she had recently read. What better name for a hyena than that of a witch? The fact that it was a Russian witch didn't really matter; a witch is a witch in any language. So Babayaga she became.

Of course, this quickly got shortened to 'Baba,' and then further deteriorated into 'Babushka' and 'Babushkeleh mushkeleh,' and all sorts of other endearments. After all, she was a baby.

Baba was still very undeveloped. I had expected her to be comparable in development to a six-week-old puppy, but she was behind; her teeth were just beginning to sprout.

She drank from a bottle and did not yet eat solid foods. Her sight, hearing and smell seemed well behind the development of a puppy of her age, and she lacked awareness of and orientation to her surroundings.

For the most part, all she wanted to do was to eat and sleep. Her preferred sleeping places were dark and constricted dens—as far back behind the sofa as she could crawl, behind the cupboards, between the bookcase and the wall—narrow, hidden spots that were dark and safe, and that were too small for other animals to get into. She did enjoy sleeping in my lap if I was sitting quietly, preferring to push her head far under my arm where it was dark, and she felt sheltered.

Her habit of trying to find the deepest, darkest, most hidden corner to sleep in was something of a problem, as I would come into the house and look in vain for her. It is amazing the places an animal that wants to hide can get into! I sometimes scoured the house, peering into all her usual sleeping spots without finding her. Sometimes I had to wait until she got hungry and came out looking for food before I found her newest hiding place.

When she was outdoors, her as-yet-incompletely developed eyesight and her difficulties in perception of heights and distances became especially apparent. She would scurry right to the edge of a terrace about to scuttle over, without showing any sign of noticing that there was a difference in ground levels.

Her typical way of progressing was simply to plunge forward, ignoring everything in her path, apparently either not aware of things that could stop her, or feeling that she could just plow through them anyway. As she was only about fifteen centimeters high, it was quite impressive to watch. All movement was, of course, accompanied by her unique grunting squeal.

If Baba was to be a house animal, she would have to be housetrained. I had a good deal of experience in housetraining puppies, but I had never house-trained a hyena, and as far as I knew, neither had anyone else. There were no handy training manuals. I was well aware that some species cannot be housetrained, simply because of lack of sufficient sphincter control. A goat, for instance, is quite an intelligent animal—some goat lovers say that it is even as intelligent as a dog—but when a goat has to go, it has to go. I had no idea what Baba's capabilities were.

The question was how to go about it. A puppy has an inbred desire to do what you want and to gain praise and avoid punishment. Punishment does not have that sort of effect on a hyena cub. So I decided to follow the principle in animal training of 'shaping'—observing Baba's natural behavior and then making use of that through reward and punishment to build the behavior I wanted.

From the beginning Baba used a few particular spots to eliminate rather than messing indiscriminately all over the house. One of her favorite spots was a corner where a floor tile had come loose. She liked to dig in the grit remaining from the loosened cement, trying to cover up what she had done. (A hyena, incidentally, does not eliminate with the frequency of a puppy, but when it does, everything is produced at once.) This behavior was a good clue to what to do. I took a plastic kitty litter pan, filled it with sand, and placed it in this spot. Sure enough, Baba came over, inspected it carefully, and began to dig. Soon she was using her sandbox to the exclusion of all other corners in the house.

Training her to eliminate outdoors was even simpler. As she spent more time outside, Baba gradually, on her own initiative, stopped using the litter box. Soon I was able to remove it entirely. She was totally reliable, and from a young age scratched on the door to attract my attention if she wanted to go out.

Another interesting habit was that of 'marking' the cat box. Hyenas have a scent gland under their tails, which can be extruded to exude a sticky yellow substance, odorless to humans but of great interest to other hyenas. Hyenas in the wild go around marking branches, blades of grass, and other objects they meet in their travels. No one is really sure why; it may be a territorial instinct, or have some communicative purpose.

Baba began marking her box, straddling it with her hind legs and smearing the edge with her 'hyena butter.' She would then turn around and with fascination inspect what she had done, and then, likely as not, mark the box again. Whatever perfume this substance has, it seemed to be very specific to hyenas as even the dogs were totally uninterested in the smell.

Baba never tried to mark anything else inside the house. But when she started spending more time outdoors, she marked anything she could get between her legs: broom handles, the chain she was tied with, water buckets, branches, blades of grass. It was quite a sight to see her holding a broom in her mouth and trying to manipulate it so that she could get her leg over the handle.

As a baby, the most important part of her day was food time. When she first arrived, she drank formula from a bottle, a concoction of milk, eggs, and vitamins. She was very attached to her baby bottle and laid contentedly in my lap, sucking away even after it was empty, with her paws wrapped around it to keep me from taking it away. Her position was very similar to that of human infants I have known. She ate three to four times a day and had a healthy appetite.

As her teeth came in, I introduced her to solid foods. I started feeding her with soft white cheese, like I did with any puppy I wanted to wean. She took to it very well, although she made it quite clear that she preferred cottage cheese. Ground raw meat was added to the menu, which she accepted enthusiastically.

By the time that Baba's teeth were well grown, she was ready to eat a wide variety of foods. She came to the table and tried anything we were eating. She proved to have very particular tastes. She liked most dairy products, although her favorites were cottage cheese and fruit-flavored yogurt. All kinds of eggs were fine, but her favorite was a nice fluffy omelet. She adored fruits, especially the sweet ones, including melon, bananas, apples, grapes, and avocado.

In the wild, melons and other fruits serve not so much as a food, but as a source of moisture for an animal living in such arid conditions where at times there is no free standing water to be found. Baba was never thirsty—she always had plenty of water, not only for drinking but for playing in as well—but she loved melons and other fruit. She picked sweet fruits out of her dish and ate them in preference to meat or other foods.

She was quite different from her wild cousins, the brown hyenas of the Kalahari, who can go for months or even years without drinking water, subsisting only on the moisture content of their food, and very much appreciating the wild desert melons that can still be found in the dry season.

Some vegetables were of interest to her: corn was a favorite, as were cooked vegetables left over from the dinner table. Meat was a basic part of her diet, but she was not a carrion eater; she wanted her meat fresh. Meat that wasn't to her taste or bones that she was not interested in were carefully inspected, rolled on thoroughly, and put aside to 'season.' Some weeks later, when the bones were thoroughly dried out, she brought them out to gnaw on. But what she would sell her soul for were the real sweets—cookies, bits of cake, or above all, chocolate.

Because of her increasing interest in food, Baba soon discovered that there were times when other people were eating and she wasn't and if she begged, she just might get some handouts. Baba's begging was very hard to ignore, as it consisted of pitiful squealing, climbing on your knee and nudging with her head. As she got larger, she discovered that the climbing was unnecessary. By the time she reached her full size, she was able to stand at the dinner table with her chin resting on the table's edge, looking over the contents of the meal and deciding just what appealed to her most. It is difficult to eat when you have a hyena head, nearly at eye level, following every bite from plate to mouth with beseeching eyes and a begging grin, accompanied by an under-the-breath whine.

Baba was always very gentle about food. Unlike the dogs, who were likely to grab offered tidbits out of one's hands, with or without fingers, depending on how quick you were, Baba first carefully sniffed anything offered her and then took it gently. Far from wolfing it down on the spot, she took it away to inspect it and enjoy it in privacy.

Despite the tremendous power of her jaws, Baba could take a raw egg out of my hand and carry it away without breaking the shell.

It was also fun to see her eat such delicate fruits as bunches of grapes or pomegranates. She would hold the fruit down with one huge paw and one by one pluck the grapes off delicately with her teeth or, with a pomegranate, she would carefully separate the fruit from the husk with her tongue. She was so fond of fruit that if offered fresh meat, dog food (which she was not so fond of but ate anyway), and fruit, she would pick out the fruit to eat first.

The only thing that made Baba lose her self control was chocolate. Just the smell of chocolate was enough to throw her into an ecstasy of anticipation. The only way I had of making her 'laugh'—a very deep throaty chuckle seeming to be indicative of deep feelings of longing—was to tease her by holding a bit of chocolate just out of reach. As a chocolate freak myself, I understood her feelings.

Chapter Twenty-Nine: Baba and the Pack

In order to take Baba with me to various places as planned, she had to learn to walk on a leash and to be tied. I could not depend on her following me around like a puppy; she was much too independent.

Baba was not at all disturbed by being dressed in a collar. She simply ignored it. A leash, however, was another matter. She took off in the direction that she wanted, impervious to the fact that she was on leash, until she ran into the end of it, whereupon she either struggled to keep on going, squealing her protest at this undeserved confinement, or she turned around and took off in another direction. After some trials, she did begin to learn that the purpose of the leash was for her to go in the same direction that I was going.

She started to respond to my calls and encouragement and to the corrections given with the lead. However, she remained subject to her own particular moods; if something interested her, she stopped and investigated it before walking on. If something frightened her, she wouldn't pass it. If the weather was hot, she was likely to choose a shady spot and lie down, not wanting to move at all. She was prone to 'sit down strikes,' in which, for one of any number of reasons, she decided she just didn't want to move, and she wouldn't budge. Even dragging her along on her bottom was not sufficient to get the stubborn little beast back on her feet again. Usually, I gave up, picked her up, and carried her. At this point she still was tiny; I didn't want to think of what would happen if she pulled such tricks on me when she was fully grown.

Most animals learn very quickly to accept the fact of being tied and to stop fighting it. Not so with Baba. She continuously paced back and forth at the end of her chain, pulling and protesting at the top of her lungs. This went on for weeks; she would not rest when she was tied, even if it was for several hours at a time. Finally, even Baba's stubbornness wore down, and she accepted the fact of being tied, and proved to be very clever about not getting tangled in her chain or getting the chain twisted around obstacles in the area.

Not all of Baba's life consisted of lessons and discipline; there was also playtime. Her favorite game was tag. Dogs also like to play a kind of tag, one dashing madly at the head of the pack, weaving and twisting, often carrying a toy or such in his mouth, while the others try to catch him. Baba's style, however, was different. She would start to dash through the house and get so caught up in the sheer thrill of racing at top speed, that she became indifferent to whether anyone else was playing or not.

After a few attempts to chase her, the dogs stood watching in amazement as she streaked back and forth through the house, rugs flying in all directions, chairs and tables knocked to the sides, books and newspapers scattered in her wake. She skidded into the furniture and ignored the bumps she got. When I tried to catch her, she expertly dodged my arms or simply barreled through them by sheer force, like a mini bulldozer. Not much in the way of dog, human or furniture can stand in the way of a racing hyena.

Finally, when the surroundings resembled a disaster area, the game would suddenly end with Baba streaking under the sofa and coming to a stop in a dark corner to catch her breath. With a great feeling of relief that most of the household effects had once again survived, I returned things to their place until the next time.

As Baba grew and became more and more aware of her surroundings, she also became more and more curious. If curiosity, as I have heard it said, is one of the signs of intelligence, then Baba was amply supplied with both. For Baba, curiosity didn't mean just looking at something new, it meant a thorough examination—tasting, touching, manipulating, pulling, tugging, taking to pieces, and trying everything possible to experience the new object in its fullness. She very soon discovered that behind cupboard doors there was a wealth of new things to manipulate: pots, pans, cleaning supplies, paper products, towels, tablecloths, tinned foods, and any number of other fascinating objects to be taken out, inspected thoroughly, and then scattered all over the house.

She was not really destructive while she was small. Unlike a puppy that pulls out books or shoes for the sheer joy of shredding them to bits, Baba was mostly interested in finding out what all these strange things were, and even more, in examining these wonderful dark hidden corners that were crammed full of such wonders.

I would come into the kitchen to find her disappearing into a cupboard, only the tip of her tail showing, as she threw things out behind her for later inspection. Often, so excited by the thrill of discovery, and perhaps by life in general, she would start to run, racing back and forth through the house, tail in the air, all her hair standing on end, scattering dogs, cats, furniture, and the contents of most of the house storage areas in all directions as she streaked back and forth.

It was clear, even while she was still small, just how tough she was. During her mad dashes, knocking into things never put her off stride. Blows that would have sent a puppy yelping for pity didn't affect her at all.

Baba loved to play with the dogs, but after a few experiences, they became more and more wary of playing with her. She never gave up; the dogs could roll her over, pin her down, and claim victory, and the minute she squirmed free she would be at them again, nipping and agitating to get on with the game. If the dogs really got fed up and snapped at her, she immediately became submissive, and the minute they turned away, she was after them again, ready for more.

I don't suppose that at the start the dogs really realized what they were dealing with. For them, Baba was just another puppy. Puppies can be nice to play with at times. The bitches especially had a lot of patience and affection for puppies. But if a puppy got pesky, a growl and a threatening nip were always enough to show them that the game was over.

This 'puppy,' though, was different. She was wild and full of energy, and unlike ordinary puppies, rough play didn't put her off at all; to the contrary, the rougher the play, the happier she was. Although she reacted appropriately to a growl and a nip—head lowered and turned sideways in submissive posture, eyes down, even sometimes rolling over on her back with her legs in the air—two seconds later she was at them again, bouncing around, nipping at legs, pushing, pawing, and agitating in any way she could think of.

Kimie, one of the younger collies, was the dog that Baba singled out for special attention. When the other dogs were fed up with her games, they snapped and snarled at her until she took them seriously and finally gave up. If they really got annoyed with her, she fled under the sofa, from which safe haven she emitted ferocious sounding, deep-throated moans. But no matter what poor Kimie tried, it never subdued Baba.

No matter how annoyed he got, snapping, snarling or nipping, Baba blithely came back for more, grabbing his tail, nipping his legs, tugging his ruff and doing anything that would cause a reaction, which for Baba was part of the game. Invariably I had to come to Kimie's rescue and drag Baba off.

If she was loose in the garden, Baba's favorite game was 'chase me.' It was amazing how fast such a clumsy-looking little animal could move. The dogs never had a chance of catching her as she raced through the garden, dodging and weaving. If they got near her, she simply plunged through any shrubbery that might be in her way, something that my educated dogs knew was not allowed. The thickest bushes or growths of cactus didn't seem to bother Baba. After a few of these crazy games, I decided that the location would have to be moved to one of the large puppy pens if I intended to save any of my garden. Baba, of course, was not very interested in running in the pen where there was nothing to demolish.

Only once did we come across a dog that could stand up to Baba's endless energy. He was a Dalmatian belonging to a family who had come for advice. The Dalmatian is a breed known for tremendous energy and endurance, something that at times makes it very difficult to keep one as a house pet. This young dog was suffering from the typical problems of a high-spirited dog confined to an apartment all day with nothing to do, and he had begun occupying himself by destroying whatever was in reach. His owners were in despair, and had come to find a solution that would turn him into a *mensch*.

Baba was asleep under the sofa when they arrived. She awoke, peeked out, and discovered that there was a new victim available. She crawled out, stalked the unaware Dalmatian, sitting quietly next to his masters, and began her play ritual.

The Dalmatian responded gladly. They began chewing on each other, rolling around on the floor, and roughhousing with all their hearts, all of this accompanied by a cacophony of ferocious sounding growls, snarls, and shrieks.

I reassured the dog's owners that Baba was just playing, as the game went on and on. Once they had started, neither of the pair was willing to call it quits. Both were determined to stick it out to the bitter end. Towards the end, the game seemed to be proceeding in slow motion, as the two young animals tried to keep it up, both stubbornly refusing to stop. Finally, the two simply collapsed simultaneously on the floor and went to sleep. This was the only time I had ever seen Baba played out.

Perhaps the Dalmatian's owners decided that our style of play therapy was a bit more than they had expected, or the dog had his energy level permanently lowered. Whatever the cause, we never saw them again. I am rather sorry that I didn't offer to buy that dog; one play session like that per day would have done wonders to keep Baba calm.

Chapter Thirty: Driving With Baba

I don't suppose there are many people who go shopping for a car with the primary criterion being that it is suitable for traveling with a hyena.

Now that I had Baba, I really had to get a car; one of the ideas behind the project was to take her everywhere with me to see if a hyena was capable of adjusting to strange surroundings and widely varied situations, when in nature it was suspicious of anything unfamiliar. Although Baba was still quite small, my experiences in bringing her home from Haifa showed that I couldn't very well go on traveling with her by public conveyance, especially when she got bigger.

During my years in Israel, I had owned a wide variety of vehicles. Their quality varied from a brand new Volkswagen van, purchased when I was a new immigrant and still allowed to buy a tax-free vehicle, down to that ancient Willys truck, purchased when my legal and financial status became purely Israeli. The last vehicle I had before Baba was the 'riksha'—a three wheeled, closed miniature van, running on a tiny Vespa engine. This little critter was not really suitable for traveling with a hyena, since it had a tendency to break down regularly. I also think that she could have chewed the whole thing to pieces without any trouble at all.

My budget was very limited, but finally I found something that looked good—my first old Subaru station wagon, beat up, dirty, with a lot of mileage on the clock, but with an engine that roared up the hills like a tiger. There was plenty of room inside, even for an adult hyena, and no one would ever notice a few teeth marks in that upholstery.

The time had come to introduce Baba to the joys of car travel. The first time out, I put her in the back of the station wagon. She did not approve of this idea at all—the whole drive was punctuated by her screeches of protest as she paced around and tried to climb over the seat. This disturbed my concentration, so the next trip I tried putting her in the back seat. This also was not to her taste. But this time she simply crawled under the front passenger seat and went to sleep. This became her regular spot. Usually, nothing could be seen but the tip of her tail sticking out.

It was very common in Israel at the time for those fortunate or rich enough to own a car to give rides to others, especially to soldiers, who have special stations along the roadside where they stand to hitch rides. Having spent a good deal of time hitching on the roadside myself while carless, I had promised the gods of vehicular travel that when the time came that I was blessed with a car, I would be considerate of those less fortunate and give them rides. However, that was before Baba!

Most of the hitchhikers I picked up didn't pay much attention to Baba; many didn't even notice the tail sticking out under their feet, and most of those that did seemed to think that it was a cat because of the stripes, or a puppy. I decided that the best thing was to let them believe what they wanted.

Occasionally, of course, there was someone who noticed that this didn't seem to be a very typical-looking dog or cat, especially on those occasions that Baba woke up, took interest in the new feet, and came out to investigate.

A young soldier I picked up one evening was apparently on his way to a heavy date. He was spruced up in Class A uniform, and had very liberally applied aftershave; I had to open the window to keep from choking, even though it was a cold night.

Baba was fascinated by scents; she investigated thoroughly any new odor she came across, and then, if she liked it, rubbed against its source, rolling and rubbing to try to allow the wonderful smell to permeate her body. So not surprisingly, when after a few moments the fragrance of the aftershave drifted down to Baba's position under the seat, she awoke. Following the lovely smell, she climbed on to the back seat, put her front feet on the soldier's shoulders, and started ecstatically licking his neck. Baba had a very rough and sandpapery tongue; when the soldier looked back to see what was rasping at his neck, he came face to face with something that obviously was not a cat or dog. The poor fellow turned white and froze in terror. I tried to reassure him that Baba was just being friendly. Meanwhile, Baba tried to press even closer against him.

I am sure that that was the longest ride the poor fellow ever experienced. He leaped from the car when we arrived at his destination, not even stopping to thank me for the ride. To Baba's joy, the smell of aftershave lingered in the car for days.

Another time I picked up an elegantly-dressed woman, standing by the road next to her broken down car. She was very grateful for the ride. But about halfway along, she started to giggle hysterically, and managed to force out, "It's, it's biting me!" For some reason Baba had become attracted to the poor lady's nylon stockings, and was licking at them from under the seat with her sandpapery tongue, a tongue designed to lick the meat off the bones of her prey.

Then there was Orit. Orit innocently asked me for a ride back to Tel Aviv, after she had been on a visit to my neighbors. On the way, however, I had to stop at the nearby village to pick up our mail. Baba had, by this time, become more exploratory, and if left alone in the car, she prowled around looking for things to chew up. I preferred the steering wheel and other equipment as they were without hyena improvements, so I asked Orit to wait for me in the car and to keep an eye on Baba while I ran up to get the mail.

"It will only take a minute," I said. "If Baba tries to climb into the front seat, just yell NO! at her and push her back."

Two minutes later I was back, to find Baba trying to climb over Orit into the front seat, and while Orit is quite a hefty girl, she was unable to stop Baba and sat waiting for me in petrified immobility. I hear that after Orit managed to recover from her ordeal, she entertained her friends for months with the tale of being left alone in a car with a man-eating hyena.

There were some advantages to traveling with Baba. There is no better way to get immediate attention and service from your auto mechanic than to drive in with a hyena in the car. To this day my mechanic is extremely fast and totally reliable about all repairs and service to my car because he knows that I can't afford to be stuck without it for long. Whenever it has to be worked on by anyone else—an electrician or whatever—he immediately notifies them that this is the car of the lady with the hyena and they had better finish it fast. I wouldn't be surprised if, when he takes my car in for the yearly licensing test, he doesn't tell the examiners, "Look guys, you'd better pass this car. The lady who owns it drives around with a hyena."

One day, when Baba was already a pretty big beastie, about the size and weight of a young retriever and she was altogether too big to crawl under the front seat, one of my nightmares came to pass. I was driving home from work with Baba asleep in the back seat, looking forward to getting home. The day was cold and gray and the rain was steadily pouring down. I am not at all fond of winter, especially not when the weather is wet. Baba was also far from enthusiastic about rain.

Suddenly, the car began to cough and sputter, and with a final whimper, it died. I coasted to the side of the road and sat there stunned. This was one of the horrible possibilities I had always tried to keep blocked out of my consciousness, against the evil eye; I was stuck with a broken-down car and Baba, miles from anywhere.

We were in the middle of the Tel Aviv to Jerusalem highway, with fields on all sides, no telephone anywhere in the vicinity, the rain pouring down, and 20 kilometers to go to get home. Baba, awakened by the cessation of movement, looked at me, looked out the window, and buried her head in her paws.

I got out and opened the hood. Using my vast knowledge of auto mechanics, I checked that all the spark plugs were connected, the battery was in place, banged on the starter a few times for good luck, and checked that there was water in the radiator. I knew that that probably wasn't the problem, but it was one of the things that I knew how to check. I closed the hood, and climbed dripping back into the car. Praying to whatever deities might be listening to at least have mercy on a poor, cold hyena, I turned the key. The starter worked, the electric system was fine, but the car wouldn't start.

All kinds of visions of possible solutions began passing through my rattled brain. I could try to stop a passing car. The driver might turn out to be a mechanical genius who would instantly fix what was wrong, or else he would give me a ride home, of course not minding that I was taking my hyena along too. Or I could try to stop a police patrol car and tell them that I was having trouble with the car and I had this animal with me that I couldn't leave alone. Of course, thus far I hadn't seen any police; some days you saw them every five kilometers or so, but not that day. I figured I could try to stop a taxi and persuade him to take me and my hyena home for a reasonable fee. I could tell him it was really a weird kind of dog.

I got out and opened the hood again. Nothing looked different. There were no loose wires dangling that looked as if they should be attached to something. Everything looked as I expected an engine to look.

I got back in and tried again to start the motor. Nothing. And again, nothing. And again, nothing. And again. Then, a spark of response! Maybe persistence does have its rewards. After a few more trials, rather reluctantly, the engine caught! Oh, blessed car!

I think I used more energy willing that car to get home than it used in petrol. But we got there.

The next day, Baba stayed home; once through that nightmare was enough. The car went straight to the garage. Once he stopped laughing my mechanic was very sympathetic.

"The engine flooded," he said.

"How can the engine flood while the car is traveling?" I asked. Even I know that things like that are not supposed to happen.

"The needle controlling the gas flow got stuck," he said. But he fixed it.

The next day, Baba rode again.

Chapter Thirty-One: "That's a What?!!"

When Baba turned two months old, I started introducing her to the wide world. She was still very much a baby, but she was much more aware of her surroundings. She had to learn that there were many new things to experience outside of her familiar home ground.

Her education began with an introduction to collar and leash. She took it very much in her stride. Unlike a puppy, which is likely to fuss, squirm and squeal the first time he is checked by the leash, Baba wasn't at all bothered. On the contrary, she just ignored the existence of any limitation and either plunged forward to wherever she wanted to go or stopped dead refusing to acknowledge all attempts to coax her to continue moving. This refusal to budge continued until she had either satisfactorily analyzed whatever unfamiliar object had attracted her attention, or until I gave up in frustration and picked her up. Whenever I gave in to her in this way, visions of a full-grown 40 kilogram hyena refusing to move until I picked it up would flash through my mind.

Traveling with Baba was indeed an experience. She did not accept anything new casually—not objects, places, people, noises—like a dog would through trust in his master and self confidence. I am sure that Baba had some feelings of confidence in my ability to protect her from all the terrifying things in her new world, but this never overcame her very strong natural suspicion and caution.

Thus, walking with Baba was a very slow procedure. She took a few steps, then came to a dead stop while she looked things over. If, after examination, everything looked safe and unthreatening, she took another few steps until the next dead stop. Trying to force her to move didn't help; she would let herself be dragged along rather than move voluntarily. Dragging was accompanied by a very vocal protest consisting of her inimitable squeal produced at the top of her lungs. This often resulted in an audience of passersby who collected to watch me 'torturing' the poor little animal. I have often been told by acquaintances that they never managed to train their dogs to walk properly on lead, as they were embarrassed to correct them in public. Well, they should try walking down the street with a hyena.

Of course, observers had a hard time identifying just what this poor screaming animal was. Guesses ranged from some strange unknown breed of dog to a cross between a dog and cat (interesting idea); rarely could they identify Baba as a hyena. People were fascinated when they found out what she was. Every time that Baba pulled one of her sit down strikes, we ended up surrounded by people inundating me with questions. I often worried that the police would get me for obstructing traffic.

One of the first questions was always, "What does it eat?" I don't know what people really expected to hear, perhaps that I kept a handy supply of dead bodies in the freezer. But they did seem disappointed to hear that Baba's diet at this stage consisted primarily of her milk bottle with additions of cheese, omelets, and chopped meat, and that she was beginning to show a love of fruits. As the word for carrion in Hebrew (*nevelah*) tends also to be a swear word used to graphically describe someone unpleasant, I was very tempted to tell people that I was making a list of *nevelahs* for use when Baba grew up. But I guessed that people might not appreciate the humor in that. The idea wasn't really original; It came from a zoologist friend of mine, who kept a list of people that she intended to bite if she ever got rabies.

I must admit that one of the most cherished comments I ever got was from a very dignified elderly gentleman in Jerusalem. He stood off to the side watching as I gave one of my impromptu street corner lectures to a group of fascinated spectators, with Baba sitting in the center of the circle making rude comments of her own. As the group drifted off, he came over and said very politely, "Madam, you shouldn't walk around with an animal like that. Everyone is looking at the animal and no one is looking at you!"

Baba was a well-known sight on the campus of Tel Aviv University. People stopped me when Baba was not with me to say, "I know you! You're the one that walks around with the hyena!"

Somewhat later, I also heard that there were various stories going around among the students as to just what I was doing with a hyena. The most interesting was that I was supposedly having an affair with one of the professors, and he, in appreciation, had arranged for me to have a hyena. An interesting idea of gratitude.

Baba had her own corner in the cafeteria, where she liked to settle down to sleep, pressed against the cool cement wall, while I ate lunch.

She was very fond of chips, and begged handouts from nearby tables. Other lunchers found it hard to turn down a pleading hyena.

Despite her familiarity with the campus, Baba never walked without caution, often stopping dead to examine anything unfamiliar in her path. She often doubled her forelegs and walked along on her 'wrists' along the hedges. I was never sure why. Was she lowering her profile to the level of the bushes in an attempt to conceal herself? One day when she walked out of the shelter of one of the hedges, she was startled to find two students sitting on the lawn. For days after that, at that particular spot, she carefully stalked up to the corner and peeked out to see if there was anyone waiting on the other side.

Students in the corridors of the buildings would be stunned to see a young hyena casually following me up the stairs. She loved my boss's office because it was air-conditioned. After only one or two visits there, we needed only to enter the building and she dragged me down the hall to his door, standing there impatiently and scratching on it if I was too slow in opening it. Once inside, she threw herself down in the corner with a deep sigh of pleasure, oblivious to all but the blissful coolness. Getting her to leave the office was another matter; she knew it was hot outside.

Baba was also well known in the office of the department secretary. I always had the feeling, though, that Adiva was disappointed when she saw me intact and whole, with no bites or missing limbs. She was convinced that Baba would eventually eat me.

People's reactions, after their first moment of astonishment, were for the most part positive. They wanted to know how she behaved, what she ate, if she could be trained like a dog, if she howled at night. There is a great deal of confusion in the public mind between the behaviors of the various carnivores. A fairly frequent comment was, "I never knew that a hyena was such a beautiful animal!" However, once in a while we ran into less pleasant comments. One man approached me in the book shop.

"You should be ashamed, dragging that poor animal around," he criticized.

"She's not a poor animal. She's very well treated and enjoys going places with me," I replied.

"An animal like that should be in nature, living free, not being kept in captivity and used for experiments!"

"She isn't being experimented on. She gets great food and sleeps in bed with me. I don't think nature would be so kind to her. Anyway, she was born in the zoo, so she wouldn't have been in nature in any case."

"But that is what I mean! She should be in nature!"

It was obvious that I couldn't change his mind; actually, I had to admit there was a lot of truth in what he was saying. Overall, I agree that animals should be left to live in nature, providing that people don't interfere with their natural surroundings. However, the spread of agriculture in this country leaves little space for the wild animals. The number of wild animals seen run over on the highways is large; I have seen hyenas among the corpses. Nature is not kind to wild animals and the modern world even less so. Baba would never have lived in the wild; she was born a zoo animal and her life would have been spent in a cage.

Of course, one of the first places I intended to visit with my little hyena was the fellow in Haifa who supposedly had several hyenas that he had raised in his backyard. A friend of mine was acquainted with him, and we made a date to go and visit.

I met my friend Ilan in Haifa. He was fascinated by little Baba, of course. Together we drove out to the home of Moshe, the 'hyena man,' who lived in a small village outside of the city in an area that was primarily agricultural. Moshe met us at the entrance to his property and escorted us in, with me clutching Baba securely in my arms.

Moshe was a hefty, middle-aged fellow with a villainous moustache. His house was a further expression of his personality. It was tiny but totally crammed with souvenirs of Moshe's life: a tremendous collection of antique copperware once dirt cheap and now worth a fortune, and an impressive collection of antique firearms, swords and knives, and all kinds of skins, skulls, antlers, horns. I didn't know where to look first. It was obvious, however, that no animals lived in that house since there was no place for them. I had all I could manage keeping Baba from getting into things as we sat and drank tea.

Where were the animals? Out in the backyard, which was not much bigger than the house. As we stepped out the door, the first thing we met was a full-grown male hyena tied in the middle of the yard.

"You can go over and pet him—he won't do anything," Moshe said. Taking him at his word, I approached. The creature's head came up to mid chest height on me; one bite and he could swallow Baba. Was she going to be this enormous?

This hyena, called Popeye, was indeed very passive. He looked us over, sniffed Baba carefully, and let me pet him on the head. Moshe then showed me Popeye's two brothers, closed in a cage in the back of the garden. He had raised them from the age of three months; they had belonged to a circus that was visiting Israel, and, on the verge of bankruptcy, had decided to sell off some of its animals. He had found that they were not aggressive, except to strange cats that came into the yard. He used to take one of them into town with him on occasion. The three hyenas were now about two years old. The idea that I intended to keep Baba in the house, though, seemed impractical to Moshe.

"You can't keep her in your house," he said. "Nothing will be left of it. Hyenas are really destructive."

"I have raised plenty of destructive puppies. If I keep an eye on her, I can keep her from doing much damage."

"That's what you think! You have no idea of the capabilities of a hyena!"

From Moshe, I learned of the extreme caution and suspiciousness of the hyena. He asked his son to put Popeye in his cage.

"Watch," he said. "Popeye knows this path perfectly well, but now there are some crates of vegetables here that weren't here when we took Popeye out in the morning. Watch how he acts."

Sure enough, as Popeye spotted the boxes, he stopped dead, the hair on his neck and back stood on end, and he stared at the obstacle. Step by cautious step, he approached and inspected it thoroughly before he was willing to pass it by.

Hyenas were not the only denizens of Moshe's back yard. There was a young wolf, a family of wild pigs, some ducks and chickens, a dog, and a few cats. One of the little wild pigs was loose in the yard and followed after us as we made our tour. Moshe had been a ranger for the Nature Reserves Authority, had raised numerous animals, and had stories without end.

I was, of course, at the moment mostly interested in the hyenas. According to Moshe, they were loyal and devoted pets. He could let them loose to run out in the neighboring fields and, he claimed, when he called they would return. They were never aggressive to people.

The time had come to leave. Baba had had her bottle and was ready to sleep all the way home. It was hard to leave this fascinating place; I certainly hoped that my hyena would turn out as successfully as Moshe's had.

There were times when I had to leave little Baba alone for short periods. Our research project was based in the university zoo, where we had an office and a very large cage for the birds we worked with. It was an ideal place to leave Baba—roomy, fenced, and with nothing that appeared dangerous to an inquisitive little animal aside from the cages of birds. We often parked our jeep in the cage; there was plenty of room.

One day, I left Baba in the cage and went off to do something or other, secure in the feeling that my little hyena was safe. On my return, I came in the gate, which was locked as I had left it, and called Baba. No response. I looked around. Nowhere did I see a little striped animal, not curled up in the hole she had dug in the corner, not inside the empty pigeon cages that she was still small enough to crawl into and not under the work table. There was simply no sign of her.

She wasn't under the jeep. She wasn't in the jeep. I examined the whole cage again but still found no Baba. Where could a baby hyena disappear? Could someone have come in and stolen her? True that a lot of people in the zoo had been fascinated by her, but stealing a hyena didn't seem to be something that could go undetected for long.

Now very worried, I searched again and again through the large empty cage. Finally, searching under the jeep for the twentieth time, I saw a movement—not under the jeep but inside the chassis. The jeep had a metal plate covering the underside as a protection against knocks in rough terrain; this of course went around the wheelbase and other underpinnings of the jeep that had to be exposed. Baba, looking for a dark, hidden, comfortable den to sleep in, as any self-respecting hyena would, had climbed up inside the metal plate and was now sleeping inside the chassis.

With much coaxing and the more alluring offer of a milk bottle, I finally managed to get her out. She was very pleased with herself, and not at all concerned about having driven me crazy with worry. But I decided that on other occasions when she was left alone in the cage, I would leave her trailing a long lead, so that at least I would know where she was and have a handle to get her out.

Chapter Thirty-Two: Life With a House Hyena

As Baba grew, she became more interested in activity and less interested in sleeping. She was constantly on the lookout for something or someone to play with. She frequently tried to tempt the dogs into a game, but although occasionally one agreed to play, they were usually indifferent to her efforts. She tried to interest the cats in playing as well, grabbing them by the scruff of the neck and dragging them around. As can be imagined, this did little to encourage the cats to play.

When she was in the house alone, Baba found many things to interest her. She learned to open cupboards, and dragged their contents out to be examined at leisure. Plastic bottles, brooms and floor mops were all lovely things to chew on, or to grab and dash through the house with in mock chase games. The havoc wreaked by a hyena running through the house with a broom in her mouth is hard to describe. Nor was it great fun cleaning up the contents of the plastic bottles punctured by her needle-sharp, little teeth.

One evening I left Baba sleeping contentedly on the sofa in the living room. Usually, when Baba was asleep, things are safe until morning. I left the room for no more than two minutes to do something else. I should have known better.

There was a funny smell in the room when I came back, rather like rubbing alcohol. Baba wasn't sleeping any longer. She was in the middle of the carpet chewing on something. It took me a minute to grasp what was going on, and about as long for Baba to get a look at my face and streak for safety under the sofa.

Everything was purple. Baba was purple, the rug was purple, the floor was covered with purple spots, and there were even purple spots on the walls. In the middle of the carpet was the container of gentian violet antiseptic spray that Baba had decided to investigate, her investigation consisting of punching a few tooth holes in the pressurized spray container.

As I picked it up, the container gave a last gasp, and then I was also purple to match the rest of the decor.

Cursing loudly, accompanied by Baba's growls of, "Leave me alone, I didn't do anything!" from under the sofa, I dashed for the kitchen to find something to clean up the mess. As I scrubbed away with a wet towel, some of the purple started to come off. But no matter how hard I scrubbed or what I used—floor washing liquid, cleanser, laundry soap—there were still purple spots everywhere, and also purple streaks and swirls.

Meanwhile, I slowly suffocated from the alcohol fumes of the aerosol container. I decided that the only thing to do was to give up and go to bed. Baba dashed for the bedroom, glad to escape from the scene of the crime. She docilely climbed up onto her corner of the bed and crept towards me until her head was just beside my hand and peered up at me with innocent eyes. "Friends again, please?" What could I do? Learn not to leave such interesting objects in reach.

Another of her favorite sports was to chew up the house plants. I had never been highly successful in raising houseplants, although I loved having them. My gift is with animals, but my poor plants struggled along; the toughest managed to survive and even to produce a few blooms, but most of them slowly gave up the ghost despite water, fertilizer, and attempts at interested attention. The addition of Baba proved to be fatal to most of the plants that had survived everything up to then. She loved tipping over plants, and made persistent attempts to climb up to reach things that I thought were out of her reach. Plants were attacked, grabbed by stems or leaves, pulled with great energy out of their pots, and shaken until they surrendered. Then she dug and scattered the mud from the pots. I can't remember how many times I cleaned up mud from all over the house, scattered out of plant pots that I was sure she couldn't reach. There was one unforgettable day when I had visitors arrive from abroad. I took them up to the house, opened the door, quickly shut it, turned to them and told them that they would have to look around outside for a while—Baba had been at it again.

Baba had a favorite playmate, Rulrul, the little boy from next door who was going on two years-old. They were very fond of each other, perhaps because they were more or less the same size. They ran around the room, romping and rolling over each other, Baba chewing on Rulrul's hair, Rulrul pulling Baba's tail, and both having a lovely time. Occasionally Baba did get a bit rough for Rulrul, as her teeth, milk teeth though they were, were quite sharp, and like a puppy, she didn't realize what hurt. But the two of them got along wonderfully.

There was only one problem between them. Baba's most important possession in the world was her nursing bottle. Although she was eating mostly solid foods of all sorts, she still liked her milk bottle, and the sight of a baby bottle was enough to set her screaming. Rulrul was also still very attached to his bottle. Like Baba, he ate all kinds of other things, but his bottle was his security.

One day Rulrul came to visit with his bottle. Baba spotted it and decided that it was hers. That was the start of the great chase, Baba running after Rulrul trying to get hold of the bottle, Rulrul running around yelling, "Mine! Mine! Phooey, Baba!!" The only thing to do was to get out Baba's bottle, whereupon they both became friends again, lying contentedly on the sofa each sucking on his own bottle, though every now and then one or the other of the friends cast a suspicious glance over to see if maybe the other bottle was better.

Chapter Thirty-Three: Meeting the Public

Baba was soon on her way to becoming a public figure. One of her first visits to the public while she was still very small was when she accompanied me to a meeting of the judge's committee of the Israel Kennel Club. These meetings had a tendency to be rather dull; I thought that Baba might liven things up a bit.

The meeting was held in the home of one of the judges, located in a very wealthy Tel Aviv suburb. The impressive house was enclosed by an enormous walled garden with a swimming pool. The entrance hall had its own lush tropical garden growing under artificial light. The furniture was plush and spotless, and of course the sitting room was floored with a thick wall-to-wall carpet. All in all, ideal conditions for a young hyena.

I had never been to this home before, and when I saw it, I decided that Baba had better wait for me in the car. But having arrived a bit early, I invited the hostess and another of the judges who had already arrived, a gal with a very puckish sense of humor, to come out to the car and see Baba. They were both fascinated by her, and my friend with the sense of humor said to me, "You have to bring her in! Just don't tell anyone what she is."

So in Baba came. She was thrilled by this new place, and immediately decided to leap into the tropical garden. I quickly dragged her out, but she looked around for new horizons and spotted the hostess' schnauzer, which, after hearing Baba's happy shriek, took off in the direction of the pool. As people started to arrive, I was busy trying to keep Baba from climbing on the coffee table to sample the refreshments.

Everyone seemed rather surprised by my new 'puppy.'

"Well, it is a very rare breed," I answered.

"Don't tell me, I know what it is, I just have to think for a minute," declared a judge of Dobermans.

Finally, though, the game was spoiled. Our Staffordshire bull terrier specialist, who also happened to be a zoologist employed by the Israel Nature Reserves Authority, came in. "OH, how great! You have a little hyena!" he exclaimed.

"I knew that's what it was," mumbled the Doberman man.

Baba did improve the spirit of the meeting. It is hard to be pompous with a hyena crawling over your lap. During the course of the evening, she managed to crawl over everyone. She spent the end of the meeting on the lap of the chairman, finishing off the cake on his plate.

Baba then made a few appearances at dog shows. I took her mainly because I didn't want to leave her home alone. But she turned out to be very popular with the spectators, who kept trying to figure out what breed she was. The other exhibitors were less enthusiastic; they claimed that Baba and her weird noises were distracting the dogs from the business of showing to their best advantage. Baba was not terribly enthusiastic either. She found sitting under a tree in a strange park with a lot of barking dogs and staring people far from an ideal way to spend a day.

One of the show managers actually wanted me to bring Baba into the center ring for the Best in Show judging when we had a famous overseas expert judging. He wanted to see how this noted figure in the dog world would react. I refused; I didn't want to be responsible for the outcome if he decided to judge Baba as a dog.

Then one of my friends came up with another wonderful idea.

"The SPCA has asked me to give a talk at their annual general meeting about dog training. Why don't you come along and help?" she suggested. Well, okay, why not? "And why don't you bring Baba along and give a lecture on hyenas? I know they would love the idea!"

The meeting was held in the Plaza Hotel in Jerusalem, a very, very classy place. The idea of walking through that lush lobby with a hyena appealed to me. The arrangements were made and the SPCA people were indeed thrilled with the idea. The hotel management was notified ("Are you sure it won't pee on the carpet?"), the specified evening arrived and we set out for town.

Maybe setting out is not a very accurate description. My friend had her champion Norwegian Elkhound dog for the training demonstration, and I had one of the Collies, also to show off his obedience, and to make Baba feel more at home. All of us piled into the car. Now Lance, the Elkhound, did not like other dogs very much, unless they were bitches in season, and he was definitely not fond of Baba. Prize, the Collie, was a placid and well behaved dog, but didn't like to be put upon and was very vocal when he felt that he was not being treated with due respect. Those two and Baba went into the back seat.

Baba loved it. Two dogs to play with at once! The dogs did not love it at all. Prize was accustomed to Baba, but Lance was not, Baba got on his nerves. Everyone got on poor Lance's nerves.

By the time we got to Jerusalem, Lance was sitting on Marra's lap in the front seat, Prize had retreated to the back of the station wagon, and Baba had conquered the back seat.

We made our entrance into the hotel. Marra walked in first with the two dogs, who were so relieved to be out of the car that they got along beautifully. Baba and I followed into the plush lobby. Baba walked in as though she had spent every day of her life in five star hotels. With as queenly a gait as a hyena can manage, she stalked through the lobby and down the elegantly winding staircase to the lower level where the meeting was to be held, leaving a trail of frozen, open-mouthed observers. "Is that what I think it is?" I heard as we strode through.

It was hard to get the meeting started. Everyone was clustered around Baba, petting her and asking questions. Baba was not impressed. She was much more interested in exploring the strange new surroundings, turning over the ashtrays and trying to eat the electrical wiring.

Although Baba was meant to be the last on the program, the organizers decided that if they wanted to get started at all, she had better be first. People seemed to be quite interested in what I had to say about the unjustly despised hyena, and were fascinated by Baba, who kept up a running commentary throughout my talk. Since she was incapable of sitting still, most of the evening was spent play-wrestling with Marra's husband, one of her favorite people.

After my talk, Marra gave a demonstration of dog training, and I walked around the back of the room with Baba, who was bored and impatient with all this nonsense. While I spoke, I had noticed a number of hotel staff, mostly waiters from the adjacent dining room, peering in the door. Now, as I walked around in the back of the room, a few of them were gathered in the doorway, and one of them, braver than the rest, came in and asked if he could touch Baba. When I said that it would be all right, he gingerly approached and reached out to touch her. What a thrill! These fellows were all Arabs, and had probably never imagined that they would be anywhere near a hyena.

"I never in my lifetime would have believed that such a thing was possible!" the waiter gushed.

Another one brought Baba a napkin full of scraps from the dining room—and such scraps: sliced roast beef and chocolate éclairs since they had heard me say that she loved chocolate. "I don't want her to be hungry, so she won't eat someone here," the waiter said.

As we finished and walked out again into the main lobby of the hotel, Baba as usual attracted a lot of attention, comments and questions. As we were about to leave, a very elegantly-gowned woman ran up to me.

"Oh, please wait! I must show her to my little one! She's up in my room; it will just take me a minute to get her! Please!"

Well, feeling that it might give a little girl a big thrill, I waited. A few minutes later, the lady reappeared, carrying her 'little one'—a tiny Yorkshire terrier.

"Oh, just look at the hyena, baby!" she gushed, putting the terrier down on the floor in front of Baba's nose.

Baba looked at the little thing in surprise. The little thing looked Baba up and down, and with typical terrier spirit, snapped "RRRRRRRRRRRRRRUUUUUUUUUUUFF!!" in Baba's face, turned, and stalked away.

That was Baba's evening at the Plaza.

Chapter Thirty-Four: Baba the Celeb

It was inevitable that as Baba's notoriety grew the media would discover her. The first call came from a well-known Israeli women's magazine. They had heard that I had all kinds of animals, including some kind of jackal or something. I told them Baba was a hyena. They wanted to write about it, naturally.

So Baba made her first appearance in print. We were subsequently written about in everything from the very proper *Jerusalem Post* to one of the local scandal sheets, whose readers, more accustomed to photos of showgirls and such, were probably stunned to find a photo of a hyena.

Next was the radio. How, one may ask, do you interview a hyena for the radio? Well, it was managed. Holding up a piece of chocolate got Baba to squeal very nicely for the radio audience, followed by a shriek from the interviewer, "My god, she's eating the microphone!" End of interview.

The pinnacle was television. There was a very popular children's program on the air, hosted by a very personable fellow who was a real animal lover; he always appeared on the air with his dog. One of the features of the show was an interview with a child with an unusual hobby or a 'different' life style. My daughter, Dorcas was 11 at the time and of course, was a natural for this; living in 'nature' with all kinds of animals, especially a hyena, was a great subject for the show.

Dorcas was thrilled. However, after three days of being filmed, over and over and over, for a film clip that would take no more than eight minutes of air time, she was fed up and sure that she had no desire to become a movie star. Baba was also fed up. There she was surrounded by all sorts of fascinating objects—cameras, lights, cables, recorders—and she wasn't allowed to chew on any of them.

The program was highly successful, though. For several years after its airing, Dorcas was recognized with comments like, "Oh, I saw you on TV, with some strange animal—a jackal or something, wasn't it?" Even today, although Dorcas certainly doesn't resemble the little girl on TV, people remember the program.

This was the period that we got invited to the 'kibbutz circuit.' Kibbutzim try to provide a full life for their members, and one of the things that they are proud of is their cultural activities. There are indeed some very outstanding programs of theatre, music and so on that are presented in the kibbutzim, and that may travel from kibbutz to kibbutz. But there are also simpler entertainments, and one of the things that was popular at the time was a sort of 'twenty questions' or 'what's my secret' sort of quiz game. The organizers tried to find the weirdest people they could, and then a panel tried to guess just what their secret was, to the great amusement of the audience.

Baba and I appeared on several of these programs, and it was really a lot of fun. Usually the kibbutz provided transportation, and we were driven in style, sometimes to places as much as an hour or an hour and a half from home. Once there, we had to hide until the beginning of the program—and it is not easy to find a place in a kibbutz where one can hide a fairly good sized hyena without anyone spotting it. I was usually the first contestant on the program; nobody wanted Baba losing patience. I sat on stage, with a volunteer from the organizers holding Baba backstage. As I answered the questions, I heard Baba scuffling around behind the scenes with the volunteer hyena handler trying to persuade her to sit still and shut up.

Nobody ever guessed my secret, and the audiences were usually quite stunned when Baba came out from behind the curtains. Baba loved the attention, and also the various tidbits that were provided for her.

I quite enjoyed seeing the others that appeared with us on the program. My favorite was a fellow who collected snakes, and showed up with a bag of various types, including vipers, which he took out and casually draped around his neck, arms, and chair while he was talking. It was very impressive.

Another result of all this publicity was that people started appearing at the farm. "We read about you," or "we saw your daughter on television, and thought it would be interesting to come and look at this strange place, and where is that weird animal?"

Baba, at the age of nine months or so, was usually very pleased to have visitors. She looked at people and made an instant decision as to whether she liked them or not. It was very clear if Baba liked someone because she came rushing up, half crouched and squealing, with her lips drawn back in a grin over her powerful jaws, and as she reached her object's legs, she crouched lower until she was on her belly. With tail high in the air, a grin on her lips, ears lolling to the side, she begged to be scratched. As her new friend scratched her back or the base of her tail, Baba slowly rolled over until she was on her back, legs waving in the air, head thrown back so that her throat could be scratched as well as her belly, and her eyes closed in bliss. It was very hard for visitors who had come expecting to see a ferocious beast barely kept under control or a cowardly cringing carrion eater to hold on to their preconceptions when they saw her greet me like an overgrown puppy with a foolish grin on her face.

Of course, greeting often led to playing. Petting was fine, but roughhousing was better, and except for me, there were not many that could stand up for long to a Baba play session. The game usually started with Baba turning her head and taking my hand in her mouth, while keeping her eyes on me to see what my reaction was. If she saw that I was in the mood, then the game started. Baba's games were very similar to those that a dog likes, involving running, chasing and mock fighting. She dashed around and around, the hair on her back standing on end, tail high in the air, grunted in excitement and mock threat, enticing me to chase her, and swerved away at the last moment. This alternated with her charging at me and grabbing my arm or leg for a wrestle.

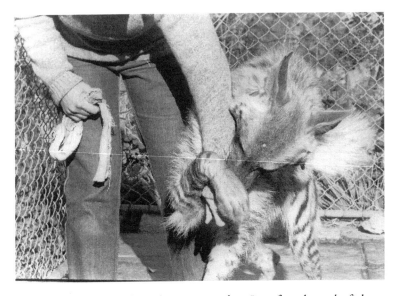

She was very gentle in hyena terms but I preferred to playfight with her only when I was wearing heavy clothes; the pressure of hyena jaws, even when the animal is being gentle, is still formidable. It was preferable, also, if the heavy clothes were work clothes—meaning things that could be discarded without hard feelings—as Baba enjoyed grabbing a sweater sleeve and playing tug of war, which didn't leave much shape to the sweater. An alternate to this game was for me to hold something—a piece of heavy rope, a section of old tire inner tube, a broom—for her to grab and pull. She galloped back and forth past me and leaped into the air to grab these objects.

Baba didn't only make use of her mouth, she also used her forepaws a great deal for manipulating and holding on to things. A favorite game of hers was to grab a strip of heavy rubber tire, stand on it, and then pull while holding it down, twisting her head around and even rolling over to try and get greater purchase on it and pull it away from me.

Visitors loved watching these games and were very impressed if I showed them Baba's teeth. None of them offered to join the game.

One of the reasons that many people don't really manage to get along with animals, I've found, even the comfortable domestic species like dogs or cats, not to mention more exotic things, is because they expect that animals, when associated with people, will stop acting like animals. People get embarrassed when their dear pet dog avidly sniffs the rear of his four legged friends, or when he gulps down with relish some particularly juicy tidbit that some foolish human has dumped in the garbage. The pampered housecat can go out on its own to hunt mice, but heaven save us from her bringing her prey home to show us. How much more so that a wild animal, even a hand-raised one, must behave according to its nature.

Baba was fascinated by smells. A great deal of her world was based on scent; she examined everything very thoroughly with her nose. There was a wide variety of scents that had particular appeal for her, from smelly meat and dead animals (to test her reactions I showed her dead mice and birds) to soap and perfume. If the source of the smell was on the ground, or if it was on an object that she could carry away and put down on the ground, she rolled on it, rubbing her neck and shoulders against the smelly object until she was saturated with the odor. When she was finished, if the object was something soft or edible like a particularly ripe banana or a piece of liver, not much was left.

If the object was something she couldn't roll on directly, she did her very best to rub against it. One of the scents that really turned her on was cigarette smoke. Smoke, being intangible, was hard to rub against, so she would rub against anything in the vicinity with her neck and ruff semi-erect and her eyes half closed in pleasure. Another scent that she particularly enjoyed could be found in human armpits. For her, this was apparently both a pleasant scent and a means of identification and security—I had seen her calm down on occasions when she was upset and nervous after she smelled my armpits and rubbed against me. Perhaps there is truth in the fact that animals can smell the scent of fear and thus she was reassured when she didn't smell fear in my bodily exudations.

Baba's fondness for smelling armpits created some rather funny reactions. In our western world, we have been taught to do everything possible to banish body odor—use of deodorants, deodorant soaps, sprays, talcum, and so on—and in general to ignore the existence of such unpleasant realities as sweat and its odor. Animals, however, are very frank in their reactions and have not learned to be subtle and polite. Baba liked these smells, and she also liked the smell of deodorants, especially sweet and flowery scents. People didn't know how to react when she rubbed up against them, poking her nose into their armpits in obvious fascination, breathing deeply, bristling and grinning.

I learned not to be embarrassed by having my hyena sniff my armpits in obvious pleasure.

From the beginning, Baba slept in my bed—another fact that shocked some people. It isn't uncommon for pet dogs and cats to sleep in bed, so why should a pet hyena be different?

Actually, it started as she grew older and more active. While Baba was very small, she disappeared into dark corners under the sofa or behind the cabinets, and only came out when she was hungry. As she grew, she began to look for more attention and social contact, and in short order learned to climb up onto my lap, where she shoved her head under my arm in contentment. If I wasn't available, any handy lap would do. Simultaneously with the development of this desire for physical contact, she also began to show an intense curiosity. This, coupled with her destructiveness, made it more and more difficult to leave her unsupervised for even a short time. As a very small animal, she really wasn't capable of doing much damage while inspecting something that aroused her curiosity. By the time she was four months old and getting her adult teeth, she could pretty well demolish anything in reach within a few minutes.

Although she usually went to sleep and slept through the night, there were times that she did wake up. I decided that for the sake of my peace of mind and the preservation of my possessions, it would be better if Baba slept in the bedroom. Being a light sleeper, I awoke if anything out of the ordinary occurred. Baba thought this was a wonderful idea. Of course, the obvious place to sleep was in my bed.

Hyenas in nature have been observed sleeping pressed against one another; physical contact with them, as with many animals, is apparently a meaningful part of their interrelations. So Baba slept curled up against me, usually with her back against mine. She liked some petting before she went to sleep, which meant that she rolled over and threw herself backwards across me so that I could scratch her throat and belly. Forty kilos of hyena plunked down hard across one's abdomen is rather hard to ignore. It also turned out, as she matured, that she did not much like getting up in the morning, especially if the weather was bad. I awoke, got dressed and called her but she didn't move. I had to grab her by the collar and drag her out of bed. Once she found herself dumped on the floor, she grudgingly got up and agreed to go out.

She was not very generous about space in bed either. She stretched in the middle of the night and then pushed with her legs until I ended up with a quarter of the bed and Baba with the rest.

She didn't sleep in the house every night. I didn't want her totally dependent on me, in the event that on occasion I might have to be away for a day or two. But this closeness, it seemed to me, was an important part of our relationship, of her trust in me, and the obvious affection she also showed. Our relationship took the place of the wild ones she would have had if she were part of a group of hyenas.

Of course, I never had to worry about being attacked in the night!

There were some other difficulties. I was at the time unmarried, having divorced from Jacques two years earlier, and did at times have male friends visiting. Most of them considered Baba very cute and sweet. But her habit of climbing onto my lap and inserting herself between my friend and me did have a dampening effect on romance. It may be that she was simply looking for the warmth and closeness of mother and littermates; there is no question that Baba found the closeness comforting. She inspected warm bodies present, licked faces, a shock to anyone not expecting a sandpaper tongue, and perhaps chewed an ear or two, before settling down to sleep. While she was small, it was not such a problem. But as Baba grew, her presence on my lap became a very difficult obstacle to get around. It was even worse to consider the possibility of telling someone serious about me that my hyena had the habit of sharing my bed at night.

Some of my houseguests were rather nervous at the idea of sharing a house with a hyena. One friend, a very formidable lady from Germany, asked me with a quaver in her voice, "What do I do if I wake up in the night and Baba is standing by the bed looking at me?"

"There is no chance that she will be at your bedside at night; she sleeps with me."

"Doesn't she ever wake up and walk around?"

"No," I answered, "she sleeps very soundly."

"But what if she does wake up?" persisted my guest.

"Well, the best thing to do would be to turn over and go back to sleep. She won't bother you; she would be much more interested in checking out what you have in your suitcase."

Probably the best sport among my houseguests was the Norwegian dog judge who was invited over by our club to judge a dog show. In order to save on expenses, various club members offered to host him while he visited, and I was of course happy to join the list. His previous host had warned him about Baba, but I had the feeling that he didn't really believe it until I came to pick him up and he saw her sitting on the back seat of the car.

He seemed rather nervous as he got in the car, but Baba was friendly and he was accustomed to animals, so by the time we got home he seemed to have decided that she wasn't all that different from a dog.

I brought him into the house, turned Baba loose—she promptly crawled under a chair for a nap; traveling is tiring—and I went off to make my visitor a cup of tea. Suddenly I heard a tremendous commotion. The cat had been hunting and had brought home an enormous rat to eat in comfort. Baba scented this wonderful object, woke up instantly and decided that she must have it. The cat and Baba were now engaged in a furious noisy battle over the carcass while my poor guest stood in the middle of the room not knowing in what direction to run.

I waded into the middle of the fray and grabbed Baba, giving the cat her chance to flee. The cat was no fool; she grabbed the rat and scrambled up to the top of the cupboard, well out of reach of Baba. Unfortunately, this was well out of my reach too, even when I climbed up on a chair. Baba, knowing her prey was up there, prowled up and down, jumping against the cupboard while the cat glared down at her.

Obviously the rat couldn't be left up there, and I couldn't reach it. However, my Norwegian visitor was very tall. Without hesitation he agreed to climb up and get the rat, which I promptly flung far out the door. The cat stayed on the cupboard in a sulk and Baba, very disappointed, went back to sleep.

The rest of the judge's visit was uneventful, but I have the feeling he was never totally relaxed when Baba was around. And I have heard that I have since become a sort of legend in parts of Norway.

Chapter Thirty-Five: Water

One of Baba's favorite games was playing with water. From a very young age, she was fascinated by it. If I watered the garden, or changed the water in cages at the zoo, she would leap around trying to catch the stream from the hose. She never seemed to be able to understand why, when she grabbed it with her teeth, it just slipped through. Of course, when she managed to catch the end of the hosepipe, she was much less frustrated. I had a lot of problems with hoses getting progressively shorter and shorter as Baba finished off the end, or turned them into an unwanted sprinkler system. Even though I tried my best to protect the hose while using it, Baba was sneaky. She would creep up behind me and grab while I wasn't watching; one good grab was sufficient for several good punctures. This was very pleasing to Baba, as now she had a lot of streams of water to chase instead of only one.

If I left her a container full of water, Baba climbed in and splashed around like a toddler in a plastic pool. The first tub she had was a large plastic box, which was just big enough for her to squeeze into. She sat in the water, splashing with her front feet and enjoying it tremendously, even though I couldn't believe that she managed to squeeze into it. As she enjoyed it so much, and obviously needed more room, I found her something larger—an old galvanized tub, large and roomy, and impervious to her teeth. She could stand in it, lie down in it and turn around in it. In hot weather she laid there submerged, only her head above water, grinning in pleasure.

One indication of intelligence in animals is their ability to learn from observation. Baba was very good at that, as regarded the things she wanted. She very easily learned, for instance, to open the water tap.

On a number of occasions I came back after leaving Baba happily playing or sleeping and found the water gushing away as she happily romped in the mud puddle she had made. She never learned to close the tap, though, since that wasn't very interesting.

As much as Baba liked playing in water, she disliked rain. Come winter, she suspiciously looked out the door in the morning before agreeing to step outside. If it was raining, I had to physically push her out. She learned to open doors so that she could come in out of the rain on her own. I even observed her making very serious attempts to turn the key in the lock, using her mouth and her forepaws, when the office door was left locked. She hated mud when it was not of her own making, and gingerly walked through muddy patches, lifting her feet high in disgust. When her feet were muddy, she was not allowed in the

371

house before they were washed off. She learned very quickly to stand still and lift each foot in turn for me to wash with the hose, so that she was allowed in out of that horrible weather.

As Baba was so fond of water, I decided to give her a treat. I would take her to the beach where there was unlimited water for her to play with. One hot summer day, we climbed into the car and headed for the nearby sea.

Baba followed me down the rocky approach, fascinated by the many new things to look at and sniff. The sand was strange to her and it was hot; she was perplexed by the funny feeling of hot sand on her feet and scratched at it and even tried to taste it.

She still hadn't noticed the water because she was still too interested in all the other new things around. We slowly walked closer. I was sure that she would be thrilled.

It was a very calm day. There was no wind, and the water was smooth as glass, with tiny waves gently stroking the shore. We walked up to the very edge of the water, and one of these little waves touched Baba's feet. I don't think that Baba had realized that she was facing water until the wave reached her. When she looked up and saw a world of water in front of her, with no end in sight, her reaction was total panic. She ran, as far and as fast as she could, at least to the safety of the familiar rocks at the end of the beach. All my attempts to calm her were useless against her instincts. She grabbed my leg in her jaws—and despite being in total panic was still very gentle—and tried to pull me away from this frightening place.

We retreated from the sea. When we reached the rocks, she crawled into the shade between two large boulders and collapsed panting in their protection. Gradually, as she saw that the sea was not going to chase her up the beach, she calmed down. After a while, she was ready—very cautiously—to come out from the rocks and return, with great relief, to the car. Baba's day at the beach was over.

Chapter Thirty-Six: Baba and the Owl

I am very fond of owls. I love their faces, the way they stare and turn their heads every which way as if trying to understand something complicated. They are also fairly easy to tame. I had raised two barn owls earlier in my career at the University, perhaps the most beautiful of all the owls, with gleaming white and tan feathers. When I set them free, they returned to be fed for some time before they became completely independent. So I was eager to try again, with a younger one that would perhaps agree to live permanently in the box I fixed on my porch.

When I heard that a bunch of barn owl hatchlings had been brought into the zoo, I saw my chance and asked if I could have one. It was fairly easy to arrange, as I had experience with the owls and had proven that I could raise them.

The fledgling was quite young, still without adult feathers and covered with soft fluff. I was told that it was eating well, and was provided with a bag of frozen day-old chicks, its food for the next few days. I put the little owl in a closed cardboard carton for its trip home.

That day was my turn to work late. Baba was wide-awake and full of energy by the time I was ready to leave. The carton with the owl was in the back of the car, and the noises and smell fascinated Baba. Instead of going to sleep as usual, she kept peering into the back.

I wasn't going straight home that day; I had an errand first in town, and then was due to stop by the house of some friends to pick up a cat that they were giving me. When I got to the first stop on my agenda, not expecting to be longer than a few minutes, I tied Baba in the car without misgivings.

When Baba was small, I could leave her in the car, and she would sleep quietly until I came back. As she grew, however, she became more independent and playful, and found being left in the car a great opportunity for exploring, which meant things like chewing up the plastic knob on the end of the gear shift, tearing up the rubber floor mats, eating the door handles, and so on. I decided that I would have to find a solution before she started chewing up more serious parts of the car interior like the steering wheel. So I tied her to the armrest of the backseat door when I had to leave her in the car. As she was well aware of the fact that acting wild and chewing things up in the car did not constitute desirable behavior, she quickly learned that being tied was connected with this, and was always very good when tied.

After my errand, I came back to the car, unsuspecting. I had never taken seriously the phrase 'my heart fell to my feet' until this moment. As I came near, I saw Baba sitting in the driver's seat. As I came closer and she spotted me, she dived into the back, crouched down on the seat with her head in the corner in a classic, "Who, me? I haven't done anything!" pose.

I opened the door. Mess is a mild description of the situation. The floor mats were turned upside down; the carton that had held the owl was torn to shreds; there was straw bedding all over; and there was a big clump of electrical wiring hanging loose under the dashboard.

My reaction was "My god, she's finished off the owl and the car too!" How the hell was I even going to get home?! At that moment, I would have given Baba as a gift to the first person that walked down the street.

All I could do was to try and find out just how bad things were. Being basically either an optimist or a fool, I got into the car, put the keys in the switch, prayed a bit, and tried the starter. The car started! I started trying everything else on the dashboard: the lights worked, speedometer worked, gas gauge, radio, horn, windshield wipers—everything seemed to be working. Feeling a bit calmer, I started to collect the debris in the car. I found that Baba had been messing around with the frozen chicks. And then, lo and behold, there was my little owl! It was hiding in the farthest, darkest corner of the car, not daring to move, but alive and well. I picked it up for examination, and it responded with a healthy peck on the hand.

After making order in the car, I answered the questions of some observers who had just come down the street and noticed odd things going on in the car. Boy, were they lucky! If they had come by just five minutes sooner, they might have had a pet hyena! We started off for the next scheduled stop on my way home. I felt very insecure with the loose wires dangling against my legs, not sure if the car would suddenly blow up or simply die in the middle of the highway. No such thing happened, and I arrived at my friends' house. Baba was very subdued during the ride, although she did try peeking at the poor little owl.

My friends also had no idea what the loose wires in the car were.

I collected the cat to add to the traveling menagerie, and we got home with no further adventures. The loose wires were still hanging there until the day I got rid of that car; I was afraid to ask my mechanic what they were and to have to explain what happened.

Chapter Thirty-Seven: Meeting the Vet

Rabies is a problem in Israel. It is endemic, which means that every now and then there is an outbreak somewhere in the country among the wild animals. This results in a terrible panic among pet owners and non-pet owners, most of whom have little idea what rabies is or how it is transmitted. Due to the hysteria caused by fear of this dread disease, people even bring their perfectly healthy house pets to be destroyed, in case they come down with rabies.

By law, all dogs in the country must be vaccinated. Of course, Baba had to be vaccinated as well, not because she was ever likely to come in contact with a rabid animal, or have the slightest chance of contracting it, but because the first question we were likely to be asked by anyone we met walking down the street was, "Is it vaccinated?" Or perhaps the second question, after "Is it dangerous?" And should Baba one day bite someone, even in play, it was imperative that her vaccinations be up to date.

The first vaccination for Baba was no problem. When she was four months old, I took her to a veterinary friend in town. We even got a city license. Dog licenses are also required by law, and you must have the vaccination to get the license. I do wonder what the city clerk thought while making out the license for a hyena.

By the time Baba needed her next vaccination, she was already quite large. Our vaccinations were ordinarily done by a vet employed by the local council, who went around from settlement to settlement vaccinating all the dogs and issuing the licenses. Many of the vets in this job were both young and just out of school, or not highly successful in private practice.

Our doctor's technique was typical of the profession; when you have hundreds of dogs to vaccinate you do it quickly. One quick jab from behind and the dog was done and on to the next. Now, with dogs this was not a problem. Doc, however, had never vaccinated a hyena. Baba was on leash, and at over a year old was already quite a large animal; at this point she was as tall as a German Shepherd and weighed about thirty kilograms. Doc, probably from bitter experience, was very wary about approaching animals. If he was wary about dogs, imagine how he felt about a hyena! He tried repeatedly to creep up on her from behind. Baba, however, was not willing to have anyone, and certainly not someone she had never seen before and who was acting very strangely, sneak up on her from behind. Although I tried to hold her head, she was not at all willing to hold still for this nonsense. She swiveled around to follow his movements, her back hair bristling to show her suspicion of this strange behavior, and her head lowered and stretched toward him, a typical hyena glare in her eyes.

"Look, a hyena doesn't like having you come up from behind. It makes her nervous. She wants to see who is coming," I explained.

"It makes me nervous to come from in front where those teeth are," he replied.

"But if you just come over and stand still and let her sniff you, then she will relax and accept you."

"What if she decides that she doesn't like my smell? My job is vaccinating dogs, not hyenas!"

Finally, I managed to hold her still long enough for him to rush in and jab her from arm's length.

The next year, Baba was considerably larger and stronger. The day Doc came to vaccinate, she was in one of the kennels. He made the rounds of the dogs and then reached her. Baba and Doc looked one another in the eye, and then Baba yawned broadly, exposing a beautiful set of teeth.

"Look," I said, "I don't think you can vaccinate the hyena this year. She is too strong for me to hold still."

Silence.

"What about letting me vaccinate her?" I asked.

"That's a great idea," he answered enthusiastically. "I'll just stand back here and watch to be sure you do it properly."

Handing me a prepared syringe, he immediately backed twenty meters away to the top of the next terrace. Baba was so fascinated watching this weird person making strange and incomprehensible maneuvers that she never even noticed when I jabbed her.

The following year there was no question. I took the syringe and went into her cage, while Doc stood a good distance away yelling helpful suggestions.

Baba never felt a thing.

Chapter Thirty-Eight: A Funny Kind of Dog

In the Jerusalem hills where we live, everything is terraced. In Biblical times, the whole area was cultivated for agriculture, and the only way of growing crops on steep hillsides was to build innumerable little terraces to hold the soil. Nowadays, this is not a practical method of agriculture, as it cannot be done by machine. But the terraces remain; despite, in some cases, hundreds of years of erosion, some are even still in very good condition.

The terrace in front of our house had collapsed, and had to be repaired immediately so that the deterioration would not continue. The real experts here in dry stone terracing were the Arabs, so the only thing to do was to go to the nearby village of Abu Gosh and find someone to come and fix the terrace.

Abu Gosh is a very picturesque village in the hills. It was started in Turkish times by the enterprising family of Abu Gosh, the family patriarch, who took up his position on the one and only road going up to Jerusalem and demanded toll from anyone who wanted to pass. This income was augmented by a bit of highway robbery on the side, it is said, resulting in the family rapidly establishing itself as rich and influential. Today, the main road to Jerusalem passes around Abu Gosh, limiting the opportunities for a self-respecting highwayman. Most of the Abu Gosh-niks, now a large village of many families, although all are related, these days work in the building trades, and they do all right. This village has been loyal to Israel throughout all the hard times, supporting the state in the war of independence and afterwards. The younger generations considered themselves 'Israelis of Muslim faith' and were very modern in outlook, not willing to chain themselves to old superstitions.

So, a few of the fellows from Abu Gosh came to fix the terrace, and they met Baba. None of them had ever met a hyena before, and they were fascinated. One of them told me that it was possible to neutralize a vicious dog by throwing a hyena skin over it. When the terrace was fixed, they asked if they could come back with the children to show them Baba. Sure, I said, why not.

They arrived back the next day, with children, cameras, and another few villagers who had not believed the story. It was very wintry outside, and Baba was in her favorite position in the house, sprawled out on the sofa. For my visitors, even more astonishing than having a hyena, was having it in the house! They didn't even let dogs or cats in their houses. They came in cautiously. Baba sat queenly on her sofa as the others all crowded into the chairs on the other side of the room.

The children soon gathered courage to come over and pet her, and the proud fathers took their photograph with the 'dangerous' hyena. But somehow, Baba didn't seem to feel that she was getting her fair share of attention. Carefully looking over her audience, she picked out one fellow who was sitting on the side, not saying much, but looking very uncomfortable. Calmly, Baba got up, stepped over to his chair, put her enormous paws in his lap, and licked his ear.

I thought I had a fair vocabulary of Arabic swear words, but this poor guy shrieked out things I had never heard before. In a total panic, afraid to move and agitate the hyena, he begged his friends to save him, as they all collapsed on the floor in gales of laughter. I rescued him from Baba. Baba thought the whole thing quite interesting.

I am sure that the poor fellow was the talk of Abu Gosh for weeks.

The reactions of Arabs to Baba have always been quite interesting. The many beliefs and tales traditionally held, in contrast to 'modern' attitudes, created some very amusing reactions. For a while, we were a high point for the JNF forestry workers in the area; many of them were Arabs. Those who had heard of Baba or who had been to the farm apparently made bets with their friends about the tame hyena and then brought them by to see that she really existed. I overheard several arguments, with one side insisting that this couldn't be a hyena, while the other side demanded payment of the bet. There was an old Arab gardener in the university zoo who, every time he met Baba and me, tried to buy her. He insisted that he would pay any price, but that he must have the hyena. Every time he saw us, he came over to pet Baba, and to bring her tidbits. It was subsequently explained to me that he felt that having a hyena would give him tremendous status in his village—enough to be worth any price.

One day I went south with a friend of mine from the Nature Reserves Authorities to visit a number of Bedouin villages. Baba, of course, came along, and settled comfortably on the back seat of the car. She was quite large by then, taking up the whole seat. She wore a bright red dog collar because I thought that red would look good in contrast to her gray and black coat. As we progressed through the villages, I noticed a number of Bedouin looking into the car at Baba. But no one said anything or asked any questions, which I thought was rather odd as it is not every day that one sees a hyena sitting in a car. Finally, my friend stopped one of the Bedouin who had been peering at Baba and asked him if he knew what she was.

"That's a funny kind of dog," he answered. My friend told him that it was no dog, it was a hyena.

"No, it's a dog. If it were a hyena, it would eat you. Who ever heard of a hyena wearing a collar?" he answered.

The Bedouin was totally unwilling to believe that Baba was a hyena. Neither he nor the other inhabitants of the village had ever seen a hyena, and believed that there was no way that a hyena could ride in a car and wearing a collar. As we drove away, he winked at us with a smile, as if to say, "You see, you can't fool me!"

Chapter Thirty-Nine: Still a Wild Animal

Not everything involved in raising a wild animal is cute or funny. People, even experienced animal people, have the tendency to forget that a wild animal remains wild, even when it is hand raised. Raising an animal from infancy accustoms it to humans, and an imprinted animal may even grow up thinking of itself as a human, but this does not change the fact that such an animal still has certain innate behavior patterns that may assert themselves at an appropriate time. Raising a wolf cub in the house from infancy does not turn it into a lap dog, nor does raising a lion cub by hand turn it into a pussycat. Many of the tragedies that have occurred with such hand-raised animals came about due to their handlers forgetting that they were dealing with a wild animal, and putting the animal into a situation that caused its instincts to take over, and the animal to behave like its wild forebears.

I always tried to keep in mind that Baba was a wild animal. Therefore, I was not really surprised that, as she became more mature, she started to show more wild behavior. With maturity, she came to the decision that not everyone in the world was her friend. The first person that she decided she did not like was a young fellow who worked as a keeper in the zoo. He passed by the cage several times a day, but never had anything to do with Baba other than stopping for a moment outside the fence to say hello. Then one day he called to me to come and see how Baba was acting. She ran back and forth along the fence, hair bristling, tail straight up in the air, mouth open, snapping at the wire. The hyena in play will wrinkle up its lips in an aggressive grin; when seriously aggressive, the mouth is open with no wrinkling of the lips. This was obviously aggressive behavior, but I had no inkling why she had suddenly developed a hatred for Gaddi. I asked him if he had teased her and the answer was no.

I tried to stop Baba by yelling "No!" at her, which was usually effective in stopping her from doing things, but there was no effect this time. Then I tried to grab her by the collar to hold her back. That was a mistake, I quickly found out. She turned her head, grabbed my arm and bit me—obviously a warning, as she did not bite hard nor hold on. She immediately let go, but the meaning was obvious—she was angry and did not want to be interfered with.

As the days went by, she became more and more aggressive to Gaddi. We tried to figure out what had set her off. Was it some particular smell on him? The other hyenas and most of the other predators in the zoo did not like him either.

Then, gradually, Baba began to choose other people that she didn't like. Some of them were people that she had been friendly to and had played with, while others were people she had never met, but who simply passed by her cage. To all of them Baba displayed the same classic aggressive behavior—bristling, running back and forth, jumping at the fence with open mouth. I could see no common denominator between these people to explain why Baba had decided that she didn't like them.

She also began differentiating between dogs that she knew and dogs that she didn't know; she showed aggression, although not nearly as pronounced, to dogs she didn't know. However, if a dog reacted with self confidence or aggression, Baba backed down.

One morning, as I was outside of the cage fetching food for the birds, I heard screams. Racing back, I found one of my coworkers, Inga, in a confrontation with Baba, and this time it was serious. Baba had gotten worked up when one of the people she had decided she hated passed by outside of the cage. Inga, never thinking that Baba would do anything to her, as Baba had always been friendly to her, had ignored the animal's agitated state and had come over in reach of Baba's chain to fill a water dish at the tap.

From Inga's description, Baba had looked at her ferociously. How well I knew that black look of nerves and anger, and how hard it is for anyone who is not intimately familiar with an animal's facial expressions to discern things like that. Inga talked to Baba for a minute, then approached to get water when Baba jumped at her, first grabbing her slacks and not managing to get a good hold, and then jumping again and grabbing Inga's leg. Inga, had panicked—and it is certainly justifiable to become panic stricken when being bitten by a hyena—and had screamed at Baba and pulled back. The action of pulling back, of course, only made Baba hold on tighter.

By the time I got to the cage, Baba had released Inga. Inga was in a state of shock, with a few deep holes in her leg from the canine teeth, and a good deal of bruising from the pressure. Hyenas do not have very sharp teeth, but they can exert tremendous pressure with their jaws. I was somewhat relieved to see that the bite did not look much worse than a dog bite. We took Inga to the doctor for treatment ("You were bitten by what?!!") and she was advised to take sick leave for a week or two. It was indeed very painful, especially for someone not accustomed to taking animal bites in stride.

But now the real problems began. Inga developed a total and irrational terror of being anywhere near Baba; she was sure that Baba would see her, rip her chain free, and rush to attack. There is no way to control a fear like this. So Baba could not be anywhere in Inga's vicinity.

Then Professor Mendelson, the department head, gave the final word that Baba could not come to the zoo anymore. There were too many people that she was showing aggression toward, and it was too dangerous. There wasn't much to say. The fact was that Baba was at times aggressive and I had no way of being sure that she might not attack someone else. Baba was banished and from then on she had to stay home.

Chapter Forty: Baba at Home

Now that Baba had to stay at home, she had to have a secure and comfortable pen to be left in for the many hours that I was at work. With the help of my coworkers who came out to the farm to help, I built a roomy pen with a strong fence and a large and comfortable shelter against sun and rain. (The fence one needs for a hyena is not the same as the fence one needs for a dog!) Baba was quite content there once she became accustomed to the idea of being confined.

However, the pen had a dirt floor. During the summer it was fine, although Baba did some extensive excavating, including digging a very comfortable den underneath her shelter. However, as soon as the rains started, it became a sea of mud. Baba hated mud, and she made it even worse with her restless pacing back and forth in disgust at the situation. She churned it up to the texture of a thick goulash, sinking in up to her pasterns. When I took her out of the muddy pen, she had to be forced to go back in, and she tiptoed into the mud, lifting her feet like a hackney horse to try to keep them clean, with an expression of utter disgust on her face. Although she really tried to stay clean, she ended up covered with mud from head to foot. Even her face was caked with mud. She tried to clean it off with her forepaws and made it even worse. She hated it so much that she was even amenable when I washed her down with the hose, lifting one paw at a time for me to wash and lifting her head up so that I could reach her neck and chest.

The only thing to do was to lay a cement floor. For a week Baba was moved to one of the dog kennels, and we worked on Baba's floor. This involved bringing pickup truckloads of gravel from a nearby quarry; the Arab watchmen there was absolutely stunned to see me, a woman, shoveling gravel, but they happily cheered me on. Then we had to mix and lay the cement, which looks easy when someone else is breaking his back at it, but is different when you have to do it yourself. I managed, during the days that this work took, to get just about every male on the farm to participate, and even some of the females—partly using the Tom Sawyer principle; "See how much fun I'm having, wouldn't you like to join in?" And partly by just plain pestering.

Another improvement in the pen was an old bathtub, cemented in so that Baba couldn't turn it over. Her old plastic water container was slowly being chewed to bits, and she overturned it constantly. The old galvanized tub that Baba had loved so much was now much too small for her when she climbed into it to take a cooling dip. This new one was much roomier, it couldn't be overturned, she always had water which could be changed and cleaned easily, and she had plenty of room for water play.

When Baba was brought back to her improved living conditions, she was very suspicious of all the changes. She slowly walked in and made a circuit of the pen, avoiding the bathtub. All of her hair stood on end in reaction to the changes to her familiar territory. She inspected every centimeter of the pen over and over. It was obvious that, through her nose, she read the whole story of the building project. Every now and then she would, out of the corner of her eye, sneak a look at the bathtub to be sure that it was not going to creep up and attack her while she wasn't looking. Gradually she worked her way over to it and reached out to smell it, ready to run if it should make a threatening move. The final stage, when she had decided that the tub was not going to move after all, was to lift her leg over the edge and mark it. Now it was hers!

Baba probably liked the dirt floor better than the cement, but certainly did not miss the mud. The bathtub, though, became one of her great pleasures. During the summer she laid in it, covered over with water, cool as could be.

Baba became very possessive of her pen and defended it against any one she didn't like. She put on quite a display, running back and forth, tail up and hair standing on end, jumping at the fence, and presenting a frightening appearance.

I still never really knew why Baba decided that she liked some people and hated others; there seemed to be nothing in common between the people that she hated. It was pretty obvious, however, why she hated our neighbor Amatzia. Amatzia was a very macho type, physically strong and very self confident. His normal way of moving was to stride along confidently in his heavy army-type shoes, as though nothing could stand in his way. Animals tend to interpret this kind of behavior as aggressive and threatening. One day I came out of the house to find Baba and Amatzia in a confrontation. Baba was tied in the center of the yard and Amatzia had tried to pass her by. They stood face to face, glaring at each other. Baba's hair was on end. Neither man nor beast was willing to give an inch. From that day on, Baba decided that she hated Amatzia. He just had to pass by her pen and she would run back and forth in full aggressive display.

So one day when Amatzia was showing a workman something in the yard and stood on the terrace just above Baba's pen, she got very annoyed as usual. She raced back and forth along the wall of the terrace, leaping into the air trying to 'get' Amatzia. Amatzia, macho as ever, ignored her snapping jaws as he casually stood on the terrace edge.

It was a very hot day, and putting on aggressive displays is hard work, especially when it doesn't seem to be making an impression. As I watched the performance, Baba suddenly turned around, ran full speed to her bathtub, leaped into the water, submerged herself except for her head, sat there a minute, and then, refreshed, leaped out and started running and displaying again. After a few more minutes of running, she again returned to the bathtub, plunged in, soaked herself thoroughly, and went back to her display.

I guess that could be called 'keeping cool.'

When Baba was about six or seven, we had a very harsh winter. There were tremendous windstorms, and one night I woke up, opened the front door, and found an enormous pine tree lying across the porch. The winds had been so strong that they had pulled down an old pine that had stood by the steps. The tree fell across Baba's pen and covered the yard, missing the house by inches, but taking with it the telephone and electric lines.

As I took stock, I suddenly realized that Baba was somewhere under the tree. It was hard to see what had happened in the dark, but some probing with my flashlight revealed that the tree, although it had partly crushed the fence of Baba's pen, was resting on the roof of her shelter, and peering through the branches covering the opening I saw the shine of her black eyes.

The next morning, in daylight, with winds still gusting far above normal, we could assess the situation more clearly. Baba's pen was completely covered by the tree, but it was held off the ground by the fence and the shelter, and by the fact that it had fallen on the upper terrace as well. There was no way to repair everything without first sawing the tree into pieces and taking these out bit by bit.

I didn't know how Baba, no doubt extremely upset by having a tree fall on her, would react to having strangers with power saws working in her pen to get rid of the tree. The only thing I could do was to crawl under the tree to where Baba was sitting crouched in her shelter, to reassure her and keep her calm while the work was going on.

I wasn't sure how she would react to me under these circumstances. This was exactly the sort of situation that could make a wild animal dangerous, if it felt that it had to defend itself from danger. With some misgivings, I worked my way in under the branches, taking to Baba and soothing her as I approached.

Far from being aggressive, Baba was very glad to see me. She pressed herself against me with her head on my lap, looking for comfort from the strange happenings of the night. The workmen started on the tree, and Baba and I sat together, half smothered by flying sawdust. It took hours for the tree to be cut up and removed and during the whole time, Baba sat with me calmly, watching these strange people and their strange activities and never showing the slightest aggression. As pet owners are fond of saying, it was as if she understood that they were trying to help.

Chapter Forty-One: Goodbye

Baba is buried in the *wadi* not far from the house, in a place overlooking the valley; it is the kind of landscape that would have been home to a wild hyena. She lived the last years of her life peacefully on the farm, in her familiar and comfortable surroundings, and she died peacefully and without fear at twelve years of age.

I have had many animals over the years, and have been attached to them all but there are always those that are special, which hold a place in the heart that can't be held by anyone else.

I have had many dogs that loved me truly, and even those who would, perhaps, have given their lives for me, though they never had an opportunity to prove it. But Baba was a special animal entirely, and our relationship was totally different.

Somehow, it was tremendously satisfying to have a hyena 'love' me, to be for her the universe; her security, her source of food, affection, fun, discipline, and her protection from all the frightening things she faced in the course of her life. In some ways it was more satisfying to have a hyena happy to see me when I came home than to have the same response from a dog, to have her roll over to be petted and then leap into the air and jump around in playful joy. A dog is expected to act like that, but a hyena is wild and belongs to itself unless it willingly gives its affection.

The experience was unforgettable, and worthwhile, as it taught me, more than ever, that a wild animal remains ever wild and is not meant to be a household pet. The relationship I had with Baba will remain a cherished memory, but I will never do it again.

Chapter Forty-Two: Bringing Bayud Home

It had been several years since I had visited the Bedouin to look for dogs. A woman cannot travel around among the Bedouin tribes on her own; this is unacceptable in the Bedouin culture. The warden of the Nature Reserves Authority who I had traveled with in the past had been transferred to another area, and I did not know the new warden. It was definitely advisable to visit with someone who knew the tribes and was respected by them.

It was the spring of 2001. Israel was hosting a very important international dog show, the European Winner Show. This show was held each year in a different European country and awarded a special title to the winning dogs, European Winner. Although it was true that Israel was not really in Europe, the FCI, the international association that controls official dog activities, had problems deciding in what category we fit, and Europe was easiest and least likely to cause conflict. The Israel Kennel Club hoped that we would be able to attract many exhibitors from outside the country. We had indeed hoped for a surge of tourism in the country from the millennium celebrations on. Unfortunately, the Intifada, (the beginnings of a new surge of Arab terrorism in Israel) had begun in the fall of 2000, and many people who had planned to come to visit in Israel were afraid to do so.

In fact, many exhibitors from abroad who had intended to come to the show cancelled, out of fear of the supposed conditions in Israel. But the European Winner Show was going forward as planned, with or without foreign exhibitors. In conjunction with the show, we were planning an International Canaan Dog Convention. Canaan fanciers from all over the world were invited, and we hoped that many would come to see the dogs in their natural surroundings. The exhibitors for the other dogs may have cancelled, but Canaan people are a unique breed, like their dogs. Canaan fanciers registered from all over, including the U.S., England, Finland, France, and Italy, and were indeed eager to go to the desert and look for dogs when they arrived.

I decided that it would be worth trying to make some new contacts with the Bedouin so that we would have a chance of seeing some Canaans when, as one of the activities that we planned, we took our visitors to the desert. I called up Matti, the warden that I knew, and he gave me the telephone number of a Bedouin, Hassen, who he said would be willing to help out.

How the Bedouin have changed in some ways! They now have cellular phones, pickup trucks, and generator-powered TVs, but in most other ways their lifestyle is very much the same as it has been for thousands of years.

The day of the trip to the desert came, and on the way south, our tour guide and I called Hassen. He was willing to meet us in the afternoon and take us back to his own camp. So, after a lovely visit to Massada and the Dead Sea with our overseas guests, we headed for Tel Arad, where we were to meet Hassen.

Hassen's son was waiting for us on the edge of the highway, where a rocky trail headed off over the low dusty hills. There was no possibility that our bus could navigate that trail. Several of the guests were able to get a ride with Hassen's son in his pickup truck and the rest of us began to walk along after him.

At first, there was nothing in sight except the dry brown undulating landscape. The hilly layout of the land here is very suited to the Bedouins' temperament; the camps are completely hidden from one another and from any visitors until you actually climb the rise behind which the tent is hidden. You could be standing fifty meters away from a camp, and not have the slightest idea that it is there. After walking for a while, first we came to a group of very nice camels in very good condition, that were hobbled and grazing on the very sparse vegetation. Camels are very valuable livestock so of course, as we came closer, we heard the dogs that were guarding them begin to bark.

Ahead of us on the hillside, we could see the encampment, and several dogs started running towards us. And they clearly were Canaans! There was a large cream-colored male with cut ears—a very nice type of dog that I would have been happy to have; the Bedouin cut the ears of their best watch dogs so that they will guard better—they believe that this makes them more alert. There was also a red bitch, and in the distance a few more dogs, including a puppy. As we came closer to the camp, another dog came over the rise barking, a very pale cream dog, nearly white, of a lovely type, with erect ears and very dark nose and eye pigment. This one was even better than the first male!

Hassen and his family greeted us with the typical Bedouin hospitality, inviting us all into their tent for tea. We all sat on the carpets spread out for us on the ground, and the women, who appeared to have dressed in their best in honor of the visitors, served the sweet tea.

As we were getting ready to leave, after the visitors photographed the Bedouin and the dogs, camels, sheep, and so on, I decided that I would try to convince them to let me have one of the dogs. They seemed to have quite a large number, and I thought they might be amenable to letting me take one home. At first, I was offered the puppy that was running around the camp, but after they had caught him and brought him over, I saw that he was of a different type, with a longish coat, and not really what I was looking for. He was not from their dogs, the Bedouin told me when I asked who his parents were, but came from the neighbors. This could mean that he was from another tribe kilometers away.

Getting up my nerve, I asked about the white dog. Yes, I could have him, they said. Not the one with the cut ears, he was their best watch dog, but the young one, his son, could be spared.

I was overjoyed—that was just the one that I wanted! We agreed that I would come back to get him. It was impossible to take him now on the bus. I would call the day before I intended to come down to the desert, so that Hassen could catch the dog and tie him.

The prospect of getting a new dog from a new bloodline was very exciting and I didn't want to waste any time. The Bedouin move around a lot, and their animals move with them, and chances were, if I waited too long, the dog would be gone. So I talked to a friend of mine in Arad who had spent years working for the Nature Reserves Authority, and knew the Bedouin and their customs, and arranged for him to accompany me; once again, as a woman alone, I could not go to visit the Bedouin. We were also joined by a friend who is a professional photographer, in particular of dogs, who very much wanted the chance to photograph this event. Two weeks after my first visit, we were again on the way to the desert.

I wasn't sure that I could identify the turn off onto the dirt track, but when we got to the area, I found that I did remember the landmarks, and found the turn without trouble. Getting up the track was another story, though. My car was a little Fiat Uno, not very powerful and very low to the ground. As we jounced over the rocks studding the trail, I had major misgivings over what this was doing to my poor little car, especially when we got stuck at one point and all of us had to get out and push the car out of a rocky ditch. Was getting a new dog worth wrecking my old car?

But we did manage to make it to the camp, with the car still in one piece and the Bedouin were waiting for us. Hassen was there with a son in his twenties, and some of the younger children. They had prepared the tent for us to sit in, with colorful carpets and cushions, and we were invited in.

We were again welcomed with typical Bedouin hospitality— plenty of hot sweet tea, and then hot and very strong and bitter coffee. Hassen's son proved to be quite well educated and up to date on what was going on. He even knew that there had been a big dog show in Tel Aviv a few weeks earlier with dogs and visitors from abroad, though he really wasn't sure he understood the point of such a thing. At this point, after some casual conversation, I asked if they had managed to tie the dog for us. Yes, they said, he was tied right outside the tent. And indeed, there he was, a few meters away, tied to a pole and hiding under an old tractor, very unhappy about the situation. We had passed right by and not seen him!

Hassen and his son wanted to know how we intended to take the dog home and I responded that I had a collapsible crate in the car for the dog. That idea seemed to be acceptable to the Bedouin. However, they said that they had had a very hard time catching him, and were very hesitant about how they would get him into the crate. They suggested I take the crate out of the car, that we would then put the dog into the crate, and lift it back into the car. But, once the crate was out and was standing next to the tractor, the men seemed very hesitant about approaching the dog or even touching the chain. They seemed to be afraid of him, and when they moved a bit closer, the dog growled softly.

This looked like it was going to be more complicated than I had expected. If the Bedouin were afraid of the dog, I was not going to have an easy time with him. And how would we get him into the crate? I could put the chain through the bars and try to pull him in that way...

The problem was solved much more easily than that. Hassen's wife suddenly appeared. When she saw what was going on, she walked over, took the chain, and pulled the dog out from under the tractor. He immediately submitted to her, with his head lowered and his tail wagging a bit. Obviously the dog was accustomed to the women of the family.

This was what we had always observed about the Bedouin; it is not the men who ever deal with, feed or relate to the dogs, it is the women and children. The Bedouin men can't get near their dogs, but the women and children can. This was a superb illustration of this fact. The Bedouin woman pulled the dog over to the crate, the dog passively accepting what she was doing, and pushed him in. Once the dog was in the crate, the men were ready to come over and lift it into the car. The dog flattened himself to the floor of the crate and remained passive.

Once the dog was in the car, it was time for more tea and talk; in this culture, things cannot be rushed. We were offered a meal, which it would have been impolite not to accept. However, it was lovely fresh salads in wonderful olive oil, fresh pita bread, olives—the Bedouin have a very healthy diet and it is very rare to see one that is overweight. I asked if the dog had a name. Yes, they said, his name was Bayud, which they could not translate for me exactly but they said it had to do with his white color, and he was two years old. He was a son of the older dog and the red bitch, and they had kept him to guard, as his father was an excellent guard dog.

In return for the dog, I offered presents. It would have been an insult to the Bedouin if I had offered money, and I had to be very careful to choose gifts that would be correct. I brought the photos that had been taken of them at the previous visit, which they were thrilled with, a tea set for the women of the household, and a game for the children.

Finally, it was time to go. After invitations to return, and an invitation from me to stop in and visit if they were ever in my vicinity, we left for home.

Bayud took the trip amazingly well. This dog had of course never been in a car, but he did not panic, but rather sat and inspected his surroundings and watched what was happening. He did not get travelsick. He allowed me to touch him through the bars.

When we got to Sha'ar Hagai, he let me put a collar on him without any resistance. I put him in a kennel in isolation from the other dogs, until he settled in a bit.

Survival is the first priority of an animal like this so from the first day, he was prepared to eat. He would not eat dry dog food; of course this wasn't food to him, but he would eat canned dog food. He moved around the kennel, eating and drinking when there was no one around. When he heard me coming, he lay down in the corner of the kennel. But he allowed me to approach him, to touch him and stroke him. He never, despite being cornered in a totally unfamiliar environment, showed the slightest inclination to attack or even to growl, and was never in a state of panic. I found him to have a very steady temperament. And after a few days, when I came into the kennel, he did not lower his head and he slightly wagged his tail. A relationship was starting to develop!

The breakthrough came soon after he let me pet him. There had been a few other dogs in the area of the kennel where he was, but I had now taken them out and brought them back up to the kennel next to the house. Bayud was alone in the lower kennel—and this obviously was not to his liking. The next morning when I came down, he was standing with his feet on the wall, watching for me, and came up to greet me when I came in—he did not want to be alone. I put him on a leash and took him out and he followed me as if he had been walking on a leash all his life.

Bayud bonded to me totally. As our relationship developed and he gained more and more trust in me, I was able to do anything with him. He was as totally devoted as if I had raised him from puppyhood. He was a fierce guardian of his territory, however, was not at all interested in having anyone else touch him. For him, I was the only person in the world, though he after some time he did allow me to hold him to permit the vet to vaccinate him. I am still amazed by the trust and devotion he gave me. For me, this is a perfect example of what a dog is—willing without question to give up the total freedom of the wild to become friend and partner of a human.

Bayud adjusted very well to kennel life. He never looked for problems or quarrels with other dogs, but was perfectly capable of holding his own when it was necessary. He also proved to be a very interested and efficient stud dog, and several months after his arrival, his first puppies were born.

Bayud sired lovely puppies, very much like himself in type, and many of them also the same color, cream so light that it looked white until you noticed the faint white markings. His puppies also had very strong temperaments. Like their sire, they were self-confident and able to cope well with all sorts of situations. Over the years, a number of his children and grandchildren became champions both in Israel and abroad.

Bayud, however, never went to a dog show. I decided it would be too stressful for him to have to cope with all the strange people and strange dogs and would not be justified. He was happy at home in his own territory. So, he stayed at home and let his offspring represent him in the outside world.

It is funny to make a connection between modern technology and Canaan Dogs, but sometimes these things happen...

Laurence Aries, a serious Canaan breeder in France, very much wanted to breed Sufat (French and Luxembourg Ch. Sufat Hol me Sha'ar Hagai), a bitch she had gotten from me, when she came into season in the spring. But she felt that there was nothing really suitable to breed her to in France or indeed in most of Europe. The available dogs were all related to Sufat in one way or another, and Laurence was interested in trying to use a new bloodline. Sufat is an outstanding bitch who despite at the time still being quite young had already had a great show career, and Laurence hoped that her puppies would carry on in the same tradition.

So she contacted me to ask if there was any possibility of sending semen to France. The dog that she wanted to use was Bayud. We do have a veterinarian in Israel who is an expert in artificial insemination, and in collecting and cooling or freezing semen. He was willing to do the job, no problem. The only problem facing me was Bayud.

Bayud was totally devoted to me and I could do anything with him, but he still had no interest in having anyone else touch him. He also had not been in the car or away from Shaar Hagai since I had brought him home from the Bedouin camp. I couldn't imagine what he would think of the idea of going to the vet and being handled in the most intimate way possible to collect semen...The vet suggested that I do a 'trial run' at home to see if he would let me handle him. No problem, he let me do everything necessary. So I put him in the car and took off for the vet's clinic.

Bayud was not very happy about the car ride. He did not act up, but I could see that he was definitely not comfortable. He was glad to get out of the car when we arrived at the vet's place, but was not very happy to see that he was in a strange place. The vet still had some other clients with their dogs waiting to be seen, so I walked around with Bayud outside, letting him sniff the area, mark the bushes, and settle down. He behaved amazingly well, staying close to me and trying to ignore the fact that there were strange people and strange dogs around. Never a growl or sign of aggression, though I could feel how tense he was about the strange situation. But someone who was not as aware of dog body language as I am would never have imagined that this dog wasn't accustomed to walking around on a leash among dogs and people. The Canaans continuously surprise us with their adaptability.

Finally, it was our turn. I had warned the vet that I didn't think Bayud would let him touch or take sperm from him, so he provided me with the receptacle, stood back and instructed me how to do it. But despite all my efforts to arouse him, Bayud stood there looking suspicious and definitely not showing any signs of sexual interest—his attitude seemed to be more, "*You must be kidding*! Here??? Like this???" I finally was too tired to try any longer, so the vet offered to try—he had more experience (that was for sure!) and maybe he would succeed...

I had brought a muzzle along, so I muzzled Bayud and held his head and the vet took his turn. Nothing at all—no surprise to me. Bayud did not growl or attempt to show any aggression to the vet, but I could see that it was just because he knew that I wouldn't allow it, not that he wouldn't have liked to try.

So what now? Well, I would have to go home, taking the receptacle with me, take the sperm at home, and come back to the vet with the sperm (over an hour drive each way) so he could prepare it and it could be shipped to France.

Bayud was glad to be home, and after giving him a rest, I collected the semen with no problem at all. I brought it back to the vet and it was prepared, packed in a special thermos in ice, and was picked up by the express shipping company.

We were, as is common in Israel, in a period of on and off strikes, and there was a possibility that there would be an airport strike and then the sperm would not get shipped. The shipping itself would take almost two days to get from Israel to Laurence's vet in France. But the shipment did depart on time and I was hoping that there would be no trouble in France.

Not only Israel has labor problems. There was a strike in France, and it took even longer than expected for the sperm to arrive at its destination. And then Laurence called to tell me that there was a problem. The package had arrived, and when the vet opened the thermos, he found that the receptacle containing the prepared sperm had come open and most of the contents had spilled out into the melted ice in the thermos. There was only a tiny amount left. He had inseminated Sufat with the tiny remainder, but told Laurence that he saw few sperm in it under the microscope and he didn't believe that this would be successful.

Laurence wanted me to try and ship another batch—but meanwhile, a strike had started in Israel and the airport was closed. I had to tell Laurence that I was sorry but we would have to wait until next time.

Almost two months later, I got a call from France. It was Laurence. She had been at a show with Sufat the week before and thought that Sufat was sitting strangely. When she got back, she took her to the vet, and an examination showed that Sufat was in whelp. An ultrasound check showed three pups!

A week later, Sufat whelped FIVE fat healthy puppies.

My vet was stunned when he heard the story. I was not as surprised—that survival drive is very strong in the Canaan Dog—even while the dog is still in the form of sperm!

Bayud was very protective of his territory and had the habit of starting to bark when a stranger came to visit and to continue barking nonstop until that person left. This barking could go on for hours. The other dogs would bark a bit, see that I had allowed the visitor in, and would then settle down and ignore the person. Bayud, however, felt that as long as a stranger was in his territory, he had to continue giving warning.

There was only one occasion that defeated his guardian instincts. My granddaughter's school class was studying the various settlements in which the children in the class lived. As this was a 'country' school, there were children from a variety of villages, moshavim and kibbutzim (agricultural settlements). The class learned the history of each settlement and then went to visit; the whole class came to Sha'ar Hagai and, of course, one of the things they were interested in seeing was the kennel and the dogs.

The dogs were in their kennels, and the children came into the yard adjoining them. There were about 30 children plus several parents and teachers. As the first children came into the yard, Bayud, as usual, jumped on his kennel fence and started barking ferociously.

But the children kept coming. There were more and more standing in the yard looking at him. Bayud started looking very confused, as no one seemed to be taking his barking very seriously, and the crowd in the kennel yard grew larger and larger. He had never seen so many people at once—and in his territory!

Finally, with a disgusted expression, he shook himself, turned around and went into his dog house with his back to the crowd. This was just too much to cope with on his own, so he was better off ignoring it. If he ignored them, maybe they would go away...which indeed they did, in time. As the last of the children left the kennel yard, Bayud came out of his dog house, looked around, shook himself, and gave a few barks—"See, I chased them away after all!"

With time, Bayud did learn to grudgingly accept the fact that there were other humans in the world and that at times he would have to deal with them. He even became willing to allow a few of the kennel help I had to touch him. He never seemed to miss his wild life in the desert, never trying to run off into the forest, though he could have if he really wanted to. He trusted me completely, and was totally devoted.

He had sired quite a number of lovely puppies, which were already contributing to the breed in other countries as well as in Israel. But now, I really had no need to use him further at stud; he had played his part and now it was necessary to go on and look for new bloodlines in the wild. Not having unlimited room or budget for keeping the dogs, I would often try to find a 'retirement home' for the older dogs that were retired from breeding for one reason or another, so that I would have the space for new stock. But finding such a home for Bayud would not be easy.

The solution was to offer him to my good friend Isabella in Italy. She had been breeding Canaans for a number of years, producing excellent puppies, and understood the breed very well. Her dogs were based on bloodlines she had obtained from me, and she very much needed some outcross lines, unrelated to the dogs she had; Bayud would be ideal for her, and if there was anyone I could count on to understand and get along with Bayud, it was her. Isabella was thrilled with the idea of getting him. Isabella planned to come to Israel to get acquainted with him and then to take him home. However, her son became ill, and she had to cancel the trip. So, I made arrangements to ship Bayud to Italy by air freight.

He was accustomed to going into a crate, so he had no trouble entering his crate at the airport. He also was very calm, despite walking through the noisy and bustling freight terminal, the sort of place he had never experienced. He was not enthusiastic about all the confusion, but trusted me so much that he was willing to accept that I would not take him into danger.

It was hard to see him taken away. He had been with me for six years. But I knew he would have a good home. I wondered how he would react at the end of his journey, when a stranger came to take him out of his crate.

I anxiously awaited the report from Italy. Not only did Isabella call to tell me that he had arrived safely and was adjusting well, but she e-mailed me a photo to prove it. Bayud was happily sleeping in Isabella's bed next to her and one of her bitches. Obviously he was going to have a very good life!

The adaptability of the Canaan never ceases to amaze me. What other dog can go from being a wild animal in the desert to sleeping in bed without blinking an eye?

Chapter Forty-Three:
In Search of the Origins of the Dog

For years, whenever there has been a good opportunity, I have gone down to the desert to the areas where the Bedouin live, in the hopes of finding good dogs there to add to our Canaan Dog gene pool. There is still a wild or semi-wild population, unrelated to the 'domesticated' stock we have been breeding from for the last years. The dogs are still valued by the Bedouin as guard dogs, and are kept for this purpose in their camps and with their herds. However, this population is rapidly disappearing, and we are worried that soon we will not be able to find Canaans in the desert. The government has a policy of encouraging the Bedouin to live in towns with all the modern comforts of permanent houses, such as electricity, telephones and so on, and to work at 'normal' jobs, rather than living from nomadic herding. The Bedouin in these new towns bring home dogs of various breeds—this is a status symbol for them, but these new conditions are not very conducive to the preservation of the Canaan. And of course, the attempts by the government to destroy populations of stray dogs that might be reservoirs for rabies are also dangerous to the survival of the Canaan—those charged with implementing these policies can't really differentiate between true Canaans and packs of abandoned strays. It is very important, therefore, for us to us to take advantage of any opportunities we might have to bring in new wild bloodlines while they still remain available.

In the fall of 2003, we were faced with a special challenge. A film production company that was preparing a film for the *National Geographic Channel* contacted me. This film was a study of the origins of the dog—a subject that is attracting more and more interest as a result of the genetic research being done in the last few years. The film was to include a quest for the most ancient breeds of dog, those that were the closest to the original ancestor of the dog, that were still the most natural and the least changed by the influences of humans. The breeds featured in the film were the Carolina Dog, the Indian pariah dog, the Dingo, the New Guinea Singing Dog—and the Canaan Dog of Israel.

The producers were interested in as much footage as possible of dogs in a more 'natural' environment—which in this case were the dogs that lived in and around Bedouin camps. Filming actual wild dogs would have been virtually impossible considering the limited amount of time that was available for filming this portion of the program—the schedule was to complete all the filming in two days. But the dogs that lived around the Bedouin camps were close to being wild, hunting and scavenging to feed themselves, and were unapproachable and uncared for. Even the dogs that 'belonged' to the Bedouin were for the most part dogs that had been born in the wild and caught as puppies, tied up in the camp until they became accustomed to it, and then released to live in the camp as guardians and to accompany the grazing herds as their protectors. These dogs could rarely be touched or caught by anyone but the children. Bedouin children, as is true of children everywhere, have a special relationship with animals and especially with dogs.

Filming in Bedouin camps was not something that could be done without a lot of planning and prior arrangement. The Bedouin are very protective of their privacy and are not fond of having strangers wandering around unless they have been invited. The most traditional do not want outsiders seeing their women, and when strangers arrive, the women are hidden in closed tents. Some also still have a belief that by taking photographs of them, the photographer is stealing the soul of the subject—we have been warned a number of times over the years that we could photograph the dogs, but under no circumstances could we photograph the people. So, advance arrangements were necessary to gain the Bedouins' cooperation. This was the task that I and my friend Yigal Pardo, a stills photographer who is especially known for his great animal photography, were entrusted with. We already had developed an excellent relationship with one group of Bedouins. A year and a half earlier, they were the tribe that had been willing to let me take Bayud from their camp. Bayud had adjusted very well to 'civilization,' and had, in the year following, sired several excellent litters. The old sheikh, father of the family, had passed away about six months earlier, and the camp was being run by one of the younger sons, a very friendly and outgoing fellow named Salame, who spoke excellent Hebrew and was quite 'modern.' Yigal had been in touch with him regularly over the year since our last visit, and so when we called to ask if he would be willing to let us come with a film photographer, he agreed without hesitation.

We soon found out that the Israeli producer who was working with the U.S.-based production company also had an excellent Bedouin contact. This was Mahmud, who had for many years worked for Israeli production companies, providing various livestock and extras for the films being made in the south of Israel. Israel is a very popular film location—there are typical desolate and barren desert landscapes that could really be anywhere, without all the political problems of filming in places like Afghanistan. Mahmud was from a completely different area than Salame, knew everyone and everyone respected him—after all, he provided them with work at times. The only problem was that Mahmud didn't really know what sort of dogs we were looking for—he had never paid much attention to dogs before.

I was thrilled to have this opportunity to make an organized trip to Bedouin camps, some of which I had never visited before. I had great hopes of finding new stock that we could obtain from the Bedouins, either adults or puppies that could bring new bloodlines into the gene pool, or to locate dogs that we could possibly breed to in the future.

The Israel Canaan Dog is in a rare situation in that it is still considered by the Federation Cynologique Internationale to be a 'breed in development'—a breed that has a pure population living in natural surroundings that has not yet been entered in a studbook. Dogs from this population can be entered in the studbook appendix of the Israel Kennel Club only if they fulfill certain requirements: they must come from a suitable and remote area where it is very unlikely that any mixing with other dog populations has occurred; they must be judged by an expert judge of the breed to be typical of the breed at a minimum of nine months of age; and then they must be test bred to a Canaan Dog with a full pedigree that has already produced puppies, and the offspring must be judged at a minimum of nine months of age. After three generations, the results can be fully registered in the regular studbook and the grandchildren of the wild dog are considered regular purebred Canaans; the earlier generations are registered in the studbook annex.

As Canaans are one of the few breeds that still have such a population existing, we have been making great efforts in the last few years to obtain new stock while it still exists. Due to the encroachment of 'civilization' on what were formerly isolated and barren areas, and the pressure on the Bedouin to settle in towns and abandon their nomadic life style, the niche that the Canaan Dog has inhabited for generations is rapidly disappearing and so, therefore, are the wild and feral dogs.

As we were planning the details of the trip, we had another great piece of luck. About a week and a half before we were due to go down to the desert, one of my Canaan bitches, Timmie, came into season. She would just be ready at the time we were going down, and we might have an opportunity to do a breeding in the desert. This was great! The National Geographic people thought this could be interesting. We called Salame, and he was willing for us to bring the bitch and try to breed her to one of the camp dogs.

The planned day of the trip, we set off for the desert—the local producer, Eitan, the photographer, Lloyd, Yigal, Timmie and me. Timmie was not really enthusiastic—she has not spent a lot of time in cars, and like most Canaans, prefers to stay at home in her own territory. But she settled in on the back seat of the SUV between Yigal and me, and soon began to feel quite comfortable.

The first location to be visited was in the vicinity of Tel Arad, where the camp of Salame's family was located. As always, it took a bit of searching before we found the track that led to the camp. The tracks through the desert, once you get off the paved roads, are not easy to follow if you are not a Bedouin. Salame and his family were waiting to greet us.

Those who have never been in the desert tend to have a very romanticized notion of what life there is like, influenced perhaps by Laurence of Arabia and similar epics. Those notions are very far from the truth. The Bedouin life is not romantic and glamorous; it is very difficult and rather squalid.

What is referred to here as desert is not an area of picturesque sand dunes, but barren, hard hills where little grows except rocks. Everything is in shades of grey. Even the limited plant life that does grow is a dull greyish-green. Most of the time it is very hot during the day, with little protection from the burning sun, and at night it can be very cold. There are strong winds, especially in the late afternoon when the sun is setting and the land is cooling. There is no running water; the only water is from wells, or what is brought from town in small tankers. Even in the winter, when there is rain, most of it runs off in flash floods because little soaks into the cement-hard ground.

The Bedouin life is very harsh, not one of flowing white robes and prancing Arabian stallions. They have very few possessions, as their traditional life is built on the ability to be mobile—to pack all their belongings on a camel or a donkey and follow the herds to wherever there might be grazing. They do not have furniture—in a Bedouin tent, you sit on carpets on the floor with cushions to support you if you are a welcome guest. This is the same way that the Bedouin sleep. But although they do not have many personal possessions, the Bedouin are a very practical people, and so they collect things. Anything that has been thrown out by someone else might be found in a Bedouin camp, stacked around in piles on the chance that it might be of use some time for something—old pieces of tin roofing, old wooden pallets, barrels, old fencing, boards... However, what they really value are the things they need to survive, and these needs have changed—nowadays they have pick up trucks in place of donkeys, and tractors in place of camels, and many of them have cell phones and generators, which they turn on in the evening to watch TV.

Important to the Bedouin are their honor and their traditions, and one of the most important traditions is that of welcoming guests. So, we were warmly welcomed, ushered into the guest tent, and offered thick, bitter Turkish coffee, and then sweet herb tea.

Obviously, manners dictated that first we must sit around and accept the Bedouin hospitality and discuss all manner of topics, before we could get down to the subject of dogs. Everything was open to discussion, from which sort of pickup truck was the most practical for them (the Bedouin are particularly partial to the Toyota these days), to politics, to the rights of Bedouin women (they do have a choice as to whether to agree to marry a certain man or not). And finally, we got around to the dogs.

Salame had caught one male and tied him, so that we could photograph him and possibly use him to breed to Timmie. There were quite a number of dogs around the camp, quite typical Canaans, but all stayed well out of reach. There was one particularly nice young red and white male that, according to Salame, could be approached by no one, not even the children. A number of the dogs were out with the sheep and would return with the flocks in the evening.

The dog that had been tied was a young white male that Salame called 'Bayud' the same as the dog I had taken the year before. According to Salame, all white dogs were called 'Bayud' which referred to their color, and all red dogs were called 'Foxie.' We got a collapsible crate out of the car and set it up; part of what we wanted to film was how I transported home the dogs I got from the desert. The new Bayud's chain was pulled through the mesh of the crate and he was pulled inside.

Many dogs of the more domesticated breeds who were not accustomed to being crated would, no doubt, have done everything in their power to escape the confinement, from crying and screaming to trying to tear apart the crate with their teeth. This Bayud, showing the intelligence and adaptability of the Canaan, a breed that has had to be able to adapt rapidly in order to survive, did not act up. He turned around in the crate a few times, saw that he was confined, and then lay down and waited to see what would happen. I was able to put my hand in to him—he sniffed it but did not try anything else. After a few minutes, I was even able to lift his lip to check his teeth—he appeared to be between one and one and a half years old. This dog had never been tied or handled before, other than perhaps being fed by the children, but although wary, was ready to 'withhold judgment' until he saw what was happening.

After photographing him in the crate and being loaded into the car, we let him out and tied him back in the spot he had been in originally. Now was the time to attempt the breeding.

When I took Timmie out of the car, the Bedouins were fascinated to see that she really was the same as their dogs. I slowly approached with Timmie, not sure how this Bayud would react. Would he attack a strange dog in his territory, without being interested in the fact that she was a bitch in season?

Bayud immediately realized that this was a bitch in season, and to my surprise, was interested enough to ignore me—a total stranger in his territory—and to start courting Timmie. Timmie was happy to sniff him and start to play with him, but when he started to attempt to mount her, she objected. "I've never seen this male before and you expect that just like that I will let him have me???? *You must be joking!!!*" was Timmie's reaction. I could see that this would all take time.

Canaans are dogs that tend to be devoted to their one mate permanently, if they have a chance, and are certainly not ready to accept just anyone for breeding. It is known for a Canaan bitch running free to refuse all other males until a Canaan dog comes along. Even when dog and bitch are acquainted, they like to go through an entire play ceremony before they will consider breeding. So Timmie and Bayud played, and Lloyd, who was fascinated, filmed all of it. At one point, Timmie tried to show dominance by mounting Bayud. Although he had been extremely tolerant of her to this point, this was not acceptable—he flipped her over and pinned her to the ground with a fierce snarl, to show her who was the boss here. I was careful not to interfere, even though I wasn't entirely sure of how far this would go— but I had confidence that the ritual would not result in injury to either of the dogs.

Finally, I decided that there had been enough play—Bayud was getting tired and Timmie was still acting coy, though I could see that she had decided that he was acceptable. I decided to hold her to see if we could finally get a breeding. I was not sure how Bayud would react to having me standing there holding his bitch—some dogs can get quite aggressive to protect a bitch from perceived rivals.

But he totally accepted me and got about his business, and soon we had an accomplished breeding. I was even able to touch him lightly on the head and body while this was going on.

After the breeding, we released Bayud from the chain. I was sure that he would take off for the edge of the camp. Not at all! He started walking around the camp, marking everything in sight—now he was a man, and he was showing the others! He followed after us as we went towards Salame's tent for another round of coffee and tea—after all, maybe these interesting strangers had another bitch for him in their car....

Salame told us that there was also a litter of puppies in the camp. The bitch had dug a deep den in a hillside, behind piles of rubble and trash—getting near was really difficult. The seven pups were about ten days old and were fat, healthy and shiny, and all of them were red or red and white. We decided we would have to come back again in another month or so to see how they had developed.

All the dogs in the camp looked in good condition, not underweight for the most part and with coats that looked healthy, and the puppies were obviously well fed by their mother. It is important to keep in mind that most of this was the result of the dogs hunting and scavenging for themselves. The Bedouin told us that they 'fed' the dogs—they threw them all the scraps and leftovers, they said. But anyone familiar with Bedouin life knows that scraps and leftovers are few and hard to come by—nothing is wasted in their harsh lifestyle. The dogs scavenged around the camp and in the garbage dumps of any towns within a reasonable distance, and hunted for themselves, mostly catching small rodents and insects. Other breeds of dog would never survive on this regime, or if they did, they would be very thin and scruffy. The Canaans, strong, hardy and tough, made efficient use of every scrap they found, hunted efficiently despite the difficulties of the terrain, and were in excellent body condition and obviously healthy. We have also found over the years that dogs that we brought in from the desert were almost completely free of external and internal parasites; obviously they have natural defenses. Keeping these valuable natural characteristics in the breed was essential, and introducing new wild stock as much as possible was the way to do so.

The rest of our day was spent driving around the area and photographing some shepherds, mostly young boys, with their flocks and their dogs. Many of the dogs were Canaans, although some of them were dogs that had been picked up in town and brought back. None of the shepherd boys spoke Hebrew, but they didn't object to being photographed with their animals.

That night we stayed over in a hotel in Beersheba. Timmie had refused to urinate since we left Sha'ar Hagai, though I had taken her out of the car several times—this was not her territory! Even though I walked her for a long time that night, she refused, and was content to sleep in my room at the hotel. She behaved with perfect manners, though it was the first time she had ever been in such surroundings.

The next morning we left to meet Mahmud and to explore a new area. Timmie was very happy to get back into 'her' car—she had decided that this was her property, and she was feeling very comfortable. Unquestionably, she had been more comfortable all day than we were—while we were sitting on the hard ground drinking tea, she was curled up on the plush car seat with the air-conditioning on... The Bedouin found it very hard to understand why we would leave the car engine on so that a dog could have air-conditioning. For the rest of the day, Timmie simply refused to get out of the car at all—it was hot outside, and anyway, who knew if we wouldn't decide to introduce her to another strange male! When I tried to get her to come out of the car to relieve herself, she set her feet against the seat and simply refused to move.

The new area, which was between Arad, Massada, and the Dead Sea, was much more remote than Tel Arad, and the Bedouin there were extremely isolated, traditional and less social. Had we not come with Mahmud, who was known and respected in this area, we would not have been allowed in the camps. We were warned in each camp that we visited that we were welcome to photograph dogs, but we must stay away from, and not photograph in the direction of the tents, as the women were there. The tents were closed to keep us from seeing the women.

However we were welcomed with typical Bedouin hospitality. We were also told that it was difficult these days to find the real Bedouin dogs—the dogs were disappearing. Once there had been many, but now there were few and they were becoming very hard to find, because in many places dogs were being brought from town that were mixing with the 'good' dogs. However, the Bedouin had no idea or plans of selective breeding to try to preserve these dogs that were so useful to them.

We visited a number of camps in the area, and in all of them we found excellent dogs. Most of the dogs were hidden on the hillsides around the camp, and until we started walking around, you would never have noticed that they were there. They blended in perfectly with their surroundings and never moved or made a sound—until we 'crossed the line' into what they considered their territory and then they jumped up and started to bark. It was possible to walk right past a dog that was a few feet away, lying in the rocks, or under a tractor or a pile of rubble, and not to see it at all. But should we turn in the direction of what the dog considered his territory, he would leap to his feet, barking and circling and very efficiently guarding. It was rare that a dog would exhibit real aggression towards us, though. The task of these dogs was to warn the Bedouin that something was happening that required their attention, not to attack. The only dogs that were aggressive were those few that we found tied in the camps—these dogs, unable to move away to protect themselves, took the only alternative and were ready to bite if necessary.

The dogs here were mostly cream, gold or reddish in color, and there were many I would have been pleased to take home with me. But these dogs were unapproachable. The Bedouin themselves were not always sure how many dogs were 'attached' to the camp or where they were—we had to go climbing up the surrounding hills to look for them. And then they stayed well away from us.

In a few camps we saw bitches that were obviously nursing puppies. For the most part, the puppies were so well hidden that the Bedouin didn't even know where they were. One litter was in a place that the Bedouins knew about, but hidden so deep under a pile of huge bales of hay that there was no chance of getting near the pups.

However, in another camp, there were two pups of about five or six weeks of age that were hidden under some barrels in the center of the camp. We were told that we could take them if we wanted. The parents were nice type dogs—both father and mother were in the camp. The Bedouins pulled the pups out for us—though litter brothers, one was very small, half the size of the second. But both looked well fed and healthy. I accepted the gift of the two pups, knowing that if I took only the bigger and better developed one, the small one would certainly be killed now that he had been caught—they had a number of dogs in this camp and didn't need any more.

The two pups were terrified when I put them in the car at my feet, and Timmie was not enthusiastic either. How could I even consider putting those Bedouin dogs in HER car?!!!! She turned her back and ignored their existence.

It was now dusk and time to head for home. It had been an amazingly successful trip—we had seen many dogs, most of them excellent Canaans, and found areas that we hadn't been in before, therefore probably giving us completely new bloodlines. The filming had gone very well, and much material had been gathered for the film—I couldn't wait to see what came out of this. We had achieved a breeding and brought home two puppies, as well as developed some excellent contacts for the future. Tired and happy, we got back to Sha'ar Hagai. Timmie, though reluctant to leave her car, looked out, saw that she was home, heaved a sigh of relief, climbed out, squatted and peed. Her territory!

The film was broadcast on the *National Geographic Channel*, under the name *The Search for the First Dog*. It was very well made and we were very pleased with the results. It has been showed many times all over the world, and has attracted a good deal of attention and comment. People do sometimes identify me from having seen the film; not many people have a claim to fame based on an appearance on international television helping dogs have sex in the desert...

Timmie, unfortunately, did not have puppies from the desert breeding. However, the two pups we brought back grew up to be very typical Canaans. The larger of the two we named Pereh, or Wild One me Nachal Yealim, which was the name of the place where we found him. He stayed with us at Sha'ar Hagai. His pet name at home was 'Monster'—this was a dog that had definite opinions of his own which he expressed at every opportunity. He sired several litters and has offspring that are champions in several countries. We were successful in bringing in a new bloodline that has been beneficial to the breed.

Pereh was a very dominant dog who became quite a problem with the other males. He wanted to be top dog. We found a home for him with a friend who lived on the outskirts of Jerusalem and had an orchard; he needed some dogs to guard the orchard and the supplies and equipment that he kept there, and knew that Canaans would be the ideal choice. Pereh and a few Canaan bitches were very effective for some time in preventing thefts. However, the thieves realized that as long as the dogs were there, they would not be successful; the next time they attempted a theft, they killed the dogs. Pereh lost his life because he was so good at doing what he was meant to do—guarding his territory.

Pereh's brother, Pashosh, became a home watchdog for a friend who ran a plant nursery, and is highly effective at the job. An easier life than in a Bedouin camp, for sure!

Chapter Forty-Four: Down Under and Dingoes

One of the places I have always dreamed of visiting is Australia. What I had read about it in books and seen in films fascinated me; it seemed rather like the Wild West with an exotic flavor, that was both romantic and exciting, and plenty of animals around everywhere. The people, according to books and films anyway, were casual, friendly, open, welcoming and usually involved in exciting and challenging activities. Just my sort of place, I thought! So I was really thrilled when I received an invitation from the Collie Club of Victoria to judge the 9th National Collie Show on July 7-8, 2007. Not only would I be able to visit Australia, but I would also be able to see the Australian collies—with a reputation for being high quality; this was of great interest to me. Now there were only two and a half years to wait— judges for important shows are invited well in advance, to make sure that they are available.

I am not very fond of flying, to put it mildly. It is not that I am afraid to fly, but rather that I find it extremely uncomfortable. There is never a comfortable place to put my legs, and it is not that I am tall and have long ones. My neck is always at an uncomfortable angle, no matter which pillows I try to use, and I am never able to sleep. Flying also has a strong effect on my stomach. Not that I am airsick, just a frequent visitor to the toilet. This is not so bad when I sit on the aisle, my preferred place, but if I get a window seat and have to frequently climb over other passengers, this makes things even more uncomfortable. The thought of the long, long flight to Australia was not something I looked forward to, but the end goal was worth it. Finally, after over two years of waiting, I boarded the plane for the 20 hours or so in the air to get to Melbourne.

Myrna Shiboleth

Israel in July is very hot—in the 30s centigrade, or 90s Fahrenheit. The first thing that hit me as I left the airport in Melbourne was the weather—it was really cold, and rainy. True, I knew that it was winter in Australia, but I hadn't imagined that it would be that cold!

I am sure that everyone I met down under thinks I am quite fat—I spent the next two weeks wearing at least five layers of clothes just to try to keep warm. Australians seem to be very hardy and immune to feeling cold—even indoors, it was cold. Homes and buildings seemed to be heated only very minimally.

But, other than the weather, everything was just marvelous. I was welcomed by Judy, not a collie person, but very active in the dog world. She had lived in Israel some time back for a number of years and her husband is Israeli. I had met them briefly when they visited Israel that June; they had come to meet me and visit the kennel and we had immediately felt a connection. They welcomed me warmly into their home.

Friday before the show, there was time for some sightseeing, so Judy took me for a drive up into the mountains around Melbourne. Although it was still somewhat rainy, the scenery was fabulous. I was especially impressed by the huge tree ferns, something I had never seen before, which were absolutely beautiful. The variety of plant life and the constantly changing terrain were fascinating. I never knew there were so many varieties of gum and eucalyptus trees! And what I found particularly thrilling was to see the huge flocks of parrots of all types and colors living wild and free and fearless everywhere! It was fantastic! When we stopped for lunch at a small road side restaurant, flocks of birds congregated all along the huge plate glass window hoping for handouts, and looking in at us as if we were on display. The restaurant owners were obliging, providing a feeding station for the birds; this, after all, was great for the tourists.

424

The dog club venue in Melbourne was the site of the show, a really impressive complex of fields and buildings for every possible canine activity. There were indoor and outdoor rings, facilities for meetings, for meals, training grounds, fenced fields where you could exercise your dog off lead, and even a wonderful dog museum. The collie show was indoors in a huge building, very fortunate as it rained on and off during the day. The ring was huge, which was very pleasing to me, as I really like to see dogs moving when I judge. I was warmly welcomed by the committee, and met face to face for the first time the people who had invited me and made the arrangements. How nice to put faces to the names!

The show was started with a ceremony of blessing by a well-known local aboriginal. He also demonstrated how to throw a boomerang, making it look easy. I was introduced to him and while we were waiting for the final arrangements in the ring, we went outside and he again demonstrated the use of the boomerang, giving me one he had made by hand as a gift. I didn't dare try, being sure that if I did, the boomerang would disappear and never be seen again. There was a flag ceremony and a nice demonstration of canine freestyle, a dog sport that I really like, so it was lovely to see it being done.

And then it was time to get to work—with an entry of 254 collies, it would be a long day. I was eager to see the dogs, and I was not disappointed. Throughout my long day of judging, I was continuously impressed by the high quality of most of the entries.

One of the first things that stood out was the beautiful grooming and presentation of the dogs. They were in superbly groomed, with every hair in place, and were also in excellent muscular condition, something that is not so common in other countries; apparently, Australians give their dogs sufficient exercise and activity. I was impressed by the overall good construction and movement—there were almost no problems with cow hocks, a common structural fault in many countries, and most of the dogs were smooth and powerful movers, something I feel is essential in the collie. Toplines were strong and level—another common fault is soft or swayed backs—and the necks were sufficiently long and elegant. Tails were set and carried correctly. In Europe, there is a tendency towards broad short heads with wide skull and heavy ears that are set quite wide. Here, heads and expressions were overall quite good, with good length of head, few problems with heaviness or thickness of head, and nice high earset, although there were some problems with rather large eyes that were not of the best in shape. The one problem that I observed was a tendency to narrowness in the chest and a lack of forechest, in particular in the younger dogs. It appears that these bloodlines are slow maturers, as this issue was much better, overall, in the fully mature adults.

It was also super to also have such a large entry of smooth collies (collies with a short coat but otherwise the same as the long coated collies)—I love smooths, and it is rare to see more than a few at shows, and here, as well as a large entry, they were of excellent quality.

There were a number of dogs that I would have been happy to take home with me, both in roughs (the long coated variety) and smooths. What a shame it is so far away!

After my long and tiring but very satisfying day judging, there was the official dinner—delicious food, fabulous company, and wonderful prizes for the winners.

The following day were the obedience and agility competitions. I have always worked with my collies, have done obedience, agility, and herding over the years, so am always interested in seeing the working dogs. I think that a dog in general, and collies in particular, are happiest when they have active and challenging things to do, and always really enjoy seeing them working. So, it was lovely to see so many entries, and the collies working happily and enthusiastically. I sat by the ringside—this was an outdoor ring. The day was pleasant and mostly sunny, although the ground was very wet from all the rain the day before, and exhibitors and dogs squelched around in various spots. The agility judge invited me to walk the course with him before the competition started, which I was pleased to do. This is done by all the competitors, similarly to what is done in equestrian jumping competitions—the competitor walks the course as it has been set out, calculating the correct speed and approach to the obstacles, where to turn, and so on, in order to be able to direct and help the dog to do his best.

Afterwards, I was told that the collie people were really impressed. Conformation judges are rarely interested in anything but the looks of the dog, and they were really surprised to see me spending the day watching the performance dogs, and even walking the course As someone who is interested in natural dogs that are not only beautiful but functional and able to perform either to survive or to do a job, I like to see dogs working at tasks that suit the breed, and that prove that they are not just beautiful standing still, but strong and healthy. The qualities that result in a dog that is healthy and functional are not there by chance; they are genetic factors that must be selected for just as carefully as the points that make him a successful show dog, and are perhaps even more important. My dogs spend a minimal amount of time in the show ring, compared to the time spent living with me and doing things together.

Following the working trials, there was the seminar, with interesting presentations on DNA testing and collie eye testing. Collies are a breed that has genetic eye problems. Careful testing of breeding stock over the years has resulted in the almost total elimination of one eye problem, PRA, which can result in blindness, but is now rarely found in collies. Breeders are interested in preventing the reappearance of this disease and in eliminating, in time, other less serious problems, so DNA testing is very much a part of the program of all serious collie breeders all over the world.

As well, I gave my own presentation of "Collie Silhouettes," which was very well received. My idea was not to criticize modern dogs, but to contrast them with famous dogs of the past. I took a lot of photos of past and present dogs and presented them only as a black silhouette—this way, it was possible to really see the shape of the dog, without the distraction of markings or of knowing who the dog was. The participants in the seminar were really shocked to see how different some of the modern dogs were from the best-known dogs in the breed in the past.

Unfortunately, most modern breeds, including the Collie, are no longer working dogs. Instead of breeding them for the qualities that would make them good workers, they have become pets and show dogs, and selection has gone in the direction of what is pretty. The result can be dogs that look lovely when standing still or relaxing on the sofa, but that don't have the correct body construction to be efficient or functional. The collie was always an agile and athletic dog, and one of the most important characteristics was its elegance. Nowadays, many collies seem to be just a huge pile of fur, without elegance, and without a well-built body under the coat. It makes me very sad to see this, and is another reason that I am so drawn to the Canaans, which are a breed still natural in construction, is functional, and also beautiful, with the beauty of nature.

The following weekend, when I had the opportunity to judge a number of other breeds at the Melbourne Dog Club Ch. show, I was again impressed by the quality of the dogs. It is unfortunate that Australia is so far away and isolated from a large part of the dog world. Breeders in many other countries are not familiar with the Australian dogs and their high quality, and are unable to make use of them. The Australian breeders, on the other hand, despite the great difficulties and expense involved in importing new stock do import out of their obvious dedication to improving their breeding and producing the best possible dogs. Impressive!

Now was my chance to play tourist.

When I started making plans to visit Australia, my first thoughts, of course, were, "I have to see the dingoes!"

The dingo of Australia is perhaps the only truly wild dog that still exists. Geneticists have found that the dingo is unique from the modern dog in his genetic makeup: pure dingoes can be identified positively by DNA examination. There is even some question among scientists and researchers as to whether the dingo is a dog or a wolf. Australia's dingo experts tend to consider it a wolf. Although there are some dingoes that have been 'domesticated' and live as family pets, the great majority are still wild animals that are scattered throughout Australia.

The dingo is generally assumed to have reached Australia some five thousand years ago from its origin in Asia. There is some question as to how this happened. One popular theory is that it accompanied the ancestors of Australia's aboriginals in their migration from Asia. Another theory that is well accepted today is that the dingo is in fact the descendent of dogs that arrived in Australia with seafarers from Asia, perhaps even of only one pregnant bitch that remained to whelp on the new continent. This theory is based on the very limited genetic variation that is found between dingoes.

However the dingo did travel to Australia, it found an ideal habitat there. There were no large predators on the continent, and there was plenty of game to hunt. The dingo spread throughout the continent very successfully, inhabiting a niche that was highly suited to its needs.

A type of symbiosis developed between the aboriginal people and the dingo. One fact that we all tend to forget, and one of the major reasons, perhaps, that the dingo has not become domesticated as have the other primitive breeds of dog all over the world, is that the aboriginals were hunter-gatherers, nomads that traveled from place to place searching for their needs. They did not develop settled villages and they did not keep livestock, so there was no use for herd or guard dogs. The dingoes were most likely camp followers, picking up scraps left behind, following on hunts and perhaps alerting the aboriginals to the presence of game or running forward to catch the prey and then being chased off by the human hunters. Dingoes were never selectively bred or chosen to fill a task, and therefore remained truly wild dogs, opportunistic but not domesticated. The Canaans, on the other hand, associated themselves with a herding population that found the dogs of great use in helping them with the herds and protecting the animals and the camps from predators. Thus, a much closer relationship was built up between the dogs and the humans.

However, the dingoes do play an important role in the aboriginal culture, appearing in their dreams and symbolism, and even now many are still found in and around aboriginal settlements and are a familiar part of village life, although many of these are not pure dingoes, but mixed with other breeds.

The dingo's problems began with the arrival of the white man in Australia. Settlers introduced cattle and sheep as a primary source of livelihood. Initially, there were few problems, as here was sufficient hunting for the population of dingoes and there was no need for them to prey on the sheep. However, things changed as the settlers had a greater and greater impact on their environment, and caused serious changes in the local ecology. One of the greatest changes was caused by the introduction of the rabbit. Although this was not intentional, the rabbits found Australia an ideal habitat and spread rapidly and in huge numbers throughout the country. On the one hand, they endangered the sheep and cattle industry by competing for the grazing, and on the other hand, their great numbers resulted in a large increase in the number of dingoes, as there was plentiful food. When man acted to decimate the numbers of rabbits, the dingoes were left without their major source of food, and turned to the relatively easy prey available in quantity—the sheep.

The dingo has been classified for many years as a predatory pest in Australia. Hunting them was encouraged, with a bounty being paid in some areas. To protect livestock from potential dingo predation, a 3,307 foot long fence has been built in southeast Australia, the longest manmade structure on the continent.

The dingo is a skilled hunter. He is a pack animal, like most of the canids, with the size of the pack depending on the resources available in his territory—the pack may consist of two or three, which is most common, or can have a larger number. The pack is skilled at bringing down a variety of prey, including the large red kangaroo, which is difficult and even dangerous to hunt. However, the dingo is not averse to hunting on his own, going off to scavenge or hunt smaller prey such as rodents, and then later making contact with his pack. The female comes into season once a year, with litters usually consisting of four to six pups.

Despite its reputation as a savage killer, the dingo is actually shy and prefers to avoid confrontations with humans. If you meet a dingo, fanciers told me, it will not attack—its typical behavior will be to run away into the bush. Even dingoes that have been raised as pets are usually quite shy with strangers.

My first face to face encounter with dingoes was at the home of John Ring, a dingo fancier who lives outside of Melbourne. As I stepped inside his kitchen door, I was almost bowled over by two furry missiles streaking at me, jumping and trying to lick my face. Were these the savage and dangerous beasts of stories?

John has two young females of just over a year of age. They have been separated from their mothers and raised by hand from about four weeks of age. The dingo breeders feel that this is necessary to imprint them on humans and socialize them effectively to living in human society. From this age on, they are handled extensively, exposed to people, other animals, noises, cars, and all the various stimuli they will experience in their life with people.

Laws for keeping dingoes as pets in Australia are very strict. A potential owner must obtain a license, which requires him to build an escape-proof enclosure for the dingoes, according to very exacting criteria. A dingo can never be left off leash if it is not in the enclosure or inside the owner's house.

John's two females, very well socialized and living in a family with small children, were very friendly, happy to be petted and ready to lick my face. However, John told me that they are not usually so outgoing with strangers. They are much more likely to stand back and look people over from a distance, and then perhaps to approach and sniff the visitors. This behavior is very typical of many of the primitive or pariah dogs, as well as of the dingo. According to John, the dogs are never aggressive to people, and are totally reliable with his small children. They live in the house much of the time, and sleep in bed with John and his wife. When they are not in the house, they must be in their enclosure, or on leashes—John often takes them walking, or for rides in his car. Having been very thoroughly socialized, they are accepting and familiar with most things they may see on their walks, but are immediately aware and somewhat suspicious of anything strange or new in their surroundings.

My next chance to get up close and personal with dingoes was at the Healesville Sanctuary, a lovely park in the mountains outside of Melbourne which has been set up to present to and educate the public about the Australian native animals. There are several enclosures of dingoes there, with the dingoes being kept in pairs of neutered male and female; there in no interest in breeding at this facility. These dingoes have also been raised from a young age and exposed to the public—they are taken out and walked on leash around the park so that people can meet them and see that the dingo is not fearsome, but approachable.

When I entered their enclosures with the chief keeper, Adrian Mifsud, the dingoes were again quite friendly, coming over, sniffing me, ready to be petted and even to lick me. However, their interest was much more in Adrian and other staff members who were familiar 'pack members' and known to bring treats as well. They were affectionate and friendly, but still retained a certain aloofness and independence, never showing the real submission we are often accustomed to receiving from our familiar canine pets. Adrian also told me that the dingoes are never aggressive to people. As well as the dingoes in the sanctuary, Adrian has two as pets at home, and has worked with them extensively in the wild. His pets, he said, although also hand raised and socialized from an early age, are very shy of strangers, and when someone comes to visit, they run off to the far side of their enclosure, generally showing little interest in being friendly.

Although not aggressive to people, tame dingoes still have a very well-developed hunting instinct and may attack other animals, including dogs. They make use of various vocalizations including howling, but they do not bark, another thing that separates them from the average dog.

The dingo's bad reputation has developed, in part, as a result of two cases of dingoes supposedly attacking children. Both of these cases, Adrian explained, were in tourist areas where the dingoes had become very accustomed to people being around and feeding them, and had therefore lost their natural reluctance to come close to humans. Other possible dingo attacks have been found to have been dingo crossbreds, not true dingoes.

The greatest threat to the survival of the dingo today in Australia is the large and growing number of crossbreds. Dingoes and dogs crossbreed easily, and with the growing population of domestic dogs throughout Australia, pure dingoes are becoming more and more scarce and crossbreds more and more common. Dingo fanciers believe that the pure dingo may disappear in the wild in 20 to 25 years, and feel that the only way to preserve these dogs is in sanctuaries or fenced reserves, and by developing breeding groups. There are a number of breeders who are attempting to do just that, keeping stud books, doing careful selective breeding to preserve the dingo characteristics, and looking for additional bloodlines to preserve as much as possible genetic diversity in the breed.

Why is it important to save a dog that is for the most part scorned and despised in its own home? The dingo is extremely valuable to our understanding of the dog. As the only true wild dog still existing, we can learn from its behavior, lifestyle, and relation to man; about what the dog was originally, at the very beginning of its development as a separate species from the wolf; and the beginnings of its association with man. The more we learn about these ancient dogs, the better we can understand our modern ones, their descendents. The dingo is a treasure that is rapidly disappearing. We can only hope that the Australians will realize the importance of preserving it.

And for me, of course, the similarities in appearance and behavior to the Canaans were fascinating. The connection between them, both being breeds of primitive dogs, was clear. I felt that meeting the dingoes gave me more insight regarding the Canaans as well. Being able to meet face to face with another breed of primitive dog, to see how they behaved with one another and with the people around them, to observe their body language and communication, to learn about their history and development and the way that they survived, and then to compare this with the Canaans was really valuable to my understanding of the pariah type of dog,

Healesville was not just a sanctuary for dingoes, but for all Australian native animals. It was great to see all of these weird species up close. I was treated like a visiting dignitary, quite a strange feeling for me, and given the greatest possible privilege—that of meeting and stroking a platypus. Healesville has the only duck billed platypus in the world that has been successfully hand raised, and I was allowed to come 'behind the scenes' and meet him. What a strange little animal, and what a thrill to be able to touch him!

Part of my visit involved also meeting some of the Melbourne Jewish community. My hostess, Judy, was very active in the community, and had arranged for me to give a lecture to WIZO (Women's International Zionist Organization).

Her idea was that people were tired of hearing visiting Israeli politicians and generals, and would enjoy something different. I was to give a talk on the use of dogs in Israel for various purposes, in particular as service dogs to help physically- and mentally-challenged people. I am quite proud of the progress in these fields in Israel, so was very glad to talk about it.

The talk was very well received—people had little knowledge of how much dogs can contribute to the quality of life of the disabled, and were thrilled that Israel was making progress in these programs. Judy had been quite nervous beforehand; she knew that I was experienced in lecturing, but had never heard me talk, and didn't know what the results would be. What a relief for her to discover that people really enjoyed and were interested in what I had to say.

One thing that I learned from my visit to Australia is that two weeks is not nearly enough time—such a huge and fascinating country and so much to see! I also had a chance to spend two days in the Perth area, which was again completely different in scenery and plant life.

What made my visit most enjoyable were the people—everyone was friendly, hospitable, outgoing, helpful, and did all possible to make my visit a success. I feel that I have made new friends that I will certainly want to stay in touch with. And I have no doubt that I will be doing everything possible to be able to go back again to visit Australia!

On the way back, I spent a night in Hong Kong, as there are no direct flights from Israel to Australia. To get home, it was necessary for me to fly through either Hong Kong or Bangkok—I thought that Hong Kong would be interesting, and if I was already flying through there, I could take one extra day and see a bit of the sights. And it would be a welcome break from the long hours in the plane.

The Hong Kong airport is built on landfill into the sea. Coming in to land, circling over the island, was fascinating. From the air, it was possible to see just about all of Hong Kong and the various islands making it up. There were steep mountains rising high, covered with what looked to be dense forest, and these areas, which made up a large percentage of the land area, seemed to be free of human habitation. All of the huge population of Hong Kong is concentrated in a small area of coast line, in enormous high rise buildings clustered very closely together. A fascinating view, and a huge contrast from Australia, where there is endless land, nothing is crowded, and tall buildings are few.

Hong Kong was very hot and humid, another huge contrast from Australia. Here it was summer—funny how you can go from one extreme to another so quickly! I had booked a hotel in the center of town. It was not a five star hotel; I had only looked for something reasonable and comfortable for one night. But the facilities were amazing—the room was huge, and the enormous bathroom provided anything you might need—not just shampoo and soap, but shaving cream, toothbrush and toothpaste, hand cream, body lotion—I wondered what the five star places provided.

I walked around the streets, amazingly clean and well kept for such a huge, teeming city. There was a lot of traffic, and some people walked around with face masks—apparently there is a serious air pollution problem. But there were also a number of lovely green parks. There were few dogs around, but the only ones I saw were a few little breeds like pugs being walked by their owners. Certainly there weren't any strays in this part of town. I saw a few areas with large and modern shopping centers, but most of the shops along the streets were small, traditional, family-type places.

That evening, as I had a quiet meal in the hotel restaurant, a Chinese woman approached and started to talk to me. She spoke in broken English, and at first I didn't really understand what she wanted. It slowly dawned on me that she was hitting on me! A tourist woman, eating alone, apparently was a tempting mark! I was quite flabbergasted—this was not an experience I had had before. I tried politely to discourage her, but this was obviously not going to be effective, it just made her more persistent. Finally, I managed to convey to her that I was really not interested in having her come back with me to my room. Poor woman, what a way to make a living...

It was good to arrive home and have all the flights, traveling and adventures behind me. Dogs and family were all fine. I, of course worried, like any good Jewish mother—I had been away for two weeks which was the longest trip I had taken for quite a while. But although everyone was glad to see me, they had all managed very well without me. Dogs, of course, can't count the days—for them a few days or a few weeks is about the same, either I was there or not. They are always just as happy to see me at the end of a short trip as at the end of a long one.

Chapter Forty-Five: Adventures in Boratland

When I was asked to speak at a planned international conference on primitive and aboriginal dogs in Almaty, I didn't have the slightest idea where Almaty was, but research showed that it was the largest city in Kazakhstan. The only information I had about Kazakhstan was what could be gleaned from the movie *Borat,* a big hit of the season. When would I ever have another chance to visit Kazakhstan? So I accepted the invitation and started planning.

When friends heard that I was planning on traveling to Kazakhstan, they were really surprised. "Didn't you see *Borat*?" was the first thing they asked. Well, yes, I had, but that was just a movie, after all. It was just fiction.

The conference was on a subject that was of great interest to me. Titled "Aboriginal Dog Breeds as a Part of Biodiversity and of the Cultural Heritage of Humankind," it seemed to tie in with the work I have been doing for years to preserve the Canaan Dog.

When I told Adrian Mifsud, my Australian friend who works on the preservation of the dingo, about the conference he decided also to come, and was asked to give a presentation on the dingoes. Dr. Rita Trainen and Dr. Zafra Sirik, devoted and serious dog judges and cynologists, decided that the topic was highly interesting and that they would also come along. Before the conference, Adrian came from Australia to spend a week with me here in Israel to learn more about the Canaan Dog.

So, there were four of us who caught the flight from Israel through Istanbul to Almaty, Kazakhstan on September 9, 2007. There were about 12 hours between our connecting flights, so we had a very enjoyable day touring Istanbul. In good spirits, we caught the flight to Almaty, arriving there at 4 in the morning.

The airport was very small. The first indication that things might be different than expected was the toilet in the arrivals hall—it was what we used to call a Turkish toilet, basically a hole in the floor. It was quite surprising to find this in the arrivals hall of an international airport. Flashbacks of *Borat* started to pop up in my mind.

Adrian had not received his visa in advance so now he had to apply at the special window, and I accompanied him. Visas are not automatically granted to visit Kazakhstan—you must apply in advance with an invitation showing the purpose and length of your visit, where you are staying, and photos and other personal information and then it takes a few weeks. If you don't have an invitation, you must request that the Kazakhstan government office provides one. The visa itself is a large and colorful page that is glued into your passport—no simple stamp for these people.

The organizers of the conference had promised that a visa would be waiting at the entry point for those who had not managed to get one in advance. Of course, this was not the case. After filling out stacks of paper work and waiting while they considered the situation, the visa was finally provided, and we moved on to the next line, the passport inspection.

There were only a few booths, and the lines moved slowly. Our line, of course, was the slowest, at times not moving at all—it seemed that someone at the head of the line was having problems, and we stood and waited and waited and waited. The line wasn't more than about ten people. Finally, after an hour and a half we got to the window. The officer in charge told us sternly, "Camera!!!!" and indicated a camera above his head. We had to stand and look into the camera while he thoroughly inspected our passports; it was forbidden to look around.

Finally, we were through. Rita and Zafra were waiting for us in the arrivals hall, with a number of other participants in the conference that had also arrived in the last few hours. The organizers, as promised, were there to meet us, and we expected to be taken to the hotel which had also been reserved by the Khazakhi organizers.

The person who had handled most of the arrangements, as far as we knew, was Vladimir, a Russian who had been living for many years in the U.S., and who was a long time member of PADS (Primitive and Aboriginal Dogs Society—an international group involved in the preservation of the primitive breeds). He himself had laikas, a primitive Russian breed rather similar in appearance to huskies that are used for hunting, and was very knowledgeable and involved with the primitive hunting breeds in particular. He was the one who had invited me to make a presentation on the Canaan dogs, and seemed to be responsible for much of the program and arrangements. In part, this seemed to be because the organizers in Kazakhstan spoke only Kazakh or Russian. The flights to Kazakhstan were quite expensive for all of us participants, as it was quite remote and not on the common tourist routes, so to encourage participation and lower the costs, there was no charge for the conference itself. In addition, we had been promised hotel accommodations for free. This would not be a luxury hotel, Vladimir had told us, but it would be comfortable and scenic. Anyone who wanted to reserve a luxury hotel was welcome to do so—but the prices in Almaty were very high.

As far as I was concerned, if there was a bed, a toilet and a shower, I would be satisfied, as long as it was free. My companions agreed.

Now, we were hoping to get to the promised hotel, have a shower and some breakfast, and then go to the opening session of the conference which was due to start in about two hours. We had had little or no sleep for two nights, and a long and tiring day touring Istanbul. It was a long time since the last meal we had had on the flight, and we really felt the need for a bit of refreshment. However, there were still a few participants that were due to arrive shortly on another flight.

Vladimir, a little balding gnome of a man, was one of the group meeting us at the airport. He told us that we could go on with Camilla, the daughter of one of the organizers. She and her boyfriend had a car and could drive us, so that we didn't have to wait for the others. This sounded like a good idea at the time.

Camilla was quite young, seeming to be in her late teens. Fortunately, she did speak fairly good English. We followed her out of the arrivals hall to the parking lot where her boyfriend was waiting in the car.

It was hard to tell if the car was meant to be rust colored or was simply totally rusted over. The age was hard to determine, but it was certainly considerably older than Camilla.

Her boyfriend opened the trunk with some difficulty, and loaded in our suitcases. The trunk lid didn't close, so he bounced up and down on it with all his weight until the contents were squashed down sufficiently for the catch to click closed. We wondered if we would be seeing our suitcases again.

We all climbed into the back seat, trying to avoid sitting on the springs that were sticking up through the upholstery in various places. The windows were in a permanently fixed position, some partly open and some closed; the handles to open or close them were totally useless. The only way to change their position was to pull the glass up or push it down.

With a lot of coughing and sputtering, the engine started, accompanied by strange vibrations throughout the car. But we were distracted from the condition of the car by what was happening around us.

The Almaty airport was not very big or very busy, and the parking lot was also not very large, but there was apparently only one entrance and exit with room for only one car at a time to go through. And it seemed that half of the population of the city was in the airport parking lot this morning and all of them wanted to get out, quickly, and simultaneously. The cars were packed together like a herd of cattle all trying to push out through a gate at once, accompanied by revving engines, clouds of exhaust fumes, and shouts and curses from all sides. Luckily, we didn't understand the language! No one was willing to give way and it was a game of nerves and display of force to get out of the parking lot.

Finally we managed to get out and on to the highway. Still totally unnerved by our introduction to Kazakhi customs, we began to look around at our surroundings. It was very hot and everything was extremely dusty. The road was lined with what seemed to be rather ramshackle shacks and small houses, but it was very hard to see them clearly, as they were all thoroughly fenced in with large pieces of tin roofing. There was plenty of litter scattered all along the roadside, and here and there were small shops and roadside stalls selling fruits and vegetables and various other items.

The car was making very strange noises and there was a strong smell of exhaust fumes, even though the windows were open. The radio was on full blast; Camilla shouted to us that the engine noises were annoying to her boyfriend, so he kept the radio on as loud as possible so that he wouldn't hear them. The music seemed to be some sort of local pop.

We were going to stop first at her house for a few minutes, Camilla explained. She had to take care of her dogs, and thought we might be interested in seeing them. She was a breeder of Tazys, the local form of Saluki, and used them for hunting. She also had a few Asian Ovtscharkas, a very large breed known for its aggression, and therefore useful for guarding.

We pulled into the yard of a small, rundown little house, with several old rusted cars, and piles of car parts and other trash scattered around. It rather reminded me of Bedouin camps—the Bedouin are great hoarders of everything, sure that there will at some time or other be a use for these things. It seemed that here in Kazakhstan the attitude was similar. There also was a large old bus. It looked to be at least forty or fifty years old, but it was freshly painted in a bright poison green. "That is for you," Camilla commented. We were not quite sure what she meant.

She had about ten or twelve Tazys of various ages running around, and a few Ovtscharkas; some of them were very good looking. The conditions they were kept in certainly were not luxurious kennels, or what one would expect to see when visiting a breeder in a more modern country, but they seemed to be well fed and happy, and Camilla was very proud of them, telling us of the hunting prowess of the ones that she worked with.

Time was passing, and soon the conference was due to begin. We were very hungry by now, and very hot and tired and really desperately wanted a chance to refresh ourselves. But this was not to be.

When we finally left Camilla's house, we were told that we had to go directly to the conference. The hotel was at least half an hour's drive away, and there wasn't time, we would go there only in the evening. "What about breakfast?" we asked in despair. From the blank look on Camilla's face, it seemed that no one had considered that we might want to eat. After phoning someone for a consultation, she told us that she would take us to the hotel where some of the other participants were staying, which was near the conference hall, and we could have something to eat there.

The place we were brought to seemed more like a hostel than a hotel, and the dining room was rather reminiscent of one in a kibbutz. We sat at a long trestle table, and there was no menu, we were simply provided with a few plates of food—thick slices of rather dry bread, a saucer of jam, a big bowl of rice, and some pieces of boiled chicken. There was weak tea to drink. This was breakfast.

I didn't care. I was hungry and was about ready to eat anything, especially when I thought about spending the next few hours sitting in a conference.

We were now really in the center of Almaty. This part of town was the total opposite of the areas we had passed through earlier. Construction was going on everywhere, of huge and totally modern high rise office and apartment buildings. Kazakhstan is apparently a country that is developing very rapidly, with very large oil reserves, and is attracting business and investments from all over the world. It is even a launch site for space satellites—Israeli satellites have been launched from there. The contrast between the modern and the old was enormous. People in this part of town were well dressed and fashionable.

Tails of Sha'ar Hagai

Traffic was insane—this seemed to be a characteristic of the country. The streets in Almaty were excellent—wide, at least four lanes and in some places six lanes, and in excellent condition. But where there were four lanes, there seemed to be at least six lanes of traffic, and where there were six lanes, it seemed there were at least ten rows of cars moving frantically, zipping from lane to lane, honking, and often ignoring traffic lights and signs. Pedestrians took their lives in their hands whenever they had to cross the road. There were many expensive and luxurious cars, and SUVs and jeeps were very popular and included in the mayhem were cars with both right hand and left hand steering, although Kazakhstan was a country where driving was on the right. We were told that although it was really illegal to have the opposite steering, Japan often had excess cars that had been made for the English, Australian, or S. African market, and sold them to Kazakhstan cheap. So who cared if it was against the law to drive them? Apparently no one...

Having had our breakfast, we were now all expected to get to the conference. No time for showering or changing clothes; as we were would have to do. We were all escorted out, and there, waiting for us, was the poison green bus.

We all climbed into the green monster that reeked of exhaust fumes and cigarette smoke—it seems that the Kazakhi population for the most part is unaware of the dangers of smoking, or couldn't care less. The seats were far from comfortable, but were in good repair for the most part—there were no springs sticking out, although a few of the seats didn't seem to be completely fastened to their frames and jiggled around. There were lacy curtains on the bus windows, perhaps to keep us from seeing too much outside, or from noticing that most of the windows couldn't be opened. Air conditioning, of course, was nonexistent.

The bus started up with a roar which quickly died down into a cough, and we moved off in a belch of smoke. The venue for the conference was only a few minutes away, even with the terrible traffic.

The conference was being held in one of the buildings of the local university. The building looked quite old and was rather classical in style, with very high ceilings, but was not in the greatest of repair; the paint was rather shabby, corridors dingy, and all was permeated by a mild, moldy smell. The conference room was a large auditorium with huge windows all around, and luckily these windows could be opened to let in some air, as here also air conditioning was unknown, and the day was already quite hot. Fortunately, despite the state of the building, there was all the audio visual and computer equipment that the participants might need for their presentations. There were also a team of translators to translate from Russian to English and the reverse, and everyone was provided with headphones so that they could follow the simultaneous translations.

We were all welcomed by representatives of the Kazakhstan government and those who were responsible for organizing the conference. These included a representative of the university, a representative of the Ministry of Agriculture, and the secretary of the Ecological Union, who were the official sponsors of the conference.

The topics on the agenda were really interesting, and covered a much wider range than I had expected. The primitive dogs being discussed here were not only the 'original' types, like the Canaan and the dingo, but included sight hounds and herd guard dogs that have been used, in some cases, in the same capacity and in the same geographical areas for thousands of years. The presentations were made by internationally-known experts on the breeds from their native countries. Not only was there information on the dogs themselves, but a lot about the cultures that made use of them. This was not the kind of information that was readily available and now was being presented by people who lived that way, so it was really fascinating. The Canaan was one of the very few of these primitive breeds that had received international recognition and was registered by all the kennel clubs. As well as making a presentation on the breed, what we had done in Israel to gain recognition for the Canaan and to increase its acceptance and value to the average dog owner was a model for what they were trying to do in other countries. There was a great deal of interest in hearing about our successes with the breed. I was honored to be able to make this presentation in such a respected forum.

The time came for a lunch break. After our rather meager breakfast, we were ready for a decent lunch. The conference organizers told us that we would walk to a nearby restaurant.

All of the participants walked in a loose file following the organizers. The streets were even more teeming with cars than in the morning, and crossing to the other side was quite harrowing, and accompanied by a symphony of honking and some incomprehensible comments. Once again, I was happy we didn't understand the language.

The restaurant turned out to be simple cafeteria style. No luxuries such as table cloths; the tables were long, bare trestles. We lined up to get our meals, and found that the choice of food was very limited. The primary dish was a pile of rice with small amounts of rather unidentifiable bits in it, which apparently were vegetables and meat. This, it seems, was the major part of the kazakhi diet. It was called something like *plav*, and was often eaten two or three times a day, but actually was quite tasty. Not being a gourmet, I was prepared to eat just about anything, and the food was filling and quite good. But as the week went on, we discovered that this was one of the few things you could find to eat in restaurants; Kazakhstan did not seem to have much of a tradition of good eating. What was good and tasty the first time when we were hungry, started to become less so after ten or more times.

We had noticed, watching the people on the street and in the conference, that they were very good looking, many with a somewhat oriental cast to their skin and features, and it was rare to see anyone that was overweight. Apparently there wasn't a great deal of interest in food in this society.

The afternoon session of the conference's first day dragged on. It was still very interesting, but it had gotten quite hot in the hall, and after the rather heavy lunch, it was hard to stay alert, especially after two nights with almost no sleep. We were relieved when the conference session closed for the day. Now we could get back to our hotel.

The green bus was waiting for us outside. We all piled in, everyone trying to find seats towards the front to avoid the heavy exhaust fumes in the rear. With a roar of the engine, we pulled out into the evening rush hour traffic.

It was hard to imagine that traffic could be any worse than it had been during the day, but it was. The streets were crammed with cars which moved at a snail's pace, accompanied by blasting horns—apparently there was no law here against using them, or if there was, no one was very concerned. We did have a chance to see the city as we crawled past the beautiful buildings being constructed, some obviously very expensive homes, and a few large beautiful parks with lovely green lawns and masses of flowers, which we were told belonged to the wife of the president.

Finally, we were out of the town center and starting to climb up into the surrounding mountains. Traffic thinned out and there were fewer and fewer buildings. However, our speed of travel was not much improved; the bus was really laboring to climb these hills, and there were a few spots where we were sure we would have to get out and push.

But finally we were there. We pulled through a gate into a small valley among the mountains. The scenery around us was lovely, and ahead were several blue and white buildings, reminiscent of chalets in Europe. This was the hotel.

As we climbed out of the bus, we saw something even more impressive. Staked out to perches spaced along the front lawn were huge raptors. They were golden eagles, eyeing us regally as we walked by. They must have had a wingspan of about two meters, or so it seemed—a few spread their wings for us as we passed. Along the side of the buildings were many flight cages filled with birds of prey—more eagles, hawks, falcons, owls, vultures, in an amazing variety.

There was also a row of kennels, filled with beautiful Tazys, the saluki-like sighthound that is native to Kazakhstan, and a few Asian Ovtscharkas, large, fierce guard dogs bred throughout Eastern Europe, Russia, and parts of Asia, used to protect the herds from predators and thieves. In the back we could just see a stable block and fenced yard for the local breed of horse that was also being bred here.

This was all fantastic, and just the sort of thing that we had hoped to see in Kazakhstan. But when we entered the hotel, it appeared that outside impressions and inside reality were not quite the same.

This seemed to be a sort of lodge which the owner, apparently a very rich man whose hobbies were hunting and breeding dogs, birds, and horses for the hunt, used for his hunting guests. It was very simple inside, though there were some really beautiful paintings of hunting scenes throughout. The rooms were furnished minimally, with narrow beds and a chair or two, which also could be opened up into a bed. We all had to share, with three or four in a room, as there was not really enough accommodation for all of us. I ended up with one of the chair-beds. One end was broken, so I had to sleep with my head at the foot of the bed so that it would not collapse during the night.

However, to my great relief, there were normal toilets, and there was also a shower. Then again, we soon discovered that in our room, the door to the bathroom could not be kept closed unless someone on the outside latched it, and then opened it for the user when she was finished. We always had to have someone else around to close and open the door when we wanted to use the facilities. Another point that we discovered during the first night was that the water was turned off at about ten at night and only came on again at about eight.

There was also no food provided at this lodge. Of course, since we were getting the accommodations for free, we really couldn't complain. We were told that there was a restaurant a few minutes walk away, and that we would have to go to a grocery store to buy food for breakfast, and then the woman in charge of the hotel would prepare it for us.

We all bought a variety of things for breakfast and then walked over to the restaurant. It was very simple, with a grill outside, and tables outside as well. The menu was very limited—this, we were discovering, was standard in Kazakhstan—with the main dish being a sort of kebab, chunks of meat with onions and tomatoes on a skewer. There was also heavy country bread. This was pretty much it, but it was tasty and we were hungry. It took a long time to get served, as there were communication problems—the owners of this restaurant spoke only local languages, and none of us could speak to them. Sign language and smiles was pretty much the only way to try and communicate.

Exhausted, we were all ready for bed. The next day was another long session of lectures, and I would also have to give my presentation on the Canaan Dogs.

The conference proceeded in a similar fashion the next day. I was feeling rather nervous about my presentation. There were some much-respected people at this conference, and although I had been doing a good deal of public speaking over the last few years, to be addressing an international conference was intimidating. Some of the participants were really very well known in the field, and one was even a British lord. These were people who were really experts in the subject, not an audience with little knowledge that would accept unquestioned what I had to say. However, my presentation on the Canaans went well, and was well received. That said, we were starting to get the feeling that the reasons behind this conference might be a bit different than what had been expressed until now.

It turned out that the major topic of discussion was the Kazakh Tazy. We had seen these dogs at Camilla's house and also in the kennels of the hotel. To us, there were no apparent differences from salukis, a breed that is known and registered all over the world. Some of the Bedouin in Israel keep salukis as hunting dogs; their dogs were of desert type, not as large and feathered as the show dogs seen in the U.S. and Europe. The Tazys looked very much like these desert salukis, and Zafra, who is a real expert in the breed, felt that this was not a different breed, but a slight variation in type—but still salukis. However, it seems that the Kazakhstan dog world felt that it was an insult to their national pride to call these dogs salukis. They were their national dog, and they wanted them to be accepted by the international dog world as a separate breed, the Kazakh Tazy. And for some incomprehensible reason, they had decided that we, the delegates of PADS, were the ones to bring this about.

We were supposed to pass an official declaration at this conference that Kazakhstan was entitled to its own national breed and that it should gain FCI (the Federation Cynologique Internationale, the international organization responsible for setting breed standards) recognition. The third day of the conference was dedicated to preparing this declaration.

Emotions ran high as the subject was discussed. The local representatives refused to accept our repeated explanations of the FCI system, and the fact that we had absolutely no influence on the FCI. By the end of the day, everyone was hot, tired, frustrated, a few people were probably hoarse, and nothing had been decided.

The next day there was a trip planned. All of us wanted to see more of Kazakhstan than the hotel and the university building and the traffic jams of Almaty. We were scheduled to have a day tour out of town into the surrounding desert. Our transportation was—what else! —the green bus.

The drive was supposed to be about an hour and a half, to get out of the city and into the desert and surrounding mountains. As we crawled along in Almaty traffic, it seemed that it would take at least that long if not longer just to get out of the center of town. It was stiflingly hot, and the exhaust fumes of the surrounding traffic and of the bus did not help the situation. We then noticed that there was not just one driver, but a whole crew lined up in the front of the bus— rather like the crew of an aircraft. There seemed to be a pilot, co-pilot and another crew member whose function was not yet clear.

The pilot/driver was in the driver's seat, steering. Next to him was the co-pilot, crouched next to the seat in something that looked rather like a yoga position. He was holding something in his hands, but we couldn't see what. We soon discovered just what his task was. The bus frequently seemed to sputter and die, and apparently it was necessary, in order to get it started again, for the co-pilot to put together two wires that he was holding to spark the starter into action. It was hard for us to accept that this was what was happening, but after it happened a few times, it became obvious that this was really the case.

We also soon discovered what the job of the third crew member was. After about half an hour's travel, we pulled over to the side of the road and stopped. The third man got off, grabbed two jerry cans that were behind the driver's seat, and ran off down the road. As we sat there, a few of our companions that could speak Russian tried to find out what was happening. We were informed that we were out of gas, and the third man was running off to a gas station to bring some. But we had passed some gas stations! Why, we asked, hadn't we filled up there? "That gas is too expensive," we were told. We just didn't have enough in the tank to get to the cheaper gas station.

This would have been an amusing incident, if it hadn't been repeated numerous times during the day. The bus, apparently, was a huge guzzler of gas, and frequently ran out. It also had to be pampered with frequent additions of water, and at times, the driver and his co-pilot would stop, get out, open up the panel over the engine, and climb inside, banging around until the bus once again roared into action.

At least we were now out of the center of town and driving past numerous villages. The roadside was lined with markets selling everything from fresh produce to housewares, and was very colorful, and there were a variety of fragrances from the various dishes being cooked at the roadside stands. Some of the people were dressed in colorful local tradition.

This was very interesting at first, but as we drove on, quite slowly, it became clear that the bus was having a problem with engine power. With numerous stops to pamper it with water, fuel, and emergency technical care, we began to wonder if the only thing we would see on this trip was these roadside markets. There were also no rest stops as the hours passed. We were rather hesitant to buy refreshments at the roadside stands we passed, considering the surrounding 'sanitary' conditions. There were, of course, no public restrooms either—the options were to hike off into the surrounding fields and find a convenient bush, or to use one of the outhouses scattered around behind the houses. One whiff at the door of one of these was a great argument for finding a tree.

But after a few hours we found the signs of habitation thinning out and the scenery changing. We were now driving through a desert landscape of barren rocky plains surrounded in the distance by barren mountains, all in typical desert colors of sand, brown, tan, and red. The scenery was actually very similar to the Negev desert in Israel.

There were no signs of civilization out here, and there was little traffic on the road. Other than a few groups of horses grazing on the very sparse vegetation, there were no signs of life. I worried what would happen if the bus broke down or ran out of gas this far out.

As we got close to the mountains, we turned off onto a dirt trail, the bus jouncing along over the rocks. We found that we were being accompanied by a car carrying a few of the organizers and a few of the more VIP-level participants. They had left several hours after us, but not having to cope with breakdowns and gas refills, had indeed arrived in an hour and a half, the time it was expected to arrive at this location. There was a sign identifying the location as a national park. We soon came to the end of the trail; the bus could go no further, now we had to walk.

The scenery was indeed impressive. There was a deep gorge running through with a small river at the bottom. We were on the top and could look down and see all the layers of rock that had been carved away over the millennia by the river which now looked so insignificant at the bottom. Along the river there were green trees and other vegetation, while the rest was dry and barren.

A few of the local participants had also driven out to join us, and had brought some of their tazys. Seeing these dogs running free in their natural environment was truly a beautiful sight.

We had all brought along sandwiches and some watermelons and other fruit had been purchased at one of our roadside stops. We had a refreshing rest, spoiled only by the amount of garbage scattered around at the picnic site. It seems that in any location that was visited by people, much garbage was left behind—something that is unfortunately common not only in Kazakhstan...

The time had come to turn back. It had been quite hot during the day, but there was plenty of wind in the desert, and as the sun started sinking, the wind began to turn cold. We climbed into the bus, hoping that the return would be uneventful.

We were scheduled to stop at a local yurt for a light meal on the way back.. This was the tent belonging to one of the local tribes and was organized for tourist visits. It was supposed to be only about half an hour's drive from where we were, being located near one of the villages on the edge of the desert.. Of course, the drive took considerably longer.

The bus again overheated and ran out of gas, and the crew member responsible for the jerry cans had to hitch a ride into town, fill up, and hitch a ride back, leaving us sitting in what felt like the far end of nowhere for over an hour. Finally, the bus was ready to move again, and we arrived at the yurt.

The place was quite fascinating. These people were from a tribe that followed the tradition of hunting; not the kind of hunting we are familiar with, but a form that has existed in this part of the world for many centuries. The hunters here went out on horseback, carrying their trained birds of prey and accompanied by their dogs—tazys and laikas. They hunted everything from rabbits to wolves, and the hunting was actually done by the dogs and the raptors. The bird was released and searched from above, the dogs hunted the prey on the ground, and when the prey was found, they attacked and killed it. The dogs were trained to submit to the raptors; they had first priority on the kill. The most valued birds were the huge golden eagles, and there was no question that such birds were even capable of killing a wolf.

The family that lived in this yurt was very proud of their tradition and very skilled at it. The father of the family told us that he had competed in an international falconry competition in England a year ago and had won the first prize. He proudly showed off his golden eagle. His oldest son also had an eagle, and the younger children, learning the profession, had hawks of various sorts. They had a number of tazys that were kept also for hunting, a laika, and several Asian Ovtscharkas. These huge dogs, fierce guardians, were lying calmly around the camp sleeping. We were able to walk past them and even step over them and they didn't move. But at night, woe to the uninvited visitor that tried to pass these dogs.

There was a small museum of the hunt which we were allowed to see, with all sorts of equipment for flying the birds, traditional clothing, and the pelts of animals that had been hunted. We saw wolf and fox pelts among the others.

Finally we were invited into the yurt for a light meal. The yurt is a traditional tent, very large and very high with a smoke hole in the center of the roof. These tribes were traditionally nomadic, often moving from place to place, so all their possessions needed to be portable. It was beautifully decorated with all sorts of colorful embroidered panels. The food was set out on low tables, and everyone sat on rugs and cushions on the floor—very reminiscent of the Bedouin style of hospitality in Israel. There were many small dishes with a variety of traditional foods and sweets. I have to admit that, in keeping with the obvious culinary skills we had seen until now in Kazakhstan, there was nothing here that was particularly special or unique. But we were quite hungry and were happy to also have some hot tea.

It was getting dark, and we were all ready to head back to the hotel. It was about 8 p.m. when we climbed back on the bus; the ride back to the hotel should have taken about an hour to an hour and a half. However, after our long day, we were not optimistic. To pass the time, we laid bets on what time we would get back to the hotel.

As expected, the bus did not behave any better on the way back than on the way out. And the traffic in Almaty, although it was already quite late at night, was almost as heavy as during the day. We finally arrived at about 1 in the morning. The winner of the bet was not very happy that he had been right. We all collapsed into bed with relief that we had actually arrived at the hotel and were not sleeping in the bus along the roadside.

We had hoped that, now that the presentations to the conference were completed, we would have time to tour around and see more of the country. But the next morning at breakfast, we were told that we were all expected to participate in a meeting on the subject of the Kazakh tazys. The local breeders were determined that we sign a declaration that this was indeed a unique native breed that deserved to be recognized internationally. Our continued protests that we had no influence on things like that were ignored, and most of the day was spent on trying to write a declaration that would be acceptable to everyone—an impossibility, especially considering the language difficulties. Finally, after hours of arguing, with everyone hungry and exhausted, it was decided that a declaration would be prepared and sent to everyone by e-mail. We are still waiting to receive it.

The only advantage was that we did not have to depend on the old green bus—the meeting was held at our hotel.

In the afternoon, we were treated to a demonstration of the training of the raptors, presented by the master of falconry who was responsible for the training. It was thrilling to see these huge and beautiful birds following his commands and returning to his glove. He presented the golden eagles, a few types of falcon or hawk, a huge owl, and even a vulture. The vulture was not very impressed by having an audience, and after diving into the little decorative pond where the bait had been thrown, he decided to take off for his home cage by foot, followed cautiously by the falconry master's son who wanted to regain control without getting in range of the powerful beak. Just another proof that animals are not computers, and have a mind of their own at times...

One interesting comment made by the master was that it was important never to start thinking that these birds loved you—they worked only because they were trained to and that was the source of their food, no affection was involved. To become sentimental about them was looking for trouble...

I think that this is one of the major differences between mammals and birds. Mammals do seem to develop real affection for the people who raise and care for them. Of course, we all know that our dogs are attached to us, but even an animal like Baba the hyena was very attached to me, and very affectionate. Birds don't seem to have the emotional capabilities, although perhaps a few species like parrots do develop a connection.

That evening, celebrating the end of the conference and the imminent departure of the participants, we had a festive meal in the hotel. Food was ordered in from a local restaurant. There were huge quantities of food, most of it plav. There was also some local liquor, and many toasts. I took one taste and decided that pretending to drink was the best idea.

It was now our last day in Kazakhstan. We were determined to have at least one good day of touring, so abandoning the others and the green bus, we hired a real guide. There were four of us, and we had two sturdy jeeps with two brothers who ran a tourist business. The plan was to drive up into the mountains and see some of the scenery for which the country was known.

We climbed up and up, through forests clinging to the steep and rocky mountainsides. The roads were not paved, but carved out of the rock and the higher we got, the narrower they became. It had been a pleasant sunny day, but the higher we got, the colder the air, although the sun was still shining brightly. Finally we reached our first goal— a gorgeous mountain lake, clear and sparkling, like a gem in the green of the forest, with high and barren peaks surrounding it all. We walked along the rocky shore, enjoying the total silence.

Our guides had provided a picnic for us. We sat and ate what was probably the best meal we had had in Kazakhstan—wonderful country-style dark bread with cheese and sliced meat, fresh tomatoes and fruit, and hot tea.

The next part of the trip was to continue on to another and higher mountain. We drove up past a very modern sports complex, and at a vantage point above it, we met our old green bus. The other conference participants had managed to get up this high with the bus, but it could go no further. We felt very smug as we continued on in our jeeps, higher and higher. The road disappeared, and we found that we were driving through fields of various-sized boulders. Our drivers obviously knew the way, but it certainly wasn't visible, and there were very few cars going this high.

Finally, after jouncing along for some time, we got as far as the jeeps could go. Above us were the rocky peaks, still covered with snow, even though it was September at the end of a hot summer. Up here, some three thousand meters above sea level, there was snow all year around. We climbed through the rocks to try and reach the snow line, and almost got there. But the thin air made the effort exhausting, and we finally sat on the rocks in the bright sun and enjoyed the stunning scenery, fresh cool air, and total silence.

The sun goes down quickly in the mountains, and the stark contrasts of sun and shadow are amazing. It was time to go back down and rejoin the world.

This day of touring had helped make the trip worthwhile, and we were grateful to our guides. They took us to the airport; our plane was due to leave in a few hours and there was no point in going back to the hotel. We had already said our goodbyes.

Now all we wanted was to get on board our plane and get out of Kazakhstan. The country was beautiful and the people were fascinating, but there were still too many remnants of the attitudes and bureaucracy of the former regime to let us feel really comfortable there. The *Borat* image remained in our minds, although I have to say that the local people we met were very pleasant and friendly, and we felt no signs of anti-Semitism, despite being from Israel.

We stood in the passport control line. As my turn came, I presented my passport to be stamped, and glanced around to see where my companions were.

"No! Camera!!" strictly ordered the uniformed clerk. I quickly lifted my glance and stared into the camera for the last time—I was not going to break any rules now!

It was great to be at home. Kazakhstan was a fascinating experience, but I don't know if I would care to go back there again. But who knows what the future may bring...

465

Chapter Forty-Six: Dogs in the Service of Man

Breeding dogs is, for me, very rewarding. I enjoy living with my dogs and having them as friends. I take great pleasure in showing them and gaining titles, and I am really happy to provide dogs as friends and family members to people who take my puppies. But for me, the most satisfying thing of all is to be able to breed dogs that will become service dogs and provide support, assistance, love and improved quality of life to people with various difficulties and handicaps.

Collies are wonderful as service dogs, as they have unending love and patience for their masters and are very amenable to training. The Canaans serve in other ways, as guards and protectors. Each breed has its own characteristics. I have always appreciated the particular qualities of each breed and tried to do things with them that were suited to them. Service dogs have to be very calm and able to accept anything going on around them without doing anything that might endanger their partner. They have to be friendly to everyone and willing to be touched and petted and their reactions to their surroundings always have to be calm. Any sudden reactions on the part of a dog that is guiding a blind person or providing physical support or guidance for someone who is disabled, for instance, can be dangerous. A Canaan, on the other hand, has a very different nature; he is a dog that is by nature very alert, aware and reactive to anything different or possibly threatening in his surroundings, always ready to protect his 'pack' and not happy about being petted by any stranger, which is not what is required of a service dog.

One day, in 2000, I got a phone call from a fellow who introduced himself as Yariv Ben Yosef, a dog trainer. From his impassioned deluge of words, I began to understand that he was a trainer of service dogs and that he was looking for a smooth collie puppy for a special project.

Although I didn't know him, it was clear that he was totally involved and passionate about what he wanted to do; I just wasn't sure just what that was.

As the conversation continued, I found that he had an idea for using dogs to help early-stage Alzheimer's patients. This had never been done before, but he was sure it could be successful. After researching a number of breeds, he decided that smooth collies would be the right dogs for this project, and since I was known as a collie breeder, maybe I could help.

People suffering from Alzheimer's and other degenerative brain damage diseases suffer loss of cognitive skills, including memory of people and places, judgment, and orientation in time.. The loss of orientation hinders their ability to get home safely, so that any time they leave home, they run the risk of getting lost. The ability to get home becomes a major survival issue for these people.

People with dementia and other degenerative brain diseases also feel terrible loneliness, frustration, anger and helplessness. Against their will, they are prisoners in their own homes and are dependent on others to get out. Often they feel ashamed, and start to isolate themselves from contact with others. It becomes a vicious circle, and often the lack of activity results in physical deterioration in addition to the mental problems.

The idea was that with the help of a specially trained dog, the patient can get home by simply giving the dog the command to take them home., which returns to them their freedom of movement and makes it possible for them to leave their homes without requiring the help of family members. This was a revolutionary idea, but made a lot of sense. If a dog could guide the blind, then why not those suffering from periodic memory loss? There were no smooth collies in Israel, so my part in the project was to try to find a suitable puppy abroad that could be brought to Israel for training.

After researching breeders of smooths, I got in touch with a few that seemed to have dogs that fit the requirements we thought were suitable for the project. We were pleased to receive a reply from a very well-known breeder in Finland who had a puppy she thought would be right for the purpose. Arrangements were quickly made to bring her to Israel.

Belle, as she was named, went to a foster home where she would be raised until she was old enough to work with her future master and immediately started learning her future task. It was important that puppies start their training from about two or three months of age, so that their responses were very well imprinted. Yariv immediately began to teach her to go home, first just by standing outside the door of the apartment she lived in and giving her a treat for any reaction—touching the door, barking, pushing, scratching—and then encouraging an increased reaction. He began to teach her to come to the door from a few steps away and gradually increased the distance. As she grew, she learned to bring Yariv "home" from greater and greater distances, through the busy streets of the town she lived in. She also began to learn to react to strange behavior—part of her task would be to alert and get help if her master stumbled, fell, or had any other physical problems.

After about a year of intensive training, Belle was ready to go to her new master. Yehuda was a 62 year-old Alzheimer's patient who had been a highly-respected professional, and was very depressed by the diagnosis of the disease; he began to stay at home more and more, sometimes not even getting out of bed. He had less and less contact with people other than his immediate family, and felt ashamed that he might have an attack and behave in a way that would be embarrassing. He was very skeptical that a dog would be able to help in any way, but he and his family were so hopeless that they were willing to try anything.

Belle was introduced to Yehuda and his family. First, there were just visits to get acquainted and for Belle and Yehuda to start learning to work together. Once they had started to bond and to work efficiently, Belle became a permanent member of the household. Yariv was constantly available to work with them and assist them to become an efficiently functioning pair, and to solve any problems that might arise.

Yehuda now says, "The dog has given me a quality of life by releasing me from the prison walls of my own home. This is the best thing that has ever happened to me..."

Belle was the first dog to be trained for this task, and we were not sure just what she would be able to do. The first part of her training was to bring Yehuda home. He would not have to be afraid to go to out of the house, because if he got lost, Belle would lead him back. She also was taught to guide him around obstacles such as holes, dangerous curbs, parked cars and traffic—very much like a guide dog. Yehuda also was not so steady on his legs, at times stumbling and falling, and Belle was taught to provide support as necessary.

Part of the tragedy of this disease is the feeling of loneliness, isolation, and anxiety felt by the patient. Belle was very responsive to all of Yehuda's mood changes, and stayed close to him, touched him, and provided comfort and reassurance just by her presence. Even at the times that an Alzheimer's patient is not cognizant of what is happening to him or around him, he can still feel the presence and reassurance of a loving dog.

A dog also needs regular care and a normal routine. Belle learned to nudge Yehuda in the morning to encourage him to get up and out of bed. Walking with Belle helped improve his physical health and as she loves to play, by bringing her toys to Yehuda, encouraged him in additional physical activity. It is known that regular physical activity is one of the factors that helps to slow down the progression of

Alzheimer's. Yehuda also tried to keep to a set routine in Belle's care, with regular feeding, walking and grooming—a way to maintain a more normal way of life.

Walks with Belle are also a source of contact with other people. Yehuda is able to talk to others about his dog, and to let them pet her. Belle is friendly and happy to be noticed and her special harness also attracts interest. This type of social contact is relaxed, and the interaction relieves feelings of loneliness; Yehuda can feel that he is still part of his community, and can still retain the possibility of independent action—he can go out to walk with Belle without having to wait for a family member to have the time to accompany him.

Belle is a full-time companion to Yehuda, and bonded to him and his needs. When Yehuda is depressed and does not want to get out of bed, Belle plays with him, pulls the blankets away from him, brings him her toys, and will not stop until Yehuda responds. She is with him when he can't sleep at night, and is with him when his family is busy with other activities. Because she is always there with him, Yehuda does not feel so dependent on having a family member with him all the time.

Alzheimer's Aid Dogs are trained to sense their owner's condition and warn when irregular situations such as breathing distress, falling, epileptic fits, etc. occur. Yehuda choked on food one day. Belle barked and ran between the family members until they understood there was a problem. On another occasion, Belle clung to Yehuda after he tripped in the yard and was very attentive until he got up. Belle is also specially trained to react to crisis situations by barking to alert help or to press a special emergency button. In one case, Belle began barking and would not stop, although Yehuda was not in any trouble or distress. It was then discovered that Yehuda's wife, in another room, had fallen and could not get up, and Belle was alerting to this situation as well.

The main role of the Alzheimer's Aid Dog is to return its owner safely home when it hears the verbal command "Home!" from its owner. To be prepared for situations where the person might forget the command, get confused, not be aware of the passing time, or to the fact that he has left the familiar physical area, a special electronic homing device has been developed. If Yehuda is gone from home and his family suspect he might have gotten lost and forgotten to give Belle the command "Home," they can signal Belle through the device on her collar to bring him home now. The collar also has a GPS transmitter so that the family can locate Belle and Yehuda wherever they might be. Belle is trained to never leave Yehuda, and if he is unable to come home with her, she stays with him, tries to attract attention by barking, and waits for them to be found. This is crucial since a disoriented person who is lost could be in a life-threatening situation.

Belle has proven her ability to find her way home over long distances and through unfamiliar areas and to find the safest way, changing a normal route for a new one when the usual way was obstructed due to construction work. In the past, Yehuda's daughter would not allow him to pick up his grandchildren from the kindergarten and walk them home due to fear of him becoming disoriented. Now he is able once again to bring his grandchildren home—his daughter knows that Belle will find the way, and Yehuda can once again enjoy the role of grandfather.

Belle has amazed us with her fantastic ability to orient herself to the vicinity. Since Belle was the first dog to do this job, we didn't really know what to expect, and her perception and initiative are beyond what we could have imagined. On one occasion, Yehuda was visiting in a different community and went for a walk. He got lost, but Belle was able to take him directly back to the house he was visiting, even though this was the first time she had been there. On another occasion, Yehuda and his wife, accompanied of course by Belle, took a trip to

Paris. He left the hotel to buy a newspaper, and got lost. Belle not only brought him back to the hotel, but to the room they were staying in.

The success of this first dog brought a fantastic satisfaction to me and to Yariv. To me, Alzheimer's disease seems like the cruelest possibility of aging. It is not a matter of losing health, but of losing yourself, your memories, and the things that make you unique. Being able to do anything to help is wonderful.

With Belle proving that this project could be successful, the next stage was to find more dogs able to do the job. Working with dementia patients, in my opinion, is the hardest task a service dog can have; guide dogs for the blind do a marvelous job of giving mobility to the blind, but are guided by the commands of their masters. However, Alzheimer's Aid Dogs have to cope with the inability of their masters to direct them. These dogs have to have the ability to take the initiative and bring their partners home, whether the person is capable of giving the command "home," or is totally unaware of his surroundings and what is happening. The dog must be tough enough to persist even when his person may resist, and to call for help if he can't bring them home. He must be totally devoted and loving to his master and willing and eager to spend 24 hours a day with them and at the same time, this dog must be strong enough mentally to be able to absorb and ignore the changing and unstable moods of an Alzheimer's patient, who may forget that they have a dog, and even behave abusively when they are having an attack. Alzheimer's dogs provide unconditional love, so total that they can continue loving and working with their partner no matter what his mental state or mood.

Obviously, it is extremely difficult to find dogs that can fill these requirements. We imported several more smooth collies, tried a few rough collies, and a few dogs of other breeds, but they were not up to the task. These dogs, which had wonderful temperaments and working ability, simply were not up to the stresses of the Alzheimer's program, and went on to work as service dogs in other capacities.

I was sure that if we had succeeded with one dog, we could succeed with more. The problem was finding the right dogs. I got in touch with a well-known breeder of collies in the U.S., the Rapaport family of Kings Valley Collies. I knew their name as breeders of very successful show dogs, but I discovered that they had, for many years, also been breeding collies as service dogs for a variety of tasks. Here, I felt, might be the right line of dogs to work as Alzheimer's Aid Dogs.

The Rapaports were excited by the project, and offered us two smooth collie puppies. One lovely sable female, Sunny, went for training, and the second, a tricolor, came home with me to grow up as potential breeding stock. She was named Freckle, because of one little black freckle in her wide white collar.

Sunny progressed very well in her training. By the time she was a year old, she had proven her abilities and was ready to meet her future master.

In this case, the patient was a woman in the late fifties, another highly-educated professional. Gila had always been interested in sports as well, and was fit and healthy looking. She was supported by a close and loving family; all found it very difficult to cope with the bleak future.

I was present at a few of the sessions where Yariv worked with the patient, to teach her how to work with her new dog. My job in this project was to try and provide puppies that would be good working dogs, but I could do this best if I knew as much as possible about the needs of the patient and their interactions with the dog.

It was heartbreaking. This lovely and attractive woman, who could carry on an intelligent and interesting conversation one minute, the next might not be able to remember the name of the dog which she had been told a moment ago, or whether the dog was to walk on her right or left. Yariv had unlimited patience, repeating things again and again, and building up a habit pattern so that Gila could react correctly to the dog without thinking about it or even realizing what she was doing. I would never have been able to do it, and it was hard to keep a cheerful demeanor even just as an observer. Sunny, however, was ever attentive and alert to all needs of her new partner.

Seeing the whole procedure made me even more aware of the importance of this project and of its value. With Sunny, Gila could now go for walks as she had always done, and live as close to a normal life as possible, without being afraid of not getting home again. Sunny was so connected to her master and so aware of everything associated with her, that when Gila began to develop epileptic attacks, Sunny began to respond to them, giving warning in advance and even refusing to leave the house or let her charge go out when she felt an attack was imminent. And Sunny was proven to be right every time—her warnings were taken very seriously.

Freckle quickly became a happy member of the pack at home. She proved to be a very intelligent, very active, and very opinionated girl, who always liked to be in the center of any activity. She did very well in the show ring, quickly becoming a champion.

The time arrived for her to have her first litter. The father was my smooth boy, Spirit. Freckle produced nine fat and healthy puppies, seven smooths and two roughs, and was a devoted mother, taking excellent care of her puppies and not losing patience, even with nine plump little rascals running after her.

From this litter, one daughter became a working Alzheimer's Aid Dog, proving again that this was a job that a dog could do. To date, the only dogs that have succeeded in this task are smooth collies.

Another daughter became an epilepsy alert dog. She went at the age of three months to a severely epileptic woman. Efrat's attacks were so frequent and so severe, that she was afraid to go anywhere alone, even to take a bus, from fear of having a serious attack and suffering injury, and the embarrassment of experiencing it in a public place.

The puppy she received, that she called Sky, started to warn her of imminent attacks from the age of three months, from 15 minutes to 2 hours before the attack. This gave Efrat the possibility to prepare, to sit down in a safe place, or to call for someone to help her, and thus to be ready and in control of the situation.

Over the last two years that Sky has been working, Efrat has been having fewer and fewer attacks. Presently, she has gone for a long period without any. The doctor attributes this in part to the feeling of security and confidence that her dog gives her. I think this must be true. The feeling of calm and confidence we get from having a dog on hand to stroke and talk to is significant to a person without any particular problems, so I am sure that this is even more significant to someone with a service dog.

Several other of Freckle's pups became service dogs for autistic children. These dogs, first of all, provide unconditional love. Autistic children, who have trouble communicating, are able to develop a relationship with a dog that does not anything of them and is ready to love them and stay with them no matter how they behave. As well, these dogs help to teach these children responsibility and a framework, as they learn to help take care of the dog, feeding it, grooming it, 'training' it and so on. The dogs also learn to prevent the child from running away or into the street, making use of their natural herding abilities, and can distract the child from attacks of anger or other undesirable behavior, just by their presence, by touching or licking the child.

Freckle has indeed proved that she has the ability to pass on the required characteristics for service dogs.

From her second litter, she has another daughter that is close to completing training as an Alzheimer's dog, and several others that are also service dogs in other capacities.

Our vision for the future is to develop this line of excellent working dogs, so that we can provide more solutions for more challenged people, in particular Alzheimer's sufferers.

Freckle's second litter is now 15 months old. One daughter has graduated training as an Alzheimer's Aid Dog and is now working with the patient, and a few others of the litter are also service dogs of various types. One of her sons has stayed here with me. Freckle is now, I hope, pregnant with her third litter, for which people are eagerly waiting, and I am importing a new smooth bitch and dog from the U.S. to expand this essential program.

Chapter Forty-Seven: Some More Special Dogs

There have been a lot of wonderful dogs over the years, but there are always those that stand out in particular. Canaans are not always easy dogs to live with, with their unique temperament; people who don't understand them sometimes find that these dogs have taken over the leadership of the household. Over the years, I have taken back several dogs that I sold as puppies, but that had not worked out successfully in their new homes. Some of them were successfully rehomed with people that appreciated them, but some stayed here, and became some of the best dogs I ever had.

One of these was Lehitraot. He was a son of Shachmat, and his mother was a sister to Chami. There were five puppies in the litter and they were all really beautiful. As usual, the puppies were all named with Hebrew names; *Lehitraot* is Hebrew for, 'Be seeing you,' and little did we suspect when he left for his new home that this would soon be true.

The little cream-colored fellow went to a family living in a nice house in the Tel Aviv area, and he was given the pet name of Nockie, short for Knock-out, as he was so beautiful. Little Nockie was brought up with plenty of love and affection, but apparently with little discipline. Canaans are very clever dogs, and when they see an opportunity to become pack leader, they take it. Nockie quickly decided that it was his job, as the pack leader, to defend all property belonging to the pack, and he became more and more aggressive in fulfilling his self-appointed task. He was always sweet and affectionate to his family, but outsiders were not allowed.

After Nockie managed to bite a few people that had 'invaded' his territory, he was brought back to us. His owner, sad at having to give him up but worried about the consequences of having such an aggressive dog, put him in the kennel and left.

As far as Nockie was concerned, after five minutes in the kennel, this was his new territory. All of us at Shaar Hagai were strangers to him, and no one was allowed in to his kennel. He was quite ferocious in the defense of his new territory, and attacked the fence when we came near. After all, he had been abandoned by his pack (his former family), and who knew what we were going to do to him.

It took about two weeks for Nockie to calm down. The first few days, we could not enter his kennel, unless we were holding the turned on water hose in front of us. This was the only way to put in his food and do some cleaning of the kennel without being bitten. Dorcas had a particular interest in Nockie, since he was a son of Shachmat. The two of us spent a lot of time sitting outside his kennel and talking to him, and offering to let him sniff our hands through the wire. After a few days, he began to come over to sniff instead of attacking the fence, and began to show an interest when we came near.

Finally, it seemed to be time to go in and make friends. I entered his kennel without the hose in hand, and let him come over and examine me. Once he had done so, I offered my hand for him to sniff and gently touched him. This was the breakthrough—he now decided that we were his new pack, and was willing to allow us in his territory.

The next step was to start taking him out on leash. As a dog that had never been disciplined or properly trained, he was happy to go out to walk, but wanted to go at his own pace and in his own direction. He was after all, the pack leader, or at least he thought so. Any limitations we imposed on him with the leash were likely to result in growls and threats. But persistent work led to the desired results—Nockie learned to follow the basic commands, as he realized that behaving would bring him more walks, praise, and attention, and therefore was definitely worthwhile.

He was about a year and a half old, and was a really beautiful dog. I was sure that he would easily become a champion, so we started taking him to shows. The first few times we took Nockie to dog shows, he was very excited by all the strange dogs and was ready to attack any that came near enough. This was not acceptable. But we discovered that he absolutely loved riding in the car. Any car with an open door was an invitation for him to jump in. He soon discovered that if he behaved, he could ride more often. So good behavior away from home also became highly worthwhile.

At shows or other events where there were many dogs, I could often feel, through the leash, that Nockie was muttering under his breath at having to be close to the other dogs, but he always controlled himself and behaved like a gentleman.

He quickly became an Israel champion, and now the plan was to travel with him to some shows abroad. I was planning to go to the World Show in Brussels in 1995 and decided that this would be an opportunity to start showing him in Europe. He and one of the collies, Stargazer, traveled with me by plane and we then stayed in a hotel room in the center of Brussels. Nockie behaved perfectly in the hotel, during our walks around the city, and at the show, and won the title of World Winner 1995.

I was so pleased with his behavior that I decided the next year to take him again. In 1996, the World Show was in Vienna and Budapest. The show was four days, two days in each city. There was also to be a meeting of the International Collie Society. I was very interesting in attending that and seeing European collie friends that I hadn't seen for some time.

I was sharing a room with a Collie Society friend. Nockie met her and quickly learned that she belonged in our territory, though she was expected to stay in the area of her own bed and not to come near ours. However, I had not thought to warn others there for the meeting that the dog in the room did not behave like a collie. One afternoon, a few other friends just walked in without being invited. Nockie immediately ran forward and stood in the entrance, growling. My friends, being dog people, immediately understood the hint and stopped until I could call him back and assure him that it was all right.

My roommate was astonished. "But he has been so sweet to me all the time," she said. Well, of course, she belonged to his territory.

Nockie went on to win another World Winner title. He sired some lovely puppies, and remained sweet and devoted to us for his lifetime, although he never neglected his job as guardian of the pack.

Barak was a double great grandson of Nockie and a grandson of Solo, and had many others of the greats of Shaar Hagai in his pedigree. So, it was obvious that he would be something special. He was red, a color that I really like, but that we don't get very frequently.

However, we had a lot of puppies and too many dogs, as was usually the case, so Barak was sold. The family that chose him lived in Gush Etzion, a rather troubled area near the border, and they wanted him as a watchdog first of all, and then as a pet for the children. There were quite a number of children of all ages in this family.

About a year later, I got a call from the family. Barak was causing trouble and they didn't want him anymore, could I come to get him? I drove out to their village, about an hour and a half away. As I came close to their very isolated little settlement, I passed by many Arab villages. The entrance to the village had soldiers stationed to check cars entering; unfortunately, a fact of life in many parts of Israel, especially near the border.

At their house, I asked to see Barak. He was tied on a long cable around the side of the house, and as soon as he saw me approaching, he began to bark. He was a really beautiful young dog, a typical Canaan with a deep red color.

"What is the problem with him?" I asked.

"He is a coward," they told me.

I walked towards him. He stood his ground, barking and baring his teeth. He did not remember me and this was his territory that I was invading. This definitely was not the behavior of a coward.

A bit more questioning revealed that he was a highly alert and effective watch dog—at night, when the soldiers went on their regularly security inspection, he barked, and this annoyed the family and the neighbors. Of course, it was much easier to get rid of the dog than to try and educate him about what he should be barking at and what wasn't necessary.

I was happy to take Barak home. As I left, I told the family, "If I lived in a place like this, I certainly would not want to be without a good guard dog!"

One of the things that I have found very hard to accept in Israel is that people in sensitive or dangerous areas often do not have dogs. Whenever I hear of an attack on a settlement, where a terrorist has cut the fence and attacked people in their own home, I feel very sad and frustrated—just having a little noisy dog that would bark at strange noises could have been enough to have saved lives...

Barak adjusted quickly to being back at Shaar Hagai. He was far from being cowardly; actually, he was a very self-confident dog, and was extremely affectionate. It appeared that the family, having no previous experience with dogs, had paid little attention to him, and he had really felt that lack. He had been kept tied almost all the time, and had little experience with other people or dogs.

His problems were not with people; he was quite outgoing and friendly. However, he didn't really know how to get along with other dogs and spent a lot of time at first fighting through the fence with the other dogs. His lack of experience was obvious—he was the one that always ended up with a bite in the foot when he was stupid enough to put his foot through the fence, or a scratch on the face when he got too up close and personal. In time, he learned correct communication and the fence fighting slackened off.

His first few times at shows he was confused, but he quickly began to enjoy these experiences. He was a very showy dog, one of those rare reds, and stood out from the others. He quickly became a champion.

I was eager to take him abroad to shows—he was such a striking dog, I had no doubts that he would be a real success. The World Dog Show in 2000 was being held in Milan, Italy, and that seemed like it would be a good start. My good friend Isabella, a devoted Canaan breeder, had decided that this was a good opportunity to have an international Canaan meeting, and Canaan fanciers were coming from many countries—the U.S., England, Finland, Germany, France—so of course we had to have an Israeli representation.

Barak and I flew to Milan where the show was to be held. He was very calm about his first experience on a plane. We were picked up by other Canaan friends that had already arrived and were taken to the location of the Canaan meeting, where we would all be staying for a few days. It was not far from the show venue—quite an important consideration in Italy where traffic jams can be interminable. The place was actually a riding stable owned by friends of Isabella. Since various events were held there which required the riders to stay over, there were a few dormitory rooms which had been offered to us.

The conditions were quite primitive. It seemed to be a converted stable that had been furnished with camp beds. There was one toilet and shower downstairs adjoining the club room. It was June and quite hot during the day, and, of course there was no air conditioning or even a fan.

There was however, a plethora of hungry mosquitoes. But we would not be spending a lot of time there, and the evenings were cool and comfortable. There were also some really nice horses around which I enjoyed watching.

I was quite accustomed to traveling on a shoestring budget and having this sort of accommodations. Some of the others were rather surprised, to say the least.

The first day was when everyone was arriving, of course all at different times. There was no restaurant nearby, and no plans to go anywhere until all the participants had arrived. So, the owners kindly provided us with a home-cooked Italian meal.

I really love Italian food; it is probably my very favorite. There was, of course, pasta, and a very tasty sauce with all kinds of things in it. There was a bit of a language problem, but we finally understood that it was all sorts of seafood. I like fish and have even learned to like some of the odder things like shrimps and calamari. But as I started to eat, I saw all sorts of little pieces that I soon identified as legs. Tiny little legs.

I am not sure what sort of creature was cooked into this sauce, but I decided to stick with the pasta without the legs.

The show was held in a huge conference center on the outskirts of Milan. We had a few rented cars for the group, and the next morning set off for the show.

World Shows are huge events and as the number of entries, which can be as many as 20,000 or more, are too many to be judged in one day, and are divided up into four days. Even then, the shows are crowded, but it is fascinating to see both the variety of dogs and of people as well.

There was a good number of Canaans entered, both from breeding in Italy and from abroad—a number of participants in the conference also brought dogs with them. Barak was entered in the Champion class with a number of other good-looking Canaans, but I was sure he would impress the judge. At ringside, to support the Israeli entry, was my friend Avi, the president of the Israel Kennel Club and a Canaan owner himself, and a few of the Israeli judges who were present at the show.

As my turn came to show Barak, I stood him for the judge to examine, and then started running around the ring to show off his beautiful movement. Since he was such a good mover, I ran quite fast to give him the chance to show himself off to best advantage. I was watching him as I ran, and did not notice that someone had left a chair at the ring side with the legs inside the ring. I connected with the chair and ended up flat on my face in the ring, with Barak cringing at the end of the leash wondering what was happening.

Red faced but unhurt except for my dignity, I got up, tried to reassure Barak that it wasn't his fault, and continued. But the impression had been spoiled; Barak got only third place in the class, one of the only times in his career that he wasn't the winner. And I discovered, to my horror, that not only were the Israelis at ring side to see my embarrassment, but they had recorded it with a video camera!

A really nice young dog of Isabella's was the winner that year.

The conference went well, and after the official program was over, we were all invited to come to visit Isabella. She lived in a very picturesque part of Tuscany a few hours drive from Milan.

The nearest town was Rufina. From there we had to take a narrow road up into the mountains. The road soon ended and we were left with a narrow dirt track, very rocky and pitted, that climbed up and down and around at quite extreme angles. It was indeed beautiful, but it required strong nerves. Finally we arrived at Isabella's house, a very old stone building, obviously quite historic, but in the process of being renovated. Like many dog people, Isabella did not have a lot of money, and most of what she had went to the comfort of the dogs. People comforts tend to be secondary.

I loved the country atmosphere, the absolute quiet, the mountain air. Barak found all the new smells fascinating. Isabella had quite a lot of dogs, both Canaans and Siberian huskies, and some of them were really lovely. They had plenty of space to run around and enjoy life.

All too soon, it was time to fly home. Barak had behaved like a true gentleman the whole trip, and had impressed everyone, other than the judge, apparently. I had enjoyed the trip as well, aside from those few moments in the ring.

Barak made up for his loss in the spring of 2001, when the European Winner show was held in Israel, and together with that, we had another international Canaan meeting and a specialty show. There were also many guests from abroad, some with their dogs—many of the people who had been at the event in Italy now came to Israel. Barak redeemed himself completely by winning the European Winner title and the Best in Show title at the specialty.

But, I felt that Barak deserved to win a World Winner title, and since he had lost it in Italy mostly due to my fault, in 2001 I decided to take him to Portugal, where the show was going to be held. I also had two puppies that had to be delivered to my friend Laurence in France, who was unable to come to the show in Portugal, so I arranged to fly with the dogs to Italy, meet Isabella who was driving to Portugal in a large van with a number of dogs to show, and on the way to deliver the puppies. I knew that it would be fun to spend a few days traveling with Isabella; she is an outspoken and funny woman and a good friend.

Living in Israel tends to make you forget how big other countries are and how long the distances. In Israel, you can drive from one end of the country to the other in less than a day; Europe is a bit different.

We had allowed about two and a half days for the drive. Theoretically, this is possible. In reality, there are traffic jams, road work, closed roads, detours, rest stops, and all sorts of unplanned things that take up a lot of time. We arrived at the meeting point in the south of France where we were to deliver the puppies to Laurence, but we were already behind schedule. So, we decided to drive straight through without stopping at hotels for the night, but just taking a few hours break to sleep at the roadside.

To keep awake and alert, we talked. We told each other our life stories, including all the intimate details—after all, those were the sort of things that kept you alert and interested. We sang. We giggled. And we kept traveling, only stopping to give the dogs a chance to stretch their legs every few hours.

Finally, we crossed the border into Portugal. But the show was being held in Porto in the north, so we still had a long way to go. There were some excellent highways in Portugal, but they were all toll roads. This was before the Euro became the currency for all of Europe and all we had was some Italian money and U.S. dollars. A Portuguese friend that we would be meeting in Porto had told me in advance about the toll roads, and said that it was necessary to pay in Portuguese money; they would not accept other currencies or credit cards. We searched for a bank or currency exchange, but this was an area of small sleepy country towns and there didn't seem to be any place that was open.

So we started down the side roads in the direction of Porto. This was also before it was common to have GPS systems in the car, so all we had was a book of maps. There seemed to be little in common between what was in the book and where these roads actually went. It was quite mountainous in this part of Portugal, and the roads seemed to meander in various directions, anything other than a straight line. The countryside was really pastoral and beautiful—but the driving was very slow.

Finally, we arrived late in the evening at the hotel where we were staying. Luckily, it was summer and the days were very long, so it was still light when we unpacked the car and got the dogs settled. We finally had a chance to have a decent meal, and met my friends in the restaurant. We explained why we were so late.

"Oh my," we were told, "you can pay on the toll road with anything—cash or credit cards, no problem!"

The show in Portugal went well, with Barak winning the title of World Winner this time.

The drive back was much easier, as we were able to travel on the highway. Again we met Laurence in the south of France. She had asked to borrow Barak for a few months to use for breeding, and she would show him in France. It was hard for me to let him go. We had developed a really close relationship, and you can't explain to a dog that he will be coming home again in a few months—he would not understand why I was leaving him behind. But he was needed for the development of the breed in France, and I knew I could depend on Laurence to take good care of him and keep him happy. She was very experienced with Canaans and understood the breed well.

Barak sired a number of litters in France, producing some lovely puppies, had some very nice show wins, and won a lot of friends for the breed there. After some months, I came back to pick him up, on my way to the U.S. this time. He would be going with me to some shows there, and would stay there for a while with another friend of mine, Cheryl, a keen Canaan breeder and exhibitor who very much wanted to use him in her breeding program.

Laurence was meeting me in Paris with Barak and a few other dogs, as there was a big show there. When I came out to the car, Barak looked at me intently for a minute and then, very deliberately, turned his back. "You abandoned me here," he seemed to be saying, "and now I don't want to know you!" I couldn't really say that he wasn't right.

But that night in the hotel, he climbed onto my bed and lay down next to me. He had forgiven me—as long as he could sleep in bed.

By now a very experienced traveler, Barak took the trip to the U.S. and the shows there in his stride. I was again very sad to leave him, but he now knew that I would be coming back.

He was very successful in the U.S., winning Best of Breed at specialty shows and in all breed shows as well, and taking a Group 1 and two Group 2's, a rare achievement for a rare breed like the Canaan. His puppies were also starting to gain titles.

Then I got a call from Cheryl. They were at a big show where Barak had won Best in Show at a breed specialty. But somehow, after the judging, when he was resting in his crate, he had gotten hold of a towel and had chewed it up and swallowed part of it. He had an intestinal blockage and was being operated on.

I was sure that he would come out of the operation okay—after all, Canaans are very strong dogs, they are survivors, and he would certainly survive this. But there had been too much damage to his stomach and intestines, and after a valiant fight, Barak died.

I was heartbroken. I had been looking forward to his return, with plans for his future. The kennel seemed so quiet without him.

Barak lives on in my memory and in his great descendents, but I still miss that flash of red as he came running to greet me. It is always very difficult for me to part with any of my dogs for a period of time, but to help develop the breed in other countries it is quite important for the best dogs to be seen at shows there and used for breeding. Since I can't spend a lot of time away from home, there is no choice but to let some of the dogs go for a while to trusted friends. But every time I say goodbye for a while to one of my dogs, I feel a pang in my heart. This time, the pang was justified. It is no one's fault, accidents do happen and animals are unpredictable, but whenever I think of Barak, I will always feel that moment of doubt as to whether I made the right decision in leaving him in the U.S..

Shaked is a great grandson of Barak. His father is one of the 'miracle' puppies born in France from Bayud's sperm that we shipped that defrosted on the way. His full name is Nes HaBedouim, literally miracle of the Bedouins, and he's related to Barak through his daughter Sufat Hol. His mother, known as Pandora, spent some time in France at shows and came back pregnant, producing a lovely litter. Shaked was sold as a puppy to a young guy who had been eagerly waiting for a show quality Canaan puppy, and he chose Shaked from the litter.

Shaked developed into a beautiful young dog. His owner indeed came with him to shows, and I was very pleased to see how good he was looking.

Then, when Shaked was about a year and a half old, his owner turned up on my doorstep with the dog in tow. Shaked had bitten his wife, and he had no choice but to get the dog out of the house. Apparently, Shaked had become very protective of his food. Aggression over food is a very common behavior problem which can occur in almost any breed. The wife had never had a dog before, and was quite nervous about having a dog in the house, even though he had been raised in their home since he was an eight week old puppy. Dogs, of course, are very aware of people that are afraid of them. He began to growl at her when she came near his food dish. The couple sought advice from a dog trainer and they were told that, in order to show Shaked that no one wanted to take his food away, he should be given a smaller portion, and then, while he was eating, the wife should come and add more food to his dish. So while he was eating, she came over and stuck her hand in the dish, and Shaked, sure that she was going to take his food away, bit her.

Any one who understands dog behavior would understand that Shaked felt that he was doing the appropriate thing. But, although I tried to explain to the couple that this was a problem that could be solved, and that Shaked could easily learn to behave calmly even around food, the wife refused absolutely to have him come home.

The husband was actually crying when he left; he was very attached to Shaked and had done all he could to raise him properly. Unfortunately, he had never contacted me to ask for advice while the pup was growing and developing his behavior patterns. He had then gone to a trainer that worked with very harsh methods, not at all suitable for a Canaan, and this had created an even higher level of stress in the dog. And the final result was a bite.

Shaked was a beautiful dog that was certainly suitable for the show ring. But I didn't really need him—I had his mother, his litter sister, and his half sister. My initial idea was to keep him and educate him about good manners and proper dog behavior, and then to find a good home for him.

He remembered me and remembered the kennels, although he hadn't been back since he left as a puppy for his new home. I do find that almost all of the dogs that leave here as puppies, not to mention those that may go to new homes when they are a bit older, do remember me, even if they haven't seen me for years. They seem to be thrilled to see me, jumping on me joyfully with wagging tails and face licks. After all, I was second only to their mother, and that is something that is imprinted on their brain. It doesn't surprise me, but many people are surprised to see a dog that I haven't been in contact with for many years so very happy to see me.

Although Shaked remembered me and was glad to see me, he was very tense. He seemed to be worried all the time, and waiting to be reprimanded. I discovered that his owner had taken him to a dog trainer to learn obedience (the same one that had given the wife such unsuccessful advice), and this trainer was known to use old fashioned methods that were quite harsh. Shaked had learned to follow commands in order to avoid being punished, rather than learning to follow commands because doing so would bring positive rewards of praise, treats and petting, the methods that are so common and successful these days. Aside from the fact that aggressive training methods based on punishment tend to produce dogs that are worried and unenthusiastic about obeying, Canaans are not very responsive to harsh methods. These methods can either make them shy and afraid or aggressive. Canaans are natural dogs that are very oriented to pack behavior, and the relationships in a pack are not built on harshness and violence, but rather on mutual respect. What appears to the dog to be unjustified aggressiveness results in a response of trying to evade this treatment in any way that may prove effective.

Shaked was very surprised when I started to give him treats and lots of affection for whatever I asked him to do. It took him a long time to overcome the worried attitude that he had developed—it was close to a year before I felt that he was really rehabilitated. But when you are working with dogs like this, there seems to be a day when a light goes on in the brain and the dog has a moment of revelation: "Gee, life is different now! Things are good!" And this moment arrived in my relations with Shaked.

Suddenly he was a different dog. He was happy, he played, he jumped on me to lick my face, and wanted to be with me as much as possible.

By now, I had become as attached to him as he was to me. He is really a very sweet dog, very affectionate, and not at all a trouble maker. He tries to avoid confrontations with other dogs, walking past them when they are lunging at him through the kennel fence with his head turned away and with great dignity. There was no question that he would stay at Shaar Hagai—I could never put him through another move, and the need to adjust and learn to trust someone new, after the hard time he had had.

Shaked easily finished his Israel Champion title. I then took him to a few shows in Greece. He behaved like a true gentleman throughout the trip, in the airport, at the hotel, at the show, and won Best of Breed and CACIB (candidacy for International Champion) at both shows. This year, 2008, he completed the requirements to become an International Champion. He has also had two litters with lovely puppies.

I am sure that there will be more chances to travel with him. He was so well behaved and a pleasure to be with on the trip to Greece, and he likes traveling and seeing new places. But mostly, I enjoy his companionship. It is a pleasure to me to see him happy and relaxed and to trust me completely after his difficult start in life. His home will always be at Shaar Hagai.

Of course, aside from all the Canaans, there were also special collies. The most special of those that live with me now is DoJo.

DoJo's mother was a blonde bombshell that I imported from Brazil. The breeder there, who I had known for a number of years, had a very lovely type of collie that I very much admired, and his dogs also had excellent temperaments. In my opinion, collies in Europe were not as good as they had been years ago—they were small, not very well constructed which meant that they didn't have much endurance, lacking the typical elegance of the breed, and were quite passive in temperament. I had always done various activities with my collies, having them run with me when I was riding, work with the sheep and goats that we had, and do various dog sports like agility. For me, a collie was a bright, active, intelligent dog that always wanted to participate, not a dog that preferred to spend its time sleeping on the sofa. So I decided to bring in some new blood, and Menina, a Brazilian champion, arrived in Israel. She was a beauty, and very much fit my image of what a collie should be. She also was a real Brazilian—full of life and energy, interested in everything, and with strong intentions of being the queen of the pack.

When she came into season, she was bred to a dog that I had bred who was living with my very good friend Ruth. Shawn had a super temperament, and was very much the type of collie I liked. He was dark and handsome—a tricolor —so the two were an excellent match.

There were eight puppies, fat and healthy, a mix of sables and tricolors and males and females. Menina was an excellent mother, and they grew well and started getting up on their feet and taking an interest in their surroundings.

There was one little tricolor male who, from the day that he opened his eyes, seemed to always be watching me. Whenever I approached the puppy box, he would leave the others and come running over, trying to climb over the side of the box to get even closer to me. I began to understand that the look he was giving me meant, "I am yours! I am here to stay!"

There was no resisting, he stayed. He was named Don Juan officially, but his name at home became DoJo.

DoJo developed into a lovely youngster, but he had a lot more than beauty. He had a wonderful temperament—happy, outgoing, ready to be a friend to anyone who was willing to give him a pat, and totally devoted. Nothing in life was better than coming with me wherever I went. He was very bright and learned very quickly. Because of his great desire to learn and to please, and the strong bond between us, I decided to train him to do heelwork to music (also called 'dancing with dogs'), a fairly new dog sport that I found a great challenge and a lot of fun. It was based on all the movements common in obedience—heeling, sitting, down, stay, and so on, with additional movements added, from pivots and turns to weaving between the handler's legs—all done to music. I suppose it is something like gymnastics, but for dogs. DoJo loved it, and we put on our first performance at a club show when he was only ten months old. It was highly successful, done to the music of "Cecilia" by Simon and Garfunkel.

DoJo also brought me one of my greatest dog show successes, winning Best Puppy in Show at one of our international all breed shows. He easily became an Israel and International champion, and has sired some lovely puppies, with his sweet and bright temperament.

But mostly, he is my friend. He is a permanent house dog. Since there are so many dogs here at Shaar Hagai, most of them have to take turns to spend time in the house. But DoJo, king of the collie pack, has the right and privilege of always being a house dog. I think that sometimes he is not so happy that this position of privilege has to be shared with other dogs, and that part of his job is to help to educate the puppies in the pack. But to be with me, he is willing to put up with anything.

He watches me all the time, with a quizzical expression, as if to say, "What can I do now? I am here for you!" It is rare for me to look out the window, when he is out in the yard, and not find him looking up at me. In the house, he lies next to my favorite spot on the sofa, or next to the bed, where he can always see me. His eyes speak better than any words.

Then there is T.G. She was born on the day that my mother passed away. I don't really make any connection between these two events, it is a coincidence, but somehow her birth helped me to get through a hard time.

She was a daughter of Tia, a lovely bitch who had had a large litter of healthy puppies previously. But this litter, born as I was waiting to hear the final news of my mother's condition, was composed of very tiny and very weak puppies. Several of them were born dead, and the others, it was obvious, had little chance of survival, and indeed began dying one by one.

T.G. was no more than 100 grams at birth, nothing compared to a normal collie puppy that weighs between 250 and 350 grams at birth. But unlike the others, this puppy was not ready to die. She was too tiny to grab hold of her mother's nipples to nurse, but when I milked Tia and gave her the milk in an eye dropper, she eagerly guzzled it down.

After a few days, she had grown enough to be able to nurse on her own. She was the only survivor, and seemed determined to eat as much as possible and to grow as fast as possible, to get to the size she should be. She was extremely alert, and interested in the world outside of the whelping box from the day she opened her eyes. After all, there were no siblings to keep her busy. Entertainment and activity would have to come from the household. By four and a half weeks of age, she was climbing out of the box and running around the kitchen, and although I tried to set up fences and barriers to keep her confined to one part of the room, nothing worked. She was a very determined little thing, and managed to find a way over, under, around or through any barrier. Once she was out, she proudly pranced around the room, very pleased with herself.

Her name came from her attitude and determination. She was named True Grit after the John Wayne movie with the character of a young girl who was determined and would never give up. True Grit she was, and T.G. for short.

T.G. is now three years old, a lovely sable and white girl who became a champion before she was two years old, and is well on her way to becoming an international champion. No one, looking at her now, could imagine what a tiny scrap she was when she was born. But she has remained strong and determined and bosses the other bitches around, even though most of them are older than her.

There have been and are so many lovely dogs...but I can't talk about all of them, or this book will never end...

So I will end this chapter with my current puppy, a very special little fellow who shows signs of becoming one of the most special.

Habibi, a Canaan of course, is now seven months old. He is an immigrant from France. Why, you might ask, do I need to bring in a puppy from France when I have so many of my own? Well, therein lies his story.

In January 2008, I took a quick trip to France to pick up two dogs. One was Lilo, one of my champion Canaan bitches, who had spent a year with my friend Laurence going to shows. She managed to finish the title of Luxembourg Champion and had some wins in France as well, but I didn't want to leave her away from home any longer. I was also bringing back Bedouim, one of the 'miracle puppies' born from Bayud's sperm I sent over. Bedouim had grown into a very beautiful dog and had completed several titles in Europe, as well as having sired a number of excellent puppies, including Shaked. Laurence was now interested in sending him home with me for a while so that he could become an Israel champion. For a Canaan, no matter how many titles he may have, there is no title more coveted and valuable than to be an Israel Champion, proving that he is up to the standard in the land of origin of the breed.

Laurence lives in the south of France, and there are no direct flights to anywhere near her. So we made arrangements to meet in Paris. She was coming to a show there, and would bring the dogs, and I could take them home.

She had a number of dogs with her when she picked me up from the airport. She was planning to show several Canaans and several Australian shepherds which she also breeds, and she had a puppy to deliver to someone who was coming from Germany to pick it up. So that the puppy would not be lonely on the trip, she brought two more puppies with her, a little red female and a cream male.

We were sleeping at the house of a friend, and when we got there, Laurence began to take the dogs out of the van for some exercise and fresh air. This was my first chance to see the puppies, which had been in a big crate in the van. She brought them into the house—it was a very cold and rainy day. They were all very attractive and happy puppies, but the little cream male—he walked in as if he was the king and we were all his court. His tail was up and tight over his back, his ears stood straight up, although he was only just over two months old, an age when most puppies' ears are going every which way, and he looked like a perfect Canaan in miniature. But most impressive was his temperament. Nothing fazed him, nothing frightened him. He explored his surroundings and was submissive to no one, not even the adult dogs. When the puppies were fed, his intention, before we prevented it, was to take all three portions for himself.

The puppy was named Chabib, a Frenchified version of *Habibi*, an Israeli slang term for buddy. He was a son of Bedouim and Sissie, a bitch I had sent to Laurence a few years before, and this was the breeding I had planned for her. Habibi was the only surviving puppy in the litter, the others had died of an infection while tiny, so he grew up as the center of attention. And he certainly felt that he deserved it.

I had no intentions of bringing home a new puppy. As ever, there were too many dogs at Shaar Hagai. But this little fellow fascinated me. He reminded me so much in appearance of one of his ancestors, Sirpad, who had also been a single puppy in the litter.

Laurence denied having any hidden intentions; she had brought the puppies for socialization, and so they could get more accustomed to riding in the car. And she wanted me to see them and give her my opinion. She was worried, she told me, about finding the proper home for Habibi. He was so beautiful, she wanted him to be in a show home, but he had such a strong temperament that she was worried that someone who didn't have a lot of experience with Canaans would not be able to manage him. I could see that he might, indeed, be a difficult puppy to raise, but in the right hands, he could be fantastic. I tried to be noncommittal; yes, I agreed that he was a beautiful puppy, who indeed should have a show career. I found myself, as the days of my visit went by, watching the little fellow more and more.

The day before the show, we took the dogs for a walk in a huge park. The weather was very cold and windy with a hint of rain, so there were few people around, and it was possible to let the dogs, which were quite obedient, run off lead. The puppies were also allowed to run after us off lead; they were not confident enough in this strange place to go far, but were thrilled to run around us and explore the new smells and sights.

We walked a long way, several kilometers at least, it seemed to me. Laurence's dogs were accustomed to having a lot of exercise, and the last few days of being cooped up in the van while traveling had been hard on them. We wanted them to have a chance to expend their excess energy before the show the next day, when again they would be confined to an indoor venue. The puppies ran along with us all, keeping up very well with the adults and not showing signs of fatigue, even though they were still so small. Habibi had his tail up all the time, showing no fears or worries about being in a strange place.

There was a pond and a stream going through the park, and we had to cross a little bridge. The bridge was just a few iron rods fastened together, and it was wet and slippery. We had to be very cautious as we crossed it, although it was only a meter or so long.

The puppies, however, were not familiar with bridges, certainly not of this kind. The two of them stood at the far end as we crossed, worriedly looking after us. Well, they were not going to be left behind! Habibi took the lead and stepped out onto the bridge, and immediately slipped and fell into the stream beneath. It was not deep, only about twenty or thirty centimeters, but for a puppy it was swimming depth. Poor Habibi, very surprised to find himself in the cold water, paddled around not quite sure what to do. The little red female, seeing that Habibi was in the water, decided that this must be what they were supposed to do, and jumped in after him.

Laurence fished the two soaked puppies, looking like drowned rats, out of the water. I was really worried—the water was very cold, the weather was wintry and windy, we were still a good way off from the car, and we had nothing to dry them off with. But the puppies took it all in stride. They thoroughly shook off, and continued running after the other dogs. The little female was a bit subdued, with her tail down, but Habibi was his usual cheerful dominant self, ignoring the soaking and running along with his tail up.

As I found myself worriedly watching him for signs that he was chilled, I realized that it was a lost cause—I had already, in my mind, accepted that Habibi was mine.

Laurence was very happy to hear my decision to take him home; this of course had really been her intention when she decided to bring him along. She knew me too well, and knew I wouldn't be able to resist a puppy like this.

So now we had to call the airline and see if they would accept a puppy as cabin baggage—he was too young to travel in the freight section—and to find a bag that I could use to carry him on board. Pets in the cabin have to be small enough to fit under the seat, and this requires a soft carrier that can be squeezed under.

There was no problem with the airline; they agreed that Habibi could travel as cabin baggage. At the show, we made the rounds of the commercial stands, and finally found a bag that seemed suitable. It was just large enough for Habibi to sit in fairly comfortably, and although there wasn't much room to move around, there was an open corner where he could stick his head out to look around.

Travelling with dogs always attracts attention. Coming up to the check in desk with the two large dog crates containing Lilo and Bedouim was attraction enough, but with Habibi sitting on top in his bag, his head out, watching all the interesting things happening around him, we were irresistible. People gathered around asking questions, and of course wanting to pet Habibi. He had such a sweet and appealing expression, that no one could pass him by.

Finally, the check in was completed, and the crates were taken away to be loaded. I went on through passport control and to the gate; there was still an hour or so to wait until boarding.

Habibi was bored and cramped in his little bag, so I took him out on leash so that he could stretch his legs, and perhaps work off some energy—there were five hours on board during the flight when he would have to sit still. He found everything fascinating, and wanted to play with anything he could get in his mouth—the leash, paper drink cups, the carpet... Habibi was a constant source of interest to the other waiting passengers.

The flight was quite crowded when we finally boarded. Habibi was not at all tired, and not at all happy about having to get back in the bag. This was no fun, and he kept trying to wriggle his way out, as I tried to stuff the bag under the seat where it was supposed to be. Fortunately, the other passengers seated next to me were not dog haters, and found my struggles quite amusing. I could see that this was not going to be an easy flight.

Then I was approached by one of the stewardesses. There were a few empty seats at the back of the plane, she told me. Maybe I would like to move there with the puppy? There would be more space.

Oh yes! That was a marvelous idea! I was moved to the very last row, and there I had a row of three seats entirely to myself. Rather than having to stuff Habibi under the seat, he could sit on the seat next to me. I was even able to open the bag and let him stretch out on the seat. He loved it—this way he could keep his head on my arm or lap and be able to see everything that was going on. Passengers and crew that passed by on their way to and from the toilets or the galley all stopped to coo over him, which he accepted as his due. It was an exhausting flight for me. There was no chance to nap; I had to keep an eye on Habibi all the time as well as answer all the questions and comments of the passersby. Habibi did sleep much of the time, very comfortably spread out on the seat.

We arrived at last, and I collected my suitcase and the crates with Lilo and Bedouim. It was four in the morning and I was eager to get home. There were few flights coming in and the airport was quite empty. The customs officials were quite bored, and when they spotted me coming through with three dogs, they decided that now they could have a bit of action.

This was what I had been dreading. Usually, there is no inspection when you come into Israel with a pet. People who go through all the trouble and additional arrangements and expense of traveling with an animal will also have all the required documents. But I was coming in with three dogs, and the inspectors decided that this must be a commercial situation, I was bringing dogs in to sell. Of course, I had all the documents required, but Habibi was two weeks younger than the age at which a puppy is allowed to enter the country, even though he had already had his vaccinations. I was worried that they would inspect the date of birth, and then there would be trouble.

I was stopped, and the inspectors asked for all the documents, which I provided. Glancing through them they did not seem to notice Habibi's date of birth, and they didn't find anything wrong, but then they asked me, "Do you have an import permit?"

Dogs being imported into Israel need a permit, which is issued in advance. But this applies to dogs that are being imported by cargo, and not usually to pets that are traveling with a passenger. However, the permit is required by law for an accompanied pet, even though it is rarely asked for.

I explained that these were show dogs, that I had taken them abroad to shows and now was bringing them back. Well, what about the puppy, they asked. I told them that Bedouim was his father. But they were not ready to let me through.

The clerk from the veterinary department who was on duty was called to come and inspect the dogs and the documents. I sat waiting, as all the other passengers from my flight passed on through. Habibi was very restless, and I took him out of the bag. It soon became apparent why he was restless; he had been astonishingly good for the whole time we were in the airport in Paris and on the plane, but this trip had already taken many hours, and he was a small puppy...he squatted and peed, producing a very large puddle on the shiny tile floor. Fortunately, I had a good supply of tissues in my bag, and managed to mop it all up fairly unobtrusively.

I know most of the clerks that work for the veterinary department, because of my frequent trips with dogs and shipping and receiving them. I had told the customs officer that if he told the clerk on the phone that it was me, he would be given approval to let me go. But the officer was not prepared to do that.

The clerk arrived—of course, someone who knew me.

"Oh, it's you!" he said. "Why didn't you say so before?" He stamped the papers, and I was finally on the way home with all the dogs.

Habibi was not worried at all about meeting my pack of dogs: he walked right in as though he had spent his whole short life there, tail up and full of self-confidence. I knew that I was going to have to keep a close eye on this puppy, he was sure to annoy the adults with this attitude.

There was from the first time I saw him a strong bond between Habibi and me, and our flight together had strengthened it. He wanted to be with me as much as possible. He also revealed another characteristic which was rare in Canaans—he was a natural retriever. He would bring back toys that were thrown for him, and would bring me presents—any toys that he found or interesting objects that he could pick up, which could be anything from a leaf or stick to a shoe, he would bring over and drop at my feet. He had an expression that could not be ignored; when he looked at me with those dark, dark eyes and sweet face, I had to respond.

This strong bond and desire to do things with me made me decide that Habibi was meant to be a working dog. I decided that he would be perfect for nose work, and more specifically for search and rescue.

I had worked with a few dogs in the past on tracking, most notably Nova the collie and Shachmat the Canaan. The most effective method was to start the training while the dog was still quite a young puppy, and build up the desire to work and to use the nose. So at three months of age, with the assistance of a friend who had done a lot of work with sniffer dogs of all sorts in the army, Habibi started his training.

First of all, he had to be very well socialized and learn to cope with all sorts of conditions, places, people, and so on. So, he began to come with me everywhere. To start with, his place was on the passenger seat of the car next to me. He loved to sit and watch the traffic and scenery

506

go by. This remained his place until he got too big and had to move to the back seat.

Habibi is now eight months old and his training is going very well. He loves working and will search an area of about two hundred meters to find someone who is hidden. He shows great promise as a working dog. People ask me what my ultimate goal is with him. I can't really answer. It will take time to see what he is capable of, but the important part to me is the great pleasure we both get from working together and meeting the challenges.

Habibi is a house dog and my constant companion. He is very well behaved for a puppy, though he does have plenty of energy, and is very popular with everyone who meets him. His expression is irresistible. He is very special, but future adventures with him will have to wait for the next book...

Chapter Forty-Eight: To the Desert—in Quantity

The Canaan Dog has been officially recognized by the Israel Kennel Club as the national breed of Israel for about 25 years. But not much was done in recognition of this other than making use of the Canaan as part of the kennel club's logo until 2005, when a decision was made that all Israeli dog judges, no matter what other breeds they judge, must do a course of seminars and apprentice judging on the Canaan. It was felt that any Israeli judge invited to judge in another country should also be an expert on the national breed.

This was a popular decision, as the Israeli dog people have become proud of the Canaan, a natural resource that has changed over the years from a rather scorned animal found on the fringe of modern life, 'just an Arab dog' to a breed recognized and growing in popularity all over the world.

Becoming a dog judge is not an easy process. It requires years of learning and experience. To be accepted as a student judge here in Israel, a candidate must first have proven his long-term interest in dogs and cynology, which is more or less the science of dogs, by having been a breeder and exhibitor of their own preferred breed, and having been active in the breed club. The club must give the candidate a recommendation to the kennel club, that he is fit and suitable to become a judge. He must then work in the ring at dog shows as ring secretary, ring steward, or judge's secretary for a number of shows, to learn the procedure and gain experience and knowledge. He must attend the canine college run by the Israel Kennel Club, where he has to do a series of courses on a wide variety of doggy subjects, including anatomy and physiology, structure and movement, breed development, dog behavior, health and nutrition, and rules and regulations of the kennel club and of the international organization to which the Israel

Kennel Club belongs, the Federation Cynologique Internationale. Once the candidate has passed these courses, which are on a high academic level, including examinations, he must write a detailed paper on the first breed she is learning to judge (which is usually the breed he has been showing and exhibiting), which includes the history of the breed, an analysis of the breed standard, and the history and development of the breed in Israel. The candidate must serve as a student judge in the ring with experienced judges at a number of shows, and be evaluated by the judges he works with. Then, finally, he must pass two examinations, one theoretical and one practical, where he actually judges the dogs and is evaluated by a judge who is expert in the breed. Once all of this has been completed successfully, the candidate becomes a qualified judge of his first breed. He is provisional for a while, until he has proven that he indeed is a qualified judge, and then he is added to the list of FCI International judges.

For each additional breed that a judge wants to add to his list, he must go through the student judging, writing of the paper on the breed, and examinations. So, becoming a dog judge is far from easy, but this is all justified, as breeders and exhibitors expect to receive an expert and non-biased opinion when they present their dogs to a judge at shows. This opinion will help them to evaluate their dogs and to make breeding decisions in the future.

There were eight 'students' in the course I was asked to give on Canaans, all of them coming from breeds that were very different, such as miniature pinschers, Bernese Mountain dogs, Rottweilers, and German shepherds.

I gave them several seminars on the development of the dog as a species. The Canaan, as well as a few other primitive breeds that still exist, such as the dingo, the Carolina dog, and the New Guinea singing dog, are considered to be the direct descendents of the first dogs that developed about 150,000 years ago and are still very similar to what they were then. The students then had several chances to do practice judging at a few shows, including a Canaan dog specialty that we organized for this purpose. But the high point of the course was to be a trip to the desert, to see the dogs in their natural environment.

Arranging this trip was not easy; it had to be at a time of year when the weather was suitable, which is never a simple thing in the desert. In the summer it was very hot, and the dogs usually could only be seen very early in the morning or late in the evening when the sun was not out in full strength—not very compatible with the schedules of the aspiring judges. In the winter, there was always the chance of rain. Rain in the desert was not pleasant as there could be very heavy rainfall in a very short time, which could even cause severe flash floods. The arid desert ground did not readily absorb the water; rather the rain tended to just run over the top of the ground, creating very slick mud which was very difficult to walk or drive in. And the dogs, of course, were not stupid—why should they stand out in the rain so that a bunch of strangers could look at them?

Finally we set a date for the beginning of November 2007 for the field trip, hoping that indeed the weather would stay good.

Another requirement was to make arrangements with the Bedouins. If we tried wandering around the desert on our own looking for dogs, there was very little chance we would see anything, especially when it was such a large group. We needed a guide, and fortunately our friend Salame was willing to take on the job.

The day dawned sunny but with a haze in the air. Temperatures were quite comfortable. We all met at a prearranged spot to pick up two jeeps we had rented for the day—normal cars were not suitable for the sort of terrain we would be traveling on. The first stop was Salame's camp.

Of course when we arrived, we had to stop and drink tea with the family. As we sat in the tent, discussing the plans for the day and enjoying the Bedouin tea, we could see in the distance some of the flocks of sheep passing, accompanied by the women who were herding them, and some dogs. Although they were a fair distance away, we could see that they were beautiful Canaans. How I would have loved to be able to bring one of those home! But these were working dogs, highly valued and never to be parted with.

A number of Salame's relatives and neighbors came by to take a look at this big group of crazy people coming down to look for dogs. Even the children thought it was worthwhile to come over and see us—after all, if we were crazy enough to be interested in dogs, maybe we would also have sweets or presents for them.

We spent time as usual with the Bedouin; drinking tea and coffee and talking about everything except the reason that we were there, while the judges, not very familiar with the Bedouin culture, were getting fidgitier and fidgitier. Finally, Salame was ready to get on with the search for dogs. We all climbed into the jeeps and set off along the nearly invisible desert tracks, following his instructions.

We moved from camp to camp, attracting a lot of attention wherever we stopped. The Bedouin in each camp had to come over and look at all these strange people who were asking about dogs. We would be answered with a casual wave of the hand—sure, there are dogs, somewhere around. Often the children were sent to look for dogs that should be there but were not showing themselves.

I love the desert: the wild and barren landscape, the impressive mountains and valleys, the colors which can be very bright in the sunlight and very subtle when it is cloudy. The harsh, rocky landscape, with very little growing there for most of the year, with no apparent sources of water makes it obvious how very hard survival is there. Most of my companions, although like most Israelis they had been in the south on vacations and weekend trips, had never really looked at the surroundings as having to support a population of both people and animals, and how very difficult living there was; to truly understand the Canaans, they had to. Just walking around the camps, up and down the rocky hillsides, dressed in sturdy hiking shoes, was difficult. Now they could appreciate the necessity for sturdy tough feet in the dogs that lived there, as well as all the other characteristics they needed just for survival.

It was also a shock to them to see the conditions that the dogs were kept in. In many places, the dogs were tied on a short chain or piece of rope with little shelter and no water. These dogs were often tied during the day and released at night to perform their guard duties. No one felt that they needed pampering or special care—at night, when they were set free, they could go and find water and food. Some of my companions were really shocked by this, especially in one camp where several two month old puppies were tied in this way. They wanted to bring the puppies water, and it was necessary for us to explain to them that it would not be appreciated if they interfered in the Bedouins' care of their animals. As cruel as it seemed, these dogs had survived for generations in these conditions—and most of them were in excellent condition despite this.

The dogs that we saw, however, were disappointing. In one camp after another, we found dogs that were not Canaans, but apparent mixed breeds. The Bedouin, who were more and more abandoning their nomad existence and starting to work at regular jobs in the surrounding towns, were also bringing home various 'town' dogs, which were mixing with the natural population. We could see that the true nomadic Bedouin and wild Canaans were becoming more and more scarce.

It was already mid afternoon, and soon we would have to be returning home. There was one more camp to visit, not far from where Salame himself lived. As we drove in, we heard barking. As we got out of the jeeps and started to look around, we were thrilled to see that here, in this village, there were indeed Canaans that looked completely pure, and were of excellent type. We walked around the camp, photographing the many dogs, some running free and some tied to guard their owner's territory.

As we approached the edge of the village, we saw a fawn-colored bitch circling and barking at us. She was obviously a nursing mother, but her puppies were not with her. This meant that they were still quite young, not old enough to run after their mother. We passed by a small, ramshackle goat pen backing on to a high rocky terrace, and then, just past the pen, we saw a hole in among the rocks with bright eyes peering out.

As we came closer, we saw how cleverly the bitch had sheltered her litter. The entrance to the den was just barely large enough to allow the bitch to squeeze in, but when we knelt down in front of the den and peered in, we could see that the den inside the cave she had made was quite large. It was dark inside, so we could not see how far back it went. But we did see a litter of four puppies, well protected from all harm. We were able to reach two of the puppies and gently pull them out, as the bitch circled just out of reach, barking her worry.

They were both males, looking to be between four and five weeks of age, and were sandy brown with white markings. The other two puppies were out of reach, and refused to respond to our attempts to lure them out.

The Bedouin who owned the goats in the pen came over. It seems that the bitch was the guardian of his herd of goats, and the puppies made her even more keen in her task. When we asked him who the father of the puppies was, he pointed to an impressive red and white male who was standing next to a neighboring hut and barking at anyone who came near. This was a wonderful opportunity to get a new desert puppy. I asked him if he would be willing to let me take one.

The Bedouin came over to the den, reached in and pulled out another puppy, also a male, that was cream colored. This puppy, he said, was promised to one of his children. But I could have one of the others.

That was fine with me. I was very attracted to one of the little tan males I was holding, and decided that this was the one that would come home with me.

All of this was quite an experience for my companions, who had not expected to have a chance to see how I went about bringing in new stock. They found it hard to believe that I wanted to take a tiny puppy home. Of course, at this age, the little fellow, covered with dust and dirt from the den, was far from being impressive. But I had seen the parents and the other dogs in the vicinity, and they were of a good type, so I was confident that this pup would also grow up to be a good-looking Canaan.

On the drive home, the puppy slept quietly on my lap. The conversation revolved around trying to find a suitable name for him.

When we got home, the puppy showed that he was perfectly capable of standing up for himself. When the big dogs came over to inspect the little scrap of dogdom, he stood up to his full height of about 20 centimeters, and snarled at them with the confidence of a Great Dane. My house dogs were used to such things, so didn't take him very seriously, but he was certainly no pushover.

I named him Zuk, which is Hebrew for 'a rocky cliff,' suitable to his desert origin. He quickly learned to eat and to drink water—I think that until I brought him home, he had never had a taste of water. Desert puppies do not have anyone to offer them drinking water; only when they are big enough to run after their mother do they learn to drink. Before that they got all their liquid from nursing. Zuk was extremely clean, from the first night asking to be taken out when he had to eliminate. And he was very strong, despite his tender age and small size—he would grab hold of toys and hang on, even letting himself be lifted off the ground rather than let go.

Zuk is now five months old and developing very well. It is hard to remember how tiny he was when he came home. He has a wonderful temperament, and learns everything quickly and happily. I think he will be a worthy addition to the Canaan gene pool.

I wonder if he remembers his early days in a den in a rock wall, and appreciates the life of luxury that luck has brought his way.

Meanwhile, four of the eight student judges have become qualified to judge Canaan dogs. And not only have they learned about this breed, but I think that seeing natural dogs and how they live and survive has also had an effect on how they look at dogs of the other breeds that they are involved with.

Myrna Shiboleth

Afterword

It has been thirty eight years since I first found my way up the road to Sha'ar Hagai. My daughter was born here, and unable to stay away, came back to live here with her new husband. My grandchildren have been born here. And, of course, many, many generations of dogs and other animals.

We live in the modern world these days. We have a telephone, as well as the amazingly popular cellular phones—how wonderful it would have been if they were available twenty or thirty years ago! We have electricity and all the necessary appliances, as well as some that are not really necessary like a microwave, air conditioner, and satellite TV.

I can't say that I live in luxury, although in comparison to what we had when we started, life is certainly much more luxurious. But I was never looking for luxury.

I have lived as I chose to live, and have accomplished at least part of what I set myself to accomplish. The Canaan Dog has become accepted as a breed all over the world, and I am confident that it will survive, even when the time comes that I can no longer be active as a breeder. I have achieved a lot with the dogs. Maybe most important is that I have provided many people with four-footed friends and companions that have brought much joy to their lives.

Life hasn't been easy, but then, who says it should be? But it has certainly never been boring! It is a new century and a new millennium. Who knows what new 'tails' await us in the future?

Made in the USA
Columbia, SC
27 December 2024

50739414R00319